Jon E. L   on history and military history are sold worldwide.   e editor of many *The Mammoth Book of* anthologies, including the best-selling *Cover-Ups*.

Other titles by Jon E. Lewis

The Mammoth Book of Antarctic Journeys
The Mammoth Book of Cover-Ups
The Mammoth Book of Native Americans
The Mammoth Book of How It Happened
The Mammoth Book of On the Edge
The Mammoth Book of Pirates
The Mammoth Book of True War Stories
The Mammoth Book of Wild Journeys

London: The Autobiography
Rome: The Autobiography
World War II: The Autobiography
Survivor: The Autobiography
SAS: The Autobiography
Spitfire: The Autobiography

The Mammoth Book of

CONSPIRACIES

JON E. LEWIS

RUNNING PRESS
PHILADELPHIA · LONDON

Constable & Robinson Ltd
55–56 Russell Square
London WC1B 4HP
www.constablerobinson.com

First published in the UK by Robinson,
an imprint of Constable & Robinson Ltd, 2012

Copyright © J. Lewis-Stempel, 2012

The right of Jon E. Lewis to be identified as the author of this work has been asserted by
him in accordance with the Copyright, Designs & Patents Act 1988.

A copy of the British Library Cataloguing in Publication
Data is available from the British Library

UK ISBN: 978-1-84901-363-5 (paperback)
UK ISBN: 978-1-84901-730-5 (ebook)

1 3 5 7 9 10 8 6 4 2

First published in the United States in 2012 by Running Press Book Publishers,
A Member of the Perseus Books Group

Books published by Running Press are available at special discounts for bulk purchases in
the United States by corporations, institutions, and other organizations. For more
information, please contact the Special Markets Department at the Perseus Books Group,
2300 Chestnut Street, Suite 200, Philadelphia, PA 19103, or call (800) 810-4145,
ext. 5000, or e-mail special.markets@perseusbooks.com.

US ISBN: 978-0-7624-4271-3
US Library of Congress Control Number: 2011930502

9 8 7 6 5 4 3 2 1
Digit on the right indicates the number of this printing

Running Press Book Publishers
2300 Chestnut Street
Philadelphia, PA 19103-4371

Visit us on the web!
www.runningpress.com

Printed and bound in the UK

CONTENTS

INTRODUCTION

These are, of course, *theories*. If they were proven beyond all doubt they would be conspiracy *facts*.

This book, a companion to *The Mammoth Book of Cover-Ups*, is a guide to the weirdest, wackiest and the most dangerous conspiracy theories around. I have, hopefully, steered a path between the Scylla of outright scepticism and the Charybdis of wide-open gullibility, the latter constantly boosted by the Internet, a self-referring universe where one blogger's claim becomes one researcher's proof. As a measuring stick of a theory's veracity, I have included an "ALERT" guide, with a 1 to 10 rating, with 1 being "No way, Jose" and 10 being "It's a cert". A small number of cases have appeared in *Cover-Ups*, but reappear here in the light of more and new information.

There are conspiracy theories that cross the edge of madness – David Icke's "reptilian-humanoid takeover" and Vril-powered UFOs driven by Nazis come hurtling to mind – but there are plenty out there that raise real issues about the abuse of power by secretive groups of politicos, CEOs, medicos and military honchos. Everyone should sleep a little less easy and be a little more vigilant after reading about the US Army's "Operation Northwoods" (which proposed false-flag terrorist outrages on the American people and the sticking of the blame on Cuba) and you may want to give the bio-research facility at Plum Island a wide, wide detour.

As they say: just because you are paranoid, it doesn't mean that they aren't out to get you ...

Jon E. Lewis

APPLE

Ever wonder how two tech geeks like Steve Jobs and Steve Wozniak made their billions?

Conspiracists know the answer. Jobs and Wozniak built the first Macintosh computer in a California garage and when it failed to raise interest they did a deal with the devil, selling their souls in exchange for success on earth. The proof was on the price tag of the first Mac: $666.66. The mark of the Beast. Rounding off the evidence is the Apple logo. There's a bite taken out of the apple, the forbidden fruit.

Alternatively, Apple did a deal with Big Brother. Take a look at an iPhone. It plays, unknown to its owner, iSpy on you. A secret file stores latitude and longitude, complete with a dater. The file is unencrypted and is transferred to any device the iPhone syncs with. Thus anyone with access to the owner's computer can track his or her movements. Invasion of privacy anyone? Apple's snooping habit doesn't end with the locator file. The "Hackintosh hacker" alleged that Apple has stuck a code into the iPhone that tracks keyboard use, so every time the user taps in information this is relayed to Apple HQ. The claim has never been verified but Apple's appetite for gathering personal information is infamous; in 2010 the company applied for a patent ("Systems and Methods for Identifying Unauthorized Users of an Electronic Device") that could record the heartbeat of iPhone users, as well as covertly photograph them and their surroundings. If Apple collects information, as sure as God made little green apples, law enforcement agencies will one day come calling to use it. All of which has made dark rooms full of pale conspiracy theorists wonder if Apple is not doing the CIA/FBI's job for them.

Apple justified the patent application as a security measure to prevent thieves using stolen phones, but as the Electronic Frontier Foundation (EEF) watchdog pointed out the technology also enabled Apple to cut off customers who pimped (quite lawfully) their devices. Improper use would also be reported to the Orwellian sounding "proper authorities". The EEF christened the patent "traitorware". Apple's inclination to control is almost as great as its inclination to spy. On prudishly deciding that cartoonist Mark Fiore's NewsToons app was too satirical for its taste Apple rejected it. When Fiore won a Pulitzer though they installed the app. Never one to miss a commercial opportunity, Apple.

Of course, Apple likes to keep its own secrets very close to its chips: the company is heavily controlling of image and market share. When *Consumer Reports* had the brazen gall to say it couldn't recommend the iPhone 4 until the antenna was improved, threads discussing the issue on Mac.com forums mysteriously disappeared overnight. And only an absolute cynic would claim that Apple's 2010 litigious spat with internet mag *Gizmodo* about its review of an iPhone 4 prototype left in a bar and passed on to the website was a staged publicity stunt, what with the new phone getting oodles of free publicity, and security at Apple HQ being Fort Knox tight.

Byte into an Apple. Indeed.

Big Brother Apple is Watching You: ALERT LEVEL 8

Further Reading
www.eff.org/deeplinks/2010/08/
  steve-jobs-watching-you-apple-seeking-patent-0

AREA 51

"Warning. Restricted Area. Photography of This Area is Prohibited".

So read the signs staked around Area 51, a high-security military base in the Nevada desert, 90 miles (145 km) north of Las Vegas. Also known as Groom Lake, the facility, which comprises thousands of acres, is surrounded by security fencing and intruder detection systems, and is regularly patrolled. A no-fly zone operates above it. The US Government, you get the feeling, wants to keep peeping eyes away from what happens in Area 51.

Why? There is a long-standing belief by conspiracists that Area 51 houses the UFO disc found at Roswell, as well as other crashed alien spaceships. At Area 51, the theory goes, the recovered UFOs are back-engineered so that their technology can be utilized by the US military. The latter are helped – either willingly or unwillingly – by captured alien pilots.

Few of the human government employees who work at Groom have ever talked about their work, but two who did were Leo Williams and Bob Lazar. Williams claimed to have worked in alien technology evaluation, the results of which informed the design of the B-2 stealth bomber. In 1989 Lazar announced on local TV that he too had been involved in "back-engineering" at Groom's S-4 hangars complex, including assessment of the Roswell craft's propulsion system. He had even uncovered "Gravity B", a force arising from the manipulation of a new nuclear element, "ununpentium".

Neither Williams nor Lazar proved very convincing witnesses. Lazar had invented his purported MIT physics qualification and before working in back-engineering had been engaged in the rather less than cutting edge employment of managing a photo shop. A steady stream of sightings of strange lights and craft at Groom, however, kept alive the notion of Area 51 as a top-secret UFO lab, perhaps the manufacturing plant of Black Helicopters.

Certainly, Area 51 has been the testing ground for weird and wonderful aircraft. The U-2 spy plane was flown there; so was the SR-71 Blackbird, the B-2 stealth bomber, the F-117 stealth fighter, and the unmanned aerial vehicle known as the "Beast of Kandahar" (and officially as RQ-170 Sentinel) that spied on the Abbottabad compound of Osama bin Laden. And these are only the craft the public has been informed about. It's reasonable to suppose that other prototype and avant-garde aircraft have taken to the air at Groom, less reasonable to suppose that they have been developed from alien technology.

There was, though, one conspiracy taking place at Area 51. Bill Sweetman, editor-in-chief of defence technology for *Aviation Week*, maintains that the government absolutely encouraged "deliberate disinformation campaigns to generate a lot of noise about UFOs back in the 1950s and 1960s to cover secret flights of planes like the U-2, and then again in the late 1970s and early 1980s to link area 51 to UFOs through 'fake' documents and eye-witness accounts of alien technology and even alien bodies".

The object of the disinformation was to mask the real reasons for the building of the base, namely the R&D of air-machines to best the Ruskies.

The Government, in other words, conspired to create a conspiracy theory.

> Area 51 is a factory for alien-human top secret flying objects: ALERT LEVEL 2

Further Reading
David Darlington, *Area 51: The Dreamland Chronicles*, 1998
Eric Elfman, *Almanac of Alien Encounters*, 2001
Annie Jacobsen, *Area 51: An Uncensored History of America's Top Secret Military Base*, 2011
Phil Patton, *Dreamland: Travels Inside the Secret World of Roswell and Area 51*, 1998

JULIAN ASSANGE

During 2010, the whistle-blowing website WikiLeaks released troves of classified US cables. They made fascinating reading, and Joe and Josephine Public learned a thing or a hundred it never knew its government and allies were up to, from the US CIA's 3,000-strong secret army in Afghanistan to Saudi Arabia's plea for a missile strike on Iran. WikiLeaks justified the release of the information as being in the "public interest", while embarrassed establishments in the West complained about the endangering of national security. Julian Assange, the Australian founder of WikiLeaks, became, depending on your point of view, a hero or an Osama bin-Laden-style bogeyman. In the latter camp, Sarah Palin called for the "anti-American" Assange to be pursued "with the same urgency we pursue al-Qaeda and Taliban leaders". But Palin had a particular hard spot for WikiLeaks; the site had published her emails from her unsuccessful run for VeePee of the USA, one of its highest profile coups since its foundation in 2007.

Not long after Palin blew her hunting horn, the US Government announced its intention to try Assange under the Espionage Act of 1917. Then there were cyberspace sabotage attacks on WikiLeaks, the US Air Force started blocked access on its computers to any website which posted the cables (including the *New York Times*), and PayPal, Mastercard, Visa, Amazon and Bank of America all refused to handle donations to WikiLeaks.

To put the cherry on the conspiracy cake, Julian Assange was then arrested in Britain, at the request of Swedish prosecutors, on a completely unrelated matter. The Swedes maintained that Assange was guilty of rape, unlawful coercion and molestation in their bailiwick. Assange directly accused the US of smearing him on trumped-up charges; meanwhile, the two Stockholm women allegedly assaulted by Assange – who were left-wing fans of his – explicitly denied being "set up by the Pentagon or anyone else". In a prime case of wheels within wheels, WikiLeaks staff apparently blocked Assange from using the site to claim he was a victim of a conspiracy in the Swedish case. Citing Assange's autocratic style and courting of publicity, other staff left, others called for his replacement. Some defectors allied with a new site that published leaks about – WikiLeaks.

All, clearly, was not well down in WikiWorld. As WikiObservers sagely noted, the US might not need to conspire to destroy Assange and his operation. He might do that himself.

For his part Assange uploaded an "Insurance File" onto the internet, which is reputed to be bursting with more top secret government information. Only Assange knows the password, and this is to be released posthumously – should he suffer an "accident".

> US conspired with Stockholm to frame WikiLeaks leader on sex charges: ALERT LEVEL 4

Further Reading
Daniel Domscheit-Berg, *Inside WikiLeaks: My Time with Julian Assange at the World's Most Dangerous Website*, 2011
David Leigh and Luke Harding, *WikiLeaks: Inside Julian Assange's War on Secrecy*, 2011

AUM SHINRIKYO

Nipponese yoga teacher Shoko Asahara founded the Aum Shinrikyo ("Supreme Truth") sect in 1984 on a religious programme that combined Buddhism with **Nostradamus** and End-is-Nigh Christianity. A standard issue cult leader, Asahara boasted a beard, plus messianic powers (the ability to make the sick rise from their beds) and supernatural abilities. He couldn't quite walk on water, but he could walk through walls, a feat made difficult for his followers because he made them scald their feet. Despite – or maybe because of – Asahara's certifiable lunacy, Aum Shinrikyo attracted over 50,000 members. In the material world of Japan, it did at least offer something more than the pursuit of the yen. That said, like many a cult leader, Asahara was an accomplished businessman, raising sect funds through software enterprises and outright extortion at gunpoint.

Asahara promised the faithful that one day Aum Shinrikyo would rule Japan. When an electoral bid for power failed miserably in 1989, Asahara determined on a terrorist takeover instead. Representatives of Aum travelled to the HQ of the International Tesla Society in New York looking for documents detailing Tesla's weapons of doom (see **Free Electricity** and **HAARP**) but the FBI had long before seized the brainbox's research notes. Frustrated in their search for advanced sci-fi weaponry, Aum settled on buying arms from Russia (including a military helicopter), making an **Ebola** bomb and the building of chemical weapons. After murdering and assassinating individuals not to its taste, in 1994 Aum launched a mass sarin gas attack in the city of Matsumoto. Eight died. On 20 March 1995, Aum committed the deed by which it became internationally infamous: the attack on Tokyo Subway System with sarin nerve gas in which twelve people died and thousands were injured. Asahara was apprehended by the Japanese police and, after a lengthy trial, was sentenced to death. To date the sentence has not been carried out.

To no great surprise, the reviled Aum rebranded itself in 2000, becoming "Aleph".

> Secret Japanese cult sought terrorist takeover of the Land of the Rising Sun: ALERT LEVEL 10

Further Reading
D. W. Bracket, *Holy Terror: Armageddon in Tokyo,* 1996

BAVARIAN ILLUMINATI

It is the conspiracy whose name hardly dare be spoken. Through front organizations such as the Freemasons and the Bilderberg Group, the Bavarian Illuminati are poised to usher in the **New World Order**.

Such is the fear of serried ranks of conspiracy theorists. The Illuminati, then, have come a long way since their foundation in the smallsville Bavarian town of Ingolstadt on 1 May 1776 by Professor Adam Weishaupt, a lecturer at the local university. Like other intellectual groups which flourished in the Enlightenment, the Ancient Illuminated Seers of Bavaria (a.k.a. the Illuminati, a.k.a. the Order of Perfectabilists) flirted with progressive and subversive ideas, not least atheism and republicanism. Initiates were required to undergo a rigorous study of philosophy, beginning with the Ancient Greeks and ending with contemporaries such as Helvetius; graduates, enlightened and eager, would then – went Weishaupt's plan – enter leading positions in Bavarian government and society, and so transform Catholic Bavaria into a utopia of liberalism and rationality. Like other such groups, the Illuminati adopted esoteric rituals and signs, partly for reasons of security, partly for the excitement of clubability. Each member had a code name: Weishaupt was Spartacus, and his right-hand man Zwack was Cato.

The Illuminati soon attracted the unwelcome attention of the state's autocratic ruler, the Elector Prince Karl-Theodor, who in 1784 banned all secret societies in an attempt to halt the tide of Jacobinism (republicanism). In the following year the 650-strong Illuminati were proscribed by name and Weishaupt quit

Bavaria in a hurry. His hopes of rebuilding the Illuminati were dashed when a police raid on Zwack's house seized hundreds of Illuminati documents and membership lists. Besides, the Illuminati's main recruiting ground, the Freemasons, had wised up to Illuminati methods and had begun blocking infiltration. Weishaupt himself settled down to a quiet life as a university lecturer in Saxony.

Ironically, just at the moment the Illuminati project failed, the paranoid myth that it was an omniscient, omnipotent secret society was born. In 1797, Augustin de Barruel published the first of his two volume *Memoires pour server a l'histoire de Jacobinisme* ("Memoirs serving as a history of Jacobinism"). An ex-Jesuit, de Barruel blamed the recent French Revolution on an inner sanctum of Masons – the Illuminati. A year later, Professor John Robison fingered the Illuminati in his *Proofs of a Conspiracy Against All the Religions and Governments of Europe, Carried on in the Secret Meetings of Free-Masons, Illuminati and Reading Societies*. In the febrile atmosphere of late eighteenth-century Europe, de Barruel and Robison's claims caused a furore, and the Illuminati became the favourite bogeymen of conservatives on the continent.

That there was no hard evidence for the continued existence of the Illuminati troubled not one of these writers, just as it failed to trouble the British author Nesta Webster a century later. Webster's colourful *Secret Societies and Subversive Movements*, published in 1924, detected the fingers of the Illuminati in the French Revolution (see Document, p.12) and the Russian Revolution just gone by. Webster's book enjoyed only modest influence in her home country, but in America it became the conspiracy gospel of the Far Right. Today, the Illuminati are Public Enemy Number One for the John Birch Society, survivalists, the patriotic militias and Christian fundamentalists, who all claim to have detected the Illuminati's real goal: a single, authoritarian, satanic global government – a **New World Order**. As an alert on the Christian Science University website in 2000 had it: "A diabolical and Satanic ... scheme has been designed and is being prepared for global implementation by anti-Christ agents of an organization called 'The Illuminati'."

There is a secret sign of America's special role in the Illuminati's plans: the Latin motto *Novus Ordo Seclorum* (translated as "New World Order") on the US dollar bill. Unfortunately for conspiracists, the actual translation of the Latin tag is "New Order of the Ages", or, colloquially, "a fresh start". The desperate mistranslation of *Novus Ordo Seclorum* is typical of the "evidence" Illuminati-watchers hold up as evidence of conspiracy. Free of the constraints of actual evidence, contemporary conspiracists speculate wildly. David Icke considers the Illuminati to be a front for shape-shifting **Reptilian Humanoids** from planet Draco, while one major Illuminati conspiracy theory claims that the order was founded in Mesopotamia around 300,000 BC. That is, before the Neanderthals staggered around the Earth, dragging their knuckles on the ground. In the archetypal Illuminati conspiracy theory, however, the pyramid of power is, from the top down: Lucifer, or the All-Seeing Eye; the Rothschild Tribunal, being the inner circle of the Rothschild banking family; the Great Druid Council; below them, the Council of Thirty-Five, consisting of leading Freemasons; the **Committee of 300**, which is led by the black nobility, notably the British Royal Family.

That whirring sound you can hear? That is Adam Weishaupt, who believed that Illumination was about moral and intellectual perfection, spinning in his grave.

> The Illuminati are a secret order preparing to install a global satanic dictatorship: ALERT LEVEL 1

Further Reading
William Cooper, *Behold a Pale Horse*, 1991
John Robison, *Proofs of a Conspiracy Against All the Religions and Governments of Europe*, 1798

DOCUMENT: NESTA WEBSTER, *SECRET SOCIETIES AND SUBVERSIVE MOVEMENTS*, LONDON, BOSWELL PRINTING & PUBLISHING CO., 1924

Illuminism in reality is less an Order than a principle, and a principle which can work better under cover of something else. Weishaupt himself had laid down the precept that the work of Illuminism could best be conducted "under other names and other occupations", and henceforth we shall always find it carried on by this skilful system of camouflage.

The first cover adopted was the lodge of the "Amis Réunis" in Paris, with which, as we have already seen, the Illuminati had established relations. But now in 1787 a definite alliance was effected by the aforementioned Illuminati, Bode and Busche, who in response to an invitation from the secret committee of the lodge arrived in Paris in February of this year. Here they found the old Illuminatus Mirabeau – who with Talleyrand had been largely instrumental in summoning these German Brothers – and, according to Gustave Bord, two important members of the Stricte Observance, the Marquis de Chefdebien d'Armisson ("Eques a Capite Galeato") and an Austrian, the Comte Leopold de Kollowrath-Krakowski ("Eques ab Aquila Fulgente") who also belonged to Weishaupt's Order of Illuminati in which he bore the pseudonym of Numenius.

It is important here to recognize the peculiar part played by the Lodge of the "Amis Réunis". Whilst the "Loge des Neuf Soeurs" was largely composed of middle-class revolutionaries such as Brissot, Danton, Camille Desmoulins, and Champfort, and the "Loge de la Candeur" of aristocratic revolutionaries – Lafayette as well as the Orléanistes, the Marquis de Sillery, the Duc d'Aiguillon, the Marquis de Custine, and the Lameths – "the Loge du Contrat Social" was mainly composed of honest visionaries who entertained no revolutionary projects but, according to Barruel, were strongly Royalist. The rôle of the "Amis Réunis" was to collect together the subversives from all other lodges

– Philalèthes, Rose-Croix, members of the "Loge des Neuf Soeurs" and of the "Loge de la Candeur" and of the most secret committees of the Grand Orient, as well as deputies from the "Illuminés" in the provinces. Here, then, at the lodge in the Rue de la Sordière, under the direction of Savalette de Langes, were to be found the disciples of Weishaupt, of Swedenborg, and of Saint-Martin, as well as the practical makers of revolution – the agitators and demagogues of 1789.

The influence of German Illuminism on all these heterogeneous elements was enormous. From this moment, says a further Bavarian report of the matter, a complete change took place in the Order of the "Amis Réunis". Hitherto only vaguely subversive, the Chevaliers Bienfaisants became the Chevaliers Malfaisants, the Amis Réunis became the Ennemis Réunis. The arrival of the two Germans, Bode and Busche, gave the finishing touch to the conspiracy. "The avowed object of their journey was to obtain information about magnetism, which was just then making a great stir", but in reality, "taken up with the gigantic plan of their Order", their real aim was to make proselytes. It will be seen that the following passage exactly confirms the account given by Barruel:

> As the Lodge of the "Amis Réunis" collected together everything that could be found out from all other masonic systems in the world, so the way was soon paved there for Illuminism. It was also not long before this lodge together with all those that depended on it was impregnated with Illuminism. The former system of all these was as if wiped out, so that from this time onwards the framework of the Philalèthes quite disappeared and in the place of the former Cabalistic-magical extravagance ['Schwärmerei'] came in the philosophical-political.

It was therefore not Martinism, Cabalism, or Freemasonry that in themselves provided the real revolutionary force. Many non-illuminized Freemasons, as Barruel himself declares, remained loyal to the throne and altar, and as soon as the monarchy was seen to be in danger the Royalist Brothers of the "Contrat Social" boldly summoned the lodges to coalesce in defence of King and Constitution; even some of the upper Masons, who in the degree of Knight Kadosch had sworn hatred to the Pope and Bourbon monarchy, rallied likewise to the royal cause. "The French spirit triumphed over the masonic spirit in the greater number of the Brothers. Opinions as well as hearts were still for the King." It needed the devastating doctrines of Weishaupt to undermine this spirit and to turn the "degrees of vengeance" from vain ceremonial into terrible fact.

If, then, it is said that the Revolution was prepared in the lodges of Freemasons – and many French Masons have boasted of the fact – let it always be added that it was "Illuminized Freemasonry" that made the Revolution, and that the Masons who acclaim it are illuminized Masons, inheritors of the same tradition introduced into the lodges of France in 1787 by the disciples of Weishaupt, "patriarch of the Jacobins".

Many of the Freemasons of France in 1787 were thus not conscious allies of the Illuminati. According to Cadet de Gassicourt, there were in all the lodges only twenty-seven real initiates; the rest were largely dupes who knew little or nothing of the source whence the fresh influence among them derived. The amazing feature of the whole situation is that the most enthusiastic supporters of the movement were men belonging to the upper classes and even to the royal families of Europe. A contemporary relates that no less than thirty princes –reigning and non-reigning – had taken under their protection a confederation from which they stood to lose everything and had become so imbued by its principles that they were inaccessible to reason. Intoxicated by the flattery lavished on them by the priests of Illuminism, they adopted a religion of which they understood nothing. Weishaupt, of course, had taken care that none of these royal dupes should be initiated into the real aims of the Order, and at first adhered to the original plan of excluding them altogether; but the value of their cooperation soon became apparent and by a supreme irony it was with a Grand Duke that he himself took refuge.

But if the great majority of princes and nobles were stricken with blindness at this crisis, a few far-seeing spirits recognized the danger and warned the world of the impending disaster. In 1787 Cardinal Caprara, Apostolic Nuncio at Vienna, addressed a confidential memoir to the Pope, in which he pointed out that the activities carried on in Germany by the different sects of Illuminés, of Perfectibilists, of Freemasons, etc., were increasing:

> The danger is approaching, for from all these senseless dreams of Illuminism, of Swedenborgianism, or of Freemasonry a frightful reality will emerge. Visionaries have their time; the revolution they forebode will have its time also.

A more amazing prophecy, however, was the "Essai sur la Secte des Illuminés", by the Marquis de Luchet, a Liberal noble who played some part in the revolutionary movement, yet who nevertheless realized the dangers of Illuminism. Thus, as early as 1789, before the Revolution had really developed, de Luchet uttered these words of warning:

> Deluded people ... learn that there exists a conspiracy in favour of despotism against liberty, of incapacity against talent, of vice against virtue, of ignorance against enlightenment ... This society aims at governing the world ... Its object is universal domination. This plan may seem extraordinary, incredible – yes, but not chimerical ... no such calamity has ever yet afflicted the world.

De Luchet then goes on to foretell precisely the events that were to take place three and four years later; he describes the position of a king who has to recognize masters above himself and to authorize their "abominable régime", to become the plaything of an ambitious and fanatical horde which has taken possession of his will.

> See him condemned to serve the passions of all that
> surround him ... to raise degraded men to power, to
> prostitute his judgement by choices that dishonour his
> prudence ...

All this was exactly fulfilled during the reign of the Girondin
ministry of 1792. The campaign of destruction carried out in
the summer of 1793 is thus foretold:

> We do not mean to say that the country where the Illuminés
> reign will cease to exist, but it will fall into such a degree of
> humiliation that it will no longer count in politics, that the
> population will diminish, that the inhabitants who resist
> the inclination to pass into a foreign land will no longer
> enjoy the happiness of consideration, nor the charms of
> society, nor the gifts of commerce.

And de Luchet ends with this despairing appeal to the powers
of Europe:

> Masters of the world, cast your eyes on a desolated multi-
> tude, listen to their cries, their tears, their hopes. A mother
> asks you to restore her son, a wife her husband, your cities
> for the fine arts that have fled from them, the country for
> citizens, the fields for cultivators, religion for forms of
> worship, and Nature for beings of which she is worthy.

Five years after these words were written the countryside of
France was desolate, art and commerce were destroyed, and
women following the tumbril that carried Fouquier-Tinville
to the guillotine cried out: "Give me back my brother, my
son, my husband!" So was this amazing prophecy fulfilled.
Yet not one word has history to say on the subject! The
warning of de Luchet has fallen on deaf ears amongst poster-
ity as amongst the men of his own day.

De Luchet himself recognizes the obstacle to his obtaining
a hearing: there are too many "passions interested in supporting the system of the Illuminés", too many deluded rulers

imagining themselves enlightened ready to precipitate their people into the abyss, whilst "the heads of the Order will never relinquish the authority they have acquired nor the treasure at their disposal." In vain de Luchet appeals to the Freemasons to save their Order from the invading sect. "Would it not be possible," he asks, "to direct the Freemasons themselves against the Illuminés by showing them that whilst they are working to maintain harmony in society, those others are everywhere sowing seeds of discord" and preparing the ultimate destruction of their Order? So far it is not too late; if only men will believe in the danger it may be averted: "from the moment they are convinced, the necessary blow is dealt to the sect." Otherwise de Luchet prophesies "a series of calamities of which the end is lost in the darkness of time, ... a subterranean fire smouldering eternally and breaking forth periodically in violent and devastating explosions." What words could better describe the history of the last 150 years?

The "Essai sur la Secte des Illuminés" is one of the most extraordinary documents of history and at the same time one of the most mysterious. Why it should have been written by the Marquis de Luchet, who is said to have collaborated with Mirabeau in the "Galerie de Portraits" published in the following year, why it should have been appended to Mirabeau's "Histoire Secrète de la Cour de Berlin", and accordingly attributed to Mirabeau himself, why Barruel should have denounced it as dust thrown in the eyes of the public, although it entirely corroborated his own point of view, are questions to which I can find no reply. That it was written seriously and in all good faith it is impossible to doubt; whilst the fact that it appeared before, instead of after, the events described, renders it even more valuable evidence of the reality of the conspiracy than Barruel's own admirable work. What Barruel saw, de Luchet foresaw with equal clearness. As to the rôle of Mirabeau at this crisis, we can only hazard an explanation on the score of his habitual inconsistency. At one moment he was seeking interviews with the King's ministers in order to warn them of the coming danger, at the next he was energetically stirring up insurrection. It is therefore not impossible that he may have encouraged de Luchet's exposure of the conspiracy, although meanwhile he himself had entered into the scheme of destruction. Indeed, according to a pamphlet published in 1791 entitled "Mystères de la Conspiration", the whole plan of revolution was found amongst his papers. The editor of this "brochure" explains that the document here made public, called "Croquis ou Projet de Révolution de Monsieur de Mirabeau", was seized at the house of Madame Lejai, the wife of Mirabeau's publisher, on October 6, 1789. Beginning with a diatribe against the French monarchy, the document goes on to say that "in order to triumph over this hydra-headed monster these are my ideas":

We must overthrow all order, suppress all laws, annul all power, and leave the people in anarchy. The laws we establish will not perhaps be in force at once, but at any rate, having given back the power to the people, they will resist for the sake of their liberty which they will believe they are preserving. We must caress their vanity, flatter their hopes, promise them happiness after our work has been in operation; we must elude their caprices and their systems at will, for the people as legislators are very dangerous, they only establish laws which coincide with their passions, their want of knowledge would besides only give birth to abuses. But as the people are a lever which legislators can move at their will, we must necessarily use them as a support, and render hateful to them everything we wish to destroy and sow illusions in their path; we must also buy all the mercenary pens which propagate our methods and which will instruct the people concerning their enemies whom we attack. The clergy, being the most powerful through public opinion, can only be destroyed by ridiculing religion, rendering its ministers odious, and only representing them as hypocritical monsters, for Mahomet in order to establish his religion first defamed the paganism which the Arabs, the Sarmathes, and the Scythians professed. Libels must at every moment show fresh traces of hatred against the clergy. To exaggerate their riches, to make the sins of an individual appear to be common to all, to attribute to them all vices; calumny, murder, irreligion, sacrilege, all is permitted in times of revolution.

We must degrade the "noblesse" and attribute it to an odious origin, establish a germ of equality which can never exist but which will flatter the people; [we must] immolate the most obstinate, burn and destroy their property in order to intimidate the rest, so that if we cannot entirely destroy this prejudice we can weaken it and the people will avenge their vanity and their jealousy by all the excesses which will bring them to submission.

After describing how the soldiers are to be seduced from their allegiance, and the magistrates represented to the people as despots,"since the people, brutal and ignorant, only see the evil and never the good of things", the writer explains they must be given only limited power in the municipalities:

Let us beware above all of giving them too much force; their despotism is too dangerous, we must flatter the people by gratuitous justice, promise them a great diminution in taxes and a more equal division, more extension in fortunes, and less humiliation. These phantasies ["vertiges"] will fanaticise the people, who will flatten out all resistance. What matter the victims and their numbers? spoliations, destructions, burnings, and all the necessary effects of a revolution? nothing must be sacred and we can say with Machiavelli: "What matter the means as long as one arrives at the end?"

Were all these the ideas of Mirabeau, or were they, like the other document of the Illuminati found amongst his papers, the programme of a conspiracy? I incline to the latter theory. The plan of campaign was, at any rate, the one followed out by the conspirators, as Chamfort, the friend and confidant of Mirabeau, admitted in his conversation with Marmontel:

The nation is a great herd that only thinks of browsing, and with good sheepdogs the shepherds can lead it as they please ... Money and the hope of plunder are all-powerful with the people ...

Mirabeau cheerfully asserts that with 100 louis one can make quite a good riot.

Another contemporary thus describes the methods of the leaders:

Mirabeau, in the exuberance of an orgy, cried one day: "That 'canaille' well deserves to have us for legislators!" These professions of faith, as we see, are not at all democratic; the sect uses the populace as revolution fodder ["chair à révolution"], as prime material for brigandage, after which it seizes the gold and abandons generations to torture. It is veritably the code of hell.

It is this "code of hell" set forth in the "Projet de Révolution" that we shall find repeated in succeeding documents throughout the last hundred years – in the correspondence of the "Alta Vendita", in the "Dialogues aux Enfers entre Machiavel et Montesquieu" by Maurice Joly, in the Revolutionary Catechism of Bakunin, in the Protocols of the Elders of Zion, and in the writings of the Russian Bolsheviks today.

Whatever doubts may be cast on the authenticity of any of these documents, the indisputable fact thus remains that as early as 1789 this Machiavellian plan of engineering revolution and using the people as a lever for raising a tyrannical minority to power, had been formulated; further, that the methods described in this earliest "Protocol" have been carried out according to plan from that day to this. And in every outbreak of the social revolution the authors of the movement have been known to be connected with secret societies.

It was Adrien Duport, author of the "'Great Fear'" that spread over France on July 22, 1789, Duport, the inner initiate of the secret societies, "holding in his hands all the threads

of the masonic conspiracy", who on May 21, 1790, set forth
before the Committee of Propaganda the vast scheme of
destruction:

> M. de Mirabeau has well established the fact that the for-
> tunate revolution which has taken place in France must
> and will be for all the peoples of Europe the awakening of
> liberty and for Kings the sleep of death.

But Duport goes on to explain that whilst Mirabeau thinks it
advisable at present not to concern themselves with anything
outside France, he himself believes that the triumph of the
French Revolution must lead inevitably to "the ruin of all
thrones ... Therefore we must hasten among our neighbours
the same revolution that is going on in France."

The plan of illuminized Freemasonry was thus nothing less
than world-revolution.

At the beginning of the Revolution, Orléanism and
Freemasonry thus formed a united body. According to
Lombard de Langres:

> France in 1789 counted more than 2,000 lodges affiliated
> to the Grand Orient; the number of adepts was more than
> 100,000. The first events of 1789 were only Masonry in
> action. All the revolutionaries of the Constituent Assembly
> were initiated into the third degree. We place in this class
> the Duc d'Orléans, Valence, Syllery, Laclos, Sièyes,
> Pétion, Menou, Biron, Montesquieu, Fauchet, Condorcet,
> Lafayette, Mirabeau, Garat, Rabaud, Dubois-Crancé,
> Thiébaud, Larochefoucauld, and others.

Amongst these others were not only the Brissotins, who
formed the nucleus of the Girondin party, but the men of the
Terror – Marat, Robespierre, Danton, and Desmoulins.

It was these fiercer elements, true disciples of the Illuminati,
who were to sweep away the visionary Masons dreaming of
equality and brotherhood. Following the precedent set by
Weishaupt, classical pseudonyms were adopted by these

leaders of the Jacobins, thus Chaumette was known as Anaxagoras, Clootz as Anacharsis, Danton as Horace, Lacroix as Publicola, and Ronsin as Scaevola ; again, after the manner of the Illuminati, the names of towns were changed and a revolutionary calendar was adopted. The red cap and loose hair affected by the Jacobins appear also to have been foreshadowed in the lodges of the Illuminati.

Yet faithfully as the Terrorists carried out the plan of the Illuminati, it would seem that they themselves were not initiated into the innermost secrets of the conspiracy. Behind the Convention, behind the clubs, behind the Revolutionary Tribunal, there existed, says Lombard de Langres, that "most secret convention ['convention sécrétissime'] which directed everything after May 31, an occult and terrible power of which the other Convention became the slave and which was composed of the prime initiates of Illuminism. This power was above Robespierre and the committees of the government, ... it was this occult power which appropriated to itself the treasures of the nation and distributed them to the brothers and friends who had helped on the great work."

What was the aim of this occult power? Was it merely the plan of destruction that had originated in the brain of a Bavarian professor twenty years earlier, or was it something far older, a live and terrible force that had lain dormant through the centuries, that Weishaupt and his allies had not created but only loosed upon the world? The Reign of Terror, like the outbreak of Satanism in the Middle Ages, can be explained by no material causes – the orgy of hatred, lust, and cruelty directed not only against the rich but still more against the poor and defenceless, the destruction of science, art, and beauty, the desecration of the churches, the organized campaign against all that was noble, all that was sacred, all that humanity holds dear, what was this but Satanism?

In desecrating the churches and stamping on the crucifixes the Jacobins had in fact followed the precise formula of black magic: "For the purpose of infernal evocation ... it is requisite ... to profane the ceremonies of the religion to which one belongs and to trample its holiest symbols under foot." It was this that formed the prelude to the "Great Terror", when, to those who lived through it, it seemed that France lay under the sway of the powers of darkness.

So in the "great shipwreck of civilization", as a contemporary has described it, the projects of the Cabalists, the Gnostics, and the secret societies which for nearly eighteen centuries had sapped the foundations of Christianity found their fulfilment. Do we not detect an echo of the Toledot Yeshu in the blasphemies of the Marquis de Sade concerning "the Jewish slave" and "the adulterous woman, the courtesan of Galilee"? And in the imprecations of Marat's worshippers, "Christ was a false prophet!" a repetition of the secret doctrine attributed to the Templars: "Jesus is not the true God; He is a false prophet; He was not crucified for the salvation of humanity, but for His own misdeeds"? Are these resemblances accidental, or are they the outcome of a continuous plot against the Christian faith?

We shall now see that not only the Illuminati but Weishaupt himself still continued to intrigue long after the French Revolution had ended.

Directly the Reign of Terror was over, the masonic lodges, which during the Revolution had been replaced by the clubs, began to reopen, and by the beginning of the nineteenth century were in a more flourishing condition than ever before. "It was the most brilliant epoch of Masonry," wrote the Freemason Bazot in his *History of Freemasonry*. Nearly 1,200 lodges existed in France under the Empire; generals, magistrates, artists, savants, and notabilities in every line were initiated into the Order. The most eminent of these was Prince Cambacérès, pro Grand Master of the Grand Orient.

It is in the midst of this period that we find Weishaupt once more at work behind the scenes of Freemasonry. Thus in the remarkable Masonic correspondence published by M. Benjamin Fabre in his "Eques a Capite Galeato" – of which, as has already been pointed out, the authenticity is admitted by eminent British Freemasons – a letter is reproduced from Pyron, representative in Paris of the Grand Orient of Italy, to the Marquis de Chefdebien, dated September 9, 1808, in which it is stated that "a member of the sect of Bav." has asked for information on a certain point of ritual.

On December 29, 1808, Pyron writes again: "By the words 'sect of B... .' I meant W... ."; and on December 3, 1809, puts the matter quite plainly: "The other word remaining at the end of my pen refers enigmatically to Weis-pt." So, as M. Fabre points out:

There is no longer any doubt that it is a question here of Weishaupt, and yet one observes that his name is not yet written in all its letters. It must be admitted here that Pyron took great precautions when it was a matter of Weishaupt! And one is led to ask what could be the extraordinary importance of the rôle played at this moment in the Freemasonry of the First Empire by this Weishaupt, who was supposed to have been outside the Masonic movement since Illuminism was brought to trial in 1786!

But the Marquis de Chefdebien entertained no illusions about Weishaupt, whose intrigues he had always opposed, and in a letter dated May 12, 1806, to the Freemason Roettiers, who had referred to the danger of isolated masonic lodges, he asks:

In good faith, very reverend brother, is it in isolated lodges that the atrocious conspiracy of Philippe [the Duc d'Orléans] and Robespierre was formed? Is it from isolated lodges that those prominent men came forth, who, assembled at the Hôtel de Ville, stirred up revolt, devastation, assassination? And is it not in the lodges bound together, co- and sub-ordinated, that the monster Weishaupt established his tests and had his horrible principles prepared?

If, then, as M. Gustave Bord asserts, the Marquis de Chefdebien had himself belonged to the Illuminati before the Revolution, here is indeed Illuminist evidence in support of

Barruel! Yet disillusioned as the "Eques a Capite Galeato" appears to have been with regard to Illuminism, he still retained his allegiance to Freemasonry. This would tend to prove that, however subversive the doctrines of the Grand Orient may have been – and indeed undoubtedly were – it was not Freemasonry itself but Illuminism which organized the movement of which the French Revolution was the first manifestation. As Monsignor Dillon has expressed it:

> Had Weishaupt not lived, Masonry might have ceased to be a power after the reaction consequent on the French Revolution. He gave it a form and character which caused it to outlive that reaction, to energize to the present day, and which will cause it to advance until its final conflict with Christianity must determine whether Christ or Satan shall reign on this earth to the end.

If to the word Masonry we add Grand Orient – that is to say, the Masonry not of Great Britain, but of the Continent – we shall be still nearer to the truth.

In the early part of the nineteenth century Illuminism was thus as much alive as ever. Joseph de Maistre, writing at this period, constantly refers to the danger it presents to Europe. Is it not also to Illuminism that a mysterious passage in a recent work of M. Lenôtre refers? In the course of conversation with the friends of the false Dauphin Hervagault, Monsignor de Savine is said to have "made allusions in prudent and almost terrified terms to some international sect ... a power superior to all others ... which has arms and eyes everywhere and which governs Europe today."

When in "World Revolution" I asserted that during the period that Napoleon held the reins of power the devastating fire of Illuminism was temporarily extinguished, I wrote without knowledge of some important documents which prove that Illuminism continued without break from the date of its foundation all through the period of the Empire. So far, then, from overstating the case by saying that Illuminism did not cease in 1786, I understated it by suggesting that it ceased even for this brief interval. The documents in which this evidence is to be found are referred to by Lombard de Langres, who, writing in 1820, observes that the Jacobins were invisible from the 18th Brumaire until 1813, and goes on to say:

> Here the sect disappears; we find to guide us during this period only uncertain notions, scattered fragments; the plots of Illuminism lie buried in the boxes of the Imperial police.

But the contents of these boxes no longer lie buried; transported to the Archives Nationales, the documents in which the intrigues of Illuminism are laid bare have at last been given to the public. Here there can be no question of imaginative abbés, Scotch professors, or American divines conjuring up a bogey to alarm the world; these dry official reports prepared for the vigilant eye of the Emperor, never intended and never used for publication, relate calmly and dispassionately what the writers have themselves heard and observed concerning the danger that Illuminism presents to all forms of settled government.

The author of the most detailed report is one François Charles de Berckheim, special commissioner of police at Mayence towards the end of the Empire, who as a Freemason is naturally not disposed to prejudice against secret societies. In October 1810 he writes, however, that his attention has been drawn to the Illuminati by a pamphlet which has just fallen into his hands, namely the "Essai sur la Secte des Illuminés", which, like many contemporaries, he attributes originally to Mirabeau. He then goes on to ask whether the sect still exists, and if so whether it is indeed "an association of frightful scoundrels who aim, as Mirabeau assures us, at the overthrow of all law and all morality, at replacing virtue by crime in every act of human life." Further, he asks whether both sects of "Illuminés" have now combined in one and what are their present projects. Conversations with other Freemasons further increase Berckheim's anxiety on the subject; one of the best informed observes to him: "I know a great deal, enough at any rate to be convinced that the 'Illuminés' have vowed the overthrow of monarchic governments and of all authority on the same basis."

Berckheim thereupon sets out to make enquiries, with the result that he is able to state that the "Illuminés" have initiates all over Europe, that they have spared no efforts to introduce their principles into the lodges, and "to spread a doctrine subversive of all settled government ... under the pretext of the regeneration of social morality and the amelioration of the lot and condition of men by means of laws founded on principles and sentiments unknown hitherto and contained only in the heads of the leaders." "Illuminism," he declares, "is becoming a great and formidable power, and I fear, in my conscience, that kings and peoples will have much to suffer from it unless foresight and prudence break its frightful mechanism ['ses affreux restorts']."

Two years later, on January 16, 1813, Berckheim writes again to the Minister of Police:

Monseigneur, they write to me from Heidelberg ... that a great number of initiates into the mysteries of Illuminism are to be found there.

These gentlemen wear as a sign of recognition a gold ring on the third finger of the left hand; on the back of this ring there is a little rose, in the middle of this rose is an almost imperceptible dint; by pressing this with the point of a pin one touches a spring, by this means the two gold circles are detached. On the inside of the first of these circles is the device: "Be German as you ought to be"; on the inside of the second of these circles are engraved the words "Pro Patria".

Subversive as the ideas of the Illuminati might be, they were therefore not subversive of German patriotism. We shall find this apparent paradox running all through the Illuminist movement to the present day.

In 1814 Berckheim drew up his great report on the secret societies of Germany, which is of so much importance in throwing a light on the workings of the modern revolutionary movement, that extracts must be given here at length. His testimony gains greater weight from the vagueness he displays on the origins of Illuminism and the role it had played before the French Revolution; it is evident, therefore, that he had not taken his ideas from Robison or Barruel – to whom he never once refers – but from information gleaned on the spot in Germany. The opening paragraphs finally refute the fallacy concerning the extinction of the sect in 1786.

The oldest and most dangerous association is that which is generally known under the denomination of the "Illuminés" and of which the foundation goes back towards the middle of the last century.

Bavaria was its cradle; it is said that it had for founders several chiefs of the Order of the Jesuits; but this opinion, advanced perhaps at random, is founded only on uncertain premises; in any case, in a short time it made rapid progress, and the Bavarian Government recognized the necessity of employing methods of repression against it and even of driving away several of the principal sectaries.

But it could not eradicate the germ of the evil. The "Illuminés" who remained in Bavaria, obliged to wrap themselves in darkness so as to escape the eye of authority, became only the more formidable: the rigorous measures of which they were the object, adorned by the title of persecution, gained them new proselytes, whilst the banished members went to carry the principles of the Association into other States.

Thus in a few years Illuminism multiplied its hotbeds all through the south of Germany, and as a consequence in Saxony, in Prussia, in Sweden, and even in Russia.

The reveries of the Pietists have long been confounded with those of the Illuminés. This error may arise from the denomination of the sect, which at first suggests the idea of a purely religious fanaticism and of mystic forms which it was obliged to take at its birth in order to conceal its principles and projects; but the Association always had a political tendency. If it still retains some mystic traits, it is in order to support itself at need by the power of religious fanaticism, and we shall see in what follows how well it knows to turn this to account.

The doctrine of Illuminism is subversive of every kind of monarchy; unlimited liberty, absolute levelling down, such is the fundamental dogma of the sect; to break the ties that bind the Sovereign to the citizen of a state, that is the object of all its efforts.

No doubt some of the principal chiefs, amongst whom are numbered men distinguished for their fortune, their birth, and the dignities with which they are invested, are not the dupes of these demagogic dreams: they hope to find in the popular emotions they stir up the means of seizing the reigns of power, or at any rate of increasing their wealth and their credit; but the crowd of adepts believe in it religiously, and, in order to reach the goal shown to them, they maintain incessantly a hostile attitude towards sovereigns.

Thus the "Illuminés" hailed with enthusiasm the ideas that prevailed in France from 1789 to 1804. Perhaps they were not foreign to the intrigues which prepared the explosions of 1789 and the following years; but if they did not take an active part in these manoeuvres, it is at least beyond doubt that they openly applauded the systems which resulted from them; that the Republican armies when they penetrated into Germany found in these sectarians auxiliaries the more dangerous for the sovereigns of the invaded states in that they inspired no distrust, and we can say with assurance that more than one general of the Republic owed a part of its success to his *understanding with the "Illuminés"*.

It would be a mistake if one confounded Illuminism with Freemasonry. These two associations, in spite of the points of resemblance they may possess in the mystery with which they surround themselves, in the tests that precede initiation, and in other matters of form, are absolutely distinct and have no kind of connexion with each other. The lodges of the Scottish Rite number, it is true, a few "Illuminé" amongst the Masons of the higher degrees, but these adepts are very careful not to be known as such to their brothers in Masonry or to manifest ideas that would betray their secret.

Berckheim then goes on to describe the subtle methods by which the Illuminati now maintain their existence; learning wisdom from the events of 1786, their organization is carried on invisibly, so as to defy the eye of authority:

It was thought for a long while that the association had a Grand Mastership, that is to say, a centre point from which radiated all the impulsions given to this great body, and this primary motive power was sought for successively in all the capitals of the North, in Paris and even in Rome. This error gave birth to another opinion no less fallacious: it was supposed that there existed in the principal towns lodges where initiations were made and which received directly the instructions emanating from the headquarters of the Society.

If such had been the organization of Illuminism, it would not so long have escaped the investigations of which it was the object: these meetings, necessarily thronged and frequent, requiring besides, like masonic lodges, appropriate premises, would have aroused the attention of magistrates: it would not have been difficult to introduce false brothers, who, directed and protected by authority, would soon have penetrated the secrets of the sect.

This is what I have gathered most definitely on the Association of the "Illuminés":

First I would point out that by the word hotbeds [foyers] I did not mean to designate points of meeting for the adepts, places where they hold assemblies, but only localities where the Association counts a great number of partisans, who, whilst living isolated in appearance, exchange ideas, have an understanding with each other, and advance together towards the same goal.

The Association had, it is true, assemblies at its birth where receptions [i.e. initiations] took place, but the dangers which resulted from these made them feel the necessity of abandoning them. It was settled that each initiated adept should have the right without the help of anyone else to initiate all those who,after the usual tests, seemed to him worthy.

The catechism of the sect is composed of a very small number of articles which might even be reduced to this single principle:

"To arm the opinion of the peoples against sovereigns and to work by every method for the fall of monarchic governments in order to found in their place systems of absolute independence." Everything that can tend towards this object is in the spirit of the Association ...

Initiations are not accompanied, as in Masonry, by phantasmagoric trials, ... but they are preceded by long moral tests which guarantee in the safest way the fidelity of the catechumen; oaths, a mixture of all that is most sacred in religion, threats and imprecations against traitors, nothing that can stagger the imagination is spared; but the only engagement into which the recipient enters is to propagate the principles with which he has been imbued, to maintain inviolable secrecy on all that pertains to the association, and to work with all his might to increase the number of proselytes.

It will no doubt seem astonishing that there can be the least accord in the association, and that men bound together by no physical tie and who live at great distances from each other can communicate their ideas to each other, make plans of conduct, and give grounds of fear to Governments; but there exists an invisible chain which binds together all the scattered members of the association. Here are a few links:

All the adepts living in the same town usually know each other, unless the population of the town or the number of the adepts is too considerable. In this last case they are divided into several groups, who are all in touch with each other by means of members of the association whom personal relations bind to two or several groups at a time.

These groups are again subdivided into so many private coteries which the difference of rank, of fortune, of character, tastes, etc., may necessitate: they are always small, sometimes composed of five or six individuals, who meet frequently under various pretexts, sometimes at the house of one member, sometimes at that of another; literature, art, amusements of all kinds are the apparent object of these meetings, and it is nevertheless in these confabulations ["conciliabules"] that the adepts communicate their private views to each other, agree on methods, receive the directions that the intermediaries bring them, and communicate their own ideas to these same intermediaries, who then go on to propagate them in other coteries. It will be understood that there may be uniformity in the march of all these separated groups, and that one day may suffice to communicate the same impulse to all the quarters of a large town ...

These are the methods by which the 'Illuminés', without any apparent organization, without settled leaders, agree together from the banks of the Rhine to those of the Neva, from the Baltic to the Dardanelles, and advance continually towards the same goal, without leaving any trace that might compromise the interests of the association or even bring suspicion on any of its members; the most active police would fail before such a combination ...

As the principal force of the "Illuminés" lies in the power of opinions, they have set themselves out from the beginning to make proselytes amongst the men who through their profession exercise a direct influence on minds, such as "littérateurs", savants, and above all professors. The latter in their chairs, the former in their writings, propagate the principles of the sect by disguising the poison that they circulate under a thousand different forms.

These germs, often imperceptible to the eyes of the vulgar, are afterwards developed by the adepts of the Societies they frequent, and the most obscure wording is thus brought to the understanding of the least discerning. It is above all in the Universities that Illuminism has always found and always will find numerous recruits. Those professors who belong to the Association set out from the first to study the character of their pupils. If a student gives evidence of a vigorous mind, an ardent imagination, the sectaries at once get hold of him, they sound in his ears the words Despotism –Tyranny – Rights of the People, etc., etc. Before he can even attach any meaning to these words, as he advances in age, reading chosen for him, conversations skilfully arranged, develop the germs deposited in his youthful brain; soon his imagination ferments, history, traditions of fabulous times, all are made use of to carry his exaltation to the highest point, and before even he has been told of a secret Association, to contribute to the fall of a sovereign appears to his eyes the noblest and most meritorious act ...

At last, when he has been completely captivated, when several years of testing guarantee to the society inviolable secrecy and absolute devotion, it is made known to him that millions of individuals distributed in all the States of Europe share his sentiments and his hopes, that a secret link binds firmly all the scattered members of this immense family, and that the reforms he desires so ardently must sooner or later come about.

This propaganda is rendered the easier by the existing associations of students who meet together for the study of literature, for fencing, gaming, or even mere debauchery. The Illuminés insinuate themselves into all these circles and turn them into hot-beds for the propagation of their principles.

Such, then, is the Association's continual mode of progression from its origins until the present moment; it is by conveying from childhood the germ of poison into the highest classes of society, in feeding the minds of students on ideas diametrically opposed to that order of things under which they have to live, in breaking the ties that bind them to sovereigns, that Illuminism has recruited the largest number of adepts, called by the state to which they were born to be the mainstays of the Throne and of a system which would ensure them honours and privileges.

Amongst the proselytes of this last class there are some no doubt whom political events, the favour of the prince or other circumstances, detach from the Association; but the number of these deserters is necessarily very limited: and even then they dare not speak openly against their old associates, whether because they are in dread of private vengeances or whether because, knowing the real power of the sect, they want to keep paths of reconciliation open to themselves; often indeed they are so fettered by the pledges they have personally given that they find it necessary not only to consider the interests of the sect, but to serve it indirectly, although their new circumstances demand the contrary ...

Berckheim then proceeds to show that those writers on Illuminism were mistaken who declared that political assassinations were definitely commanded by the Order:

There is more than exaggeration in this accusation; those who put it forward, more zealous in striking an effect than in seeking the truth, may have concluded, not without probability, that men who surrounded themselves with profound mystery, who propagated a doctrine absolutely subversive of any kind of monarchy, dreamt only of the assassination of sovereigns; but experience has shown (and all the documents derived from the least suspect sources confirm this) that the "Illuminés" count a great deal more on the power of opinion than on assassination; the regicide committed on Gustavus III is perhaps the only crime of this kind that Illuminism has dared to attempt, if indeed it is really proved that this crime was its work; moreover, if assassination had been, as it is said, the fundamental point in its doctrine, might we not suppose that other regicides would have been attempted in Germany during the course of the French Revolution, especially when the Republican armies occupied the country?

The sect would be much less formidable if this were its doctrine, on the one hand because it would inspire in most of the "Illuminés" a feeling of horror which would triumph even over the fear of vengeance, on the other hand because plots and conspiracies always leave some traces which guide the authorities to the footsteps of the prime instigators; and besides, it is the nature of things that out of twenty plots directed against sovereigns, nineteen come to light before they have reached the point of maturity necessary to their execution.

The "Illuminés" line of march is more prudent, more skilful, and consequently more dangerous; instead of revolting the imagination by ideas of regicide, they affect the most generous sentiments: declamations on the unhappy state of the people, on the selfishness of courtiers, on measures of administration, on all acts of authority that may offer a pretext to declamations as a contrast to the seductive pictures of the felicity that awaits the nations under the systems they wish to establish, such is their manner of procedure, particularly in private. More circumspect in their writings, they usually disguise the poison they dare not proffer openly under obscure metaphysics or more or less ingenious allegories. Often indeed texts from Holy Writ serve as an envelope and vehicle for these baneful insinuations ...

By this continuous and insidious form of propaganda the imagination of the adepts is so worked on that if a crisis arises, they are ready to carry out the most daring projects.

Another Association closely resembling the "Illuminés",
Berckheim reports, is known as the "Idealists", whose system
is founded on the doctrine of perfectibility; these kindred
sects "agree in seeing in the words of Holy Scripture the
pledge of universal regeneration, of an absolute levelling
down, and it is in this spirit that the sectarians interpret the
sacred books."

Berckheim further confirms the assertion I made in "World
Revolution" – contested, as usual, by a reviewer without a
shred of evidence to the contrary – that the Tugendbund
derived from the Illuminati. "The League of Virtue," he
writes, "was directed by the secondary chiefs of the 'Illuminés'
... In 1810 the Friends of Virtue were so identified with the
'Illuminés' in the North of Germany that no line of demarca-
tion was seen between them."

But it is time to turn to the testimony of another witness on
the activities of the secret societies which is likewise to be
found at the Archives Nationales. This consists of a document transmitted by the Court of Vienna to the Government
of France after the Restoration, and contains the interrogatory of a certain Witt Doehring, a nephew of the Baron
d'Eckstein, who, after taking part in secret society intrigues,
was summoned before the judge Abel at Bayreuth in February,
1824. Amongst secret associations recently existing in
Germany, the witness asserted, were the "Independents" and
the "Absolutes"; the latter "adored in Robespierre their most
perfect ideal, so that the crimes committed during the French
Revolution by this monster and the Montagnards of the
Convention were in their eyes, in accordance with their moral
system, heroic actions ennobled and sanctified by their aim."
The same document goes on to explain why so many com-
bustible elements had failed to produce an explosion in
Germany:

> The thing that seemed the great obstacle to the plans of the
> Independents ... was what they called the servile character
> and the dog-like fidelity ["Hundestreue"] of the German
> people, that is to say, that attachment – innate and firmly

impressed on their minds without even the aid of reason – which that excellent people everywhere bears towards its princes.

A traveller in Germany during the year 1795 admirably summed up the matter in these words:

> The Germans are in this respect [of democracy] the most curious people in the world ... the cold and sober temperament of the Germans and their tranquil imagination enable them to combine the most daring opinions with the most servile conduct. That will explain to you ... why so much combustible material accumulating for so many years beneath the political edifice of Germany has not yet damaged it. Most of the princes, accustomed to see their men of letters so constantly free in their writings and so constantly slavish in their hearts, have not thought it necessary to use severity against this sheeplike herd of modern Gracchi and Brutuses. Some of them [the princes] have even without difficulty adopted part of their opinions, and Illuminism having doubtless been presented to them as perfection, the complement of philosophy, they were easily persuaded to be initiated into it. But great care was taken not to let them know more than the interests of the sect demanded.

It was thus that Illuminism, unable to provoke a blaze in the home of its birth, spread, as before the French Revolution, to a more inflammable Latin race – this time the Italians. Six years after his interrogatory at Beyreuth, Witt Doehring published his book on the secret societies of France and Italy, in which he now realized he had played the part of dupe, and incidentally confirms the statement I have previously quoted, that the Alta Vendita was a further development of the Illuminati.

BIBLE CODE

In 1997 Michael Drosnin published *The Bible Code*, in which he claimed that the holy book predicted events thousands of years before they occurred. Drosnin had decoded the Good Book to send a letter to Itzhak Rabin, the Israeli PM, warning him that he was going to be assassinated. Which he duly was.

Drosnin himself was not the discoverer of the code, only its popularizer. Bible decoding could be said to start with Jewish Kabbalists in the fourteenth century, who believed that hidden truths in the Torah could be determined by manipulation of its letters, including geometric computation (known as "Gematra"). In the 1940s, Czech rabbi H. M. D. Weissmandel applied a "skip code" to the Bible, taking the letter from the start of Genesis, "skipping" fifty letters to take the next letter, then fifty more, and fifty more until the world spelled "Torah". The word was also found in each of the other five books of Moses. Using the same system, the Jerusalem-based mathematician Eliyahu Rips, together with Yoav Rosenberg and Doron Witzum, unearthed the names of famous rabbis in the Book of Genesis in close proximity to the dates of their births and deaths, in a way that could not be explained by chance (allegedly), as outlined in their paper "Equidistant Letter Sequences in the Book of Genesis" in *Statistical Science*. Rips later used "Equidistant Letter Sequencing" (ELS) to turn up the date 18 January 1991 – the start of the Gulf War.

Rips, however, was circumspect about the use of the Bible code to foretell the future. Drosnin showed no such caution. In

Drosnin's hands the ELS method gave the date of the atomic Armageddon which would end the world.

2000. Or then again, 2006.

Drosnin was clearly not on a fortune-telling roll. In *The Bible Code II*, his sequel to his 1997 bestseller, Drosnin asserted that Palestinian Authority leader Yasser Arafat would be shot to death by Hamas gunmen. (He wasn't.)

Faced with as much ridicule as respect, Drosnin defied anyone to find a message about the assassination of a national leader in *Moby Dick*. An Australian expert in probability theory, Brendan McKay, soon found "Kennedy" and "he shall be killed".

The Bible can be decoded to foretell the future: ALERT LEVEL 3

Further Reading
Michael Drosnin, *The Bible Code*, 1997

BIG BROTHER: INFRAGARD AND ECHELON

George Orwell in his novel, *1984*, described a society in which civil liberties had gone out of the window and the government – with the help of snitches and electronic surveillance – monitored every aspect of its citizens' lives. The said citizens were constantly reminded "Big Brother is Watching You". In 1948, when the story was written, it was pure science fiction.

It may have taken a little longer than he envisaged, but Orwell's Big Brother dystopia has arrived. According to the latest studies, Britain has 4.2 million CCTV cameras – one for every fourteen people in the country. The average British citizen is caught on camera an average of 300 times daily.

Surveillance cameras, however, are obvious and overt. Much of what government and big corporations is using to watch you is not.

In the summer of 2002, US President George W. Bush posited the setting up of a corps of civilian informants as a means of helping the War on Terror. Under "Operation TIPS" (Terrorism Information and Prevention Systems), Americans would be recruited to spy on Americans at work and in the neighbourhood. Dubya planned to have a million civilian snitches. Even TIPS backers, such as Attorney General John Ashcroft, could see the flaw in the system – there was no way for the public to know if they were being observed, or if any information gathered was accurate. Such a snoopers' charter also opened the door to people laying false charges to settle personal grudges. Although straight from the pages of the training manual of the Stasi, the former East German secret police, the Bush government ploughed ahead with TIPS until *Sydney Morning Herald* journalist Ritt Goldstein reported on the operation, which then shrivelled and died in the light of public disquiet.

The demise of TIPS, however, did not leave the US Government unable to eavesdrop on its citizens, because it already had the InfraGard and ECHELON projects.

A private non-profit group, InfraGard was founded in 1996 by the Federal Bureau of Investigation (FBI) office in Cleveland, Ohio, in an attempt to co-opt industry and academia as crimebusters in cyberspace. The scheme really took off after **9/11**, when InfraGard's brief was broadened to protect America from physical as well as cyber-attack. InfraGard does this by, in the programme's own words, promoting "ongoing dialogue and timely communication between members and the FBI. InfraGard members gain access to information that enables them to protect their assets and in turn give information to government that facilitates its responsibilities to prevent and address terrorism and other crimes."

InfraGard is organized into individual, geographically based chapters, which meet with the local G-man. Members have access to an Eyes-Only InfraGard website that provides members with the hottest information on what domestic enemies are doing, the latest research on protective measures, and the ability to communicate securely with other members.

And who are the citizens who make up the secret, non-accountable InfraGard chapter? There's the rub. Of the 32,000 InfraGard members the identities of few are known, although the best guess is that the majority are suits from Fortune 500 companies. In return for participation in InfraGard, its members receive extraordinary benefits. According to one InfraGard whistle-blower, members

> get privileges, special phone numbers to call in times of emergency. They can get their family out maybe in times of an emergency or their friends, so they know about these threats. They're getting secret intelligence on almost a daily basis that the American public isn't getting, so they're in the know in a way that we aren't in the know.

Paranoid? You will be. InfraGard, however, is but the little brother of ECHELON.

ECHELON is the name given to the system of signal-collection and analysis networks run by the United States, the United Kingdom, Canada, Australia and New Zealand. ECHELON was created in 1947 during the Cold War to monitor the military and diplomatic communications of the Soviet Union and its satellite countries. Initially, the project eavesdropped on wireless and telephone communications, but with the advent of the World Wide Web it covered email and chat rooms too; with the ending of the Cold War, the focus of ECHELON turned to terrorism and crime. The centrepiece of ECHELON is a "virtual dictionary", a vast resource of keywords, names and telephone numbers. The billions of daily communications around the world are automatically scanned by ECHELON, and matches are referred to a human analyst. Estimates suggest that ECHELON can sift through a billion emails an hour. Although the US and UK are barred from spying on their respective citizens without court warrants, ECHELON cleverly avoids national law by enabling each country to monitor each other's citizens. Then swap the information.

Countries excluded from ECHELON have alleged that the system is used in commercial and industrial espionage. The French press have claimed that Boeing was provided with information by ECHELON to deprive Airbus, Boeing's European competitor, of contracts. A 1998 report prepared by the European Parliament cited "wide ranging" evidence that ECHELON information was used to provide certain companies with "commercial advantages". The French press named names, claiming that Boeing was prioritized in contracts over Airbus, its European rival. Similarly, the US Raytheon company was able to muscle in on a radar deal between a French company and Brazil courtesy of ECHELON intercepts. Meanwhile, journalist Patrick Poole speculated that AT & T took a cut of a $200 million deal between Indonesia and Nipponese satellite-manufacturer NEC due to ECHELON-obtained intelligence.

Manifestly, InfraGard and ECHELON have a role to play in fighting crime and terror; ECHELON is said to have played a "key role" in nabbing 9/11 mastermind Khalid Sheik Mohammed.

But the state's invasion of privacy, the use of citizens as spies, the misuse of information for financial ends are perils to citizens. Big Brother is watching you. You need to watch big brother.

> The Big Brothers of InfraGard and ECHELON are watching you: ALERT LEVEL 10

Further Reading
Nicky Hagar, *Secret Power*, 1996

OSAMA BIN LADEN

"Got Him!" trumpeted the *New York Post*. "Rot in Hell!" urged the *Daily News*.

Relief, revenge and jubilation came to New York in equal measures on Monday, 2 May 2011, following the announcement that a US Navy SEAL team had just killed Osama bin Laden, the leader of al-Qaeda. However, the circumstances surrounding bin Laden's death raised the big question: Had the US really got its man? Although US officials said DNA testing proved the al-Qaeda leader was killed in the villa in Pakistan, as did a facial recognition test, they refused to release photographs of his corpse. This contrasted absolutely with US policy when Uday and Qusay Hussein – the sons of Iraqi dictator Saddam Hussein – were killed in a firefight with US troops, after which the US relied on photographs of their bodies to convince people they were dead. And when Saddam himself was executed, video footage of his death and subsequent photographs were offered up as final proof of the tyrant's demise.

The lack of documentation offered by the White House was pure fodder for a conspiracy that bin Laden wasn't offed on the morning of 2 May 2011. The conspiracy was only pumped by the US Government's choice of burial site for bin Laden: the middle of the trackless ocean.

Two main conspiracies centre on bin Laden's death:

1) bin Laden died years before in the Tora Bora mountains (either from a US bomb or kidney disease), but the US and Allies hushed this up to justify the continuance of the War on

Terror. Barack Obama announced bin Laden's death for the bragging rights, and as a poll boost. Against this, most al-Qaeda websites have since claimed that their leader is now fish food. Also, the files seized by the SEALS during the mission suggest that the man in the compound was top of the organizational pyramid, and the information gleaned has allowed the "neutralization" of subordinates.

2) The SEAL raid was a fake op, bin Laden wasn't there, and is alive and well and living in the Af-Pak borderland with his VCR and hookah pipe. The Bush administration never had any real intention of huntin' the al-Qaeda leader down, because the Bush and bin Laden clans were friends, and commercial allies.

The special relationship between the Bushes and the bin Ladens *is* a matter of record; George H. W. Bush was actually meeting with bin Laden's brother on the morning of 9/11.

In this murky conspiracy scenario, George Bush Jnr and Osama bin Laden are engaged in a pleasant series of quid pro quos: Bush leaves bin Laden untroubled in his cave, and the hirsute terrorist releases an inflammatory video statement days before the October 2004 US presidential election, which proves to be crucial in helping George secure a second term in office. Helping the conspiracy along is a Facebook campaign, "Osama bin Laden Is NOT DEAD".

A minor riff in the bin Laden death conspiracy is that he tried to surrender but was killed anyway. The meat of this theory is that the US Government wanted to avoid a lengthy show trial so always intended the raid to be an assassination mission. One anonymous White House official did unhelpfully (from the PR point of view) let slip it was a "kill operation". If so, it would explain the White House's reluctance to release snaps of the al-Qaeda's cadaver, since these presumably show the classic assassination technique of a bullet through the brains.

Bin Laden was not killed by Navy SEALS in Abbottabad, Pakistan, on 2 May 2011: ALERT LEVEL 3

Bin Laden was deliberately assassinated:
ALERT LEVEL 7

Further Reading
Brandon Franklin Hurst, *Osama Bin Laden: The Final Days,* 2011
Howard Wasdin, *Seal Team Six,* 2011

BLACK DEATH

The Black Death was an outbreak of plague caused (possibly) by the bacterium *Yersinia pestis* which swept through Europe between 1348 and 1351, perhaps reducing the population of the continent by a third, from 54 million to 37 million. The chronicler Henry Knighton described the onset and aftermath of the disease in England:

> The dreadful pestilence penetrated the sea coast by Southampton and came to Bristol, and there almost the whole population of the town perished, as if it had been seized by sudden death; for few kept their beds more than two or three days, or even half a day. Then this cruel death spread everywhere around, following the course of the sun ... After the aforesaid pestilence, many buildings, great and small, fell into ruins in every city, borough, and village for lack of inhabitants, likewise many villages and hamlets became desolate, not a house being left in them, all having died who dwelt there, and it was probable that many such villages would never be inhabited.

As Knighton noted, ports were the point of the entry for the disease, because the responsible bacterium was carried by fleas of the black rat, of which medieval ships carried scores. While some contemporaries saw the Black Death as an act of God, a punishment for sins, others saw the pandemic as the handiwork of humans – in other words, the Black Death was an early exercise in germ warfare. The Indian princedoms were much suspected, because they had become discontented with the trade rules imposed by the European countries. Consequently the Indian princelings – or at least their hirelings – placed germladen rats on Europe-bound ships. When the Black Death had KOd the population of the white-skinned enemy, the Indian Army would march in and take over.

Biowarfare was not unknown in the fourteenth century; there are accounts of the Mongols catapulting disease-ridden corpses into the Genoese-held city of Kaffa, and it is true that the Black Death spread from the East. Furthermore, the pestilence may not have been bubonic plague. Medieval accounts of Black Death symptoms do not match precisely with the symptoms of *Yersinia pestis*-caused plague: the Black Death spread with extreme rapidity, whereas identified modern outbreaks of bubonic plague have been slow to expand; incidence of the Black Death peaked in summer, whereas a rat-borne disease should most likely peak in winter when people are indoors. All this said, there is no historical or forensic evidence to implicate the maharajahs. Besides, it was hardly smart business to practise genocide on your customers.

History's scapegoats, the Jews, were also alleged by contemporaries to possibly be the agents behind the Black Death. A Jew, Agimet of Geneva, did confess to having poisoned wells across southern Europe on the instructions of Rabbi Peyret of Chambery (see Document, p.50), who was himself under the control of elders in the enclave of Toledo.

Agimet's "confession", extracted under torture, was enough to start a spate of pogroms; in Strasbourg alone 2,000 Jews were pre-emptively slaughtered to stop them poisoning the city's wells. Records of similar "confessions" were sent from town to town in Switzerland and Germany, with the result that thousands of Jews in at least two hundred settlements were killed and burned in a precursor of Hitler's holocaust.

There was no international Jewish conspiracy to wipe out Christendom behind the Black Death: It is hardly credible that the Jews of Strasbourg would poison the well they themselves used. Still, the rumour of Jewish involvement made a handy excuse for not paying loans to them. As the chronicler Frederick Closener observed about the burning of the Jews in Strasbourg:

everything that was owed to the Jews was cancelled, and the Jews had to surrender all pledges and notes that they had taken for debts. The council, however, took the cash that the Jews possessed and divided it among the working-men proportionately. The money was indeed the thing that killed the Jews. If they had been poor and if the feudal lords had not been in debt to them, they would not have been burnt.

Strasbourg, incidentally, did not escape the clutches of the plague, which killed sixteen thousand inhabitants.

An **Ebola**-like haemorrhagic virus is considered by some modern disease experts to be the most plausible cause of the Black Death. If so, it would have been even more uncontrollable as a germ warfare "weapon" in the fourteenth century than *Yersinia pestis*.

> The Black Death was an Indian/Jewish germ warfare attack: ALERT LEVEL 1

Further Reading
John Kelly, *The Great Mortality*, 2005
Philip Ziegler, *The Black Death*, 1969

DOCUMENT: THE CONFESSION OF AGIMET OF GENEVA, CHÂTEL, 20 OCTOBER 1348

The year of our Lord 1348.

On Friday, the 10th of the month of October, at Châtel, in the castle thereof, there occurred the judicial inquiry which was made by order of the court of the illustrious Prince, our lord, Amadeus, Count of Savoy, and his subjects against the Jews of both sexes who were there imprisoned, each one separately. This was done after public rumour had become current and a strong clamour had arisen because of the poison put by them into the wells, springs, and other things which the Christians use – demanding that they die, that they are able to be found guilty and, therefore, that they should be punished. Hence this their confession made in the presence of a great many trustworthy persons.

Agimet the Jew, who lived at Geneva and was arrested at Châtel, was there put to the torture a little and then he was released from it. And after a long time, having been subjected again to torture a little, he confessed in the presence of a great many trustworthy persons, who are later mentioned. To begin with it is clear that at the Lent just passed Pultus Clesis de Ranz had sent this very Jew to Venice to buy silks and other things for him. When this came to the notice of Rabbi Peyret, a Jew of Chambery who was a teacher of their law, he sent for this Agimet, for whom he had searched, and when he had come before him he said: "We have been informed that you are going to Venice to buy silk and other wares. Here I am giving you a little package of half a span in size which contains some prepared poison and venom in a thin, sewed leather-bag. Distribute it among the wells, cisterns, and springs about Venice and the other places to which you go, in order to poison the people who use the water of the aforesaid wells that will have been poisoned by you, namely, the wells in which the poison will have been placed."

Agimet took this package full of poison and carried it with him to Venice, and when he came there he threw and scattered a portion of it into the well or cistern of fresh water which was there near the German House, in order to poison the people who use the water of that cistern. And he says that this is the only cistern of sweet water in the city. He also says that the mentioned Rabbi Peyret promised to give him whatever he wanted for his troubles in this business. Of his own accord Agimet confessed further that after this had been done he left at once in order that he should not be captured by the citizens or others, and that he went personally to Calabria and Apulia and threw the above mentioned poison into many wells. He confesses also that he put some of this same poison in the well of the streets of the city of Ballet.

He confesses further that he put some of this poison into the public fountain of the city of Toulouse and in the wells that are near the [Mediterranean] sea. Asked if at the time that he scattered the venom and poisoned the wells, above mentioned, any people had died, he said that he did not know inasmuch as he had left everyone of the above mentioned places in a hurry. Asked if any of the Jews of those places were guilty in the above mentioned matter, he answered that he did not know. And now by all that which is contained in the five books of Moses and the scroll of the Jews, he declared that this was true, and that he was in no wise lying, no matter what might happen to him.

CAGOULE

"La Cagoule" was the press nickname for *Organisation Secrete de l'Action Revolutionnaire Nationale* (Secret Organization of National Revolutionary Action), a French fascist organization active in the thirties. Under its leader Eugene Deloncle, La Cagoule sought to overthrow the Third Republic with a campaign of assassination and terror. Some Cagoulards borrowed the Ku Klux Klan habit of wearing a "cagoule" or hood to conceal their identity, though the leadership were well known in French society, and included Eugène Schueller, founder of the French cosmetics company L'Oréal, whose HQ proved handy for Cagoule meetings. (The firm's connection with French fascism did not end with Schueller; Cagoulards Jacques Correze and Jean Filliol, among others, enjoyed prestigious posts as L'Oréal executives post-war.) From its foundation in 1935, Cagoule recruited heavily from other French far-right groups, and its membership, which topped 150,000, was organized into a military structure of armed cells, with guns and explosives being shipped in from the fascist regimes of Spain and Italy, or stolen by Cagoulards in the French military. Politically, La Cagoule shared common ground with the **Synarchy** movement. In September 1937, La Cagoule blew up industrial employers' buildings in Paris with the intention of pinning the blame on the Communists, and two months later prepared for the overthrow of the Third Republic, intending to place Marshal Petain as chief of state. When Petain refused to participate in the plot, they chose instead Louis Franchet d'Esperay. By now, however, La Cagoule had been heavily infiltrated by the police, and the Interior Ministry ordered the arrest of seventy leading Cagoulards, among them Deloncle. A search of La Cagoule's arms dumps revealed 2 tons of explosives, 500 machine guns and several anti-tank guns. Stripped of leadership and arms, La Cagoule fell apart, though numerous Cagoulards later collaborated with the Nazi regime in Occupied France and its puppet state in Vichy. A minority of Cagoulards took the opposite path and joined the Resistance or De Gaulle's Free French Army.

French fascist group plotted overthrow of the Third Republic: ALERT LEVEL 10

Further Reading
Michael Bar-Zohar, *Bitter Scent: The Case of L'Oréal, The Nazis, and the Arab Boycott*, 1996

FIDEL CASTRO

For years Fidel Alejandro Castro Ruz complained about CIA plots to kill him. For years the CIA denied doing anything so improper. As it turned out, the Bearded One was right. The CIA had Castro in its crosshairs for a decade or more.

Born in 1926, Castro led the 1959 Cuban Revolution, which established a socialist state ninety miles off the coast of Florida. As Wayne Smith, former head of US Interests Section in Havana, once memorably put it, socialist Cuba's effect on the capitalist US was that of "a full moon on a werewolf". Neither was Castro's socialist makeover of Cuba exactly popular with the Mafia (which had interests in Havana's casinos), or the supporters of the overthrown Fulgencio Batista. And so the CIA, the Mafia, the Batistas all started hatching schemes to rid Cuba of the hirsute leader. Initially the CIA's plots centred on merely humiliating Castro; in the psy-op, "Good Times" postcards were to be dropped over Cuba showing a corpulent Castro living the high life ("should put even a Commie dictator in the proper perspective with the underprivileged masses" stated the authorizing memo); another plan called for an LSD-like drug to be sprayed in the air at the radio station Castro used for his speeches so he would start ranting nonsense. No less whacky, was an idea to dust the Cuban leader's shoes with a depilatory powder so the hair on his beard would fall out.

When humiliating Castro failed, the CIA tried invading Cuba (the Bay of Pigs debacle) before settling on assassinating him. Most of CIA's assassination plans were apparently drawn from a bad Bond novel, and included:

- Contaminating Castro's cigars with botulin.
- Contaminating Castro's drink with botulin.
- Popping poison pills into Castro's food at his favourite restaurant, with a little help from the Mafia (including Santos Trafficante, Johnny Roselli and Sam Giancana – all incidentally contenders for killing **John F. Kennedy**).
- Contaminating Castro's scuba-diving gear with tubercle bacilli, and his wetsuit with a skin-disfiguring fungus.
- Placing an eye-catching conch on the seabed off Cuba – Castro was a keen diver – that contained an explosive device, which would detonate on being lifted.

No less than eight separate plans were drawn up by the CIA between 1960 and 1965 for the final solution of the Castro problem, only one of which was rooted in reality. Rolando Cubela Seconde, a major in the Cuban army and head of Cuba's International Federation of Students, handily contacted the CIA offering to do their job for them. (Cubela had form as an assassin; as a young student he'd murdered Antonio Blanci Rico, head of Batista's secret police.) The CIA gave Cubela the code name AMLASH and a syringe disguised as a Paper Mate pen and told him to inject Black Leaf 40 (an insecticide) into Castro. Eventually, the CIA gave Cubela what he asked for: a Belgian FAL rifle so he could pot Castro from afar. Before Cubela could pull the trigger, however, he was arrested by Castro's security service. With quite remarkable generosity, Castro asked the court for clemency on Cubela's behalf, and the putative assassin was sentenced to jail instead of a firing squad. Cubela was released in 1979 and went to live in Spain.

By then the truth of the CIA's "Get Castro!" campaign had been dragged into the open, following an investigation by US Senator Frank Church. The Church Committee's "Interim Report" of 1975 detailed the CIA's hapless history of trying to undermine, then kill, Castro, and for good measure delineated CIA involvement in the assassination of Patrice Lumumba of Congo, Rene Schneider of Chile, Rafael Trujillo of the Dominican Republic and Ngo Dinh Diem of Vietnam. The most spectacular proof of the CIA's anti-Castro antics, however, came in 1993, with the declassification of the "Inspector

General's Report on Plots to Assassinate Fidel Castro" (see Document, p.57), which had been commissioned by President Johnson in 1967. So controversial, incriminating – and maybe embarrassing – was the report that the CIA refused its declassification for thirty-six years. Even presidents were refused access to the full document.

On the recommendation of the Church Committee, President Gerald Ford issued Executive Order 11905, which ruled that "no employee of the US government shall engage in, or conspire to engage in, political assassination". Jimmy Carter strengthened this proscription with Executive Order 12036, as did Reagan, through Executive Order 12333. Because no subsequent executive order or piece of legislation has repealed the prohibition, it remains in effect.

Only a smooth White House lawyer, however, was able to reconcile EO 12333 with the Reagan administration dropping bombs on Libyan leader Moammar Gadhafi's home in 1986, or President Bush's instruction to the CIA and US military to engage in "lethal covert operations" against Osama bin Laden, or indeed Obama's green light for the eventual offing of the al-Qaeda leader. According to the White House, the ban on political assassination does not apply to wartime or counter-terrorist operations.

Meanwhile, back in Cuba jokes about Castro's apparent indestructibility ran rife. One told of him being given a present of a Galapagos turtle. He declined after learning that it was only likely to live for a hundred years, saying, "That's the problem with pets. You get attached to them and then they die on you."

Central Interference Agency plotted to kill "The Beard", a.k.a. Fidel Castro: ALERT LEVEL 10

Further Reading
Fabian Escalante, *Executive Action: 638 Ways to Kill Fidel Castro*, 2007

DOCUMENT: CIA INSPECTOR GENERAL'S REPORT ON PLOTS TO ASSASSINATE FIDEL CASTRO [EXTRACTS]

The report was drawn up in 1967 at the insistence of President Johnson – who was not allowed by the Agency to see the full version. Neither was President Nixon. Indeed, the CIA regarded their own report as so incriminating that all but one copy was destroyed. The report was only approved for release in 1993.

23 May 1967: MEMORANDUM FOR THE RECORD

SUBJECT: Report on Plots to Assassinate Fidel Castro

This report was prepared at the request of the Director of Central Intelligence. He assigned the task to the Inspector General on 23 March 1967. The report was delivered to the Director, personally, in installments, beginning on 24 April 1967. The Director returned this copy to the Inspector General on 22 May 1967 with instructions that the Inspector General:

Retain it in personal, EYES ONLY safekeeping

[...]

This ribbon copy is the only text of the report now in existence, either in whole or in part. Its text has been read only by:

Richard Helms, Director of Central Intelligence
J. S. Earman, Inspector General
K. E. Greer, Inspector (one of the authors)
S. E. Beckinridge (one of the authors)

All typing of drafts and of final text was done by the authors.

[...]

It became clear very early in our investigation that the vigor with which schemes were pursued within the Agency to eliminate Castro personally varied with the intensity of the U.S. Government's efforts to overthrow the Castro regime. We can identify five separate phases in Agency assassination planning, although the transitions from one to another are not always sharply defined. Each phase is a reflection of the then prevailing Government attitude toward the Cuban regime.

a. Prior to August 1960: All of the identifiable schemes prior to about August 1960, with one possible exception, were aimed only at discrediting Castro personally by influencing his behavior or by altering his appearance.

b. August 1960 to April 1961: The plots that were hatched in late 1960 and early 1961 were aggressively pursued and were viewed by at least some of the participants as being merely one aspect of the over-all active effort to overthrow the regime that culminated in the Bay of Pigs.

c. April 1961 to late 1961: A major scheme that was begun in August 1960 was called off after the Bay of Pigs and remained dormant for several months, as did most other Agency operational activity related to Cuba.

d. Late 1961 to late 1962: That particular scheme was reactivated in early 1962 and was again pushed vigorously in the era of Project MONGOOSE and in the climate of intense administration pressure on CIA to do something about Castro and his Cuba.

e. Late 1962 until well into 1963: After the Cuban missile crisis of October 1962 and the collapse of Project MONGOOSE, the aggressive scheme that was begun in August 1960 and revived in April 1962 was finally terminated in early 1963. Two other plots were originated in 1963, but both were impracticable and nothing ever came of them.

We cannot overemphasize the extent to which responsible Agency officers felt themselves subject to the Kennedy administration's severe pressures to do something about Castro and his regime. The fruitless and, in retrospect, often unrealistic plotting should be viewed in that light.

Many of those we interviewed stressed two points that are so obvious that recording them here may be superfluous. We believe, though, that they are pertinent to the story. Elimination of the dominant figure in a government, even when loyalties are held to him personally rather than to the government as a body, will not necessarily cause the downfall of the government. This point was stressed with respect to Castro and Cuba in an internal CIA draft paper of October 1961, which was initiated in response to General Maxwell Taylor's desire for a contingency plan. The paper took the position that the demise of Fidel Castro, from whatever cause, would offer little opportunity for the liberation of Cuba from Communist and Soviet Bloc control. The second point, which is more specifically relevant to our investigation, is that bringing about the downfall of a government necessarily requires the removal of its leaders from positions of power, and there is always the risk that the participants will resort to assassination. Such removals from power as the house arrest of a [?] or the flight of a [?] could not cause one to overlook the killings of a Diem or of a Trujillo by forces encouraged but not controlled by the U.S. government.

There is a third point, which was not directly made by any of those we interviewed, but which emerges clearly from the interviews and from review of files. The point is that of frequent resort to synecdoche – the mention of a part when the whole is to be understood, or vice versa. Thus, we encounter repeated references to phrases such as "disposing of Castro," which may be read in the narrow, literal sense of assassinating him, when it is intended that it be read in the broader, figurative sense of dislodging the Castro regime. Reversing this coin, we find people speaking vaguely of "doing something about Castro" when it is clear that what they have specifically in mind is killing him. In a situation wherein those speaking may not have actually meant what they seemed to say or may not have said what they actually meant, they should not be surprised if their oral shorthand is interpreted differently than was intended.

The suggestion was made that operations aimed at the assassination of Castro may have been generated in an atmosphere of stress in intelligence publications on the possibility of Castro's demise and on the reordering of the political structure that would follow. We reviewed intelligence publications from 1960 through 1966, including National Intelligence Estimates, Special National Intelligence Estimates, Intelligence Memorandums, and Memorandums for the Director. The NTE's on "The Situation and Prospects in Cuba" for 1960, 1963, and 1964 have brief paragraphs on likely successor governments if Castro were to depart the scene. We also find similar short references in a SNIE of March 1960 and in an Intelligence Memorandum of May 1965. In each case the treatment is no more nor less than one would expect to find in comprehensive round-ups such as these. We conclude that there is no reason to believe that the operators were unduly influenced by the content of intelligence publications.

Drew Pearson's column of 7 March 1967 refers to a reported CIA plan in 1963 to assassinate Cuba's Fidel Castro. Pearson also has information, as yet unpublished, to the effect that there was a meeting at the State Department at which assassination of Castro was discussed and that a team actually landed in Cuba with pills to be used in an assassination attempt. There is basis in fact for each of those three reports.

a. A CIA officer passed an assassination weapon to an Agency Cuban asset at a meeting in Paris on 22 November 1963. The weapon was a ballpoint pen rigged as a hypodermic syringe. The CIA officer suggested that the Cuban asset load the syringe with Black Leaf 40. The evidence indicates that the meeting was under way at the very moment President Kennedy was shot.

b. There was a meeting of the Special Group (Augmented) in Secretary Rusk's conference room on 10 August 1962 at which Secretary McNamara broached the subject of liquidation of Cuban leaders. The discussion resulted in a Project MONGOOSE action memorandum prepared by Edward Lansdale. At another Special Group meeting on 31 July 1964 there was discussion of a recently disseminated Clandestine Services information report on a Cuban exile plot to assassinate Castro. CIA had refused the exile's request for funds and had no involvement in that plot.

c. CIA twice (first in early 1961 and again in early 1962) supplied lethal pills to U.S. gambling syndicate members working in behalf of CIA on a plot to assassinate Fidel Castro. The 1961 plot aborted and the pills were recovered. Those furnished in April 1962 were passed by the gambling syndicate representative to a Cuban exile leader in Florida, who in turn had them sent to Cuba about May 1962. In June 1962 the exile leader reported that a team of three men had been dispatched to Cuba to recruit for the operation. If the opportunity presented itself, the team would make an attempt on Castro's life – perhaps using the pills.

This report describes these and other episodes in detail; puts them into perspective; and reveals, that while the events described by Drew Pearson did occur and are subject to being patched together as though one complete story, the implication of a direct, causative relationship among them is unfounded.

Miscellaneous Schemes Prior to August 1960 [...]

We find evidence of at least three, and perhaps four, schemes that were under consideration well before the Bay of Pigs, but we can fix the time frame only speculatively. Those who have some knowledge of the episodes guessed at dates ranging from 1959 through 1961. The March-to-August span we have fixed may be too narrow, but it best fits the limited evidence we have.

a. None of those we interviewed who was first assigned to the Cuba task force after the Bay of Pigs knows of any of these schemes.

b. J. D. (Jake) Esterline, who was head of the Cuba task force in pre-Bay of Pigs days, is probably the most reliable witness on general timing. He may not have been privy to the precise details of any of the plans, but he seems at least to have known of all of them. He is no longer able to keep the details of one plan separate from those of another, but each of the facts he recalls fits somewhere into one of the schemes. Hence, we conclude that all of these schemes were under consideration while Esterline had direct responsibility for Cuba operations.

c. Esterline himself furnishes the best clue as to the possible time span. He thinks it unlikely that any planning of this sort would have progressed to the point of consideration of means until after U.S. policy concerning Cuba was decided upon about March 1960. By about the end of the third quarter of 1960, the total energies of the task force were concentrated on the main-thrust effort, and there would have been no interest in nor time for pursuing such wills-o'-the-wisp as these.

We are unable to establish even a tentative sequence among the schemes; they may, in fact, have been under consideration simultaneously. We find no evidence that any of these schemes was approved at any level higher than division, if that. We think it most likely that no higher-level approvals were sought, because none of the schemes progressed to the point where approval to launch would have been needed.

Aerosol Attack on Radio Station:
[deletion] of TSD, remembers discussion of a scheme to contaminate the air of the radio station where Castro broadcasts his speeches with an aerosol spray of a chemical that produces reactions similar to those of lysergic acid (LSD).

Nothing came of the idea. [deletion] said he had discouraged the scheme, because the chemical could not be relied upon to be effective. [deletion], also of TSD, recalls experimentation with psychic energizers but cannot relate it to Castro as a target. We found no one else who remembered anything of this plot, with the possible exception of Jake Esterline who may have it confused with other schemes.

Contaminated Cigars:
Jake Esterline claims to have had in his possession in pre-Bay of Pigs days a box of cigars that had been treated with some sort of chemical. In our first interview with him, his recollection was that the chemical was intended to produce temporary personality disorientation. The thought was to somehow contrive to have Castro smoke one before making a speech and then to make a public spectacle of himself. Esterline distinctly recalls having had the cigars in his personal safe until he left WH/4 and that they definitely were intended for Castro. He does not remember how they came into his possession, but he thinks they must have been prepared by [deletion]. In a second interview with Esterline, we mentioned that we had learned since first speaking with him of a scheme to cause Castro's beard to fall out. He then said that his cigars might have been associated with that plan. Esterline finally said that, although it was evident that he no longer remembered the intended effect of the cigars, he was positive they were not lethal. The cigars were never used, according to Esterline, because WH/4 could not figure out how to deliver them without danger of blowback on the Agency. He says he destroyed them before leaving WH/4 in June 1961.

Sidney Gottlieb, of TSD, claims to remember distinctly a plot involving cigars. To emphasize the clarity of his memory, he named the officer, then assigned to WH/CA, who approached him with the scheme. Although there may well have been such a plot, the officer Gottlieb named was then assigned to India and has never worked in WH Division nor had anything to do with Cuba operations. Gottlieb remembers the scheme as being one that was talked about frequently but not widely and as being concerned with killing, not merely influencing behavior. As far as Gottlieb knows, this idea never got beyond the talking stage. TSD may have gone ahead and prepared the cigars just in case, but Gottlieb is certain that he did not get the DD/P's (Richard Bissell) personal approval to release them, as would have been done if the operation had gone that far. We are unable to discover whether Esterline and Gottlieb are speaking of a single cigar episode or of two unrelated schemes. We found no one else with firm recollections of lethal cigars being considered prior to August 1960.

Depilatory:
[deletion] recalls a scheme involving thallium salts, a chemical used by women as a depilatory – the thought being to destroy Castro's image as "The Beard" by causing the beard to fall out. The chemical may be administered either orally or by absorption through the skin. The right dosage causes depilation; too much produces paralysis. [deletion] believes that the idea originated in connection with a trip Castro was to have made outside of Cuba. The idea was to dust thallium powder into Castro's shoes when they were put out at night to be shined. The scheme progressed as far as procuring the chemical and testing it on animals. [deletion] recollection is that Castro did not make the intended trip, and the scheme fell through. [deletion] remembers consideration being given to use the thallium salts (perhaps against Castro) and something having to do with boots or shoes. [deletion] does not remember with whom he dealt on this plot. We found no one else with firm knowledge of it.

Gambling Syndicate:
The first seriously pursued CIA plan to assassinate Castro had its inception in August 1960. It involved the use of members of the criminal underworld with contacts inside Cuba. The operation had two phases: the first ran from August 1960 until late April or early May 1961, when it was called off following the Bay of Pigs; the second ran from April

1962 until February 1963 and was merely a revival of the first phase which had been inactive since about May 1961.

Gambling Syndicate – Phase I

August 1960
Richard Bissell, Deputy Director for Plans, asked Sheffield Edwards, Director of Security, if Edwards could establish contact with the U.S. gambling syndicate that was active in Cuba. The objective clearly was the assassination of Castro although Edwards claims that there was a studied avoidance of the term in his conversation with Bissell. Bissell recalls that the idea originated with J. C. King, then Chief of WH Division, although King now recalls having had only limited knowledge of such a plan and at a much later date – about mid-1962.

Edwards consulted Robert A. Maheu, a private investigator who had done sensitive work for the Agency, to see if Maheu had any underworld contacts. Maheu was once a special agent of the FBI. He opened a private office in Washington in 1956. The late Robert Cunningham, of the Office of Security (and also a former Special Agent with the FBI), knew Maheu and knew that his business was having a shaky start financially. Cunningham arranged to subsidize Maheu to the extent of $500 per month. Within six months Maheu was doing so well financially that he suggested that the retainer be discontinued. Over the years he has been intimately involved in providing support for some of the Agency's more sensitive operations. He has since moved his personal headquarters to Los Angeles but retains a Washington office. A more detailed account of Maheu's background appears in a separate section of this report [...]

Maheu acknowledged that he had a contact who might furnish access to the criminal underworld, but Maheu was most reluctant to allow himself to be involved in such an assignment. He agreed to participate only after being pressed by Edwards to do so. Maheu identified his contact as one Johnny Roselli, who lived in Los Angeles and had the concession for the ice-making machines on "the strip" in Las Vegas and whom Maheu understood to be a member of the syndicate. Maheu was known to Roselli as a man who had a number of large business organizations as clients. Edwards and Maheu agreed that Maheu would approach Roselli as the representative of businessmen with interests in Cuba who saw the elimination of Castro as the essential first step to the recovery of their investments. Maheu was authorized to tell Roselli that his "clients" were willing to pay $150,000 for Castro's removal.

September 1960
Shef Edwards named as his case officer for the operation James P. O'Connell (a former Special Agent of the FBI), then Chief, Operational Support Division, Office of Security. O'Connell and Maheu met Roselli in New York City on 14 September 1960 where Maheu made the pitch. Roselli initially was also reluctant to become involved, but finally agreed to introduce Maheu to "Sam Gold" who either had or could arrange contacts with syndicate elements in Cuba who might handle the job. Roselli said he had no interest in being paid for his participation and believed that "Gold" would feel the same way. A memorandum for the record prepared by Sheffield Edwards on 14 May 1962 states: "No monies were ever paid to Roselli and Giancana. Maheu was paid part of his expense money during the periods that he was in Miami." (Giancana is "Gold.")

O'Connell was introduced (in true name) to Roselli as an employee of Maheu, the explanation being that O'Connell would handle the case for Maheu, because Maheu was too busy to work on it full time himself. No one else in the Office of Security was made witting of the operation at this time. Edwards himself did not meet Roselli until the summer of 1962.

At this point, about the second half of September, Shef Edwards told Bissell that he had a friend, a private investigator, who had a contact who in turn had other contacts through whom syndicate elements in Cuba could be reached. These syndicate elements in Cuba would be willing to take on such an operation. As of the latter part of September 1960, Edwards, O'Connell, and Bissell were the only ones in the Agency who knew of a plan against Castro involving U.S. gangster elements. Edwards states that Richard Helms was not informed of the plan, because Cuba was being handled by Bissell at that time.

With Bissell present, Edwards briefed the Director (Allen Dulles) and the DDCI (General Cabell) on the existence of a plan involving members of the syndicate. The discussion was circumspect; Edwards deliberately avoided the use of any "bad words." The descriptive term used was "intelligence operation." Edwards is quite sure that the DCI and the DDCI clearly understood the nature of the operation he was discussing. He recalls describing the channel as being "from A to B to C." As he then envisioned it, "A" was Maheu, "B" was Roselli, and "C" was the principal in Cuba. Edwards recalls that Mr. Dulles merely nodded, presumably in understanding and approval. Certainly, there was no opposition. Edwards states that, while there was no formal approval as such, he felt that he clearly had tacit approval to use his own judgment. Bissell committed $150,000 for the support of the operation [...] in the Fontainbleau Hotel. "Gold" said he had a man, whom he identified only as "Joe," who would serve as courier to Cuba and make arrangements there. Maheu pointed out "Gold" to O'Connell from a distance, but O'Connell never met with either "Gold" or "Joe." He did, however, learn their true identities. As Office of Security memorandum to the DDCI of 24 June 1966 places the time as "several weeks later." O'Connell is now uncertain as to whether it was on this first visit to Miami or on a subsequent one that he and Maheu learned the true identities of the two men. Maheu and O'Connell were staying at separate hotels. Maheu phoned O'Connell one Sunday morning and called his attention to the Parade supplement in one of that morning's Miami newspapers. It carried an article on the Cosa Nostra, with pictures of prominent members. The man Maheu and O'Connell knew as "Sam Gold" appeared as Mom Salvatore (Sam)

Giancana, a Chicago-based gangster. "Joe, the courier" (who was never identified to either Maheu or O'Connell in any other way) turned out to be Santos Trafficante, the Cosa Nostra chieftain in Cuba.

At that time the gambling casinos were still operating in Cuba, and Trafficante was making regular trips between Miami and Havana on syndicate business. (The casinos were closed and gambling was banned effective 7 January 1959. On 13 January 1959, Castro announced that the casinos would be permitted to reopen for tourists and foreigners but that Cubans would be barred. The cabinet on 17 February 1959 authorized reopening the casinos for the tourist trade. *Time* magazine for 2 March 1959 announced that the casinos had been reopened the previous week. The *New York Times* issue of 30 September 1961 announced that the last of the casinos still running had been closed.) Trafficante was to make the arrangements with one of his contacts inside Cuba on one of his trips to Havana.

Fall and Early Winter 1960
Very early in the operation, well before the first contact with Roselli, the machinery for readying the means of assassination was set in motion. The sequence of events is not clear, but is apparent that a number of methods were considered. Preparation of some materials went ahead without express approval [...]

Dr. Edward Gunn, Chief, Operations Division, Office of Medical Services, has a notation that on 16 August 1960 he received a box of Cuban cigars to be treated with lethal material. He understood them to be Fidel's favorite brand, and he thinks they were given to him by Shef Edwards. Edwards does not recall the incident. Gunn has a notation that he contacted [deletion] of TSD, on 6 September 1960. [deletion] remembers experimenting with some cigars and then treating a full box. He cannot now recall whether he was initially given two boxes, experimenting with one and then treating the other; or whether he bought a box for experimentation, after which he treated the box supplied him by Gunn.

He does not, in fact, remember Gunn as the supplier of any cigars. He is positive, though, that he did contaminate a full box of fifty cigars with botulinus toxin, a virulent poison that produces a fatal illness some hours after it is ingested. [deletion] distinctly remembers the flaps-and-seals job he had to do on the box and on each of the wrapped cigars, both to get the cigars and to erase evidence of tampering. He kept one of the experimental cigars and still has it. He retested it during our inquiry and found that the toxin still retained 94% of its original effectiveness. The cigars were so heavily contaminated that merely putting one in the mouth would do the job; the intended victim would not actually have to smoke it.

Gunn's notes show that he reported the cigars as being ready for delivery on 7 October 1960. [deletion]'s notes do not show actual delivery until 13 February 1961. They do not indicate to whom delivery was made. Gunn states that he took the cigars, at some unspecified time, and kept them in his personal safe. He remembers destroying them within a month of Shef Edwards retirement in June 1963 [...]

Edwards recalls approaching Roosevelt after Bissell had already spoken to Roosevelt on the subject; Roosevelt recalls speaking to Edwards after Bissell discussed it with Edwards. Bissell does not recall specific conversations with either of them on the technical aspects of the problem, but he believes that he must have "closed the loop" by talks with both Edwards and Roosevelt. Roosevelt recalls his first meeting with Edwards as being in Edwards' office. Edwards remembers asking to be introduced to a chemist. He is sure that he did not name the target to Roosevelt, but Roosevelt says he knew it was Castro. Roosevelt believes that he would have put Edwards in touch with [deletion], then chief of TSD's Chemical Division, but [deletion] has no recollection of such work at that time. [deletion] recalls other operations at other times, but not this one. Roosevelt did say that, if he turned it over to [deletion], [deletion] could have assigned it to [deletion].

Roosevelt remembers that four possible approaches were considered: (1) something highly toxic, such as shellfish poison to be administered with a pin (which Roosevelt said was what was supplied to Gary Powers); (2) bacterial material in liquid form; (3) bacterial treatment of a cigarette or cigar; and (4) a handkerchief treated with bacteria. The decision, to the best of his recollection, was that bacteria in liquid form was the best means. Bissell recalls the same decision, tying it to a recollection that Castro frequently drank tea, coffee, or bouillon, for which a liquid poison would be particularly well suited.

January–February 1961
Despite the decision that a poison in liquid form would be most desirable, what was actually prepared and delivered was a solid in the form of small pills about the size of saccharine tablets. [deletion] remembers meeting with Edwards and O'Connell in Edwards' office to discuss the requirement. The specifications were that the poison be stable, soluble, safe to handle, undetectable, not immediately acting, and with a firmly predictable end result. Botulin comes nearest to meeting all those requirements, and it may be put up in either liquid or solid form. [deletion] states that the pill form was chosen because of ease and safety of handling[...]

(Comment: The gangsters may have had some influence on the choice of a means of assassination. O'Connell says that in his very early discussions with the gangsters (or, more precisely, Maheu's discussions with them) consideration was given to possible ways of accomplishing the mission. Apparently the Agency had first thought in terms of a typical, gangland-style killing in which Castro would be gunned down. Giancana was flatly opposed to the use of firearms. He said that no one could be recruited to do the job, because the chance of survival and escape would be negligible. Giancana stated a preference for a lethal pill that could be put into Castro's food or drink. Trafficante ("Joe, the courier") was in touch with a disaffected Cuban official with access to Castro and presumably of a sort that would enable him to surreptitiously poison Castro. The gangsters named their man inside as Juan Orta who was then Office Chief and Director General of the Office of the Prime Minister (Castro). The gangsters said that Orta had once been in a position to receive kickbacks from the gambling interests, has since lost that source of income, and needed the money.)

When Edwards received the pills he dropped one into a glass of water to test it for solubility and found that it did not even disintegrate, let alone dissolve. [deletion] took them back and made up a new batch that met the requirement for solubility. Edwards at that point wanted assurance that the pills were truly lethal. He called on Dr. Gunn to make an independent test of them. Edwards gave Gunn money to buy guinea pigs as test animals. Gunn has a record of a conversation with [deletion] on 6 February 1961. It may have related to the tests, but we cannot be sure. What appears to have happened is that Gunn tested the pills on the guinea pigs and found them ineffective.

[deletion] states that tests of bouillon on guinea pigs are not valid, because guinea pigs have a high resistance to this particular toxin. [deletion] himself tested the pills on monkeys and found they did the job expected of them.

We cannot reconstruct with certainty the sequence of events between readying the pills and putting them into the hands of Roselli. Edwards has the impression that he had a favorable report from Dr. Gunn on the guinea pig test. Gunn probably reported only that the pills were effective, and Edwards assumed the report was based on the results of tests on guinea pigs. Dr. Gunn has a clear recollection, without a date, of being present at a meeting in which Roosevelt demonstrated a pencil designed as a concealment device for delivering the pills. Roosevelt also recalls such a meeting, also without a date. Gunn's notes record that his last action on the operation came on 10 February 1961 when he put Gottlieb in touch with Edwards. Gottlieb has no recollection of being involved, an impression that is supported by Bissell who states that Gottlieb's assignments were of a different nature. O'Connell, who eventually received the pills, recalls that he dealt with [deletion]. [deletion] has no record of delivering the pills at this time, but he does not ordinarily keep detailed records of such things.

In any event, O'Connell did receive the pills, and he believes there were six of them. He recalls giving three to Roselli. Presumably the other three were used in testing for solubility and effectiveness. The dates on which O'Connell received the pills and subsequently passed them to Roselli cannot be established. It would have been sometime after Gunn's notation of 10 February 1961.

Gunn also has a record of being approached about the undertaking by William K. Harvey (former special agent of the FBI) in February in connection with a sensitive project Harvey was working on for Bissell. According to Gunn's notes, he briefed Harvey on the operation, and Harvey instructed him to discuss techniques, but not targets, with Gottlieb. Gunn's notation on this point is not in accord with the recollections of any of the others involved. We are unable to clarify it; the note may have been in another context. O'Connell states that J. C. King was also briefed at this time, although King denies learning of the operation until much later.

Late February–March 1961

Roselli passed the pills to Trafficante. Roselli reported to O'Connell that the pills had been delivered to Orta in Cuba. Orta is understood to have kept the pills for a couple of weeks before returning them. According to the gangsters, Orta got cold feet [...]

The previously mentioned 24 June 1966 summary of the operation prepared by the Office of Security states that when Orta asked out of the assignment he suggested another candidate who made several attempts without success. Neither Edwards nor O'Connell know the identity of Orta's replacement nor any additional details of the reported further attempts.

March–April 1961

Following the collapse of the Orta channel, Roselli told O'Connell that Trafficante knew of a man high up in the

Cuban exile movement who might do the job. He identified him as Tony Varona (Dr. Manuel Antonio de VARONA y Loredo). Varona was the head of the Democratic Revolutionary Front, [1/2 line deletion] part of the larger Cuban operation. O'Connell understood that Varona was dissatisfied [...] had hired Edward K. Moss, a Washington public relations counselor, as a fund raiser and public relations advisor. The Bureau report alleged that Moss' mistress was one Julia Cellini, whose brothers represented two of the largest gambling casinos in Cuba. The Cellini brothers were believed to be in touch with Varona through Moss and were reported to have offered Varona large sums of money for his operations against Castro, with the understanding that they would receive privileged treatment "in the Cuba of the future." Attempts to verify these reports were unsuccessful [...]

Trafficante approached Varona and told him that he had clients who wanted to do away with Castro and that they would pay big money for the job. Varona is reported to have been very receptive, since it would mean that he would be able to buy his own ships, arms, and communications equipment [...] dated 24 June 1965, sets the amount as $10,000 in cash and $1,000 worth of communications equipment. Jake Esterline, who signed the vouchers for the funds, recalls the amounts as being those stated in the Office of Security memorandum.

(Comment: As a sidelight, Esterline says that, when he learned of the intended use of Varona, steps were taken to cancel the plan. Varona was one of the five key figures in the Revolutionary Front and was heavily involved in support of the approaching Bay of Pigs operation. If steps were in fact taken to end Varona's participation in the syndicate plan, they were ineffective. It is clear that he continued as an integral part of the syndicate scheme.)

When the money was ready, O'Connell took the pills from his safe and delivered them and the money to Roselli. Roselli gave the pills and the money to Varona, whom Roselli dealt with under pseudonym. Little is known of the delivery channels beyond Varona. Varona was believed to have an asset inside Cuba in a position to slip a pill to Castro. Edwards recalls something about a contact who worked in a restaurant frequented by Castro and who was to receive the pills and put them into Castro's food or drink. Edwards believes that the scheme failed because Castro ceased to visit that particular restaurant.

April–May 1961
Soon after the Bay of Pigs, Edwards sent word to Roselli through O'Connell that the operation was off – even if something happened there would be no payoff. Edwards is sure there was a complete standdown after that; the operation was dead and remained so until April 1962. He clearly relates the origins of the operation to the upcoming Bay of Pigs invasion, and its termination to the Bay of Pigs failure. O'Connell agrees that the operation was called off after the Bay of Pigs but that the termination was not firm and final. He believes that there was something going on between April 1961 and April 1962, but he cannot now recall what. He agrees with Bill Harvey that when the operation was revived in April 1962, Harvey took over a "going operation."

(Comment: As distinguished from Edwards and O'Connell, both Bissell and Esterline place the termination date of the assassination operation as being about six months before the Bay of Pigs. Esterline gives as his reason for so believing the fact that the decision had been made to go ahead with a massive, major operation instead of an individually-targeted one such as this. Whatever the intention in this respect, if the decision to terminate was actually made, the decision was not communicated effectively. It is clear that this plan to assassinate Castro continued in train until sometime after the Bay of Pigs.)

O'Connell believes that he must have recovered the pills, but he has no specific recollection of having done so. He thinks that instead of returning them to TSD he probably would have destroyed them, most likely by flushing them down a toilet. [deletion] has no record of the pills having been returned to him, but he says he is quite sure that they were.

[...]

Schemes in Early 1963

Skin Diving Suit

At about the time of the Donovan–Castro negotiations for the release of the Bay of Pigs prisoners a plan was devised to have Donovan present a contaminated skin diving suit to Castro as a gift. Castro was known to be a skin diving enthusiast. We cannot put a precise date on this scheme. Desmond FitzGerald told us of it as if it had originated after he took over the Cuba task force in January 1963. Samuel Halpern said that it began under William Harvey and that he, Halpern, briefed FitzGerald on it. Harvey states positively that he never heard of it.

According to Sidney Gottlieb, this scheme progressed to the point of actually buying a diving suit and readying it for delivery. The technique involved dusting the inside of the suit with a fungus that would produce a disabling and chronic skin disease (Madura foot) and contaminating the breathing apparatus with tubercle bacilli. Gottlieb does not remember what came of the scheme or what happened to the scuba suit. Sam Halpern, who was in on the scheme, at first said the plan was dropped because it was obviously impracticable. He later recalled that the plan was abandoned because it was over-taken by events: Donovan had already given Castro a skin diving suit on his own initiative. The scheme may have been mentioned to Mike Miskovsky, who worked with Donovan, but FitzGerald has no recollection that it was.

[...]

Booby-trapped Sea Shell

Some time in 1963, date uncertain but probably early in the year, Desmond FitzGerald, then Chief, SAS, originated a scheme for doing away with Castro by means of an explosives-rigged sea shell. The idea was to take an unusually spectacular sea shell that would be certain to catch Castro's eye, load it with an explosive triggered to blow when the shell was lifted, and submerge it in an area where Castro often went skin diving.

Des bought two books on Caribbean Mollusca. The scheme was soon found to be impracticable. None of the shells that might conceivably be found in the Caribbean area was both spectacular enough to be sure of attracting attention and large enough to hold the needed volume of explosive. The midget submarine that would have had to be used in emplacement of the shell has too short an operating range for such an operation.

FitzGerald states that he, Sam Halpern, and [deletion] had several sessions at which they explored this possibility, but that no one else was ever brought in on the talks. Halpern believes that he had conversations with TSD on feasibility and using a hypothetical case. He does not remember with whom he may have spoken. We are unable to identify any others who knew of the scheme at the time it was being considered.

CATTLE MUTILATIONS

On the evening of 7 September 1967 Colorado rancher Agnes King noted that one of her Appaloosa horses, Snippy, had not returned home for her customary drink of water. Two days later King's son Harry found Snippy dead. Her head had been de-skinned, the cadaver sucked dry of blood and there was a strong medicinal smell. When a lump of Snippy's body was touched next day by Harry's aunt, Mrs Burl Lewis, it oozed a green fluid that burned her skin. Even more bizarrely, on the ground nearby were fifteen circular burns. A subsequent radiation survey by United States Forest Service Duane Martin found high levels of radioactivity. Martin stated: "The death of this saddle pony is one of the most mysterious sights I've ever witnessed ... I've seen stock killed by lightning, but it was never like this."

Snippy was not the first farm animal to be mutilated in strange circumstances – there are cases of livestock mutilations in England in the nineteenth century – but she was the first well-publicized specimen in the modern outbreak of the phenomenon in the US. Associated Press took up Snippy's story – and neatly linked it to the UFO craze sweeping the States. Many residents of the area have reported sighting unidentified flying objects. One man said his car was followed by a top-shaped object and a student at nearby Adams State College said both his rear tyres blew out as he approached an object as it sat in a field.

A very down to earth autopsy by Dr Robert O. Adams, head of Colorado State University's Veterinary and Biomedical Science School, concluded there were "No unearthly causes, at least not to my mind" for Snippy's demise and dismemberment. He noted a severe infection in Snippy's hindquarters, and speculated that someone had come across the dying horse and slit its throat in order to end its misery. The local carnivorous fauna had done the rest of the damage to the saddle pony.

Adams' professional opinion did nothing to quell speculation about livestock mutilations, cases of which grew exponentially in the USA over the next decade, being reported from New Mexico in the south to Montana in the north. In "classic cases", evisceration was apparently done with surgical precision, the animal drained of blood, no tyre tracks or footprints were to be found in the immediate vicinity of the corpse, and the sexual organs removed. In the face of mounting public concerns, Federal authorities launched an investigation of the cattle mutilation phenomenon in May 1979, which was headed by FBI agent Kenneth Rommel. His report concluded that mutilations were predominantly the result of natural predation (see Document, p.79), but that some contained anomalies that could not be accounted for by conventional wisdom. Rommel's report left the door open for a triumvirate of prime conspiracy theories regarding cattle mutilations (mootilations?), namely that "unexplained" mutilations are the work of satanic cults, government or alien experiments.

The cult hypothesis has the merit of explaining away some of the oddities of cattle mutilations (Satanists "harvesting" bovine organs for ritual use would explain the latter's absence at the scene of the crime) and, in Idaho, forestry service employees were reported to have seen robed figures near a site of bovine excision on at least one occasion. An investigation by the Bureau of Alcohol, Tobacco and Firearms in 1975, however, found insufficient evidence of cult involvement for action to be taken.

Cattle mutilation researcher Charles T. Oliphant, meanwhile, has asserted that the phenomenon is the result of secret US Government research into "zoonotic" cattle diseases (that is, diseases transmissible to humans), chiefly Creutzfeldt-Jakob Disease (CJD)and Bovine Spongiform Encephalopathy (BSE). Oliphant notes the high levels of man-made chemicals found in some of the bovine corpses, as well as the sightings of unmarked black helicopters near mutilation sites. The use of helicopters in the mutilations would help explain why some of the dead bovines appear to have been carried and dropped – but would US officials really do such a thing as dress down, ride around in unmarked vehicles and kill animals? Er, yes, actually, according to Oliphant, who cites the case of plain clothes government officers entering a research facility in Reston, Virginia, to destroy animals suspected of carrying the Ebola virus.

Equally, those black helicopters might be doing aliens' work, because in Conspiracy World the dark choppers are often held to be "reverse engineered" with ET-technology. Why would aliens – or their Earthling stooges – want to cut up Daisy with their precision tools? Aside from fancying a burger or a T-bone steak? Who knows? The consolation must be that any alien species that needs to cut up cows by the thousand to get it right – whatever right may be – isn't *that* bright.

> Bovines carved up by ET reasearchers: ALERT LEVEL 3

Further Reading
www.rense.com/ufo/madcowufo.htm

DOCUMENT: KENNETH M ROMMEL, "OPERATION ANIMAL MUTILATION", REPORT OF THE DISTRICT ATTORNEY, FIRST JUDICIAL DISTRICT, STATE OF NEW MEXICO [EXTRACT]

Chapter Six: Conclusions and Recommendations

During the past five years, hundreds of livestock mutilations have been reported throughout the United States. Of the states affected by this phenomenon, New Mexico has certainly had its share of unusual incidents.

Since 1975, over 100 mutilations have been reported throughout the state. Ninety mutilations were reported prior to Operation Animal Mutilation. Another 27 incidents were investigated under this year-long project, which began May 28, 1979. Twenty-five of these cases were reported as mutilations. In each of these 25 incidents, as I have shown in Chapter Four, the rough jagged nature of the incisions together with the evidence at the scene clearly indicates that the carcass was damaged by predators and/or scavengers. In most cases, the animal had died first of natural causes.

Shortly after the results of my investigation were released to the press, several individuals have stated that no classic mutilations had occurred during the course of my project as though this would explain my sincere, but obviously misguided verdict of scavenger-induced damage. I agree that no classic mutilations have occurred during Operation Animal Mutilation. However, I would like to know their basis for their statement. More specifically, I wish to address the following questions to them:

1) How many of the mutilations that I investigated in this project did they also investigate?
2) Specifically, which ones did they investigate?
3) How do these mutilations differ from the "classic" cases with which they are comparing them?

Can these questions be answered, or is their observation just another one of those unsupported statements that I have encountered so frequently during the course of my project? I cannot answer this, but I can point out the results of my own analysis of the 90 mutilations reported prior to the commencement of Operation Animal Mutilation.

As I have noted in Chapter Three, a verdict of predator/scavenger-induced damage is clearly indicated in the vast majority of cases in which sufficient evidence is presented in the report. Even in those few cases in which the damage was determined to be human-induced, the resulting mutilation bore little resemblance to the "classic" case. In short, during my investigation of the 117 mutilations that have been reported in New Mexico since 1975, I have not found one single case which, after careful scrutiny of available evidence, could be confirmed as a "classic mutilation."

Are the conclusions that I have reached unique? To the contrary, the data obtained from qualified investigators and experienced veterinarians in other states only confirms what I have discovered in New Mexico. In fact, I have found no credible source who differs from this finding, nor has one piece of hard evidence been presented or uncovered that would cause me to alter this conclusion. But perhaps it is better to let the experts speak for themselves. The following statements are excerpts from letters received from veterinarians affiliated with various state veterinary diagnostic laboratories. The complete contents of these communications can be found in the appendix section of this report.

Dr. Harry D. Anthony, Kansas State University:
"It is my opinion that most of these carcass problems occur after the natural death of the animal and predators or scavengers feed on the remaining loose tissues of the carcass, such as lips, eyelids, and the external genital organs."

Dr. S. M. Dennis, Kansas State University:
"Many animal mutilation reports are a result of false or incomplete information being furnished by the rancher to law enforcement officers investigating the dead animals, and many times by inexperienced and untrained law enforcement officers putting down what they see in a manner which tends to be very dogmatic ... it appears to be a quirk of human nature for ranchers not to want to admit that an animal of theirs died either by poisoning or due to predation."

Dr. L. G. Morehouse, University of Missouri:
"It is the opinion of our pathologists that a fair percentage of animals that come to post-mortem have been eaten on by birds and carnivorous (animals). This has been observed for many years. It is also the opinion of our pathologists that the

percentage of dead animals that have lost parts to carnivorous (animals) has not increased in recent years, although the number of clients that believe their animals have been mutilated by humans or some other unexplained phenomenon have increased."

Dr. William J. Quinn, State of Montana:
"In summary, I believe that the cattle mutilations are due to flesh-eating birds and small mammals and not by an unknown person or group of persons."

L. D. Kintner, University of Missouri:
"Surprisingly as it may seem to the uninitiated, many of the scavengers make a clean cut as might be done by a surgeon with a very sharp knife. In fact, many of the animals that are presented to our post-mortem laboratory have loss of eyes, tongue, anus, and rectum within only hours after death."

Dr. Roger Panciera, Oklahoma State University:
(Commenting in a special task force report to the governor of Oklahoma in regards to cattle mutilations):

"All Investigations that have been completed have indicated death due to natural causes and death due to disease. In no case has the observation and opinion of task force indicated man has been a primary factor in death or mutilation."

Dr. M. W. Vorhies, South Dakota State University:
"Obviously, we should not dismiss the possibilities of human involvement, but it has been our experience that in all instances, we could identify evidence of predatory animals being involved in missing parts of animals dying of some natural causes.

Dr. William Sippel, Texas A & M University:
"In short, we have found no evidence of mutilation by humans of the specimens presented to our laboratory."

Dr. Robert L. Poulson, Utah Department of Agriculture:
"Livestock mutilations in Utah have been minimal, with the exception of a few cases that were reported which apparently resulted from natural or disease conditions and later mutilated by pranksters or predatory animals."

In short, as you can see from the foregoing excerpts, the conclusions of professionals from other states overwhelmingly corroborate my own findings. They all agree that the carcasses they have examined have been damaged – by animals and birds rather than highly skilled surgeons. As I have noted previously, in order to eliminate a verdict of predator/scavenger damage, it must be shown that the incisions in the carcass have been made by a knife or other sharp instrument. As I have illustrated in Chapter Four, incisions made by scavengers can resemble knife cuts, especially when viewed at a distance. In those cases in which the cut appears to be smooth, microscopic analysis is necessary to determine whether or not that cut was made by a sharp instrument. In order for such a verdict to be reached, microscopic analysis must reveal that the hair follicles have been cut perpendicular to the plain. If this cannot be shown, then the damage cannot be attributed to humans.

Although "surgical precision" is the major criterion used to distinguish scavenger-induced damage from the "classic mutilations" the latter is also attributed with other characteristics that reportedly set it apart from carcasses damaged by birds and animals. The other attributes of the classic mutilation, as I will illustrate below, can also be explained logically.

For example, one major characteristic is the removal of certain types of organs – namely the sexual organs, tongue, eye, and ear. However, as I have pointed out previously, these are the same organs normally removed by scavengers. This point is well illustrated by an experiment conducted in Arkansas on September 4, 1979. Officials of the Washington County Sheriff's Department, which sponsored this experiment, monitored a calf, which had just died, for more than 30 hours.

"By the time they completed their vigil, the animal's tongue was gone, its eye removed to the bony orbit, anus 'cored', internal organs (intestines, bladder, etc.) expelled, and little blood was evident at the scene. Who were the mutilators? Blowflies, skunks, and buzzards, who were still feeding on the carcass when the last photographs were taken September 6 at 11.00 a.m."

This experiment also illustrates another point that I have made repeatedly in this report – that the types of organs removed and the amount of damage done to the carcass depends on when the investigator arrives at the scene and which scavengers are present in the area.

Another claim made for the classic mutilation is that the animal is devoid of blood. Such a claim is rarely substantiated by a necropsy report. Rather, it seems to be based primarily on the apparent lack of blood at the scene. Such a lack, however, is easily explainable, particularly in view of the fact that most mutilations appear to be done after the animal has died. As noted previously, the blood settles to the lower port of the cavity and coagulates, thus giving the appearance that the animal is devoid of blood. Any blood on the carcass or on the ground is quickly consumed by scavengers – such as the blowflies observed in the Arkansas experiment. To quote Dr. L. D. Kintner of the University of Missouri: "It is the rule rather than the exception for these animals to do a neat job and not leave either blood or mess at the site of the carcass."

Also, it seems likely that in a number of alleged mutilations, dried blood found on the carcass has been mistakenly identified as burn marks, which are occasionally reported in classic mutilation cases. Dr. M. W. Vorhies of South Dakota University makes the following observations regarding this problem: "Often where the animal has died and the predatory animals have removed parts, there is dried blood on the hair; and this may appear to some as if the skin or hair has been burned because it will turn a very dark black color when exposed to the air."

Dr. Clair M. Hibbs of New Mexico State University, when asked to comment about the "mysterious lack of blood at the scene," sums up the situation by saying that "these statements are made by unprofessionals who do not have any real knowledge of what happens after an animal dies."

A third characteristic attributed to the classic mutilations is the deliberate avoidance of the carcass by other animals. Although many of the mutilations investigated before Operation Animal Mutilation began are considered "classic" – at least by some of the more vocal investigators – scavenger activity is cited in a large percentage of the official reports from this period.

It should also be pointed out that the deliberate avoidance of the carcass by other animals need not indicate anything mysterious or bizarre about that carcass, for scavengers will tend to avoid livestock which have died from certain types of diseases such as water belly (Urolithiasis). Water belly, according to Tommy Thompson of the Nebraska Department of Agriculture, occurs in a cow when the urinary tract gets blocked. The urine subsequently backs up into other portions of the body, eventually killing the animal. According to Thompson, an animal which has died from this condition has such a strong odor that even scavengers won't go near the carcass.

Another characteristic closely related to this one is the discovery of dead flies on some of the "mutilation" victims. In fact, shortly after it was announced that I would direct this project, Bob Erickson, a rancher from Lindrith, informed me that one of his horses had been mutilated. What struck him as so unusual about this incident was that his horse was covered with dead flies – a fact which he considered very mysterious and, in his mind, tended to authenticate the mutilation phenomenon. I later learned of a similar case which had been reported June 8, 1978 in Elsberry, Missouri. Briefly, an animal was found mutilated. Its right ear, right eye, tongue, udder, and reproductive organs were missing, according to the police report. The report also claimed that the animal's blood had been removed and that UFOs had been seen in the area. But what interested me about this particular case was the discovery made by the investigating officer of dead flies, which were fused to some branches located near the carcass.

The flies, together with the branches on which they were fused, were submitted by personnel from a local television station to the Ralston Purina Laboratory in St. Louis, Missouri, for examination.

According to the police report (1978), "[they] found [it] to be a fungus which has never before been discovered or known to exist in the wild. It has only, up to this point, been produced in a laboratory."

To investigate this incident, I obtained some letters written by Dr. J. M. Tufts (deceased) of the Veterinary Service Department of the Ralston Purina Company, who had performed the analysis. These letters, which had been sent to the Center for UFO Studies and a local television station, subsequently dispelled much of the mystery surrounding this incident. The information contained in these letters is summarized in the following paragraphs.

The flies were identified as the common "black blowfly." It was determined that they were afflicted by a fungus belonging to the genus Entomophthora, which is described in Steinhaus's *Insect Microbiology*. This volume includes a picture of clumps of flies attached to a leaf in a manner similar to that observed in the Elsberry incident.

The flies affected with the fungus attach themselves to branches and leaves in a lifelike manner and often in considerable numbers. Such flies would normally be attracted in great numbers to a decaying carcass. The disease progresses very rapidly, within 48 to 72 hours, and may completely replace the flies' internal structures. The fungus is also characterized by an adhesive material, which will cause the fly to stick to whatever it lands on. In short, the fungus could spread very rapidly and kill many flies very quickly, especially when large numbers are attracted to an area limited to the size of a carcass. Dr. Tufts concluded that the death and peculiar fixation of the flies was due to a fungal disease to which they are normally subject not to a mysterious unknown organism.

A few other characteristics of the "classic mutilation" also deserve brief mention. One common claim, as noted previously, is that the night a mutilation occurs, the family dog is unusually quiet. I have no quarrel with this observation, for as I pointed out in a recent press conference, it's hard to bark when your mouth is full of fresh meat.

Another frequently made claim is that the carcass of a mutilated animal decays either very slowly or, in some cases, extremely rapidly. There is nothing unusual about such an observation, for the rate of decay of a carcass is dependent upon a number of factors, such as the disease from which the animal died, the temperature, the weather conditions, and the types of scavengers present in the area. Depending on which factors are present, the carcass may appear to decay more rapidly or more slowly than normal.

Although not cited as a typically occurring trait, the discovery of drugs in the carcasses of some of the victims has frequently been cited as proof that these livestock are being killed and mutilated by a highly sophisticated organization. During the course of my investigation, I have found reports of only five incidents in which drugs were discovered in the carcasses of mutilated, animals – three in Arkansas and two in New Mexico.

In three of these incidents, as I have noted previously, the substances found in the animals were drugs with known veterinary use. These include the chlorpromazine found in the mutilated steer in New Mexico; the succinylcholine in the horse in Arkansas, and the santonin in the yearling steer, also in Arkansas. As I have already explained, there is reason to believe that two of these drugs had been administered to the animals, possibly by their owners. At this time I know of no reason why the chlorpromazine was found in the steer, but I have determined, as noted in Chapter Three, that the animal was on medicated feed.

The other two drugs – mescaline, which was found in a bull calf in Arkansas, and atropine, which was reportedly found in a New Mexico animal – are substances that occur naturally in plants found in the area. Since cattle are known to ingest practically anything, the discovery of such substances in the carcasses of dead livestock is certainly not remarkable.

I would like to remind you that the New Mexico case in which atropine was reportedly found has not been identified and that the only source to mention it is the same officer that made the statement that chlorpromazine was the first drug discovered in a New Mexican animal.

To account for the widespread occurrence of these so-called classic mutilations, many theories have been advocated. During the course of my 12-month investigation, I have encountered most of them. However, it didn't take me long to realize that in terms of publicity, the most popular theory in New Mexico was that these mutilations were being performed by a well-organized, highly sophisticated group who were dissecting livestock as part of a program of biological and environmental testing. The identification of this group has received less publicity, although government involvement has certainly been hinted at by a number of investigators, both amateur and professional.

Despite its popularity, I have not found one shred of hard evidence to substantiate this theory. As I have pointed out in Chapter Three, one would expect that if an organized group such as the government were somehow involved in such a conspiracy, there would be at least some information leaks – or perhaps at least one defector who would try to claim the reward money. For thousands of dollars have been offered by various state agencies for information leading to the arrest and conviction of persons responsible for mutilating livestock. To date, I know of not one single case where this money has been claimed. But then again, what use would eagles, crows, and coyotes have for money, when their food is laying in the pasture – free for the taking.

It also didn't take me long to learn that of all the theories that have been advocated to account for livestock mutilations, the predator/scavenger theory was the least popular. Although it was not within the scope of my project to determine the reason for this, the following observations made in a recent article published in the *Portales News-Tribune* (1979) aptly express my own thinking on the subject:

> Well, in our opinion, the reason that the simple explanation of these cattle first died of natural causes and almost immediately attracted coyotes, vultures or ravens, lacks credibility to the public is that they haven't been given the evidence which livestock inspectors, veterinarians and experienced cattlemen are ready and willing to provide.
>
> These knowledgeable people have become shy of answering questions from newsmen because of the Popular beliefs that have been reinforced by speculation of eerie or devilish theories by powerful public news media.
>
> It's probably simply a case of the newsmen not letting the facts get in the way of a good story.

Explanations for the Phenomenon

If there is no concrete evidence to support the claims that thousands of livestock have fallen victims to "classic mutilations," then how does one explain the livestock mutilation phenomenon. Again, although the answer to this question falls outside the framework of this project, I would like to briefly review some of the explanations offered by others interested in this phenomenon.

A possible explanation for at least some of the interest in livestock mutilations is offered by Tom Adams (1979–80) in the January issue of *Stigmata*, a newsletter devoted to the continuing investigation of livestock mutilations.

> Among items that are rumored to be in the works, however tentatively: an anthology of commentary on the mutilation phenomenon; a bibliography of published materials; a fund for research and investigation; an in-depth documentary by a Colorado TV station, a program which may or may not be circulated to other TV stations around the country.
>
> We wish we had a dollar (no, make that an ounce of gold) for every writer we've heard of within the past few

years who promised (or threatened) to turn out a serious book on mutilations.

Although the profit motive cannot be entirely discounted, the livestock mutilation phenomenon is much too complex to be explained solely on this basis. Another possible explanation is offered by Burton Wolfe (1976) in an article entitled "Demystifying all the Satanic Conspiracy Stories on the Cattle Mutilations", which appeared in the May 14, 1976 issue of the *San Francisco Bay Guardian*.

Wolfe attributes the cattle mutilation phenomenon to a hoax originally perpetrated by an astrologer named Dan Fry, host of a radio program in Minnesota called the *Cosmic Age*.

According to Wolfe, about two years ago Fry announced on his program that cattle were being mutilated "either by some weird satanic cult or supernatural creatures arriving on the range in UFOs."

Fry, apparently intending his comments as a joke, was alarmed at the impact they subsequently had on ranches and farmers.

Suddenly, farmers in Minnesota accustomed to finding dead cows with parts severed by predators began attributing the scavenging to satanists and UFO creatures. Through the mass communication media, including the Associated Press and such esteemed newspapers as the *Houston Post*, the story was disseminated to millions of people in hundreds of Midwestern cities. Reporters began to vie with each other for the most sensationalized version of how mysterious creatures from UFOs or stealthy night figures from satanic cults were mutilating cattle.

Alarmed by the results, the astrologer appeared on a number of radio and television shows "in an effort to abort his prank before the press created still more mass hysteria with it."

"'Man, there weren't any cattle mutilations,' Fry explained in a typical appearance on a Texas television talk show in March 1975. 'I just started these rumors as a joke.'"

Whether or not you accept Wolfe's explanation for the origin of the mutilation phenomenon, his observations about the role played by the media are quite revealing. Similarly, my own investigation has clearly shown that the media has played a very important role in promoting both the livestock phenomenon and the lore surrounding it.

The Truchas incident, as discussed in Chapter Four, is a classic example of how a newspaper not only can distort the facts, but also can deliberately choose to ignore them in the face of a more sensational story. This incident, as I have noted previously, would undoubtedly have gone down in history as another "classic mutilation," if I had not investigated the case myself. My own investigation, as I have shown, clearly indicated the animal had died of natural causes and had subsequently been eaten by dogs and other scavengers. Although the reporter was later made aware of the many inaccuracies contained in her articles, she never printed a retraction.

A similar incident also occurred in Roswell. However, in this case the reporter did print a retraction. On October 29, 1979, the *Roswell Daily Record* (1979a) printed an article entitled "Mutilated Cow Found". This story, which describes a cow reportedly found dead and mutilated in Carrizozo, contains the following quotes, both of which were erroneously attributed to me: "'It is definitely classified as a mutilation, but it does not hold true to form as a mutilation as are on our records,' said Kenneth Rommel, director of the New Mexico animal mutilation project. 'The difference is that the eyes and tongue were left intact on the animal,' he explained."

I have no idea where this quote came from, for I certainly did not make it. On November 9, 1979, I sent a letter to the *Roswell Daily Record* informing them of this inaccuracy.

This quotation is in error. I have not made any statements since the beginning of this project that would authenticate in any way any reported cattle mutilations. My policy in regards to this investigation has been to not give out any incorrect, or misleading information. I would appreciate it if you would make a correction in your newspaper.

The *Roswell Daily Record* (1979b) did publish a correction on November 11 issue in an article entitled, "It Wasn't a Mutilation".

The role played by the media in both sensationalizing and promoting the livestock mutilation phenomenon has also been noted by Dr. Nancy H. Owen (1980) in her study of mutilations in Benton County, Arkansas. Similarly, Dr. J. M. Tufts, whose role in unraveling the Elsberry, Missouri fly mystery which was just discussed, makes the following observation: "After all was said and done, it was obvious that Channel 2 News was more interested in creating an exciting story than in shedding any light on the occurrence of a few dead cows."

One of the most extensive studies done on the relationship between the media and livestock mutilations was conducted recently by Dr. James R. Stewart, associate professor of sociology at the University of South Dakota. In an article entitled "Collective Delusion: A Comparison of Believers and Skeptics", Dr. Stewart (1980) traces the history of livestock mutilation reports in two adjacent states – Nebraska and South Dakota. He goes on to show that there is a positive correlation between the number of reported incidents in a prescribed area and the number of news inches devoted to livestock mutilations by the media.

Another interesting point made by Stewart is the role played by law enforcement personnel in promoting the phenomenon.

Local law enforcement personnel have little, if any, experience in determining causes of cattle deaths. Consequently, they were inclined to adopt the farmer's explanations in the absence of any solid refuting evidence of their own. The same was true of some local veterinarians. Rarely do they examine dead cattle; instead they are usually asked to treat living animals.

Stewart also presents convincing evidence to support his conclusion – that the episodes just discussed represent a classic case of mild hysteria. However, as Stewart points out, not everyone in these two states believed in livestock mutilations, even in the height of the "hysteria." Curious as to the types of individuals likely to be "believers," Stewart and his students interviewed approximately 800 adults. His findings are summarized in the following quote:

> Females, persons with lower educational levels and lower socioeconomic groups seem to be more prone to subscribe to a bizarre explanation, – while males, higher educational level groups and high socioeconomic groups seem to be more reluctant to adopt the unusual explanation and are more likely to attribute cause to a natural explanation.

Recommendations

One major objective of this project was to make recommendations to the law enforcement community. Since my investigation revealed that the vast majority of reported mutilations are not a law enforcement problem, my first recommendation is that no additional money be spent to fund law enforcement investigations of this phenomenon. It should be noted, however, that this conclusion does not apply to other types of investigations, for I believe that useful and revealing studies can be done by anthropologists, psychologists, sociologists, and other behavioral scientists.

Although I believe that most reported mutilations are caused by predators and scavengers, this does not mean that you, as a law enforcement officer, might not be summoned to investigate a suspected mutilation. In the event that this occurs, you should conduct an investigation that is sufficient to determine if the facts, as alleged, are in violation of a particular state statute, such as unlawful killing, unlawful butchering, or stealing of animals.

If so, you should conduct a logical investigation to collect evidence and testimony to support a successful prosecution of the individuals involved.

If not, you should investigate the incident no further. For example, you would not conduct a homicide investigation after it had been established that the individual had died a natural death or had committed suicide. The same reasoning should be used in investigating livestock mutilations.

Don't use terms such as "surgical precision," which are conclusions. Stay with the facts, let the laboratory experts make conclusions. Also, don't be misled by statements made by non-authoritative sources, for as Adolf Hitler once said: "Tell a lie enough times and it will be believed" (KAFE, April 23, 1980).

While I would hesitate to classify these colorful reports as deliberate lies, nevertheless the principle remains the same. Constant repetition of even some of the most sensational conjectures may eventually be accepted as truth. Perhaps Dr. Samuel Johnson expressed it best when he said: "It is more from carelessness about truth than from intentional lying, that there is so much falsehood in the world."

It is my sincere hope that the conclusions reached in this report will help those engaged in the cattle industry and others to put behind them the rumors, theories and fears that some highly organized criminal activity or extraterrestrial conspiracy is responsible for these mutilations. If this year-long investigation has achieved this one result, then all of the time, effort, and research will have proved most worthwhile.

However, I tend to agree with the following observation made by Dr. Stewart in a letter which he sent to me dated May 13, 1980: "The efforts of knowledgeable experts hopefully will provide a rational explanation for this bizarre episode. Unfortunately, the histories of similar events show that reasonable, scientific explanations may deflect or deter, but never completely eliminate the fantastic explanations that gullible, naive persons adopt."

LE CERCLE

"The Circle" is an offshoot of the infamous Bilderberg group, but whereas Bilderberg jaws "The Circle" wars. Ultra-secretive and ultra-conservative, The Circle was founded in the 1950s by the French former prime minister Antoine Pinay (hence the organization's original name of "The Pinay Circle") together with the French lawyer and Nazi collaborator Jean Violet. The Circle directed its early efforts towards the creation of a unified Europe, drawing together leading politicians from the recently warring states, including German Chancellor Konrad Adenauer and French PM Robert Schuman. However, The Circle more and more came to see its role – especially after the *événements* in France of 1968 – as fighting communism and promoting a right-wing political order within the various states of Europe. This vision entirely overlapped with that of the CIA, who became major funders of The Circle. Ties between the CIA and the Circle are tight. According to Professor van der Pijl's study *Transnational Classes and International Relations*, a two-day conference of The Circle in Washington DC was attended by a former CIA official who had played a leading role in Operation Gladio, the "stay behind" network of anti-Communists prepared to rise against a left-wing government in Italy. The Circle's appetite for getting its hands dirty should not be underestimated. Circle chairman Brian Crozier used his private National Association of Freedom to smear British PM **Harold Wilson** as a KGB puppet, while across *La Manche*, Circle members in the state's Service for External Documentation and Espionage spread disinformation about socialist presidential candidate

François Mitterrand in the 1980s. (When in the Elysée Mitterrand took his revenge by closing the SEDE down.) Van der Pijl asserts that The Circle "envisaged use of provocative terrorism in Germany" to bring controversial Bavarian rightist Franz-Josef Straus to power. More controversially yet, critics of The Circle have alleged that its members in the Swedish intelligence service SAPO, assassinated Sweden's socialist prime minister Olof Palme.

Pinay discussion club doubles as anti-Left hit squad:
ALERT LEVEL 8

CERN (EUROPEAN ORGANIZATION FOR NUCLEAR RESEARCH)

No, don't press that button …

Nothing seems to go right at CERN's Large Hadron Collider (LHC) in Switzerland, with its poor old pointy-headed scientists having to cope with gremlins, explosions, arrests for membership of al-Qaeda (yes, really), which may be just as well, because according to the far fringe of conspiracy theory the particle beam accelerator is actually a doomsday weapon to bring about the end of the world. How do they know? Because the 27-kilometre-long tunnel down which the protons rage towards a collision intended to recreate the beginning of the universe has 666, the Mark of the Beast, stamped on it, while outside CERN's HQ, is a statue of the Indian goddess Shiva, the destroyer. We'll all disappear into a black hole made by the LHC in 2012 (this being the year the **Mayan Calendar**, the doomsayers' bible, ends.) Or, as Dan Brown, that well-known atomic physicist, has written in the textbook *Angels and Demons*, anti-matter will be created in the LHV for a bomb to blow the Vatican and the pontiff to kingdom come.

But the award for the most intriguing CERN conspiracy goes to two real scientists, Holger Bech Nielsen of the Niels Bohr Institute and Masao Ninomiya of the Yukawa Institute for Theoretical Physics. One of the main aims of the £3 billion LHC is to discover the Higgs boson, the missing link between mass and energy, otherwise known as the "God particle". Nielsen and Ninomiya's thesis is that all the glitches and accidents at the LHC are not accidental, but intentional, because the LHC is sabotaging itself – from the future – so it does not fulfil its function of discovering the Higgs. Such a discovery would be "abhorrent to nature". According to Nielsen: "Our theory suggests that any machine trying to make the Higgs shall have bad luck. It is based on mathematics, but you could explain it by saying that God rather hates Higgs particles and attempts to avoid them."

The repeated failures of the US Superconducting Supercollider, also designed to find Higgs, are similarly explained by God's dislike of Higgs and human attempts to impersonate his work.

This is the Hallowed Father of All Conspiracies.

> God/Time is sabotaging CERN's super collider to prevent discovery of the secret particle that holds the Universe together: ALERT LEVEL 4

Further Reading
Holger Bech Nielsen and Masao Ninomiya, "Test of Effect from Future in Large Hadron Collider: A proposal", arXiv.org

CHUPACABRA

Think ALF from the Sci-Fi TV show of that name. But not nice.
Not nice at all.

A chupacabra is, in popular lore, a vicious creature that inhabits the Americas, where it attacks livestock, prior to draining out all their blood in a Dracula-style drink. (Chupacabra is the Spanish for the carefully pronounced "goat sucker".) The first sightings of the Chupacabra came from Puerto Rico in 1995, but in recent years the critters have spotted in Michigan, Russia, the Philippines. Although eye-witnesses differ on the what exactly a chupacabra *does* look like, the creature is commonly described as being the size of a large dog, having red bulging eyes, a row of spines down its back, a scaly skin, and trailing a gut-churning stench in its wake. The chupacabra commits the exsanguinations by piercing ¼ inch holes into its prey.

Chilean chupacabra-watchers have asserted that the beast is a result of a NASA lab experiment going wrong, whereas Jorge Martin in "The Chupacabras Phenomenon" notes a different bunch of microscope-wielding gringos may be to blame:

Puerto Rico has been the site for much experimentation by the United States on the island's population and territory for decades. Examples of this can be found in the experimentation of Talidomida and anti-conceptive drugs on our women, which caused the birth of many malformed children in the 1950s. The lethal "orange agent" and other dioxine-based chemical agents were tested in several places on the island, as well as gamma radiation tests in our forests. Because of this we can't exclude the "possibility" that someone may well be experimenting with new and advanced genetic products in our country. The ABEs [Anomalous Biological Entities] could be the result – and has gone awry ... who knows?

The US government possibly? According to Martin, specimens of chupacabra were captured alive in Puerto Rico in November 1995 and dispatched stateside. The only reason the matter was not reported in the media was because chupacabra sightings tend to coincide with UFO sightings, and Uncle Sam does not want Joe and Josephine Public to know UFOs are real and/or that Uncle Sam is in cahoots with the ETs.

While the presence of an "ALF" or "alien life form" on Earth cannot be completely ruled out, until we get to shake long spindly fingers there are better explanations for the phenomenon of "El Chupacabra". A **Plum Island** genetic monster is a distant possibility, yet numerous studies of dead "chupacabras" have found them to be no more exotic than coyotes with mange. Almost as prosaically, researcher Benjamin Radford has shown that the first sightings of chupacabra coincided almost exactly with the release of the sci-fi movie *Species*. Which featured an alien/human varmint quite remarkably like the chupacabra.

> They've landed – vampiric aliens are walking the Earth: ALERT LEVEL 1

Further Reading
Benjamin Radford, *Tracking the Chupacabra: The Vampire Beast in Fact, Fiction and Film*, 2011

CLOUDBUSTER

Kate Bush had a hit single in 1985 called "Cloudbusting", which came with an eye-catching video of a machine that sucked clouds into a trumpet-like horn and blew them out elsewhere.

Both song and video were based on the "cloudbuster" machine invented by Wilhelm Reich. Born in Austria in 1897, Reich was trained as a psychoanalyst by Freud, but he eventually turned his back on the sage of Vienna to concentrate on a science centred on the study of "bions", microscopically small particles of cosmic energy. Thrown out of Austria by the Gestapo, he moved to America, where he perfected, among other inventions, the aforementioned cloudbuster. This consisted of six metal pipes strapped together, and grounded by a metal cable to a water source. Mounted on a stand, so it could be pointed at any cloud in the sky, it supposedly worked by raising or lowering "Orgone Energy", a cosmic life force like Chinese *chi*, in the atmosphere.

In the great Maine drought of 1953, with the blueberry harvest in danger of shrivelling, Dr Reich was asked by farmers to bring his cloudbuster along and do his stuff. According to the *Bangor Daily News*, within hours of Reich pointing his contraption at the sky at 10.00 a.m. on 6 July, a quarter of an inch of rain fell – despite no forecast of precipitation.

Skeptics suggested the precipitation was coincidence.

Whatever, Reich's incipient career as a rainmaker was cut short by an unholy alliance of the FBI and the Food and Drug Administration. When Reich claimed that his "Orgone Energy Accumulator" (a large wood and metal box) could cure cancer, he was sentenced to prison, where he died. The court also ruled that his inventions, their parts and his papers be destroyed.

Reich's science may have been unorthodox, but it hardly required an American court to ape the Nazis by burning scholarly books and imprisoning alternative thinkers.

Scientist Wilhelm Reich framed by Food and Drug Administration: ALERT LEVEL 9

Further Reading
Wilhelm Reich, *The Cancer Biopathy*, 1948
Wilhelm Reich, *The Orgone Energy Accumulator, Its Scientific and Medical Uses*, 1948

CLUB OF THE ISLES

You will not read about the Club of the Isles in any textbook or popular magazine. It is unincorporated and it has no membership lists. Yet, as an informal association of predominantly European-based royal households and princely families, the Club of the Isles commands an estimated $10 trillion in assets. It lords over such corporate giants as Royal Dutch Shell, Imperial Chemical Industries, Lloyds of London, Unilever, Lonrho, Rio Tinto Zinc, and Anglo American DeBeers. It dominates the world supply of petroleum, gold, diamonds, and many other vital raw materials; and deploys these assets not merely in the pursuit of wealth, but as resources at the disposal of its geopolitical agenda.

Such is the belief of *The New Federalist,* house newspaper of American politician and conspiracy theorist Lyndon LaRouche. It gets worse according to Mr LaRouche, because the goal of the Club of the Isles –which supposedly takes its name from the Prince of Wales's title "Prince of the Isles" – is "to reduce the human population from its current level of over 5 billion people to below 1 billion people within the next two to three generations; to literally 'cull the human herd' in the interest of retaining their own global power and the feudal system upon which that power is based".

How will humanity be so culled? By wars and revolutions fomented by the World Wildlife Fund (!) which, like the Club itself, is headed by the nonagenarian Duke of Edinburgh. The genocide in Rwanda is just one example of what the WWF, cunningly disguised as panda-huggers, can do. Meanwhile, that section of humanity destined to escape the chop will be made hapless and helpless by ingesting large quantities of pop music and drugs, the latter supplied by the biggest crack cartel of all – the British Royal Family. In his book *Why Your Child Became a Drug Addict*, LaRouche asserts that Queen Elizabeth II had the British Secret Service deliberately manufacture the Beatles, so as to pervert the minds of American youth with their rock 'n' roll ways.

Welcome to La-la-la-Rouche land. Mr LaRouche and his collaborators do not like the Windsors who, in the tortured minds of the LaRouchites, run, aside from drug-trafficking, the Commonwealth, the UN and pretty much the whole global shebang from their secret inner circle, the Club of the Isles. Well, not quite the entire world deal, because LaRouche also seems to think that **Synarchy** is another contender as Master Cabal of the Universe, and the good old US of A is holding out against re-becoming a British colony.

A hundred years ago, a good case could have been made for the thesis that "Britannia Rules" (with Cecil Rhodes's **Society of the Elect** as chief cheerleader), but today Britain barely scrapes membership of the G7. As with all "unified field" conspiracies LaRouche resorts to an entirely instrumentalist view of politics, by which one person pulls a lever and the world alters course: Lizzie Windsor requests MI5 to create four lovable mop heads from Liverpool, drug culture ruins the teenagers of the US.

The LaRouchites might be more convincing if they got the details correct. The title held by the Prince of Wales that gives the club its name is Lord of the Isles not Prince of. And if the Club of the Isles actually exists anywhere outside La-la-la-Roucheland it is doubtless yet another talking shop for the great and the good.

> Prince Philip and his aristo dining chums are the one ring that rules us all: ALERT LEVEL 2

Further Reading
Joan Veon, *Prince Charles: The Sustainable Prince*, 1997
"The True Story Behind the Fall of the House of Windsor", *EIR* Special Report, September 1997

KURT COBAIN

When Nirvana's lead singer Kurt Cobain exited the world on 5 April 1994 his mother exclaimed, "Now he's gone and joined that stupid club, I told him not to join that stupid club." Mrs Wendy O'Connor meant that her son had joined Jim Morrison, Janis Joplin and Jimi Hendrix on rock 'n' roll's list of twenty-seven-year-old suicides.

But did Cobain commit suicide? Within a week of Cobain's death at his Lake Washington house, Seattle journalist Richard Lee hosted a show unambiguously entitled "Kurt Cobain Was Murdered", claiming that there were discrepancies and facts difficult to reconcile with a verdict of suicide.

Kurt Donald Cobain was, admittedly, given to depression and his family had a history of suicide. Cobain himself apparently deliberately overdosed on Rohypnol and champagne earlier in 1994 while in Rome. Bandmate Krist Novoselic considered Cobain "quiet" and "estranged" in the period before his death. Cobain was also under intense financial and professional pressure, having walked out on a $9.5 million contract to headline the Lollapalooza festival.

Against this, psychologists at the rehab centre Cobain visited a week before his demise, thought he seemed far from suicidal. Neither was the "suicide note" found near his body full of the usual darknesses of such missives, and contained the statement: "I have it good, very good and I'm grateful." The last four lines of the note appear to have been written by another hand, while Cobain's body contained so much heroin – *three times* the lethal 225 mgs dose – he would have been comatose and unable to hold a gun. His body also contained significant and incapacitating amounts of diazepam (Valium). On studying the autopsy report, Canadian toxicologist and chemist Roger Lewis concluded in an article entitled "Dead Men Don't Pull Triggers": "Thus, in contrast with the 'official' verdict of suicide by shotgun, the scientific facts point to a series of events which probably included a massive, lethal 'hot shot' dose of heroin and a benzodiazepine administered to Cobain, which would have either immediately rendered him incapacitated in a comatose state or killed him instantly."

There's more. No legible fingerprints were on the pen used to write the note or on the Remington shotgun used, suggesting that both had been wiped clean. Cobain's hands, according to Seattle police reports, were free of gunpowder residue. And who fills a Remington 20 gauge shotgun with three cartridges for a suicide shot to the head, when only one is needed? And who uses their Seafirst credit card twice after their death, as timed by the medical examiner. If Cobain was murdered, whodunnit? An LA private dick by the name of Tom Grant was hired by Cobain's wife, Courtney Love, to track Cobain's credit card. Love's strange behaviour, however, soon convinced Grant that *she* orchestrated Cobain's homicide. Her motive was financial. Cobain was about to divorce Love; since ex-Mrs Cobain would get nothing in Cobain's will, she had her husband "suicided". Supporting evidence for Grant's accusation came from British documentary maker Nick Broomfield, who interviewed Eldon Hoke (a.k.a. "El Duce") a member of LA punk band the Mentors, who alleged that Love had offered him $50,000 to kill Kurt Cobain. El Duce expanded on his claim to a newspaper, saying that Love had pulled up outside the Rock Shop at 1644 Wilcox Avenue, Hollywood, and the following conversation ensued:

> **Love:** *"El, I need a favour of you. My old man's been a real asshole lately, I need you to blow his fucking head off."*
> **El Duce:** *"Are you serious?"*
> **Love:** *"Yeah, I'll give you $50,000 to blow his fucking head off."*
> **El Duce:** *"I'm serious if you are."*
> **Love:** *"Where can I reach you?"*
> **El Duce:** *"You can reach me here."*

The manager of the shop, Karush Sepedjian, overheard the conversation, and agreed with El Duce's version of it. When asked, "Did Love offer you money to kill Cobain?" with a lie detector strapped to his arm El Duce passed with a 99.7 per cent certainty. El Duce rejected Love's offer. Further attempts to interview El Duce proved impossible; he was run over by a train in 1997, so adding fuel to the conspiracy fire. Nonetheless PI Grant fingered, to his own satisfaction, the man who did take up Courtney Love's murderous proposal. Grant named the killer as Michael Dewitt. The claim is still up on Grant's website www.cobaincase.com: "After several months of intensive investigation, including dozens of taped interviews with Cobain's closest friends and family members, I reached the conclusion that Courtney Love and Michael Dewitt (the male nanny who lived at the Cobain residence) were involved in a conspiracy that resulted in the murder of Kurt Cobain."

Grant's investigation also led him to believe that the Lake Washington shooting was Love–Dewitt's second homicide attempt, and that Cobain's drug and alcohol OD in Rome was a masked murder attempt by the same duo. (According to Grant, Cobain was not a user of Rohypnol, the "date rape" drug.) Gumshoe Grant believes that the proof of Love and Dewitt's guilt is their unwillingness to sue him for defamation: "As I predicted when I first began speaking out [about Cobain's homicide], no legal action has been taken against myself or anyone in the media who have covered this story."

Unhappily for Courtney Love, her first husband, James Moreland, weighed into the controversy, telling a British newspaper: "It wasn't long before I became a battered husband ... She would go mad for no reason, and hit me time and time again ... Once she threatened to pay someone £150 to beat me up because I didn't agree with her about something."

Pointed questions also began to be asked of the coroner in the case, Dr Hartshorne, because of a conflict of interest. He knew Cobain and Love, and was known to party with the latter.

Despite the welter of evidence and allegations, the Seattle PD has so far refused to re-open the case on Cobain's death. Perhaps they should.

Smells like a conspiracy to murder Kurt Cobain:
ALERT LEVEL 7

Further Reading
Nick Broomfield, *Kurt and Courtney*, 1998 (film)
Ian Halperin and Max Wallace, *Who Killed Kurt Cobain? The Mysterious Death of an Icon*, 1999
www.cobaincase.com
www.justiceforkurt.com

CODEX ALIMENTARIUS

Latin for "Food Code" the Codex Alimentarius is a quango formed by the World Health Authority and the US Food and Agriculture Organization in 1963, with the aim of "protecting health of the consumers and ensuring fair trade practices in the food trade, and promoting coordination of all food standards work undertaken by international governmental and non-governmental organizations". Put another way, the work of the CA is to ensure that your turkey twizzler is not full of additives, has been prepared properly and is accurately labelled.

Sounds like a good idea? Not according to libertarians and alternative practitioners, who allege that Codex Alimentarius, far from being independent and "voluntary" as described, is in the hands of Big Pharma, food multinationals, agribusiness, government officials and seeks to do down local producers, organic farmers and, especially, manufacturers and sellers of vitamins – and then some. A press release from Alliance for Natural Health states:

> The WTO (World Trade Organization) is a global commercial police that ensures countries are required to purchase from transnational corporations in favour of their own locally produced goods, in the name of "lowering trade barriers".
>
> This WHO/WTO joint effort called CODEX is in the process of wiping out local supplement companies and natural health care practices, to bring in more drug based medicines, in what is euphemistically known as "creating a level playing field", while primarily giving the public a

misleading impression that someone in the World Health Organisation (WHO) is looking after its health and safety.

The frontline for anti-Codex campaigners is the humble vitamin supplement, since the Codex supposedly seeks the banning of dietary supplements for prophylactic or therapeutic use, and the classification of common foods such as peppermint and garlic as drugs, and the requirement of prescriptions for anything but the lowest potencies of vitamins. All new dietary supplements would be banned until Codex-tested. And that is where big business enters the picture: since testing is expensive, few small-scale manufacturers (runs the argument) could afford to have their products tested, so leaving the field open to the corporate colossi in the food and drink game.

Inevitably, any global regulatory body will attract charges that it is the pawn of the **New World Order** and sure enough Jon King on www.consciousape.com states "Big Brother and the New World Order (not to mention the Carlyle Group) [is] taking away your health as of April 2011." "Taking away your health" in the Codex conspiracy can equate to depopulation of the Third World, since the NWO wishes to rid the globe of useless "hungry mouths". At the very least, think NWO-observers, the Codex is not truly voluntary and supersedes domestic laws, meaning weakening of sovereignty.

It's a funny old world, the conspiracy world. Because, guess what? There is a conspiracy theory that the "Codex conspiracy" is a conspiracy. Some say that the Codex scale is all fanned up by organic foodies, homeopaths and herbalists for financial reasons. Since their products are starting to become regulated and studied by science, they are making up conspiracy theories about the nice people at Codex who simply want to make sure any and every food is safe for your body.

The verdict: Big Nanny is alive and well and living in Codex HQ in Rome. Whether the CA is the puppet of interest groups or no, it is a bureaucracy in need of democracy.

Codex Alimentarius is an unregulated body in the thrall of food corporations, politicians and scientists: ALERT LEVEL 5

Further Reading
www.codexalimentarius.net

COMMITTEE OF 300

Who is the daddy of the secret societies? Conspiracist John Coleman has the answer: the Committee of 300 is the one group that covertly runs the world.

The existence of the Committee of 300 was first mooted in a 1909 newspaper article by German civil servant Walther Rathenau; according to Rathenau the whole of the European economy was run by a group of 300 industrial magnates. He repeated the claim in his book *Zur Kritik der Zeit* ("A Critique of the Times"); in turn Erich von Ludendorff, former general and arch right-winger, maintained that the Committee was nothing less than the head honchos of the global Jewish conspiracy described in the "Protocols of the Elders of Zion". The anti-Semitic press in Weimar Germany found all necessary proof for von Ludendorff's thesis in Rathenau's person; not only was he a civil servant, he was an industrialist – the director of the German branch of General Electric – and a Jew. Thus he knew of what he spoke because he was … one of the Committee of 300 himself.

Despite all the Nazi huff and puff, they were unable to provide actual evidence of the Committee of 300's existence. (Of course, assassinating Rathenau in a fit of anti-Semitic pique, thus destroying their one "proof", hardly helped verification.) Nevertheless, the Committee of 300 continued to be a bogey-man of the Western world, and by 1992 Dr John Coleman, a self-proclaimed former MI6 officer, had decided that the Committee was actually "The Olympians", a British satanic, aristocratic sect founded in 1727. More, the Olympians/ Committee of 300 were the sponsors of all the other secret elites hell-bent on creating a **New World Order**, including the **Bavarian Illuminati**, the Council on Foreign Relations, the Club of Rome, the Trilateral Commission – to name just a few.

In all probability, Rathenau never intended the phrase "the Committee of 300" to indicate a literal cabal, or a black magic cult, but a loose alliance of industrialists. In his words, "Three hundred men, all of whom know one another, direct the economic destiny of Europe and choose their successors from among themselves."

Curiously, John Coleman is alone in finding modern evidence of the Committee of 300. He has a book to sell about the 300, titled *Conspirator's Hierarchy: The Story of the Committee of 300*, which is available from his website www.coleman300.com. So, no vested interest there, then.

> A clique of 300 satanically inclined men seek world domination: ALERT LEVEL 2

Further Reading
John Coleman, *Conspirator's Hierarchy: The Story of the Committee of 300*, 1992

CAN

The Cult Awareness Network (CAN) was founded by Patricia Ryan, daughter of Congressman Leo Ryan, who was assassinated in Guyana by members of Jim Jones's People's Temple cult. CAN was a counsel and support for families whose sons or daughters had been brainwashed by outfits like Jones's. The Network also provided information on over two hundred religious cults it considered worrisome. One such was the Church of Scientology. According to *Time*, CAN received more calls from concerned moms and dads about the Scientology church than any other group. In 1991, Cynthia Kisser, the executive director of CAN, openly criticized Scientology in a 1991 article in *Time*, saying, "Scientology is quite likely the most ruthless, the most classically terroristic, the most litigious and the most lucrative cult the country has ever seen. No cult extracts more money from its members."

Mr L. Ron Hubbard's church was very, very unhappy at such negative attention, and fought back with an expensive advertising campaign, taking out full-colour ads in *USA Today* for weeks on end. The Scientologists also sicced their house lawyer, Kendrick Moxon, on to CAN, who filed fifty civil lawsuits against the counselling group.

CAN's annual budget was $300,000 a year. Fighting the Scientologists' legal eagle in court emptied its coffers and then some. Eventually CAN was driven into bankruptcy, after CAN was found guilty of violating the religious liberties of Jason Scott, a Pentecostalist, who had been kidnapped and subjected to "deprogramming". CAN was not party to the kidnap, but was implicated because Scott's mother had called CAN's helpline, who in turn had referred her to a deprogrammer. And the deprogammer had participated in the kidnap. Usually, the Church of Scientology snubs rival religious groups, but on this occasion old man Hubbard's outfit kindly allowed its famous lawyer, Kendrick Moxon, to file a civil suit against CAN on Jason Scott's behalf. The court awarded $1 million in punitive damages against CAN.

So CAN was driven into bankruptcy. And guess who bought it? The Church of Scientology. They altered not a jot about its name or purpose. All they did was replace the staff. So when a concerned mom or dad phones the CAN helpline, they are answered by a Scientologist. That is, a member of the same sect that Cynthia Kisser thought a contender for being the "most ruthless cult" the country had ever seen.

Cult awareness group forced to close down by Church of Scientology: ALERT LEVEL 8

Further Reading
Richard Behar, "The Thriving Cult of Greed and Power", *Time*, 6 May 1991

DENVER INTERNATIONAL AIRPORT

Welcome to Denver International Airport (slogan: "Together we soar"), from where you can take flights to London, Frankfurt, Mexico City, LA and Toronto. Or, if you are a VIP, you can take a quick trip down below the runway to the subterranean HQ of the **New World Order**. Supposedly.

Denver International Airport (DIA) has been the object of conspiracy movement suspicions since it replaced the old Denver airport at Stapleton in 1995. The new airport – the biggest in the USA – was budgeted at $1.7 billion, but when the last contractor screwed in the last light bulb the cost had jumped to $5 billion. The discrepancy between the two figures, plus the vast amount of soil shifting done, gave credibility to the belief that a secret multi-level building had been constructed underground. Conspiracy researchers Alex Christopher and Philip Schneider claimed to have visited the subterranean complex, and interviewed workers there. Christopher informed radio interviewer Dave Alan:

AC: … this other man told me in private that there is a lot of human slave labor in these deep underground bases being used by these aliens, and that a lot of this slave labor is children. He said that when the children reach the point that they are unable to work any more, they are slaughtered on the spot and consumed.

DA: Consumed by who?

AC: Aliens. Again, this is not from me, but from a man that gave his life to get this information out. He worked down there for close to 20 years, and he knew everything that was going on.

DA: Hmmm. Who do these aliens eat?

AC: They specifically like young human children that haven't been contaminated like adults. Well, there is a gentleman out giving a lot of information from a source he gets it from, and he says that there is an incredible number of children snatched in this country.

DA: Over 200,000 each year.

AC: And that these children are the main entree for dinner.

DA: How many Draconians are down there?

AC: I have heard the figure of 150,000 just in the New York area.

DA: Underneath New York?

AC: Yes. In some kind of underground base there.

DA: Interesting. Now, you've seen pictures of these things?

AC: I have seen them face to face.

DA: You have?

AC: Yes. From some information that has been put out by a group or team that also works in these underground bases that is trying to get information out to people that love this country, there is a war that is going on under our feet, and above our heads, that the public doesn't know anything about, and its between these alien forces and the humans that are trying to fight them.

DA: What other types have you seen?

AC: The ones that I have seen are the big-eyed Greys and the Reptilians.

Phew. So dangerous was this knowledge that Schneider was (reportedly) murdered by the NWO. Dead men tell no tales.

Those too nervous to sneak down for a peek at the aliens can find all the proof they need about DIA's dual role as NWO HQ just by visiting the airport's main (above ground) complex, where the decor gives the game away:

- A dedication marker in the Great Hall (a Masonic term!) is unambiguously inscribed with a Masonic square and compasses. Also carved in the stone is the legend "New World Airport Commission". Spooky or what?
- A mural by the artist Leo Tanguma contains a sword-wielding

figure and a rainbow. According to Tanguma, these images are part of his themes of war and the triumph of peace, and living in harmony with Nature. Ex-Florida dentist Len Horowitz , though, maintains in his book *Death in the Air* that the rainbow is an image code for a revived Nazi plan to spray lethal toxins into the air to bring about the genocide of undesirable populations.

- The Nazi theme is continued in the design of the airport's runways. From above, they are shaped like a swastika.
- The floors in the terminal are inscribed with satanic/Masonic/NWO/Illuminati codes, such as *Dzit Dit Gaii* and *Cochetopa*.

Enough already. DIA is not the site of the NWO's HQ, and there are no below runway constructions filled with aliens eating babies and opponents of the NWO. There *are* miles of underground passages, but these have innocuous purposes. One of Christopher's photos of the NWO secret tunnels turned out to be a track for a baggage train. Tanguma's murals *are* a tad weird, probably not the sort of stuff you want to view before catching a flight, but the man's an artist for heaven's sake. (A liberal, Christian artist to boot, so hardly the sort of painter the NWO is going to hire to empathetically communicate its vision.) The codes on the floor are actually Navajo place names. Certainly, the Masons got in on the DIA project, but the Masons like to advertise with plaques and capstones (aged, they need the members because they are literally dying out), thus have been laying capstones of buildings all over America for hundreds of years. "The New World Airport Commission", declares the airport authority, was a group of businessmen who arranged the opening shindig, and came up with the name because the airport would be "new" and "world-spanning".

Denver International Airport is secret HQ for NWO:
ALERT LEVEL 1

Further Reading
Alex Christopher, *Pandora's Box*, 2007
www.mt.net/~watcher/nwodnver.html

THE DREYFUS AFFAIR

Although "*L'affaire* Dreyfus" occurred over a hundred years ago France still lives in its shadow.

Alfred Dreyfus – who was Jewish – was an artillery captain in the French Army. In 1894 he was charged with passing military secrets to the German Embassy in Paris, the evidence against him being documents found in the attaché's rubbish bin of the German written, according to graphologists, in Dreyfus's hand. Dreyfus was barred from seeing the evidence and sentenced to life imprisonment on the infamous Devil's Island off the coast of South America.

Four years later, Lieutenant-Colonel Georges Picquart discovered overwhelming evidence that the real culprit was one Major Ferdinand Walsin Esterhazy, but before Picquart could obtain a new hearing he was mysteriously transferred to Tunisia. Meanwhile, another officer who supplied clear-cut evidence that the top brass of the Army had forged documents in the Dreyfus case was interrogated. He then committed suicide. The Army, meanwhile, found Esterhazy innocent. Fearful of the public exposure of the injustice done to Dreyfus – and, let us admit it, egged on by their own anti-Semitism – high-ranking officers on the Army's General Staff and intelligence corps – had begun a cover-up of colossal dimension.

Save for the French novelist Émile Zola the conspiracy may well have succeeded. On 13 January 1898 Zola published an article, "*J'Accuse*" in the French newspaper *The Dawn* in which he publicly revealed Esterhazy as the real culprit and named the officers involved in the conspiracy. The Army leadership wrote

Zola was engaged in "one of the greatest iniquities of the century".

The military sued Zola for libel. The trial provoked anti-Dreyfus/Zola rioting in the streets of Paris. Although evidence introduced at the trial by the defence made it obvious that Esterhazy, not Dreyfus, was the traitor, and that the military was covering up the truth, Zola was convicted. To avoid prison, he fled to England. If anything, the military conspiracy escalated: the wholly innocent Picquart was arrested on suspicion of having forged the Esterhazy documents and dismissed from the Army.

By June 1899, however, public opinion had swung in Dreyfus's favour, and the libel charge against Zola was dismissed. Dreyfus himself was pardoned and, in 1906, his conviction was reversed by the highest court in France. None of the military conspirators, however, was ever brought to trial.

The Dreyfus Affair officially concluded on 21 July 1906 when Dreyfus, reinstated in the Army, was honoured by a dress parade military ceremony. Zola was absent. He had died in 1902 in his Paris home, asphyxiated by fumes from a chimney. Many believe he was murdered by right-wing extremists.

L'Affaire Dreyfus had a violent footnote. During a memorial service for Zola, Dreyfus was shot and wounded by a right-wing journalist.

The journalist was acquitted of attempted murder.

French Army leadership framed a Jewish officer for treason: ALERT LEVEL 10

Further Reading
Leslie Derfler, *The Dreyfus Affair*, 2002
Ruth Harris, *The Man on Devil's Island: Alfred Dreyfus and the Affair that Divided France*, 2010

DOCUMENT: *"J'ACCUSE"*, ÉMILE ZOLA, *THE DAWN*, 13 JANUARY 1898
An Open Letter to Mr Félix Faure, President of the Republic

Mr President,

Would you allow me, in my gratitude for the benevolent reception that you gave me one day, to draw the attention of your rightful glory and to tell you that your star, so happy until now, is threatened by the most shameful and most ineffaceable of blemishes?

You have passed healthy and safe through base calumnies; you have conquered hearts. You appear radiant in the apotheosis of this patriotic festival that the Russian alliance was for France, and you prepare to preside over the solemn triumph of our World Fair, which will crown our great century of work, truth and freedom. But what a spot of mud on your name – I was going to say on your reign – is this abominable Dreyfus affair! A council of war, under order, has just dared to acquit Esterhazy, a great blow to all truth, all justice. And it is finished, France has this stain on her cheek, History will write that it was under your presidency that such a social crime could be committed.

Since they dared, I too will dare. The truth I will say, because I promised to say it, if justice, regularly seized, did not do it, full and whole. My duty is to speak, I do not want to be an accomplice. My nights would be haunted by the spectre of innocence that suffer there, through the most dreadful of tortures, for a crime it did not commit.

And it is to you, Mr President, that I will proclaim it, this truth, with all the force of the revulsion of an honest man. For your honour, I am convinced that you are unaware of it. And with whom will I thus denounce the criminal foundation of these guilty truths, if not with you, the first magistrate of the country?

First, the truth about the lawsuit and the judgment of Dreyfus. A nefarious man carried it all out, did everything: Lieutenant-Colonel Du Paty de Clam, at that time only a commandant. He is the entirety of the Dreyfus business; it will be known only when one honest investigation clearly establishes his acts and responsibilities. He seems a most complicated and hazy spirit, haunting romantic intrigues, caught up in serialized stories, stolen papers, anonymous letters, appointments in deserted places, mysterious women who sell condemning evidences at night. It is he who imagined dictating the Dreyfus memo; it is he who dreamed to study it in an entirely hidden way, under ice; it is him whom Commander Forzinetti describes to us as armed with a dark lantern, wanting to approach the sleeping defendant, to flood his face abruptly with light and to thus surprise his crime, in the agitation of being roused. And I need hardly say that that what one seeks, one will find. I declare simply that Commander Du Paty de Clam, charged to investigate the Dreyfus business as a legal officer, is, in date and in responsibility, the first culprit in the appalling miscarriage of justice committed.

The memo was for some time already in the hands of Colonel Sandherr, director of the office of information, who has since died of general paresis. "Escapes" took place, papers disappeared, as they still do today; the author of the memo was sought, when ahead of time one was made aware, little by little, that this author could be only an officer of the High Command and an artillery officer: a doubly glaring error, showing with which superficial spirit this affair had been studied, because a reasoned examination shows that it could only be a question of an officer of troops. Thus searching the house, examining writings, it was like a family matter, a traitor to be surprised in the same offices, in order to expel him. And, while I don't want to retell a partly known history here, Commander Paty de Clam enters the scene, as soon as first suspicion falls upon Dreyfus. From this moment, it is he who invented Dreyfus, the affair becomes that affair, made actively to confuse the traitor, to bring him to a full confession. There is the Minister of War, General Mercier, whose intelligence seems poor; there are the head of the High Command, General De Boisdeffre, who appears to have yielded to his clerical passion, and the assistant manager of the High

Command, General Gonse, whose conscience could put up with many things. But, at the bottom, there is initially only Commander Du Paty de Clam, who carries them all out, who hypnotizes them, because he deals also with spiritism, with occultism, conversing with spirits. One could not conceive of the experiments to which he subjected unhappy Dreyfus, the traps into which he wanted to make him fall, the insane investigations, monstrous imaginations, a whole torturing insanity.

Ah! this first affair is a nightmare for those who know its true details! Commander Du Paty de Clam arrests Dreyfus, in secret. He turns to Mrs Dreyfus, terrorizes her, says to her that, if she speaks, her husband is lost. During this time, the unhappy one tore his flesh, howled his innocence. And the instructions were made thus, as in a fifteenth century tale, shrouded in mystery, with a savage complication of circumstances, all based on only one childish charge, this idiotic affair, which was not only a vulgar treason, but was also the most impudent of hoaxes, because the famously delivered secrets were almost all without value. If I insist, it is that the kernel is here, from whence the true crime will later emerge, the terrible denial of justice from which France is sick. I would like to touch with a finger on how this miscarriage of justice could be possible, how it was born from the machinations of Commander Du Paty de Clam, how General Mercier, General De Boisdeffre and General Gonse could let it happen, to engage little by little their responsibility in this error, that they believed a need, later, to impose like the holy truth, a truth which is not even discussed. At the beginning, there is not this, on their part, this incuriosity and obtuseness. At most, one feels them to yield to an ambiance of religious passions and the prejudices of the physical spirit. They allowed themselves a mistake.

But here Dreyfus is before the council of war. Closed doors are absolutely required. A traitor would have opened the border with the enemy to lead the German emperor to Notre-Dame, without taking measures to maintain narrow silence and mystery. The nation is struck into a stupor, whispering of terrible facts, monstrous treasons which make History indignant; naturally the nation is so inclined. There is no punishment too severe, it will applaud public degradation, it will want the culprit to remain on his rock of infamy, devoured by remorse. Is this then true, the inexpressible things, the dangerous things, capable of plunging Europe into flames, which one must carefully bury behind these closed doors? No! There was behind this, only the romantic and lunatic imaginations of Commander Du Paty de Clam. All that was done only to hide the most absurd of novella plots. And it suffices, to ensure oneself of this, to study with attention the bill of indictment, read in front of the council of war.

Ah! the nothingness of this bill of indictment! That a man could be condemned for this act, is a wonder of iniquity. I defy decent people to read it, without their hearts leaping in indignation and shouting their revolt, while thinking of the unwarranted suffering, over there, on Devil's Island. Dreyfus knows several languages, crime; one found at his place no compromising papers, crime; he returns sometimes to his country of origin, crime; he is industrious, he wants to know everything, crime; he is unperturbed, crime; he is perturbed, crime. And the naiveté of drafting formal assertions in a vacuum! One spoke to us of fourteen charges: we find only one in the final analysis, that of the memo; and we even learn that the experts did not agree, than one of them, Mr Gobert, was coerced militarily, because he did not allow himself to reach a conclusion in the desired direction. One also spoke of twenty-three officers who had come to overpower Dreyfus with their testimonies. We remain unaware of their interrogations, but it is certain that they did not all charge him; and it is to be noticed, moreover, that all belonged to the war offices. It is a family lawsuit, one is there against oneself, and it is necessary to remember this: the High Command wanted the lawsuit, it was judged, and it has just judged it a second time.

Therefore, there remained only the memo, on which the experts had not concurred. It is reported that, in the room of the council, the judges were naturally going to acquit. And consequently, as one includes/understands the despaired

obstinacy with which, to justify the judgment, today the existence of a secret part is affirmed, overpowering, the part which
cannot be shown, which legitimates all, in front of which we
must incline ourselves, the good invisible and unknowable
God! I deny it, this part, I deny it with all my strength! A
ridiculous part, yes, perhaps the part wherein it is a question
of young women, and where a certain D ... is spoken of which
becomes too demanding: some husband undoubtedly finding
that his wife did not pay him dearly enough. But a part interesting the national defence, which one could not produce
without war being declared tomorrow, no, no! It is a lie! And
it is all the more odious and cynical that they lie with impu-
nity without one being able to convince others of it. They
assemble France, they hide behind its legitimate emotion,
they close mouths by disturbing hearts, by perverting spirits.
I do not know a greater civic crime.

Here then, Mr President, are the facts which explain how a
miscarriage of justice could be made; and the moral evidence,
the financial circumstances of Dreyfus, the absence of reason,
his continual cry of innocence, completes its demonstration
as a victim of the extraordinary imaginations of Commander
Du Paty de Clam, of the clerical medium in which it was
found, of the hunting for the "dirty Jews", which dishonours
our time.

And we arrive at the Esterhazy affair. Three years passed,
many consciences remain deeply disturbed, worry, seek, end
up being convinced of Dreyfus's innocence.

I will not give the history of the doubts and of the conviction of Mr Scheurer-Kestner. But, while this was excavated
on the side, it ignored serious events among the High
Command. Colonel Sandherr was dead, and Major Picquart
succeeded him as head of the office of the information. And
it was for this reason, in the performance of his duties, that
the latter one day found in his hands a letter-telegram,
addressed to Commander Esterhazy, from an agent of a
foreign power. His strict duty was to open an investigation. It
is certain that he never acted apart from the will of his superiors. He thus submitted his suspicions to his seniors in rank,

General Gonse, then General De Boisdeffre, then General Billot, who had succeeded General Mercier as the Minister of War. The infamous Picquart file, about which so much was said, was never more than a Billot file, a file made by a subordinate for his minister, a file which must still exist within the Ministry of War. Investigations ran from May to September 1896, and what should be well affirmed is that General Gonse was convinced of Esterhazy's guilt, and that Generals De Boisdeffre and Billot did not question that the memo was written by Esterhazy. Major Picquart's investigation had led to this unquestionable observation. But the agitation was large, because the condemnation of Esterhazy inevitably involved the revision of Dreyfus's trial; and this, the High Command did not want at any cost.

There must have been a minute full of psychological anguish. Notice that General Billot was in no way compromised, he arrived completely fresh, he could decide the truth. He did not dare, undoubtedly in fear of public opinion, certainly also in fear of betraying all the High Command, General De Boisdeffre, General Gonse, not mentioning those of lower rank. Therefore there was only one minute of conflict between his conscience and what he believed to be the military's interest. Once this minute had passed, it was already too late. He had engaged, he was compromised. And, since then, his responsibility only grew, he took responsibility for the crimes of others, he became as guilty as the others, he was guiltier than them, because he was the Master of Justice, and he did nothing. Understand that! Here for a year General Billot, General De Boisdeffre and General Gonse have known that Dreyfus is innocent, and they kept this appalling thing to themselves! And these people sleep at night, and they have women and children whom they love!

Major Picquart had fulfilled his duty as an honest man. He insisted to his superiors, in the name of justice. He even begged them, he said to them how much their times were ill-advised, in front of the terrible storm which was to pour down, which was to burst, when the truth would be known. It was, later, the language that Mr Scheurer-Kestner also used with General Billot, entreating him with patriotism to take the affair in hand, not to let it worsen, on the verge of becoming a public disaster. No! The crime had been committed, the High Command could no longer acknowledge its crime. And Major Picquart was sent on a mission, one that took him farther and farther away, as far as Tunisia, where there was not even a day to honour his bravery, charged with a mission which would have surely ended in massacre, in the frontiers where Marquis de Morès met his death. He was not in disgrace, General Gonse maintained a friendly correspondence with him. It is only about secrets he was not good to have discovered.

To Paris, the truth inexorably marched, and it is known how the awaited storm burst. Mr Mathieu Dreyfus denounced Commander Esterhazy as the true author of the memo just as Mr Scheurer-Kestner demanded a revision of the case to the Minister of Justice. And it is here that Commander Esterhazy appears. Testimony shows him initially thrown into a panic, ready for suicide or escape. Then, at a blow, he acted with audacity, astonishing Paris by the violence of his attitude. It is then that help had come to him, he had received an anonymous letter informing him of the work of his enemies, a mysterious lady had come under cover of night to return a stolen evidence against him to the High Command, which would save him. And I cannot help but find Major Du Paty de Clam here, considering his fertile imagination. His work, Dreyfus's culpability, was in danger, and he surely wanted to defend his work. The retrial was the collapse of such an extravagant novella, so tragic, whose abominable outcome takes place in Devil's Island! This is what he could not allow. Consequently, a duel would take place between Major Picquart and Major Du Paty de Clam, one with face uncovered, the other masked. They will soon both be found before civil justice. In the end, it was always the High Command that defended itself, that did not want to acknowledge its crime; the abomination grew hour by hour.

One wondered with astonishment who were protecting Commander Esterhazy. It was initially, in the shadows, Major

Du Paty de Clam who conspired all and conducted all. His hand was betrayed by its absurd means. Then, it was General De Boisdeffre, it was General Gonse, it was General Billot himself, who were obliged to discharge the commander, since they cannot allow recognition of Dreyfus's innocence without the department of war collapsing under public contempt. And the beautiful result of this extraordinary situation is that the honest man there, Major Picquart, who only did his duty, became the victim of ridicule and punishment. O justice, what dreadful despair grips the heart! One might just as well say that he was the forger, that he manufactured the letter-telegram to convict Esterhazy. But, good God! why? with what aim? Give a motive. Is he also paid by the Jews? The joke of the story is that he was in fact an anti-Semite. Yes! we attend this infamous spectacle, of the lost men of debts and crimes upon whom one proclaims innocence, while one attacks honour, a man with a spotless life! When a society does this, it falls into decay.

Here is thus, Mr President, the Esterhazy affair: a culprit whose name it was a question of clearing. For almost two months, we have been able to follow hour by hour the beautiful work. I abbreviate, because it is not here that a summary of the history's extensive pages will one day be written out in full. We thus saw General De Pellieux, then the commander of Ravary, lead an investigation in which the rascals are transfigured and decent people are dirtied. Then, the council of war was convened.

How could one hope that a council of war would demolish what a council of war had done? I do not even mention the always possible choice of judges. Isn't the higher idea of discipline, which is in the blood of these soldiers, enough to cancel their capacity for equity? Who says discipline breeds obedience? When the Minister of War, the overall chief, established publicly, with the acclamations of the national representation, the authority of the final decision; you want a council of war to give him a formal denial? Hierarchically, that is impossible. General Billot influenced the judges by his declaration, and they judged as they must under fire, without reasoning. The preconceived opinion that they brought to their seats is obviously this one: "Dreyfus was condemned for crime of treason by a council of war, he is thus guilty; and we, a council of war, cannot declare him innocent, for we know that to recognize Esterhazy's guilt would be to proclaim the innocence of Dreyfus." Nothing could make them leave that position.

They delivered an iniquitous sentence that will forever weigh on our councils of war, sullying all their arrests from now with suspicion. The first council of war could have been foolish; the second was inevitably criminal. Its excuse, I repeat it, was that the supreme chief had spoken, declaring the thing considered to be unassailable, holy and higher than men, so that inferiors could not say the opposite. One speaks to us about the honour of the army, that we should like it, respect it. Ah! admittedly, yes, the army which would rise to the first threat, which would defend the French ground, it is all the people, and we have for it only tenderness and respect. But it is not a question of that, for which we precisely want dignity, in our need for justice. It is about the sword, the Master that one will give us tomorrow perhaps. And do not kiss devotedly the handle of the sword, by god!

I have shown in addition: the Dreyfus affair was the affair of the department of war, a High Command officer, denounced by his comrades of the High Command, condemned under the pressure of the heads of the High Command. Once again, it cannot restore his innocence without all the High Command being guilty. Also the offices, by all conceivable means, by press campaigns, by communications, by influences, protected Esterhazy only to convict Dreyfus a second time. What sweeping changes should the republican government give to this [Jesuitery], as General Billot himself calls it! Where is the truly strong ministry of wise patriotism that will dare to reforge and to renew all? What of people I know who, faced with the possibility of war, tremble of anguish knowing in what hands lies national defence! And what a nest of base intrigues, gossips and dilapidations has this crowned asylum become, where the fate of fatherland is decided! One trembles in face of the terrible day that there has just thrown the Dreyfus affair, this human sacrifice of an unfortunate, a "dirty Jew"! Ah! all that was agitated insanity there and stupidity, imaginations insane, practices of low police force, manners of inquisition and tyranny, good pleasure of some non-commissioned officers putting their boots on the nation, returning in its throat its cry of truth and justice, under the lying pretext and sacrilege of the reason of State.

And it is a yet another crime to have [pressed on ?] the filthy press, to have let itself defend by all the rabble of Paris, so that the rabble triumphs insolently in defeat of law and simple probity. It is a crime to have accused those who wished for a noble France, at the head of free and just nations, of troubling her, when one warps oneself the impudent plot to impose the error, in front of the whole world. It is a crime to mislay the opinion, to use for a spiteful work this opinion, perverted to the point of becoming delirious. It is a crime to poison the small and the humble, to exasperate passions of reaction and intolerance, while taking shelter behind the odious anti-Semitism, from which, if not cured, the great liberal France of humans rights will die. It is a crime to exploit patriotism for works of hatred, and it is a crime, finally, to turn into to sabre the modern god, when all the social science is with work for the nearest work of truth and justice.

This truth, this justice, that we so passionately wanted, what a distress to see them thus *souffletées*, more ignored and more darkened! I suspect the collapse which must take place in the heart of Mr Scheurer-Kestner, and I believe well that he will end up feeling remorse for not having acted revolutionarily, the day of questioning at the Senate, by releasing all the package, [for all to throw to bottom]. He was the great honest man, the man of his honest life, he believed that the truth sufficed for itself, especially when it seemed as bright as the full day. What good is to turn all upside down when the sun was soon to shine? And it is for this trustful neutrality for which he is so cruelly punished. The same for Major Picquart, who, for a feeling of high dignity, did not want to publish the letters of

General Gonse. These scruples honour it more especially as, while there remained respectful discipline, its superiors covered it with mud, informed themselves its lawsuit, in the most unexpected and outrageous manner. There are two victims, two good people, two simple hearts, who waited for God while the devil acted. And one even saw, for Major Picquart, this wretched thing: a French court, after having let the rapporteur charge a witness publicly, to show it of all the faults, made the closed door, when this witness was introduced to be explained and defend himself. I say that this is another crime and that this crime will stir up universal conscience. Decidedly, the military tribunals have a singular idea of justice.

Such is thus the simple truth, Mr President, and it is appalling, it will remain a stain for your presidency. I very much doubt that you have no capacity in this affair, that you are the prisoner of the Constitution and your entourage. You do not have of them less one to have of man, about which you will think, and which you will fulfil. It is not, moreover, which I despair less of the world of the triumph. I repeat it with a more vehement certainty: the truth marches on and nothing will stop it. Today, the affair merely starts, since today only the positions are clear: on the one hand, the culprits who do not want the light to come; the other, the carriers of justice who will give their life to see it come. I said it elsewhere, and I repeat it here: when one locks up the truth under ground, it piles up there, it takes there a force such of explosion, that, the day when it bursts, it makes everything leap out with it. We will see, if we do not prepare for later, the most resounding of disasters.

But this letter is long, Mr President, and it is time to conclude.

I accuse Major Du Paty de Clam as the diabolic workman of the miscarriage of justice, without knowing, I have wanted to believe it, and of then defending his harmful work, for three years, by the guiltiest and most absurd of machinations.

I accuse General Mercier of being an accomplice, if by weakness of spirit, in one of greatest iniquities of the century.

I accuse General Billot of having held in his hands the unquestionable evidence of Dreyfus's innocence and of suppressing it, guilty of this crime that injures humanity and justice, with a political aim and to save the compromised Chief of High Command.

I accuse General De Boisdeffre and General Gonse as accomplices of the same crime, one undoubtedly by clerical passion, the other perhaps by this spirit of body which makes offices of the war an infallible archsaint.

I accuse General De Pellieux and Commander Ravary of performing a rogue investigation, by which I mean an investigation of the most monstrous partiality, of which we have, in the report of the second, an imperishable monument of naive audacity.

I accuse the three handwriting experts, sirs Belhomme, Varinard and Couard, of submitting untrue and fraudulent reports, unless a medical examination declares them to be affected by a disease of sight and judgment.

I accuse the offices of the war of carrying out an abominable press campaign, particularly in the *Flash* and the *Echo* of Paris, to mislead the public and cover their fault.

Finally, I accuse the first council of war of violating the law by condemning a defendant with unrevealed evidence, and I accuse the second council of war of covering up this illegality, by order, by committing in his turn the legal crime of knowingly discharging the culprit.

While proclaiming these charges, I am not unaware of subjecting myself to articles 30 and 31 of the press law of July 29, 1881, which punishes the offence of slander. And it is voluntarily that I expose myself.

As for the people I accuse, I do not know them, I never saw them, I have against them neither resentment nor hatred. They are for me only entities, spirits of social evil. And the act I accomplished here is only a revolutionary means for hastening the explosion of truth and justice. I have only one passion, that of the light, in the name of humanity which has suffered so and is entitled to happiness. My ignited protest is nothing more than the cry of my heart. That one thus dares to translate for me into court bases and that the investigation takes place at the great day! I am waiting.

Please accept, Mr President, the assurance of my deep respect.

DULCE BASE

Dulce is a sleepy town in northern New Mexico (pop. 900) high up on the Jicarilla Apache Reservation. It's the sort of place where hound dogs lie sprawled on the porch, and the diner is entertainment HQ. Nothing much happens in Dulce.

Unless, that is, you believe the long running rumours that Dulce is *the* place to see UFOs and **cattle mutilations**. You probably won't glimpse the secret alien-human base there, because it is apparently deep under the Archuleta mesa. According to conspiracy researchers, the base, which extends two miles down, has no less than seven levels, is staffed by as many as 18,000 Greys (aliens), who dwell on the lower levels. The human employees occupy the top floors, unless they are being experimented on or eaten, when they disappear below. Understandably, given the alien/reptoid liking for human flesh, relations between the humans and their scaly colleagues are not always cordiale; indeed the base was the scene for a near war some years ago between the humans and the lizard-looking types. The experiments carried out on-site include the creation of hybrid alien-terrestrial life and weapons advancement. Tunnels for high-speed shuttle trains connect Dulce to **Area 51**, Los Alamos and similar military/research sites across the US.

Dr Paul Bennewitz, a businessman and electronics expert, was the first to claim (in 1979) that Dulce hosted a secret base, after he tracked alien communications to the area. Bennewitz compiled a bulging dossier of evidence regarding Dulce, from two years' worth of electronic surveillance, 6,000 feet of cine film and the case history of an encounter victim in New Mexico,

Myrna Hansen, who revealed under hypnosis that she had been abducted and taken inside Dulce. Bennewitz passed on his information to the USAF – which conceded that Bennewitz had caught something unusual on film. An Air Force memorandum later released under Freedom of Information legislation noted:

> On 26 Oct 80, SA [Special Agent] Doty, with the assistance of JERRY MILLER, GS-15, Chief, Scientific Advisor for Air Force Test and Evaluation Center, KAFB, interviewed Dr. Bennewitz at his home in the Four Hills section of Albuquerque, which is adjacent to the northern boundary of Manzano Base ... Dr. Bennewitz has been conducting independent research into Aerial Phenomena for the last 15 months. Dr. Bennewitz also produced several electronic recording tapes, allegedly showing high periods of electrical magnetism being emitted from Manzano/Coyote Canyon area. Dr. Bennewitz also produced several photographs of flying objects taken over the general Albuquerque area. He has several pieces of electronic surveillance equipment pointed at Manzano and is attempting to record high frequency electrical beam pulses. Dr. Bennewitz claims these Aerial Objects produce these pulses ... After analyzing the data collected by Dr. Bennewitz, Mr MILLER related the evidence clearly shows that some type of unidentified aerial objects were caught on film; however, no conclusions could be made whether these objects pose a threat to Manzano/Coyote Canyon areas.

It seems that the Air Force Office of Special Investigations was sufficiently jittered by Bennewitz's film to feed him disinformation; at the 1989 Mutual UFO Network convention in Las Vegas prominent Ufologist William Moore declared that he had been part of a long-running campaign to discredit Paul Bennewitz: "My role in the affair ... was primarily that of a freelancer providing information on Paul's [Bennewitz] current thinking and activities." Bennewitz, who was already having mental health problems, sank into depression and paranoia.

Some of Bennewitz's allegations about Dulce were taken up by Danny Casolaro in his pursuit of **The Octopus**, while a number of "whistle-blowers" who claimed to have worked at the base came forward. One of these was Tom Castello, a self-professed Dulce Base security officer, who proffered a stack of black and white photographs, videotape and technical papers, all "proving" the base's existence. To back up the evidence of the so-called "Dulce Papers", Castello also gave a lengthy interview about his work at the base (see Document), full of colourful accounts of the grey lizards that rule the place.

If – and it is a gigantic if – the Dulce Base exists it is so secret that at least two investigative TV crews, one Japanese and one American, have failed to find it. Quite possibly, Bennewitz snapped some strange objects out on the mesa, but these are likely to be human in origin. New Mexico has frequently been used as the testing ground for top-secret military craft, and the training terrain for special forces. Both might require the sort of diversionary disinformation that the USAF seem to have fed the hapless Dr Bennewitz.

> Dulce, New Mexico, is site of secret alien-human HQ: ALERT LEVEL 2

Further Reading
Gregory Bishop, *Project Beta*, 2005
Branton, *Dulce Wars*, 1999

DOCUMENT: INTERVIEW WITH THOMAS CASTELLO, ALLEGED SECURITY TECHNICIAN AT DULCE BASE

QUESTION – When exactly was the [upper human-occupied level of the] Archuleta installation constructed?
ANSWER – I heard Dulce was started in 1937–38 by the Army engineers, enlarged over the years, most recent work was completed 1965–66 to connect tunnels to the Page [Arizona] Base, site of one of the older underground facilities.

The four corners base is called PERICA. Most of the Native Americans [the Indians] living in that area are aware of that base, and could tell us about the underground life forms that frequently are spotted near those communities, Bigfoot, etc.

Q – By what means was the [upper] installations constructed? Are you familiar with the alleged developments made by the Rand Corporation of a highly efficient bore or mole machine capable of melting rock using nuclear powered wolfram-graphite tipped "drill-cones"?

A – According to several senior maintenance workers, part of it was blasted by nuclear devices in the sixties. There are sections, like the shuttle tunnels, that were formed by an advanced tunnelling machine that leaves the tunnel walls smooth. The finished walls in those tubes resemble polished black glass.

Q – By WHOM was the Dulce installation originally constructed?

A – Nature started the caverns. The Draco used the caverns and tunnels for centuries. Later, through RAND Corporation plans, it was enlarged repeatedly. The original caverns included ice caves and sulfur springs that the "aliens" found perfect for their needs. The Dulce caverns rival Carlsbad caverns in size.

Q – What exactly are the cattle [and human] organs such as blood, anal tissue, eyes, reproductive organs, tongues, etc. used for – i.e. the organs obtained via cattle and human mutilations?

A – Read the so-called Dulce Papers.

Q – Are the various electromagnetically controlled air or space craft – [that have been seen] leaving from and arriving at Mt. Archuleta – manned by humans, the "alien entities", or both?

A – Archuleta Mesa is a minor area ... the craft leave [and are stored] in five areas. One is SE of DULCE, one near Durango Co., one at Taos, N. M., and the main fleet is stored at LOS ALAMOS.

Q – Others have suggested that some of the entities below Dulce are not of "extraterrestrial" ORIGIN, and that they are actually descended from saurian or reptiloid beings such as the Velociraptors or Stenonychosaurus Equallus – a "serpentine" race or races similar to that hinted at in the third chapter of the book of Genesis?

A – Yes, some "reptoids" are native to this planet. The ruling caste of "aliens" ARE reptilian. The beige or white beings are called the Draco. Other reptilian beings are green, and some are brown. They were an ancient race on Earth, living underground. It may have been one of the Draconian beings that "tempted" Eve in the Garden of Eden. Reptoids rightly consider themselves "native Terrans". Perhaps they are the ones we call the Fallen Angels. Maybe not, either way, we are [considered] the "squatters" on Earth.

Q – Some have suggested that the so-called underground "E.T." bases and tunnels may, for a large part, be literally thousands of years old … constructions of an antediluvian race which attained to a considerable level of scientific complexity, and who were destroyed by a Divinely initiated cataclysm which took place after they attempted to merge their science with occult/supernatural forces.

For instance some have suggested that the Bermuda Triangle phenomena may be the result of an out-of-control Atlantean experiment that led to a space-time disaster which produced "electromagnetic fallout" in the Triangle area and elsewhere after they had accidentally loosed powerful forces and energies into the world that they knew very little about. Do your observations tend to confirm or refute such a possibility?

A – I'm not sure about the Divine part, but these "aliens" consider themselves "NATIVE TERRANS".

Q – They work for, and are controlled by, the Draco. There are other gray-skinned beings that are not in league with the Draco.

A – Where do the little gray Aliens fit in?

Q – Did you ever talk to any of the "Aliens" at the base?

A – Since I was the Senior Security Technician at that base, I had to communicate with them on a daily basis. If there were any problems that involved security or video cameras, I was the one they called. It was the reptilian "working caste" that usually did the physical labor in the lower levels at Dulce.

Decisions involving that caste were usually made by the white Draco. When human workers caused problems for the working caste, the reptoids went to the white Draconian "boss", and the Draco called me. At times, it felt like it was a never-ending problem. Several human workers resented the "no nonsense" or "get back to work" attitude the working caste lives by.

When needed, intervention became a vital tool. The biggest problem was human workers who foolishly wandered around near the "OFF LIMITS" areas of the "Alien Section". I guess it's human nature to be curious and to wonder what is past the barriers. Too often someone found a way to bypass the barriers and nosed around. The cameras near the entrance usually stopped them before they got themselves in serious trouble. A few times I had to formerly request the return of a human worker.

Q – Are there other sites tied in to the "shuttle network" other than those which you mentioned, and if so, where are the entrances?

A – WHERE!?! EVERYWHERE! THEY CRISS-CROSS THE WORLD AS AN ENDLESS SUBTERRANEAN HIGHWAY. LIKE A FREEWAY, EXCEPT THIS ONE IS UNDERGROUND ... The subterranean highway in America is like a freeway except it's underground. That highway depends on electric motors [for trucks, cars and buses] for the paved roads, and it is for limited travel.

There is another style of transit for freight and for passengers that is for rapid travel. That worldwide network is called the "Sub-Global System". It has "checkpoints" at each country entry. There ARE shuttle tubes that "shoot" the trains at incredible speeds using a mag-lev and vacuum method. They travel at a speed that excels the speed of sound. Part of your question involves the location of entrances to that base. The easiest way to answer is to say every state in the U.S.A. has them.

Frequently, the entrances are camouflaged as sand quarries, or mining operations. Other complex portals are found on military bases. New Mexico and Arizona have the largest amounts of entrances followed by California, Montana, Idaho, Colorado, Pennsylvania, Kansas, Arkansas and Missouri. Of all the states, Florida and North Dakota have the least amount of entrances. Wyoming has a road that opens directly into the subterranean freeway. That road is no longer in use, but could be reactivated if they decide to do so, with minimal cost. It's located near Brooks Lake.

Q – Are there any "bases" in the state of Utah? Have you heard anything about an alleged underground installation within the Wasatch Mountains …?

A – Salt Lake, Lake Powell Area, Dark Canyon, Dougway Grounds, Modena, Vernal. All have exits there. Others too.

Q – Does the Mt. Archuleta "shuttle system" connect with a shuttle system which allegedly radiates from Mt. Shasta in northern California?

A – Yes. Mt. Shasta is a major site of Alien – Elder Race – Reptilian Race – Human meetings. Beginning with Grover Cleveland every president in U.S. history have visited Telos City. Truman was supposed to have visited the Lower Realms as a High Archon on Earth. He was supposed to have met the King of the World there, and gave him the "Keys to the U.S.A."

Truman received assurance to new high-tech knowledge, and victory over all enemies on Earth. He then was introduced to Samaza and Khoach, aliens from Bootes and Tiphon [Draco], both reptilian "kings" or ambassadors. Truman updated the "100 Treaty" [that began IN 1933, Roosevelt] and requested magnetic advance, space knowledge and experiments. Khoach agreed, Samaza partially agreed. He exchanged hostages for genetic experiments and magnetic advance, but vetoed space and beam weaponry.

Q – Did you notice any involvement of high-level Freemasons, Rosicrucians or Jesuits within the underground installation and/or with the aliens?

A – Yes I did, but that is a loaded question, and I won't comment further. I'm not a Mason, or member of any other secret fraternal group. There is one organization I am a member of [in the U.S.A.]. That group is commonly called the "Central Unit." It is a pleasure to tell you that I AM a member of the "Sub-Galactic League" of Costa Rica.

Q – Is there any truth to the allegations that the CIA/"Aliens" have established "bases" on the moon, and also Mars?

A – I've HEARD that too, but I haven't seen proof with my own eyes. The "aliens" do allegedly have bases on several moons of Jupiter and Saturn. The CIA operates in other COUNTRIES, but I've never heard they operate on other PLANETS.

Q – Have you heard any hints or rumors suggesting that there may be lower levels beneath the ULTRA-7 level of the Dulce base, and also, where these might lead to and what they might consist of?

A – YES. Your guess is as good as mine ... Sure, there was lots of TALK but that doesn't mean it's there. However, I will tell you I saw elevators that were "off limits" unless you had an UMBRA or higher security clearance. At that base, information is supplied to me at a "need to know" basis ONLY! [My clearance was ULTRA-7.]

Q – Some insist that the U.S./Secret government has developed its own disk-craft based largely upon top-secret antigravity experiments carried out by the Nazi-German scientists during World War II. Have you heard anything referring to this?

A – When I was working in Photo-security, heard a lot of talk, never saw the proof, but once in the Air Force I developed a roll of film that showed a craft LIKE ADAMSKI'S, WITH A SWASTIKA ON THE SIDE.

Q – Tom, did you have access to the alien craft? Were you ever inside any of them?

A – Yes, I frequently saw them in the garages, there are quite a few of them. The main fleet is stored at Los Alamos. Yes, I entered several crafts. There were two things that stick in my mind, the odd spongy feeling of the floors, and the unusual pinkish-purple color of the lighting.

The crew stated the floor becomes ridged in flight, and the purple tint of the lighting changes to bright blue white. The entire inside of the aircraft are scaled down in size, when compared to the average human. The halls were curved and narrow, but some how, when inside it appears bigger than it looks. Certain areas, the outermost sections, almost felt and looked alive. I was never taken up in one.

Q – Can you give me more information on the reptilian race, what do they do on the sixth level?

A – The worker caste does the daily chores, mopping the latex floors, cleaning the cages, bringing food to the hungry people and other species. It is their job to formulate the proper mixture for the type one and type two beings that the Draco Race has created. The working caste works at the labs as well as at the computer banks. Basically speaking, the reptilian races are active at all levels of the Dulce Base. There are several different "races" of aliens that work on the east section of level six (No doubt some collaborating "Nordic" factions included. – Branton).

That section is commonly called "the alien section." The Draco are the undisputed masters of the 5–6–7 levels. The humans are second in command of those levels. I had to ARGUE with one large Draconian "boss" frequently. His name is difficult to verbalize, Khaarshfashst [pronounced throaty kkhhah-sshh-fahsh-sst]. I usually called him "Karsh," and he hated it. The Draconian leaders are very formal when talking to the human race. These ancient beings consider us a lower race. Karsh called me "Leader Castello," but it was used in a sarcastical way. However the worker caste is friendly enough, as long as you allow them to speak first.

They will answer if you address them. They are very cautious beings, and consider most humans to be hostile. They always seem surprised when they found many of the humans were open and trustworthy. There is no fraternizing with the aliens off hours. It is forbidden to speak to any alien race [in the halls or an elevator] without a clear business-oriented reason. Humans can talk to humans, and aliens can speak to aliens, but that is as far as it goes. At the work site, however, it's different. There is "free speech" in the labs.

The camaraderie found in the labs also reaches the computer banks section. In those areas, everybody talks to anybody. However, everything changes the minute you cross the threshold of the hall. Instantly, all conversations become strictly formal. Hard as it was, several times I had to arrest someone, simply because they spoke to an alien. It's a strange place.

Q – Exactly what first made you aware that something was wrong at Dulce? Seems to me that a place as obviously horrible as this one wouldn't need an Einstein to know that this is a CRIME site! What took you so long? Are you the guy who blew the whistle?

A – There are several things you should know about. I took an oath, under the penalty of death, that no matter what I saw or heard I would never divulge the information. Also, I signed a waiver that states I would willingly give up my life if I was found guilty of "treason".

At the Dulce Base treason is "ANYTHING that mentions the details of daily operations at this facility, when outside the confinement of the base." When I first arrived, a "need to know" policy was in effect. The story the "honchos" told us was that "this is a Tri-Biotransfer Facility with Advanced Technology, doing advanced adventurous methodology for medical and mental gains."

Which is a fancy way of saying they do really risky things with human life just to see what would happen. If a medical cure happens, it will be heralded on the surface of the earth as a marvelous new cure, saying it was found after years of research at some well-known medical lab. The real story of the cure is never explained.

After all, the Dulce Base IS A SECRET FACILITY! These people are very good at what they do. They do not tell the truth about the unfortunate people that end up in "Nightmare Hall." I worked with aliens. With that in mind, you should get the idea of the secrecy and the security at that place.

Yes, I know this was not the usual hospital-type job site, but in the beginning I "bought" the whole package. I was reminded daily by intercom, in the elevators, that "this site does high risk advanced medical and drug testing to cure insanity, please, never speak to the inmates, it can destroy

years of work." I'm sensible, when doctors say don't speak to
them, who was I to destroy the delicate situation?

But one man some how caught my eye. He repeatedly
stated that he was George S— and that he had been kidnapped and he was sure someone was searching for him. I
don't know why he sticks in my mind, I found I was remembering his face, thinking he sure didn't look or sound insane,
but many inmates said that. The next weekend I convinced a
friend of mine, a cop, to run a check on the guy, saying I had
a run in with him and was curious.

I didn't mention the base at all. It was a sickening feeling
when the computer confirmed that George S. was missing.
What's worse, the cops thought he was just another guy that
got tired of the daily grind and split. That was the beginning.
Am I the one that blew the whistle? No. The next Monday, I
searched for George, but he was gone.

There were no records that explained what happened to him.
It was another security officer that came to me saying he and
some lab workers wanted an off-duty meeting at one of the
tunnels, [off the record]. Curiosity took over and I said OK.
That night, about nine men showed up. They said they knew
they were risking me turning them in but they wanted to show
me some things they thought I should see. One by one they
showed records that proved many inmates were missing people.

There were newspaper clippings, and even photos that they
had some how smuggled into the base. They hoped to
smuggle them back out, without me turning them in to the
honchos. I could see the fear in their faces as they spoke. One
man stated he would rather lose his life by trying, than to lose
his soul by not doing anything at all. It was that remark that
turned the tide. I told them about George and the things I
found out about him. After a few hours we pledged to attempt
to expose the Dulce Base.

Q – The name Nightmare Hall is descriptive, but surely there
was a "regular" name, what was it called in the manuals?

A – In the manuals it was called "The Vivarium". It describes
Dulce Base as a "secured facility for tending bio-forms of all
types." In their report it is retold as "a private subterranean

bio-terminal park, with accommodations for animals, fish, fowl, reptile, and mankind." After SEEING this "park" the name Nightmare Hall is far more accurate than the manual. The "accommodations" for the inmates at Nightmare Hall fall short of the pretty picture the manual describes.

Q – You mentioned one reptilian leader, Khaarshfashst, do you know anything about him, like where is he from? Is he from Earth or some other planet?

A – His name means "keeper of the laws". They receive their name after they reach the "age of awareness". They do not recognize time as an important factor in "being aware" the way humans do. Upon their "age of awareness" they are cognitive of the station or position they are destined to fulfill. At that time they choose or allow someone to choose their name.

Their name will include the position they hold and several personally chosen letters. Each letter has a personal meaning, known only to the alien and the one that chose their name. Since Karsh's name means keeper of the laws his name includes "kaash" [memory or keep, base word for "Akashic" record] and "fashst" [law, base word fast or bind]. Reptilians choose to be not only private, but secretive of the location of their natal place. To them birth, or emergence of life, is considered as one of the sacred rites of life.

They consider Earth or Terra their "home planet", but several reptoids discuss several star maps. Most of those stars were within the Milky Way. Within those star maps lies the stars and planets of the Planets of the Allegiance.

Earth being one of the planets in their trade routes. If any human asked clear questions about the Allegiance, the Aliens referred the questions to the Draco. The Draco in turn, referred the questions to their supervisor [me]. I did not have that information about the stars, because information was supplied on a "need to know" basis. I didn't "need" that information.

Q – Did any of the working caste join in the revolt? Could you give me some names?

A – A few of the reptilian janitorial crew let us know that THEY knew WE were attempting to sabotage the work going on in the sixth and seventh levels. One of them, with the name Sshhaal, secretly formed a small group of reptoids with the same mindset as my group.

Sshhaal took upon himself the danger of informing me. He was as open as is possible in a unique situation. On the day I found out about it, I was inspecting a camera near an exit tunnel. He approached, stooped down (the tall reptiloids average about 7–8 ft. in height according to most witnesses – Branton), seemingly scraping some non-existent dirt, and he quietly said, "A few of us agreed that you are singular in your interest in missing-human reports. If true, walk away. I'll reach you. If it's untrue, destroy my life now!"

My heart almost leaped out of my chest, but I silently walked toward one of the wide halls.

For the rest of my life I'll remember those words! It was the first time I KNEW reptilians could have individual thoughts and opinions! Basically, they formed a uniform front with a small variety of interests. Or at least, that was what we had thought. It was a couple days before I heard from him again. As he walked beside me in the sixth level's infamous hall, I heard him say "Enter the exit tunnel on the sixth level, north, after your shift."

The next few hours were long and filled with thoughts of betrayal, or worse, but I shouldn't have worried. I contacted one of the original nine [resistance] men, and let him know, just in case. Gordon wanted to go with me, but I convinced him to wait a few feet from the exit and pretend he was having trouble with his cart [electric, like a golf cart]. When I got there, there were three of them.

SSHHAAL formally introduced FAHSSHHAA and HUAMSSHHAA [name base word is SSHHAA or assist]. With that, I quickly grabbed Gordon from the hall and the five of us talked and walked in the dark tunnels for about three hours. After that day, the joined resistance group got bigger and bolder. Ultimately, it ended when a military assault was initiated via the exit tunnels and they executed anybody on their list, human or reptilian.

We fought back, but none of the working caste had weapons, nor did the human lab workers. Only the security force and a few computer workers had flash guns. It was a massacre. Every one was screaming and running for cover. The halls and tunnels were filled as full as possible.

We believe it was the Delta Force [because of the uniforms and the method they used] that chose to hit at shift change, an effort that killed as many as named on their list.

We, to this day, do not know who BETRAYED us. Gordon Ennery ran beside me as we ran into the third level exit tunnels, and he died when several bullets slammed into his back. I vaporized that assassin and kept running. And I'm still running. Gordon will be remembered.

Q – Tell me more about the flash gun. Is it difficult to operate, or is it like the weapon on *Star Trek*, that can stun or kill on different modes?

A – It is an advanced beam weapon that can operate on three different phases. Phase one, like *Star Trek*, can stun and maybe kill, if the person has a weak heart. On phase two, it can levitate ANYTHING no matter what it weighs. Phase three is the SERIOUS BUSINESS mode. It can be used to paralyze anything that lives, animal, human, alien and plant.

On the higher position on the same mode, it can create a TEMPORARY DEATH. I assure you, any doctor would certify that person is dead, but their life essence lingers in some strange limbo, some kind of terrible state of non-death. In one to five hours the person will revive, slowly; first the bodily functions will begin and, in a few minutes, consciousness followed with full awareness. In that mode the alien scientists re-program the human brain and plant false information.

When the person awakes, he "recalls" the false information as information he gained through life experience. There is no way for a person to learn the truth. The human mind "remembers" and believes completely the false data. If you attempted to inform them, they would laugh or get angry. They NEVER believe the truth. Their mind always forgets the experience of re-programming.

You asked if the flash gun is difficult to operate. A two-year-old child could use it with one hand. It resembles a flashlight, with black glass conical inverted lens. On the side are three recessed knobs in three curved grooves. Each knob is sized differently. The closer the knob to the hand the less the strength. It's that simple. Each knob has three strengths also, with automatic stops at each position.

The strongest position will vaporize anything that lives. That mode is so powerful it will leave NO TRACE of what it vaporized.

Q – Is the weapon called a Flash Gun or is there a different name in the manuals?

A – Everybody calls them Flash Guns, or more commonly "The Flash" or "my Flash" when talking about it. In the manual it is first introduced as the ARMORLUX Weapon. After that, it is explained as the Flash Gun.

Q – What type of security is found at the Dulce Base? What else is used against espionage or unauthorized entry?

A – I'll mention a few, but it would be nearly impossible to cover it all. The weapon, besides the Flash Gun, mostly used is a form of sonic. Built in with each light fixture [and most camcorders] is a device that could render a man unconscious in seconds with nothing more than a silent tone. At Dulce there also are still and VCR cameras, eye print, hand print stations, weight monitors, lasers, ELF and EM equipment, heat sensors and motion detectors and quite a few other methods.

There is no way you could get very far into the base. If you made it to the second level, you would be spotted within fifteen feet. More than likely, you would become an inmate and never see the light of the surface world again. If you were "lucky", you would be reprogrammed and become one of the countless spies for the Ruling Caste.

Q – According to certain reports, the Dulce Base is host to [other] aliens that live in level five. Is that true? Can the humans freely roam or meet one-to-one in the halls or is some type of protocol in effect?

A – There is protocol from the first time you enter the base and it MUST be followed every time you SEE an alien there.

From the working caste, to the visiting aliens, to the Ruling Caste, there is a never-ending check list of rules, law, and strict protocol. There is never a chance to roam on the fifth level. The alien housing area is off limits to any human. The Hub is surrounded by security, arsenal, military and CIA\FBI sections.

The area past the security is one of the most secured areas because it houses so many classified files. The entire east side of the fifth level is off limits except for security personnel holding ULTRA-7 [security clearance] or higher. The garage on the west side of the fifth level requires ULTRA-4 clearance.

Q – Is there proof available that could confirm the allegations of the underground base, or are we just supposed to believe you?

A – Many people have asked that one. No, I don't expect people to believe with blind faith, there is tangible proof that has been seen, felt or inspected by quite a few folks. I'm in no position to go on a lecture circuit to explain to every person on a one-to-one basis. I am trying to stay alive.

All I can do is state again, that Dulce is a SECRET FACILITY. They work HARD to make sure nobody can find the place. If everyone could easily find it, it wouldn't be a SECRET facility. I've explained the extreme security methods they use. There is other proof available.

EBOLA

Ebola haemorrhagic fever is caused by the Ebola virus, from the *Filoviridae* family, and is named after the Ebola River in Zaire, Africa, near where the first outbreak was noted by Dr Ngoy Mushola in 1976. There are five sub-species of the virus: Ebola-Ivory Coast, Ebola-Sudan, Ebola-Zaire, Ebola-Bundibugyo and Ebola-Reston. Only the last does not cause disease in humans. People infected with Ebola virus suffer sudden fever, muscle pain, headache and sore throat, followed by vomiting, diarrhoea, rash, inhibited kidney and liver functions, and internal and external bleeding. Since 1976, outbreaks of Ebola have been isolated sporadic, which is just as well as the death rate of those infected is up to 90 per cent. The disease is "zoonotic", meaning it is borne by animals but transmissible to humans. However, science is still looking for the carrier animal, and also the origin of the disease is unknown.

It is these mysteries concerning Ebola's host and source that open the door to conspiracy theorists who insist that Ebola is a man-made virus. The most prominent Ebola conspiracist is Dr Leonard Horowitz, author of *Emerging Viruses: AIDS and Ebola: Nature, Accident or Intentional?* Horowitz contends that the US National Cancer Institute, Litton Bionetics, and the US Medical Research Institute created Ebola in a lab with the intention of using it in a bioterrorism campaign against gays, blacks, Jews and Hispanics in an effort to depopulate the world. Some of those wearing the white lab coats, Horowitz alleges, were Nazi scientists brought to the US under **Project Paperclip**. Dr Horowitz traces America's eugenics scheme to a 1974 memo by

Henry Kissinger (see **Kissinger Associates**), who was himself in the intellectual debt of the Sovereign Military Order of Malta, "perhaps the most powerful reactionary segment of European aristocracy, that for almost a thousand years, starting with the crusades in the twelfth century, funded military operations against countries and ideas considered a threat to its existence".

Lennie Horowitz is off track in pinning the original sin of Ebola on the Sovereign Military Order of Malta, which, these days, is a Catholic Masonic charity (which admittedly does a bit of intelligence brokering on the side). And Lennie, a former Florida dentist, goes off track quite often; his explanation for the outbreak of World War II is that the Illuminati/Rockefellers established the frequency of 440 cycles per second as the tuning frequency for the A above middle C on the chromatic scale, so causing disharmony. Nevertheless, Ebola does have the capability, as Horowitz has highlighted, of becoming an agent for biological warfare. In 1992, members of Japan's **Aum Shinrikyo** sect travelled to Zaire in a seeming attempt to acquire a virus sample with a view to weaponizing it.

As to the origin of Ebola, the answer is: nobody knows for certain, although most scientists believe the disease to be a natural occurrence.

> Ebola is a US-engineered virus designed to reduce the population of the Third World: ALERT LEVEL 2

Further Reading
Dr Leonard Horowitz, *Emerging Viruses: AIDS and Ebola: Nature, Accident or Intentional?*, 1996

FEMA

Beside a highway outside Atlanta, Georgia, are stacked approximately 500,000 plastic coffins. The coffins, which are in full view of anyone passing by, are owned by the Federal Emergency Management Agency (FEMA). FEMA is best known for handing out hot soup and blankets after national disasters. So why does it need half a million coffins? Or six hundred prison camps?

Provision of post-disaster aid is only part of FEMA's brief. It is also entrusted with the "Continuity of Government" in the event of a national emergency. At its simplest, "Continuity" entails hustling the President, the Cabinet and Executive to an underground base beneath Mount Weather in Virginia, and dispersing alternative constitutional leaders to safe havens around the US. But successive Executive Orders have also given FEMA police state-like powers to round up US citizens and detain them without trial if they are considered a threat to national security.

What some conspiracy theorists speculate is that FEMA (founded in 1979) is actually an arm of the **New World Order**, and when the NWO's head honchos give the order for martial law and the imposition of the **North American Union**, dissenters will be rounded up and incarcerated in those six hundred concentration camps. The coffins are for those who die fighting the imposition of the New World Order. Your fate, according to FEMA researcher B. A. Brooks, will be determined by which colour list your name is on:

> We are all on a Red or Blue list somewhere, those on the red list will be woken at 4.00 a.m. and taken to the camps and probably killed.
>
> Red List – These people are the enemies of the NWO. They are the leaders of patriot groups, outspoken ministers, outspoken talk show hosts, community leaders, and even probably NET leaders. These people will be dragged out of their homes at 4:00 a.m. and will be taken to FEMA detention centers and killed. This will take place approximately two weeks before martial law is enforced.
>
> Blue List – These are also enemies of the NWO, but are followers of the Red List folks. These people will be rounded up after martial law is in place, and will be taken to the detention centers and "re-educated". Various mind-control techniques will be used on them. Most will not survive this ...
>
> Yellow List – These are citizens who know nothing about the NWO and don't want to know. They are considered to be no threat at all and will be instructed as to how to behave and will most likely do whatever they are told. Unfortunately there are too many of these to be effectively controlled, so many will be killed or starved.
>
> Black List – I have recently heard that the red and blue lists have been combined into one, and is called the Black List. All black listed citizens will be marked for execution.

Trying to prove or disprove the existence of FEMA camps and coffins is one of the internet's busiest industries. But:

Fact: The plastic "coffins" in Madison, Georgia, are actually burial liners, used to protect caskets when placed underground. The much snapped depot in Georgia is actually the storage facility of the manufacturer, Vantage Products. And there are more in the region of 50,000 rather than half a mill of the liners.

Fact: Most of the so-called concentration camps are nothing

of the sort. One camp much featured on conspiracy sites, Beech Grove, is actually an Amtrak repair depot.

Fact: FEMA has in the past (and might well in the present) enjoyed powers prejudicial to civil liberties. When President Reagan was considering invading Nicaragua, he issued a series of executive orders that provided, in the event of mass internal dissent, for the suspension of the constitution, the imposition of martial law, the construction of mass prison camps, and the turning over of government to the president – and FEMA. Other scenarios in which FEMA has been touted as playing a leading repressive role are combating a national uprising by black Americans and incarcerating Arab Americans sympathetic to al-Qaeda. It should be pointed out that sections of the American establishment vigorously opposed the granting of Draconian powers to the Agency. At the time of the Reagan initiative the then attorney-general, William French Smith, wrote to the national security adviser, Robert McFarlane: "I believe that the role assigned to the Federal Emergency Management Agency in the revised Executive Order exceeds its proper function as a co-ordinating agency for emergency preparedness ... this department and others have repeatedly raised serious policy and legal objections to an 'emergency czar' role for FEMA."

Since 2003, FEMA has been part of the Department of Homeland Security. New notepaper did not mean new efficiency: the agency was much criticized for its slowness and incompetence following **Hurricane Katrina**. Which must be a crumb of comfort to those who fear FEMA's intentions. If FEMA can't set up tents after high winds and high water could it actually round anybody up in a national emergency?

> FEMA is a police state dressed in humanitarian clothing: ALERT LEVEL 6

Further Reading
B.A. Brooks, *Things You Never Knew About FEMA*, 2009
Linda A. Burns, *FEMA: An Organization in the Crosshairs*, 2007
"The Evidence: Debunking FEMA Camp Myths", 10 April 2009, www.popularmechanics.com

FOO FIGHTERS

Is it a bird? A plane? No, it's a Foo Fighter.

In late 1944 Reuters press agency reported that strange spheres, resembling the glass balls that adorn Christmas trees, "have been seen hanging in the air over German territory, sometimes singly, sometimes in clusters. They are coloured silver and are apparently transparent."

Numerous sightings of these weird balls were recorded by Allied aircrews throughout German airspace, and later in the war over the skies of Nippon. Dubbed "Foo Fighters" (from the French *feu*, meaning fire) the balls of light made no attempt to attack, although they could out-fly conventional aircraft. Allied boffins assumed that the Nazis' sky balls were a secret air defence weapon, along the lines of exploding high altitude balloons, or anti-aircraft missiles. Sifting through Nazi records after the war, investigators found all manner of interesting secret devices being plotted, from the Feuerball (a missile that emitted signals to disrupt Allied aircrafts' radio and radar) to the Wasserfall (a radio-controlled anti-aircraft missile), but none had been deployed. The consensus was that "Foo Fighters" were actually natural phenomena, such as ball lightning or St Elmo's fire. Or, later in the war, Luftwaffe jet fighters, principally the Me262.

And there the matter lay, until conspiracist Renato Vesco decided that the Foo Fighter was actually the forerunner of the Kugelblitz, the Ball Lightning Fighter. And then "alternative historian" Jim Keith determined that the Kugelblitz was actually a ... flying saucer, launched from sites in Prague and Breslau in early 1945. A "confidential Italian document" given to Keith by an unnamed, untraceable source described a dogfight between a flying saucer and Allied planes: "A strange flying machine, hemispherical, or at any rate circular, in shape, attacked them at a fantastic speed, destroying them in a few seconds without using any guns."

Without using any guns? Surely only ray-wielding aliens didn't need guns to destroy … and so, by a false syllogism, other conspiracy theorists came to believe that the Foo Fighters were actually helmed by aliens.

Of course, *someone* had to theorize that the aliens were helping the Nazis. According to Vladimir Tersiski the occult pan-German **Thule Society** and **Vril Society** made contact with extraterrestrials, who accordingly helped the Nazis mount a moon mission and, in 1945, enabled Hitler and the other Nazi bigwigs to escape by saucer to Antarctica.

Clever chaps those aliens. But not, seemingly, clever enough to win the war on behalf of their earthling Nazi collaborators.

Nazi/alien flying saucers buzzed Allied aircraft in World War II: ALERT LEVEL 2

Further Reading
Henry Stevens, *Hitler's Flying Saucers*, 2003

FORD PINTO

Named after the horse, the Pinto was Ford's rival to the Toyota Corolla, the Chevy Vega and VW Beetle in the US in the seventies. With gas prices on the up, manufacturers were desperate for a slice of the "runabout" end of the car market. Yet were Ford so desperate that they knowingly hid deadly design faults on the Pinto?

One evening in 1972, Lily Gray, pulled on to a Minneapolis highway in her new Ford Pinto. Alongside her in the car was a young boy, Richard Grimshaw. As Gray entered the merge lane, her car stalled. Another car bumped into her Pinto at twenty-eight miles per hour. The Pinto's gas tank ruptured, then the car went up in a ball of flames. Gray died hours later; Grimshaw suffered burns over much of his body.

The Pinto lacked a heavyweight bumper, or proper reinforcement between the rear panel and the petroleum tank. So when a Pinto was rear-ended in even a minor fashion, as with Gray, the fuel tank ruptured. The Pinto had another flaw: due to its cracker-box construction the doors jammed easily when heated.

The Pinto was a firetrap on Goodyears.

When Gray's Pinto exploded into flames in Minneapolis, Ford already knew about the Pinto's fuel tank defect. Indeed, the company had been alerted to the weakness during pre-production, but, because retooling the Pinto lines to fit a safer tank would cost money, did nothing about it. As many as five hundred people may have died in Pinto explosions, but all the while Ford kept schtum about the fuel tank problem. The truth only came to light because of a 1977 report by Mark Dowie in the muckraking magazine *Mother Jones*, which quoted an internal Ford memorandum entitled "Fatalities Associated with Crash-Induced Fuel Leakage and Fire". According to a "cost-benefit" analysis in the memo, the Pinto problem would likely lead to 180 burn deaths, 180 seriously burned victims and 2,100 burned-out vehicles – all of which would cost Ford $49.53 million in out of court settlements.

Against this, modifying the tank of 11 million Pintos at $11 a go would cost $121 million.

The bottom line ruled: Ford decided it would rather pay out for death, damage and injury than save its customers lives. When Richard Grimshaw took Ford to court, the California Court of Appeal upheld punitive damages of $3.5 million against the company, partly because Ford had been aware of the design defects but had determined against altering the design (see Document, p.159).

The *Mother Jones* article and *Grimshaw* v. *Ford Motor Co.* led to the end of the road for the Pinto. There were lawsuits, recalls and a tarnished reputation that could never be made better, no matter how hard the ad men at Dearborn slaved.

A number of other cars by other manufacturers on the US market were no safer than the Pinto, and also had unprotected fuel tanks behind the axle. Ford was merely unlucky enough to be exposed.

> Ford car company put the dollar ahead of customer safety: ALERT LEVEL 10

Further Reading

Mark Dowie, "Pinto Madness", *Mother Jones*, September/ October 1977

**DOCUMENT: *GRIMSHAW* V. *FORD MOTOR CO.*
(1981)**

**Court of Appeals of California, Fourth Appellate
District, Division Two [May, 29, 1981]**
***CARMEN GRAY*, a Minor, etc., et al., Plaintiffs and
Appellants, v. *FORD MOTOR COMPANY*, Defendant
and Appellant.**
***RICHARD GRIMSHAW*, a Minor, etc., Plaintiff and
Appellant, v. *FORD MOTOR COMPANY*, Defendant
and Appellant.**
**Opinion by Tamura, Acting P. J., with McDaniel, J.,
concurring. Separate concurring opinion by
Kaufman, J.**

OPINION: TAMURA, Acting P. J.
[...]

Design of the Pinto Fuel System:
In 1968, Ford began designing a new subcompact automobile which ultimately became the Pinto. Mr. Iacocca, then a
Ford vice president, conceived the project and was its moving
force. Ford's objective was to build a car at or below 2,000
pounds to sell for no more than $2,000.

Ordinarily marketing surveys and preliminary engineering
studies precede the styling of a new automobile line. Pinto,
however, was a rush project, so that styling preceded engineering and dictated engineering design to a greater degree
than usual. Among the engineering decisions dictated by
styling was the placement of the fuel tank. It was then the
preferred practice in Europe and Japan to locate the gas tank
over the rear axle in subcompacts because a small vehicle has
less "crush space" between the rear axle and the bumper than
larger cars. The Pinto's styling, however, required the tank to
be placed behind the rear axle leaving only 9 or 10 inches of
"crush space" – far less than in any other American automobile or Ford overseas subcompact. In addition, the Pinto was
designed so that its bumper was little more than a chrome

strip, less substantial than the bumper of any other American car produced then or later. The Pinto's rear structure also lacked reinforcing members known as "hat sections" (two longitudinal side members) and horizontal cross-members running between them such as were found in cars of larger unitized construction and in all automobiles produced by Ford's overseas operations. The absence of the reinforcing members rendered the Pinto less crush resistant than other vehicles. Finally, the differential housing selected for the Pinto had an exposed flange and a line of exposed bolt heads. These protrusions were sufficient to puncture a gas tank driven forward against the differential upon rear impact.

Crash Tests:
During the development of the Pinto, prototypes were built and tested. Some were "mechanical prototypes" which duplicated mechanical features of the design but not its appearance while others, referred to as "engineering prototypes," were true duplicates of the design car. These prototypes as well as two production Pintos were crash tested by Ford to determine, among other things, the integrity of the fuel system in rear-end accidents. Ford also conducted the tests to see if the Pinto as designed would meet a proposed federal regulation requiring all automobiles manufactured in 1972 to be able to withstand a 20-mile-per-hour fixed barrier impact without significant fuel spillage and all automobiles manufactured after January 1, 1973, to withstand a 30-mile-per-hour fixed barrier impact without significant fuel spillage.

The crash tests revealed that the Pinto's fuel system as designed could not meet the 20-mile-per-hour proposed standard. Mechanical prototypes struck from the rear with a moving barrier at 21 miles per hour caused the fuel tank to be driven forward and to be punctured, causing fuel leakage in excess of the standard prescribed by the proposed regulation. A production Pinto crash tested at 21 miles per hour into a fixed barrier caused the fuel neck to be torn from the gas tank and the tank to be punctured by a bolt head on the differential housing. In at least one test, spilled fuel entered the driver's compartment through gaps resulting from the separation of the seams joining the rear wheel wells to the floor pan. The seam separation was occasioned by the lack of reinforcement in the rear structure and insufficient welds of the wheel wells to the floor pan.

Tests conducted by Ford on other vehicles, including modified or reinforced mechanical Pinto prototypes, proved safe at speeds at which the Pinto failed. Where rubber bladders had been installed in the tank, crash tests into fixed barriers at 21 miles per hour withstood leakage from punctures in the gas tank. Vehicles with fuel tanks installed above rather than behind the rear axle passed the fuel system integrity test at 31-miles-per-hour fixed barrier. A Pinto with two longitudinal hat sections added to firm up the rear structure passed a 20-mile-per-hour rear impact fixed barrier test with no fuel leakage.

The Cost to Remedy Design Deficiencies:
When a prototype failed the fuel system integrity test, the standard of care for engineers in the industry was to redesign and retest it. The vulnerability of the production Pinto's fuel tank at speeds of 20 and 30-miles-per-hour fixed barrier tests could have been remedied by inexpensive "fixes," but Ford produced and sold the Pinto to the public without doing anything to remedy the defects. Design changes that would have enhanced the integrity of the fuel tank system at relatively little cost per car included the following: Longitudinal side members and cross members at $2.40 and $1.80, respectively; a single shock absorbent "flak suit" to protect the tank at $4; a tank within a tank and placement of the tank over the axle at $5.08 to $5.79; a nylon bladder within the tank at $5.25 to $8; placement of the tank over the axle surrounded with a protective barrier at a cost of $9.95 per car; substitution of a rear axle with a smooth differential housing at a cost of $2.10; imposition of a protective shield between the differential housing and the tank at $2.35; improvement and reinforcement of the bumper at $2.60; addition of eight inches of crush space a cost of $6.40. Equipping the car with

a reinforced rear structure, smooth axle, improved bumper and additional crush space at a total cost of $15.30 would have made the fuel tank safe in a 34 to 38-mile-per-hour rear-end collision by a vehicle the size of the Ford Galaxie. If, in addition to the foregoing, a bladder or tank within a tank were used or if the tank were protected with a shield, it would have been safe in a 40 to 45-mile-per-hour rear impact. If the tank had been located over the rear axle, it would have been safe in a rear impact at 50 miles per hour or more.

Management's Decision to Go Forward With Knowledge of Defects:

The idea for the Pinto, as has been noted, was conceived by Mr. Iacocca, then executive vice president of Ford. The feasibility study was conducted under the supervision of Mr. Robert Alexander, vice president of car engineering. Ford's Product Planning Committee, whose members included Mr. Iacocca, Mr. Robert Alexander, and Mr. Harold MacDonald, Ford's group vice president of car engineering, approved the Pinto's concept and made the decision to go forward with the project. During the course of the project, regular product review meetings were held which were chaired by Mr. MacDonald and attended by Mr. Alexander. As the project approached actual production, the engineers responsible for the components of the project "signed off" to their immediate supervisors who in turn "signed off" to their superiors and so on up the chain of command until the entire project was approved for public release by Vice Presidents Alexander and MacDonald and ultimately by Mr. Iacocca. The Pinto crash tests results had been forwarded up the chain of command to the ultimate decision-makers and were known to the Ford officials who decided to go forward with production.

Harley Copp, a former Ford engineer and executive in charge of the crash testing program, testified that the highest level of Ford's management made the decision to go forward with the production of the Pinto, knowing that the gas tank was vulnerable to puncture and rupture at low rear impact speeds creating a significant risk of death or injury from fire and knowing that "fixes" were feasible at nominal cost. He testified that management's decision was based on the cost savings which would inure from omitting or delaying the "fixes."

Mr. Copp's testimony concerning management's awareness of the crash tests results and the vulnerability of the Pinto fuel system was corroborated by other evidence. At an April 1971 product review meeting chaired by Mr. MacDonald, those present received and discussed a report (exhibit 125) prepared by Ford engineers pertaining to the financial impact of a proposed federal standard on fuel system integrity and the cost savings which would accrue from deferring even minimal "fixes." The report refers to crash tests of the integrity of the fuel system of Ford vehicles and design changes needed to meet anticipated federal standards. Also in evidence was a September 23, 1970, report (exhibit 124) by Ford's "Chassis Design Office" concerning a program "to establish a corporate [Ford] position and reply to the government" on the proposed federal fuel system integrity standard which included zero fuel spillage at 20 miles per hour fixed barrier crash by January 1, 1972, and 30 miles per hour by January 1, 1973. The report states in part: "The 20 and 30 mph rear fixed barrier crashes will probably require repackaging the fuel tanks in a protected area such as above the rear axle. This is based on moving barrier crash tests of a Chevelle and a Ford at 30 mph and other Ford products at 20 mph. Currently there are no plans for forward models to repackage the fuel tanks. Tests must be conducted to prove that repackaged tanks will live without significantly strengthening rear structure for added protection." The report also notes that the Pinto was the "[smallest] car line with most difficulty in achieving compliance." It is reasonable to infer that the report was prepared for and known to Ford officials in policy-making positions.

The fact that two of the crash tests were run at the request of the Ford chassis and vehicle engineering department for the specific purpose of demonstrating the advisability of moving the fuel tank over the axle as a possible "fix" further corroborated Mr. Copp's testimony that management knew the results of the crash tests. Mr. Kennedy, who succeeded Mr. Copp as the engineer in charge of Ford's crash testing program, admitted that the test results had been forwarded up the chain of command to his superiors.

Finally, Mr. Copp testified to conversations in late 1968 or early 1969 with the chief assistant research engineer in charge of cost-weight evaluation of the Pinto, and to a later conversation with the chief chassis engineer who was then in charge of crash testing the early prototype. In these conversations, both men expressed concern about the integrity of the Pinto's fuel system and complained about management's unwillingness to deviate from the design if the change would cost money.

FREE ELECTRICITY

Born in Croatia in 1856, Nikola Tesla was a scientific genius, some of whose inventions have entered everyday life (he developed AC electrical current), some of which were madcap.

Or were they? One of Tesla's most infamous ideas concerned electricity that could be transmitted through the air without the need for wires. To this end, he developed the Tesla Coil, a device to create bursts of high-voltage electricity which could be beamed to receivers without the need for wires. His biggest coil, the Magnifying Transmitter, was built at his lab in Colorado Springs, and when tested sent electricity arcing 50 metres into the air. The surge created a static discharge that lit up the earth. But the Magnifying Transmitter worked: it illuminated light bulbs twenty five miles away, without wires.

Tesla believed that the earth is a natural conductor, and that a strategically placed grid of Magnifying Transmitters could send free electricity over the world (see Document, p.167). To receive a supply, all people would need to do was stick a metal rod into their backyard, then relay the current to antennae on their electrical devices.

According to conspiracy lore, Tesla's wireless electricity scheme did not catch on because it was suppressed by big electricity manufacturers, notably J. P. Morgan, who had hitherto been financing Tesla's projects. "Where do I put the meter?" he famously asked Tesla about the latter's "free power" scheme. The scientific jury is out on whether Tesla's coils are a possible global power source, but Morgan certainly pulled the plug on free power in Tesla's lifetime. And suppression of customer-friendly electrical goods was hardly unknown in the USA. *Time* magazine reported in 1945 that Philips, Osram and GE had engaged in a conspiracy to suppress light bulb technology that would have produced cheaper and longer lasting bulbs.

Inadvertently though, Morgan may have done the world a favour by stopping the flow of dollars to the inventive Tesla. On Long Island, Tesla began construction of the monstrous Wardenclyffe Tower to run a "World System", combining wireless transmission of free energy and a global broadcasting system. There was intense press speculation – not helped by Tesla's boast that the tower's beam was so powerful it could destroy a ship in seconds – that Tesla's invention was behind the mysterious sinking of the *Iena* in 1907. More recently, it has been suggested that the 1908 explosion that wiped out half a million acres of Siberian forest was not, as officially claimed, caused by a piece of Enke's comet hitting Earth, but a misfiring from Tesla's Wardenclyffe Tower in which a colossal, trillion-watt beam of power went to the wrong place. The tower was pulled down in 1917 because German U-boats were using it as a navigational beacon

Lack of money also put paid to Tesla's 1934 plan for a particle beam weapon, which could knock aircraft out of the sky 250 miles away. Tesla christened his new invention the "Peace Ray", because he considered it so terrible a deterrent that all wars would stop. The ray gun was never built in Tesla's lifetime (he died in poverty in 1943) but the concept was revived in the 1980s by Texan physicist Dr Bernard Eastlund – and, say conspiracists, by the mysterious Project **HAARP** of the US government in remotest Alaska.

> Big business suppresses free electricity technology:
> ALERT LEVEL 5

Further Reading
Nikola Tesla and David Hatcher Childress, *The Tesla Papers: Nikola Tesla on Free Energy and Wireless Transmission of Power*, 2000

DOCUMENT: NIKOLA TESLA, *MY INVENTIONS*, 1919 [EXTRACT]

One day, as I was roaming in the mountains, I sought shelter from an approaching storm. The sky became overhung with heavy clouds but somehow the rain was delayed until, all of a sudden, there was a lightning flash and a few moments after a deluge. This observation set me thinking.

It was manifest that the two phenomena were closely related, as cause and effect, and a little reflection led me to the conclusion that the electrical energy involved in the precipitation of the water was inconsiderable, the function of lightning being much like that of a sensitive trigger.

Here was a stupendous possibility of achievement. If we could produce electric effects of the required quality, this whole planet and the conditions of existence on it could be transformed.

The sun raises the water of the oceans and winds drive it to distant regions where it remains in a state of most delicate balance. If it were in our power to upset it when and wherever desired, this mighty life-sustaining stream could be at will controlled. We could irrigate arid deserts, create lakes and rivers and provide motive power in unlimited amounts. This would be the most efficient way of harnessing the sun to the uses of man. The consummation depended on our ability to develop electric forces of the order of those in nature. It seemed a hopeless undertaking, but I made up my mind to try it and immediately on my return to the United States, in the summer of 1892, work was begun which was to me all the more attractive, because a means of the same kind was necessary for the successful transmission of energy without wires.

The first gratifying result was obtained in the spring of the succeeding year when I reached tensions of about 1,000,000 volts with my conical coil. That was not much in the light of the present art, but it was then considered a feat. Steady progress was made until the destruction of my laboratory by fire in 1895, as may be judged from an article by T. C. Martin which appeared in the April number of the *Century Magazine*.

This calamity set me back in many ways and most of that year had to be devoted to planning and reconstruction. However, as soon as circumstances permitted, I returned to the task.

Although I knew that higher electro-motive forces were attainable with apparatus of larger dimensions, I had an instinctive perception that the object could be accomplished by the proper design of a comparatively small and compact transformer. In carrying on tests with a secondary in the form of a flat spiral, as illustrated in my patents, the absence of streamers surprised me, and it was not long before I discovered that this was due to the position of the turns and their mutual action. Profiting from this observation I resorted to the use of a high tension conductor with turns of considerable diameter sufficiently separated to keep down the distributed capacity, while at the same time preventing undue accumulation of the charge at any point. The application of this principle enabled me to produce pressures of 4,000,000 volts, which was about the limit obtainable in my new laboratory at Houston Street, as the discharges extended through a distance of 16 feet. A photograph of this transmitter was published in the *Electrical Review* of November 1898.

In order to advance further along this line I had to go into the open, and in the spring of 1899, having completed preparations for the erection of a wireless plant, I went to Colorado where I remained for more than one year. Here I introduced other improvements and refinements which made it possible to generate currents of any tension that may be desired. Those who are interested will find some information in regard to the experiments I conducted there in my article, "The Problem of Increasing Human Energy" in the *Century Magazine* of June 1900, to which I have referred on a previous occasion.

I have been asked by the *ELECTRICAL EXPERIMENTER* to be quite explicit on this subject so that my young friends among the readers of the magazine will clearly understand the construction and operation of my "Magnifying Transmitter" and the purposes for which it is intended. Well, then, in the first place, it is a resonant transformer with a secondary in which the parts, charged to a high potential, are of considerable area and arranged in space along ideal enveloping surfaces of very large radii of curvature, and at proper distances from one another thereby insuring a small electric surface density everywhere so that no leak can occur even if the conductor is bare. It is suitable for any frequency, from a few to many thousands of cycles per second, and can be used in the production of currents of tremendous volume and moderate pressure, or of smaller amperage and immense electromotive force. The maximum electric tension is merely dependent on the curvature of the surfaces on which the charged elements are situated and the area of the latter.

Judging from my past experience, as much as 100,000,000 volts are perfectly practicable. On the other hand currents of many thousands of amperes may be obtained in the antenna. A plant of but very moderate dimensions is required for such performances. Theoretically, a terminal of less than 90 feet in diameter is sufficient to develop an electromotive force of that magnitude while for antenna currents of from 2,000–4,000 amperes at the usual frequencies it need not be larger than 30 feet in diameter.

In a more restricted meaning this wireless transmitter is one in which the Hertz-wave radiation is an entirely negligible quantity as compared with the whole energy, under which condition the damping factor is extremely small and an enormous charge is stored in the elevated capacity.

Such a circuit may then be excited with impulses of any kind, even of low frequency and it will yield sinusoidal and continuous oscillations like those of an alternator.

Taken in the narrowest significance of the term, however, it is a resonant transformer which, besides possessing these qualities, is accurately proportioned to fit the globe and its electrical constants and properties, by virtue of which design it becomes highly efficient and effective in the wireless transmission of energy. Distance is then absolutely eliminated, there being no diminution in the intensity of the transmitted impulses. It is even possible to make the actions increase with the distance from the plant according to an exact mathematical law.

This invention was one of a number comprised in my "World-System" of wireless transmission which I undertook to commercialize on my return to New York in 1900. As to the immediate purposes of my enterprise, they were clearly outlined in a technical statement of that period from which I quote:

The "World-System" has resulted from a combination of several original discoveries made by the inventor in the course of long continued research and experimentation. It makes possible not only the instantaneous and precise wireless transmission of any kind of signals, messages or characters, to all parts of the world, but also the inter-connection of the existing telegraph, telephone, and other signal stations without any change in their present equipment. By its means, for instance, a telephone subscriber here may call up and talk to any other subscriber on the Globe. An inexpensive receiver, not bigger than a watch, will enable him to listen anywhere, on land or sea, to a speech delivered or music played in some other place, however distant.

These examples are cited merely to give an idea of the possibilities of this great scientific advance, which annihi-lates distance and makes that perfect natural conductor, the Earth, available for all the innumerable purposes which human ingenuity has found for a line-wire. One far-reach-ing result of this is that any device capable of being oper-ated thru one or more wires (at a distance obviously restricted) can likewise be actuated, without artificial con-ductors and with the same facility and accuracy, at dis-tances to which there are no limits other than those imposed by the physical dimensions of the Globe. Thus, not only will entirely new fields for commercial exploita-tion be opened up by this ideal method of transmission but the old ones vastly extended.

The "World-System" is based on the application of the following important inventions and discoveries:

1) The "Tesla Transformer." This apparatus is in the production of electrical vibrations as revolutionary as gunpowder was in warfare. Currents many times stronger than any ever generated in the usual ways, and sparks over one hundred feet long, have been produced by the inventor with an instrument of this kind.

2) The "Magnifying Transmitter." This is Tesla's best invention, a peculiar transformer specially adapted to excite the Earth, which is in the transmission of electrical energy what the telescope is in astronomical observation. By the use of this marvelous device he has already set up electrical movements of greater intensity than those of lightning and passed a current, sufficient to light more than two hundred incandescent lamps, around the Globe.

3) The "Tesla Wireless System." This system comprises a number of improvements and is the only means known for transmitting economically electrical energy to a distance without wires. Careful tests and measurements in connection with an experimental station of great activity, erected by the inventor in Colorado, have demonstrated that power in any desired amount can be conveyed, clear across the Globe if necessary, with a loss not exceeding a few per cent.

4) The "Art of Individualization." This invention of Tesla's is to primitive 'tuning' what refined language is to unarticulated expression. It makes possible the transmission of signals or messages absolutely secret and exclusive both in the active and passive aspect, that is, non-interfering as well as non-interferable. Each signal is like an individual of unmistakable identity and there is virtually no limit to the number of stations or instruments which can be simultaneously operated without the slightest mutual disturbance.

5) "The Terrestrial Stationary Waves." This wonderful discovery, popularly explained, means that the Earth is responsive to electrical vibrations of definite pitch just as a tuning fork to certain waves of sound. These

particular electrical vibrations, capable of powerfully exciting the Globe, lend themselves to innumerable uses of great importance commercially and in many other respects.

The first "World-System" power plant can be put in operation in nine months. With this power plant it will be practicable to attain electrical activities up to ten million horsepower and it is designed to serve for as many technical achievements as are possible without due expense.

Among these the following may be mentioned:

1) The inter-connection of the existing telegraph exchanges or offices all over the world;
2) The establishment of a secret and non-interferable government telegraph service;
3) The inter-connection of all the present telephone exchanges or offices on the Globe;
4) The universal distribution of general news, by telegraph or telephone, in connection with the Press;
5) The establishment of such a "World-System" of intelligence transmission for exclusive private use;
6) The inter-connection and operation of all stock tickers of the world;
7) The establishment of a "World-System" of musical distribution, etc.;
8) The universal registration of time by cheap clocks indicating the hour with astronomical precision and requiring no attention whatever;
9) The world transmission of typed or handwritten characters, letters, checks, etc.;
10) The establishment of a universal marine service enabling the navigators of all ships to steer perfectly without compass, to determine the exact location, hour and speed, to prevent collisions and disasters, etc.;
11) The inauguration of a system of world-printing on land and sea;

12) The world reproduction of photographic pictures and all kinds of drawings or records.

I also proposed to make demonstrations in the wireless transmission of power on a small scale but sufficient to carry conviction. Besides these I referred to other and incomparably more important applications of my discoveries which will be disclosed at some future date.

A plant was built on Long Island with a tower 187 feet high, having a spherical terminal about 68 feet in diameter. These dimensions were adequate for the transmission of virtually any amount of energy. Originally only from 200 to 300 K.W. were provided but I intended to employ later several thousand horsepower. The transmitter was to emit a wave complex of special characteristics and I had devised a unique method of telephonic control of any amount of energy.

GENERAL MOTORS

Why do the cities of America have no streetcars, let alone street-cars named Desire, running along them?

In 1974 one Bradford Snell, a staff attorney for the US Senate antitrust subcommittee, advanced the startling claim that General Motors had, in alliance with Standard Oil, Firestone, and Phillips Petroleum gone into cahoots to destroy the energy-efficient streetcar in forty-five cities, so as to pave the way for the triumph of the internal combustion engine. Which they all had a big stake in. According to Snell, GM and the other firms set up a holding company, National City Lines, that bought up electric trolley systems, dismantled them and replaced them with buses. In his report to the US Government, "American Ground Transport – A Proposal for Restructuring the Automobile, Truck, Bus and Rail Industries" (see Document, p.176), he stated that General Motors was "a sovereign economic state whose common control of auto, truck, bus and locomotive production was a major factor in the displacement of rail and bus transportation with cars and trucks".

Snell's claim received a turbo-boost in 1988, when it formed the sub-plot of the movie *Who Framed Roger Rabbit?* Here the evil character Doom reveals that he bought the Red Car system so that he could junk it and force people to drive on his new freeway.

So, were the citizens of US cities taken for a ride by GM and its corporate pals?

There *is* a kernel of truth in Snell's allegation: National City Line did buy the Los Angeles Railway in 1944, and did replace streetcar lines with buses. Furthermore, General Motors and its subsidiary, National City Lines, along with seven other corporations were indicted on two counts under the Sherman Antitrust Act. They were charged with:

- Conspiring to monopolize sales of buses and supplies to companies owned by National City Lines.
- Conspiring to acquire control of transit companies with a view to forming a transportation monopoly.

The defendants were aquitted on the second count of trying to form a monopoly (although no one disputed that GM and its allies were engaged in all out war to create a transport environment favourable to its gas-powered products). GM, though, was convicted on the first. That is to say, they were guilty of conspiring to have GM companies buy only GM buses and spares.

It is not pretty, it is not ethical, but it not quite the same as maintaining that GM killed the streetcar. The streetcar was dying in its tracks before GM came along, because the rival bus was cheaper and more versatile (especially in a rapidly growing city like LA). Even transit systems which the NLC did not buy up, such as Pacific Electric, were dismantled in favour of the rubber-wheeled alternative.

> GM took US citizens for a ride by suppressing energy-efficient streetcar: ALERT LEVEL 2

Further Reading
Scott Bottles, *Los Angeles and the Automobile*, 1987

DOCUMENT: BRADFORD C. SNELL, "AMERICAN GROUND TRANSPORT", WASHINGTON: US GOVERNMENT PRINT OFFICE. A REPORT PRESENTED TO THE COMMITTEE OF THE JUDICIARY, SUBCOMMITTEE ON ANTITRUST AND MONOPOLY, UNITED STATES SENATE, 26 FEBRUARY 1974 [EXTRACT]

N.B. Snell is erroneous in claiming that GM were convicted "of having criminally conspired with Standard Oil of California, Firestone Tire and others to replace electric transportation with gas- or diesel-powered buses", as explained above.

After its successful experience with intercity buses, General Motors diversified into city bus and rail operations. At first, its procedure consisted of directly acquiring and scrapping local electric transit systems in favor of GM buses. In this fashion, it created a market for its city buses. As GM General Counsel Henry Hogan would observe later, the corporation "decided that the only way this new market for (city) buses could be created was for it to finance the conversion from streetcars to buses in some small cities." On June 29, 1932, the GM-bus executive committee formally resolved that "to develop motorized transportation, our company should initiate a program of this nature and authorize the incorporation of a holding company with a capital of $300,000." Thus was formed United Cities Motor Transit (UCMT) as a subsidiary of GM's bus division. Its sole function was to acquire electric streetcar companies, convert them to GM motorbus operation, and then resell the properties to local concerns which agreed to purchase GM bus replacements. The electric street-car lines of Kalamazoo and Saginaw, Mich., and Springfield, Ohio, were UCMT's first targets. "In such case," Hogan stated, GM "successfully motorized the city, turned the management over to other interests and liquidated its investment." The program ceased, however, in 1935 when GM was censured by the American Transit Association (ATA) for its self-serving role, as a bus manufacturer, in apparently attempting to motorize Portland's electric streetcar system.

As a result of the ATA censure, GM dissolved UCMT and embarked upon a nationwide plan to accomplish the same result indirectly. In 1936 it combined with the Omnibus Corp. in engineering the tremendous conversion of New York City's electric streetcar system to GM buses. At that time, as a result of stock and management interlocks, GM was able to exert substantial influence over Omnibus. John A. Ritchie, for example, served simultaneously as chairman of GM's bus division and president of Omnibus from 1926 until well after the motorization was completed. The massive conversion within a period of only 18 months of the New York system, then the world's largest streetcar network, has been recognized subsequently as the turning point in the electric railway industry.

Meanwhile, General Motors had organized another holding company to convert the remainder of the Nation's electric transportation systems to GM's buses. In 1936, it caused its officers and employees, I. B. Babcock, E. J. Stone, E. P. Crenshaw, and several Greyhound executives to form National City Lines, Inc. (NCL). During the following 14 years General Motors, together with Standard Oil of California, Firestone Tire, and two other suppliers of bus-related products, contributed more than $9 million to this holding company for the purpose of converting electric transit systems in 16 States to GM bus operations. The method of operation was basically the same as that which GM employed successfully in its United Cities Motor Transit program: acquisition, motorization, resale. By having NCL resell the properties after conversion was completed, GM and its allied companies were assured that their capital was continually reinvested in the motorization of additional systems. There was, moreover, little possibility of reconversion. To preclude the return of electric vehicles to the dozens of cities it motorized, GM extracted from the local transit companies contracts which prohibited their purchase of "any new equipment using any fuel or means of propulsion other than gas."

The National City Lines campaign had a devastating impact on the quality of urban transportation and urban living in America. Nowhere was the ruin more apparent than in the Greater Los Angeles metropolitan area. Thirty-five years ago it was a beautiful region of lush palm trees, fragrant orange groves, and clean, ocean-enriched air. It was served then by the world's largest interurban electric railway system. The Pacific Electric system branched out from Los Angeles for a radius of more than 75 miles reaching north to San Fernando, east to San Bernardino, and south to Santa Ana. Its 3,000 quiet, pollution-free, electric trains annually transported 80 million people throughout the sprawling region's 56 separately incorporated cities. Contrary to popular belief, the Pacific Electric, not the automobile, was responsible for the area's geographical development. First constructed in 1911, it established traditions of suburban living long before the automobile had arrived.

In 1938, General Motors and Standard Oil of California organized Pacific City Lines (PCL) as an affiliate of NCL to motorize west coast electric railways. The following year PCL acquired, scrapped, and substituted bus lines for three northern California electric rail systems in Fresno, San Jose, and Stockton. In 1940 GM, Standard Oil, and Firestone "assumed the active management of Pacific (City Lines)" in order to supervise its California operations more directly. That year, PCL began to acquire and scrap portions of the $100 million Pacific Electric system, including rail lines from Los Angeles to Glendale, Burbank, Pasadena, and San Bernardino. Subsequently, in December 1944, another NCL affiliate (American City Lines) was financed by GM and Standard Oil to motorize downtown Los Angeles. At the time, the Pacific Electric shared downtown Los Angeles trackage with a local electric streetcar company, the Los Angeles Railway. American City Lines purchased the local system, scrapped its electric transit cars, tore down its power transmission lines, ripped up the tracks, and placed GM diesel buses fueled by Standard Oil on Los Angeles' crowded streets. In sum, GM and its auto-industrial allies severed Los

Angeles' regional rail links and then motorized its downtown heart.

Motorization drastically altered the quality of life in southern California. Today, Los Angeles is an ecological wasteland: The palm trees are dying from petrochemical smog; the orange groves have been paved over by 300 miles of freeways; the air is a septic tank into which 4 million cars, half of them built by General Motors, pump 13,000 tons of pollutants daily. With the destruction of the efficient Pacific Electric rail system, Los Angeles may have lost its best hope for rapid rail transit and a smog-free metropolitan area. "The Pacific Electric," wrote UCLA Professor Hilton, "could have comprised the nucleus of a highly efficient rapid transit system, which would have contributed greatly to lessening the tremendous traffic and smog problems that developed from population growth." The substitution of GM diesel buses, which were forced to compete with automobiles for space on congested freeways, apparently benefited GM, Standard Oil, and Firestone, considerably more than the riding public. Hilton added: "The (Pacific Electric) system, with its extensive private right of way, was far superior to a system consisting solely of buses on the crowded streets." As early as 1963, the city already was seeking ways of raising $500 million to rebuild a rail system "to supercede its present inadequate network of bus lines." A decade later, the estimated cost of constructing a 116-mile rail system, less than one-sixth the size of the earlier Pacific Electric, had escalated to more than $6.6 billion.

By 1949, General Motors had been involved in the replacement of more than 100 electric transit systems with GM buses in 45 cities including New York, Philadelphia, Baltimore, St. Louis, Oakland, Salt Lake City, and Los Angeles. In April of that year, a Chicago Federal jury convicted GM of having criminally conspired with Standard Oil of California, Firestone Tire and others to replace electric transportation with gas- or diesel-powered buses and to monopolize the sale of buses and related products to local transportation companies throughout the country. The court imposed a sanction of $5,000 on GM. In addition, the jury convicted H. C. Grossman, who was then treasurer of General Motors. Grossman had played a key role in the motorization campaigns and had served as a director of PCL when that company undertook the dismantlement of the $100 million Pacific Electric system. The court fined Grossman the magnanimous sum of $1.

Despite its criminal conviction, General Motors continued to acquire and dieselize electric transit properties through September of 1955. By then, approximately 88 percent of the nation's electric streetcar network had been eliminated. In 1936, when GM organized National City Lines, 40,000 streetcars were operating in the United States; at the end of 1955, only 5,000 remained. In December of that year, GM bus chief Roger M. Kyes correctly observed: "The motor coach has supplanted the interurban systems and has for all practical purposes eliminated the trolley (streetcar)."

The effect of General Motors' diversification into city transportation systems was substantially to curtail yet another alternative to motor vehicle transportation. Electric street railways and electric trolley buses were eliminated without regard to their relative merit as a mode of transport. Their displacement by oil-powered buses maximized the earnings of GM stockholders; but it deprived the riding public of a competing method of travel. Moreover, there is some evidence that in terms of air pollution and energy consumption these electric systems were superior to diesel buses. In any event, GM and its oil and tire co-conspirators used National City Lines as a device to force the sale of their products regardless of the public interest. As Professor Smerk, an authority on urban transportation, has written, "Street railways and trolley bus operations, even if better suited to traffic needs and the public interest, were doomed in favor of the vehicles and material produced by the conspirators."

General Motors' substitution of buses for city streetcar lines may also have contributed in an indirect manner to the abandonment of electric railway freight service. During the 1930's merchants relied extensively on interurban electric railways to deliver local goods and to interchange distant freight shipments with mainline railroads. The Pacific Electric, for example, was once the third largest freight railroad in California; it interchanged freight with the Southern Pacific, the Union Pacific and the Santa Fe. In urban areas, these railways often ran on local streetcar trackage. The conversion of city streetcars to buses, therefore, deprived them of city trackage and hastened their replacement by motor trucks, many of which, incidentally, were produced by GM.

General Motors also stood to profit from its interests in highway freight transport. Until the early 1950s, it maintained sizable stock interests in two of the Nation's largest trucking firms, Associated Transport and Consolidated Freightways, which enjoyed the freight traffic diverted from the electric railways. By 1951, these two companies had established more than 100 freight terminals in 29 States coast-to-coast and, more than likely, had invested in a substantial number of GM diesel-powered trucks.

GM's diversification into bus and rail operations would appear not only to have had the effect of foreclosing transport alternatives regardless of their comparative advantages, but also to have contributed at least in part to urban air pollution problems. There were in fact some early warnings that GM's replacement of electric-driven vehicles with diesel-powered buses and trucks was increasing air pollution. On January 26, 1954, for instance, E. P. Crenshaw, GM bus general sales manager, sent the following memorandum to F. J. Limback, another GM executive:

> There has developed in a number of cities "smog" conditions which has resulted in Anti-Air Pollution committees, who immediately take issue with bus and truck operations, and especially Diesel engine exhaust. In many cases, efforts are being made to stop further substitution of Diesel buses for electric-driven vehicles ...

Three months later, in April 1954, the American Conference of Governmental Industrial Hygienists adopted a limit of 5 parts per million for human exposure to nitrogen oxides. Diesel buses, according to another report by two GM engineers, emitted "oxides of nitrogen concentrations over 200 times the recommended" exposure limit. Nevertheless, the dieselization program continued.

GLOBAL WARMING

Is a hoax, according to an array of climate change doubters who maintain that there is no scientific evidence that the Earth is getting substantially hotter. And even if the world *is* warming up the cause is not the emission of greenhouse gases from fossil fuels – the belief of the global warming orthodox – but a natural fluctuation in temperature caused by solar activity.

An inconvenient truth for global warmers is that the world temperature apparently levelled off in 1998, and if anything has dropped since 2009. Accusations that scientific supporters of man-made global warming – "anthropogenic global warming" or "AGW" in the trade – have persistently hidden information contrary to the above or hyped the dangers of warming are rife. And sometimes well-founded: an independent inquiry into "Climategate" at the Climate Research Unit at the University of East Anglia, Great Britain, cleared academics there of actually using tricks to hide data but did find a graph produced in 1999 "misleading". Stephen Schneider, Stanford University Professor and lead author for the UN Intergovernmental Panel on Climate Change (IPCC) blithely told *Discover* magazine that scientific believers needed to "'offer up scary scenarios, make simplified, dramatic statements, and make little mention of any doubts we might have" in the greater good of convincing the public that warming was happening.

Scientists lying? Scientists are meant to stare down microscopes and tell the truth. With scientists prepared to fudge and fictionalize for political ends, it is small wonder that AGW-deniers smell blood.

In the movie *The Wild One* Marlon Brando's character is asked, "What are you rebelling against, Johnny?" to which he answers, "Whaddya got?" In similar vein, denialists cite a multitude of reasons why the global warming scam (alleged) is being foisted on the public by politicians, scientists and businessmen. In ascending order of satanic magnitude the hoax exists because:

- Green charities, environmentalists, alternative energy companies, carbon-trading NGOs, pro-climate academic researchers all need to whip up fear about global warming to justify their jobs, grants, scams and budgets. Their co-conspirators are governments from left to right, who use global warming to acclimatize the population to higher taxes and more controls on lifestyle.
- The UN and its IPCC is seeking the redistribution of wealth from First World to Third World by curtailing industrial output in the West. In particular theorists charge that the Kyoto Agreement is a direct attack on the economic capability of the USA, since ratification by Washington DC of treaty obligations to restrict emissions would lead to a giant restructuring bill. De-industrialization of the West, say some theorists, together with a one-world UN-led government equals Socialism – so making "global warming" a new twist on the old Commie takeover plot.
- The **New World Order**, like the UN, is seeking the destabilisation of the USA. Retooling the economy to satisfy global warmers and Kyoto would drag billions from defence, so making the USA vulnerable to a takeover by NWO forces.

Subtract the lunacy of the "NWO" and for once the paranoid spear carriers of conspiracy theory may have a point: the global warming brigade are blowing smoke into the eyes of the public.

The public, meanwhile, along with Joe Friday, want "Just the facts, ma'am".

Global warming is a hoax: ALERT LEVEL 5

Further Reading
Michael Crichton, *State of Fear*, 2004
James Delingpole, *Watermelons: The Green Movement's True Colors*, 2011
Naomi Oreskes and Erik M. Conway, *Merchants of Doubt*, 2010

GULF WAR SYNDROME

On returning home from the first Gulf War of 1990–91, some Coalition veterans began to complain of a disturbing illness, the symptoms of which were migraine, dizziness, loss of balance, memory and motor control. Dubbed "Gulf War Syndrome", scientists and combatants alike searched for its cause, of which there were several dire possibilities. Firstly, there was the possibility of exposure to oil fumes from well fires. Secondly, Saddam Hussein may have covertly used biological or chemical weapons. Thirdly, Coalition forces were subjected to anti-nerve gas drugs and chemical weapons by their own side, which was then covered up, as with the case of GIs being exposed to Agent Orange herbicide in Vietnam.

Not everyone, however, was convinced that Gulf War Syndrome actually existed. An issue of the *New England Journal of Medicine* in 1996 declared that most cases of the illness could be put down to leishmaniasis, a parasitic disease spread by sandflies. Other cases, as with other wars, seemed to be symptoms of shell shock. A 1998 article in *Emerging Infectious Diseases* found that veterans of the Gulf War actually had better overall health than soldiers who stayed behind. The British Ministry of Defence found no correlation between illness and Gulf War service, while the Pentagon found that only 1 per cent of Gulf veterans claimed to suffer from the mysterious illness. There were dark mutterings that veterans with Gulf War Syndrome were cleverly seeking financial compensation along the lines of that awarded to Agent Orange victims.

Undeterred, Gulf War Syndrome sufferers carried on campaigning, and began to win the battle for the public mind. In the US, a panel chaired by Anthony Principi, the Secretary of the Veteran Affairs department, decided that: "Research studies conducted since the war have consistently indicated that psychiatric illness, combat experience or other deployment-related stressors do not explain Gulf War veterans' illnesses in the large majority of ill veterans"

Across the pond, in June 2003, the High Court upheld a claim by a Brit vet that the eczema, fatigue, depression and breathing problems that he experienced were the consequence of his military service. The court's ruling was supported by a British scientific study, which found that Gulf War veterans had a lower fertility count than their non-serving peers.

Over time, the focus of Gulf War Syndrome medical research became the vaccinations troops received before deployment. By an "Interim Rule" adopted by the US Food and Drug Administration, the military were allowed to use experimental drugs on staff without their consent in a time of "military exigency". Accordingly, GIs were injected cocktails of drugs of dubious provenance, efficacy and safety. A congressionally appointed Research Advisory Committee on Gulf War Veterans' Illnesses determined in 2008 that two neurotoxic exposures were "causally associated" with Gulf War illness. These were pyridostigmine bromide (PB) pills, given to protect troops from effects of nerve agents, and pesticides sprayed on clothing, bedding and tents.

Coalition soldiers given unwittingly experimental drugs:
ALERT LEVEL 7

Further Reading
www.va.gov/RAC-VI/docs/Committee_Documents/GWIand
HealthofGWVeterans_RAC-GWVIReport_2008.pdf

DOCUMENT: *GULF WAR ILLNESS AND THE HEALTH OF GULF WAR VETERANS,* RESEARCH ADVISORY COMMITTEE ON GULF WAR VETERANS' ILLNESSES, 2008

Findings in Brief

Gulf War illness, the multisymptom condition resulting from service in the 1990–1991 Gulf War, is the most prominent health issue affecting Gulf War veterans, but not the only one. The Congressionally mandated Research Advisory Committee on Gulf War Veterans' Illnesses has reviewed the extensive evidence now available, including important findings from scientific research and government investigations not considered by earlier panels, to determine what is known about the health consequences of military service in the Gulf War. This evidence identifies the foremost causes of Gulf War illness, describes biological characteristics of this condition, and provides direction for future research urgently needed to improve the health of Gulf War veterans.

Gulf War illness is a serious condition that affects at least one fourth of the 697,000 U.S. veterans who served in the 1990–1991 Gulf War. This complex of multiple concurrent symptoms typically includes persistent memory and concentration problems, chronic headaches, widespread pain, gastrointestinal problems, and other chronic abnormalities not explained by well-established diagnoses. No effective treatments have been identified for Gulf War illness and studies indicate that few veterans have recovered over time.

Gulf War illness fundamentally differs from trauma and stress-related syndromes described after other wars. Studies consistently indicate that Gulf War illness is not the result of combat or other stressors and that Gulf War veterans have lower rates of post-traumatic stress disorder than veterans of other wars. No similar widespread, unexplained symptomatic illness has been identified in veterans who have served in war zones since the Gulf War, including current Middle East deployments.

Evidence strongly and consistently indicates that two Gulf War neurotoxic exposures are causally associated with Gulf War illness: 1) use of pyridostigmine bromide (PB) pills, given to protect troops from effects of nerve agents, and 2) pesticide use during deployment. Evidence includes the consistent association of Gulf War illness with PB and pesticides across studies of Gulf War veterans, identified dose-response effects, and research findings in other populations and in animal models.

For several Gulf War exposures, an association with Gulf War illness cannot be ruled out. These include low-level exposure to nerve agents, close proximity to oil well fires, receipt of multiple vaccines, and effects of combinations of Gulf War exposures. There is some evidence supporting a possible association between these exposures and Gulf War illness, but that evidence is inconsistent or limited in important ways.

Other wartime exposures are not likely to have caused Gulf War illness for the majority of ill veterans. For remaining exposures, there is little evidence supporting an association with Gulf War illness or a major role is unlikely based on what is known about exposure patterns during the Gulf War and more recent deployments. These include depleted uranium, anthrax vaccine, fuels, solvents, sand and particulates, infectious diseases, and chemical agent resistant coating (CARC).

Gulf War illness is associated with diverse biological alterations that most prominently affect the brain and nervous system. Research findings in veterans with Gulf War illness include significant differences in brain structure and function, autonomic nervous system function, neuroendocrine and immune measures, and measures associated with vulnerability to neurotoxic chemicals. There is little evidence of peripheral neuropathies in Gulf War veterans.

Gulf War illness has both similarities and differences with multi-symptom conditions in the general population. Symptom-defined conditions like chronic fatigue syndrome, fibromyalgia, and multiple chemical sensitivity occur at elevated rates in Gulf War veterans, but account for only a small proportion of veterans with Gulf War illness.

Studies indicate that Gulf War veterans have significantly higher rates of amyotrophic lateral sclerosis (ALS) than other veterans, and that Gulf War veterans potentially exposed to nerve agents have died from brain cancer at elevated rates. Although these conditions have affected relatively few veterans, they are cause for concern and require continued monitoring.

Important questions remain about other Gulf War health issues. These include questions about rates of other neurological diseases, cancers, and diagnosed conditions in Gulf War veterans, current information on overall and disease-specific mortality rates in Gulf War veterans, and unanswered questions concerning the health of veterans' children.

Federal Gulf War research programs have not been effective, historically, in addressing priority issues related to Gulf War illness and the health of Gulf War veterans. Substantial federal Gulf War research funding has been used for studies that have little or no relevance to the health of Gulf War veterans, and for research on stress and psychiatric illness. Recent Congressional actions have brought about promising new program developments at the Departments of Defense and Veterans Affairs, but overall federal funding for Gulf War research has declined dramatically since 2001.

A renewed federal research commitment is needed to identify effective treatments for Gulf War illness and address other priority Gulf War health issues. Adequate funding is required to achieve the critical objectives of improving the health of Gulf War veterans and preventing similar problems in future deployments. This is a national obligation, made especially urgent by the many years that Gulf War veterans have waited for answers and assistance.

HAARP

HAARP is the trip-off-the-tongue abbreviation for the mouthful that is America's High Frequency Active Auroral Research Program housed near Gakona, Alaska. Here, on a 33-acre site, scientists transmit a 3.6million megawatt signal into the ionosphere so that other colleagues in white lab coats can "understand ... and control ionospheric processors that might alter the performance of communication and surveillance systems".

HAARP is about improving communications? Oh no, it is not, say a legion of conspiracists, starting with Nick Begich and Jeane Manning, authors of *Angels Don't Play This HAARP* (1995) and Jerry E. Smith, the penner of *HAARP* (1998). Smith's subtitle gives the conspiracists' game away: HAARP is "The Ultimate Weapon of Conspiracy". Since the HAARP transmitter works by heating the ionosphere, Begich, Manning, Smith et al claim it is capable of altering the world's weather systems to the advantage of the US. The cases in point being the 2004 **Indian Ocean Tsunami** (which allowed Uncle Sam to gain control over the oil rich Aceh province), and the 2008 Sichuan earthquake and the 2011 Japanese Tsunami (both of which devastated the economies of America's chief Asian competitors).

More common is the notion that HAARP's Ionospheric Research Instrument (IRI) transmitter can be used as a "death beam" capable of destroying enemy satellites. A misfire in 1993 is claimed to have caused an electricity blackout in Canada and the north-east of the USA. Technologically, HAARP does have – although officialdom tends to deny it – a striking similarity to the patented defence system designed by Dr Bernard Eastlund, which fires pulses of electromagnetic radiation at incoming missiles. As Eastlund readily acknowledged, his patent owed much to principles laid down by Nikola Tesla, pioneer of **Free Electricity**, although the exact system powering Tesla's own "weapon of doom" is unknown. On Tesla's death, many of his papers went missing, while others were seized by the FBI who still have them under wraps.

Suspicions that HAARP has an ulterior military function are roused further by following the cash trail: the programme is funded by the Office of Naval Research, and managed by the Defense Advanced Research Projects Agency.

Even so, all nefarious applications of HAARP are denied by US officialdom, who point out that the HAARP site holds open days every summer.

Which is great if you are an Eskimo or a polar bear. Otherwise, Gakona, 200 miles east of Anchorage, is the end of the earth.

But not literally. Fingers crossed.

HAARP is a secret weapon of doom: ALERT LEVEL 5

Further Reading
Nick Begich and Jeane Manning, *Angels Don't Play This HAARP*, 1995

DAG HAMMARSKJOLD

On the night of 17 September 1961 a Douglas DC-6 crashed in North Rhodesia (now Zambia), killing all sixteen passengers aboard. One of the dead was Dag Hammarskjold, the Secretary-General of the United Nations, who had been on his way to negotiate a ceasefire between UN forces and Katangese troops of Moise Tshombe.

The official inquiry, undertaken by the Rhodesians (read British, because Rhodesia was a colony) blamed the plane's pilot for the crash, concluding that he had misjudged the approach to Ndola airport. A subsequent UN inquiry largely confirmed the British findings. However, rumours of foul play began to surface, and have continued to float around. Among the early sceptics was Harry Truman, ex-president of the US, who is reputed to have said, "Dag Hammarskjold was on the point of getting something done when they killed him. Notice that I said, 'when they killed him'."

Who did Truman mean by "they"? Answer: European mining companies, with Britain and America's spies wiping away the traces. In 1961, the unhappy Congo was the scene of a rebellion by the mineral-rich Katanga region. Backing the rebellion were western mining companies, white settlers – and secretly, suspected Hammarskjold, Great Britain. The Secretary-General, on the other hand, was using all his clout to support the Congolese Government, and had recently authorized a UN military mission (Operation Morthor) against the Katanga rebels. The British were not the only enemies of Hammarskjold; the fiercely independent Swedish diplomat had enraged almost all the major powers on the Security Council with his support for decolonization. On the other hand, he was much loved by developing countries, and his re-election as secretary-general was virtually guaranteed in the general assembly vote due in 1962.

There is a deal of evidence to suggest that Hammarskjold's plane was shot down. One of the DC-6's passengers, US Sergeant Harold Julian, was able to tell investigators before he died that he had seen sparks in the sky before the crash. His account tallies with those of charcoal burners and other eyewitnesses in the Ndola area interviewed by Swedish aid worker Göran Björkdahl, who say that they saw a plane shooting at the DC-6. Two of Hammarskjold's aides, Conor Cruise O'Brien and George Ivan Smith, both became convinced after their own investigations that the Secretary-General had been shot down by mercenaries working for European industrialists in Katanga, with the British covering up the shooting and possibly sponsoring it. (O'Brien knew of what he spoke: he had been the target of assassination by pro-Katanga mercenaries.) Norwegian Major-General Egge, the first UN officer to see Hammarskjold's body, declared that the Secretary-General had a hole in his forehead, which was subsequently airbrushed from photos. Even the official reports agree that six of the DC-6 passengers' bodies showed evidence of bullet wounds, but attribute these to exploding ammunition in the fire after the plane's crash. This contention was refuted by Major C. F. Westell, a ballistics expert, who said: "I can certainly describe as sheer nonsense the statement that cartridges of machine guns or pistols detonated in a fire can penetrate a human body." He based his opinion on a large-scale experiment that had been done to determine if military fire brigades would be in danger working near munitions depots.

Is there any tangible evidence of British – or even American – involvement in Hammarskjold's death? In 1997, documents uncovered by the South African Truth and Reconciliation Commission indicated a conspiracy between the CIA and MI5 to remove Hammarskjold in "Operation Celeste". It is perhaps timely to recall here that the CIA, by its own later admission, assassinated Congolese leader Patrice Lumumba in January 1961. According to press reports, one document turned up by the Truth and Reconciliation Commission refers to a meeting between the CIA, South African and British intelligence in which CIA chief Allen Dulles agreed that "Dag is becoming troublesome ... and should be removed." Dulles, according to the documents, promised "full cooperation from his people".

The British Foreign Office have declared the documents to be Soviet disinformation.

UN leader Dag Hammarskjold was assassinated: ALERT LEVEL 7

Further Reading
Arthur Gavshon, *The Mysterious Death of Dag Hammarskjold*, 1962
Lisa Pease, "Midnight in the Congo: The Assassination of Lumumba and the Mysterious Death of Dag Hammarskjold", *Probe*, March–April 1999

HEINRICH HIMMLER

In conspiracy land, bad Nazis never die. Either they are taken by
Vril-powered UFOs to Antarctica (like Hitler) or remodelled by
plastic surgery to live in the USSR (like Martin Bormann). Then
there is the strange case of Heinrich Himmler.

In April 1945, as the end of the Third Reich loomed, Hitler's
number one – and the architect of the Holocaust – found a
sudden and urgent desire to make peace with the Allies. When
he was rebuffed, and his treason made public, Hitler ordered his
arrest. Luckily for Himmler, Hitler promptly committed suicide
in his Berlin bunker and news of the excommunication seems
never to have reached Grand Admiral Karl Dönitz, the Reich's
new chief, whose Flensburg Government Himmler joined. To
curry favour with the oncoming Allies, Dönitz dismissed
Himmler on 6 May 1945.

Himmler then tried his luck with the Americans, offering
Dwight Eisenhower the surrender of all Germany if he was
spared from prosecution. He even suggested to Ike that he,
Himmler, be the Minister of Police in the new Germany. Ike
said, "'*Nein!*" and Himmler was declared a war criminal. Now
actively hunted by the Allies, Himmler wandered around
Flensburg near the Danish border disguised as a member of the
gendarmerie. However, the stamps on his papers raised the suspicions of a British soldier, Arthur Britton, who arrested
"Heinrich Hitzinger" on 22 May 1945 on suspicion of being a
member of the SS. In captivity he was soon recognized.
According to the official account, before Himmler could be
interrogated he committed suicide in Lüneburg by swallowing a

potassium cyanide capsule. Attempts to revive him were unsuccessful. The date was 23 May 1945.

The Himmler conspiracy is two-fold: was the man who committed suicide in Lüneburg Himmler or a double? And, if it was Himmler, was he "suicided".

Among the first to proclaim that a "fake" Himmler died in Lüneburg were members of the Nazi "ratline" **ODESSA**, who maintained that the real Himmler escaped to the village of Strones in the Waldviertel, a hilly forested area in Lower Austria, where he was involved in reviving the Nazi movement. Conspiracies make odd bedfellows; the ODESSA "double" case is somewhat supported by the British forensic historian Hugh Thomas who in *SS-1* questions whether the body examined by British military authorities was really that of the ex-chicken farmer and SS leader. Certain physical details of the dead man photographed lying on a bed at Lüneburg do, indeed, seem different from Himmler's. One nostril is larger than the other; Himmler's were symmetrical. The corpse seems to be free of a duelling scar, meaning he wasn't the boy born to Anna and Dr Gebhard Himmler on 7 October 1900. Of course he might have been wearing make-up, which Nazi leaders were rather fond of. What bangs a nail into the "Himmler double" theory, grainy photography aside, is Himmler's daughter. Gudrun Himmler (born 1929) was devoted to her father (and his politics, being a member of Stille Hilfe, the SS veterans' support group), and he to her. If he had survived 1945, it is near inconceivable that they would have not been in touch. And there is not the slightest whiff of their corresponding or meeting.

Revisionist author Joseph Bellinger and British writer Martin Allen are amongst the most prominent promoters of the alternative version of Himmler's death. Both suggest that Himmler was assassinated by the British, with Allen claiming that Himmler had secretly negotiated with Britain as early as 1943. Churchill had him murdered to cover up the fact. Much of Allen's "evidence" from the National Archives turned out to be twenty-nine forged papers. Allen's protestations of innocence or deliberate planting by MI5/the Establishment/jealous historians to discredit his thesis were undone by his professional record: his two previous books also seem to have relied on documents of dubious provenance and authenticity.

The mystery surrounding Himmler's death is unlikely to be settled anytime soon. Army personnel at Lüneburg were ordered to sign the Official Secrets Act, and unusually the relevant papers – those, that is, that haven't conveniently disappeared – are not due for release until 2045. The mystery is compounded by the fact that British soldiers took Himmler's body and buried it in an unmarked grave on Lüneburg Heath. It has never been found.

> Himmler survived the war by faking his death: ALERT LEVEL 2
>
> Himmler was assassinated by the British and his death made to look like suicide: ALERT LEVEL 5

Further Reading
Martin Allen, *Himmler's Secret War*, 2005
Joseph Bellinger, *Himmler's Tod: Freitod oder Mord?*, 2005
Hugh Thomas, *SS-1: The Unlikely Death of Heinrich Himmler*, 2002

HOLLOMAN AIR FORCE BASE

Situated 15 km south-west of Alamogordo, New Mexico, Holloman Air Force Base is reputedly one of the first places where ETs and humans had a close encounter of the third kind. Conspiracists believe that a UFO landing at Holloman may have occurred as early as the mid-1950s, and was attended by no less than President Eisenhower. This saved the aliens saying, "Take us to your leader," because he was already there. The more storied UFO touchdown occurred on 25 April 1964 (twelve hours after the Soccoro, New Mexico UFO occurrence), when a trio of UFOs hovered into view, one of which landed. Three aliens got out of the craft and talked with base officials. A retired counter-intelligence officer with the Air Force's Office of Special Investigations (OSI), Richard Doty, later confirmed the event.

A busy place Holloman. In 1973, documentary film-makers Robert Emenegger and Alan Sandler were informed by Air Force officials that footage existed of a 1971 UFO visit to the base. The 16 mm film was confirmed as genuine by Paul Shartle, an officer at nearby Norton AFB. According to Shartle the film showed aliens who were "human-size. They had an odd, gray complexion and a pronounced nose. They wore tight fitting jump suits, [and] thin headdresses that appeared to be communication devices, and in their hands they held a 'translator'."

Emenegger claimed he was later given a personal tour of Holloman AFB, and shown the site where base officials chatted with the ETs; in the conversation, the AF apparently informed the ETs that they [the AF] had been monitoring signals from an alien group with which they were unfamiliar, and did their ET guests know anything about them? The ETs said, "No." When Emenegger double-checked the authenticity of the Holloman event with USAF Colonel George Weinbrenner, the latter confirmed its truth. Off the record.

Emenegger and Sandler's documentary was released in 1974 as *UFOs: Past, Present and Future*, narrated by Rod Serling.

Sceptics declare the Holloman landing(s) a hoax. Or an urban legend. Some sources suggest that new officers at Holloman were shown a training film, *What If They Land?*, which depicted a close encounter very much like the one described by Shartle.

> Holloman AFB was site of a close encounter: ALERT LEVEL 3

Further Reading
Robert Emenegger and Alan Sandler, *UFOs, Past, Present and Future*, 1974

HURRICANE KATRINA

Hurricane Katrina roared across Florida into Louisiana on 29 August 2005 to cause over 1,830 deaths. New Orleans bore the brunt of the fatalities; wind speeds topped 200 kph, and the levee (dyke) system failed, leaving much of the city deep under water. With $81 billion of damage done, Katrina was the biggest natural disaster in US history.

Hold the word "natural"; according to an army of internet alternative theorists, Katrina was anything but. One of the most popular "man-made" theories for the devastation caused by Katrina posits that the Bush Government (in alliance with the **New World Order**, naturally) bombed the levees in New Orleans to intentionally flood the city. The main evidence for this is that residents claimed to have heard explosions before the levees breached; other sources, suggest that Bush used something rather more sophisticated than a bag of gelignite, namely a **HAARP**-like device. Whatever, by flooding New Orleans, Bush achieved a triple whammy:

1) He killed blacks. In the words of conspiracist "Liberal Lil" (some mistake in nomenclature surely?), Bush "wants to destroy the blacks so he can bolster his voter base". Genocide against blacks could also "save big dollars on the Welfare money the Feds pay out".
2) Katrina allowed Bush to increase his "autocracy". In this scenario, Bush let chaos rule in New Orleans following the hurricane, because he then had an excuse to roll out **FEMA** and impose draconian policies on rioters. To quote

SwearBear, a member of the Above Top Secret forums, Katrina/New Orleans was a "beta test for the police state".

3) Yet another benefit to Bush from blowing up the levees was the resultant disruption to Louisiana's oil business, which in turn raised the price of crude. The Bush clan, of course, have close links to oil business.

It's a mad, mad world, my masters. Because there are just as many Katrina conspiracies that cite Bush's main enemy, Islamic terrorists of the **Osama bin Laden** stripe, as Bush himself as the responsible party. Why would al-Qaeda types blow up the New Orleans dykes? Payback for the USA's War on Terror against Afghanistan and Iraq.

Idaho TV weatherman Scott Stevens cites much older enemies of Uncle Sam as being the brains and brawn behind Katrina. Stevens maintains that Japan's Yakuza crime mob employed a Russian-made electromagnetic generator to cause Hurricane Katrina to avenge the Hiroshima atom bomb attack.

Other sources, however, propose that Katrina was not a human conspiracy, but an act of God. Every Islamic fanatic under the sun sees the hand of Allah pushing Katrina into the Big Easy, yet fundamentalist US evangelicals have been no less quick to suggest that Katrina was divine retribution on New Orleans, Louisiana's very own Sodom and Gomorrah. Well, it ain't called the Big Easy for nothing. Reverend Bill Shanks of the New Covenant Fellowship of New Orleans declared that post-Katrina: "New Orleans is abortion free ... Mardi Gras free ... free of the witchcraft and false religion. God purged all of that and now we start over again." Hallelujah.

Then again, there is a peculiarly Jewish take on Katrina. Rabbi Avraham Shmuel Lewin, executive director of the Rabbinic Congress for Peace, told WND, that Katrina was thrust upon the US for its support of the evacuation of Jews from the Gaza Strip: "The US should have discouraged Israeli Prime Minister Ariel Sharon from implementing the Gaza evacuation rather than pushing for it and pressuring Israel into concessions."

There is no credible evidence that any human agency caused Katrina or intentionally exploded the levees around N.O. The will of God is harder to divine. As for the tardiness of the US authorities in dealing with the post-Katrina mayhem in New Orleans, the stupidity and slowness of bureaucracy should never be underestimated.

> Bush/al-Qaeda/the Japanese Yakuza caused Hurricane Katrina: ALERT LEVEL 1

Further Reading
www.usatoday.com/weather/.../2005-09-20-wacky-weatherman

INDIAN OCEAN TSUNAMI

On Boxing Day 2004, a tsunami struck the Indian Ocean coastline of South-east Asia, killing almost 230,000 people. Like **Global Warming** and **Hurricane Katrina**, the disaster was widely attributed by conspiracists to a human agency.

A popular theory in the Muslim world is that the tsunami was unleashed by an Indian nuclear experiment. The test, conducted with Israeli/American help, took place in the earthquake-susceptible "Five Belt" area in the hope and expectation that the resultant giant wave – and it was giant, at 100 feet high – would impact on the heavily populated Muslim regions of south-east Asia, where the bulk of casualties did indeed take place. Journalist Mahmoud Bakri wrote in an Egyptian nationalist weekly that the Indian tsunami "appeared to be genuine American and Israeli preparations to act together with India to test a way to liquidate humanity. In the[ir] most recent test, they began destroying entire cities over extensive areas. Although the nuclear explosions were carried out in desert lands, tens of thousands of kilometers away from populated areas, they had a direct effect on these areas."

But "the Great Satan" never knowingly passes up an opportunity to getting his grasping Caucasian hands on oil, thus the nuclear experiment simultaneously allowed the USA to take control of the oil reserves in Aceh province, Indonesia. The first rescue reports from Aceh purportedly detailed the arrival of 2,000 marines and the contamination of local water supplies by radiation. The papers went inconveniently missing. Of course, no contemporary conspiracy featuring the USA is any good if it is **HAARP**-less, and sure enough it is frequently mooted in internet chat rooms that the High Frequency Active Auroral Research Program is to blame for the Boxing Day tsunami. Fuelling the belief that the tsunami was a US plot was the strange case of Diego Garcia. How did this US base manage to avoid casualties while other islands in the Indian Ocean suffered huge losses?

The US Navy's answer: the island wasn't damaged by the tsunami because it is surrounded by deep water and the grade of its shores prevents tsunamis building. Thus, the surge hitting the island was estimated at six-feet deep.

Conspiracy theories fingering the US/India/Israel as detonators of a nuclear bomb in the Indian Ocean tsunami flounder on this: there are hundreds of independent seismographers with state-of-the art kit the globe over, and none of them detected the signature of an atomic explosion. As for HAARP, it may be malicious in intent, it might even be effective – but powerful enough to trigger a tsunami? Unlikely. One scientist compared its power to putting the coil from a domestic immersion heater into the Yukon.

The Indian Ocean tsunami raised serious questions – chiefly about the efficacy of the area's warning systems – but whether the US and its acolytes dunnit isn't one of them.

US and/or its cronies deliberately triggered the Indian Ocean tsunami: ALERT LEVEL 2

IRS

Donald Duck a conspirator? Unlikely as it seems, Disney's famous cartoon character is alleged to be a player in the most successful financial conspiracy of all time.

It happened like this, according to Freedom Club USA. Two years into World War II, the US Federal Government realized that it was running out of moolah to best the Nazis and the Nipponese. To raise more lucre, Congress enacted into law the Victory Tax Act of 1942, a tax on income legitimized by reference to Article 1, Section 5, Clause 2 of the Constitution: "To support Armies but no apportionment for money to that use shall be a longer term than two years." But how to get Americans to pay up for these taxes?

Enter screen left Donald Duck. The Treasury approached Walt Disney, who was given six weeks to make a short film "selling income tax" for distribution in the cinemas. Disney came up with a short film in which Donald Duck listened to a radio broadcast about how paying taxes would help win the war. So enamoured with the idea of paying taxes did Donald become that he filled in his tax return pronto and raced from LA to Washington DC in person to submit it. "Taxes to beat the Axis!" quacked Donald.

Morgenthau, Secretary of the Treasury, disappointed that the short featured a cartoon character, only reluctantly approved it for release. He need not have worried; an estimated 60 million Americans saw the *The New Spirit* short, and a snap Gallup Poll discovered that voluntary payments of income tax increased by 37 per cent. A year later a Treasury official reported to Congress:

"Up until 1941 we never received as many as 8,000,000 individual income-tax returns in a year. In 1941 that number increased to 15,000,000; in 1942 it increased to 16,000,000. This year we expect 35,000,000 taxable individual income-tax returns."

Another Disney short featuring Donald Duck, *The Spirit of '43*, kept the money coming in. The Victory Tax Act was renewed in 1944 and was set to expire when the war was over. However, it remains in effect today, codified under the Internal Revenue Code at code section 3402 in subtitle C – Wage and Employment Tax. When WWII was over, Washington was simply unable to relinquish its new-found riches – the payroll tax the public had become accustomed to.

Tax, it may be said, is not a popular issue in the USA. On the morning of 18 February 2010, Andrew Joseph Stack III flew his single-engine Piper Dakota airplane at full speed into the IRS collections office in Austin, killing himself and one worker. Stack was on the libertarian right of American politics, but the Tax Protest movement spans the political spectrum: what binds it is the belief that income tax and the IRS are illegal. The words of the Tea Party Patriots will stand for the movement as a whole: "The Tea Party argues that even if the 16th Amendment to the US Constitution was properly ratified, which is debatable, the IRS still has no legal right to tax the income of American citizens."

This is why Disney's duck is a conspirator. He was part of a plot to persuade Americans to do something mandatory that should be something voluntary.

Actually, the two main claims of the tax protestors are dubious. Article 1 of the Constitution states unambiguously: "Congress shall have power to lay and collect taxes, duties, imposts and excises."

It was Article I that allowed Lincoln to raise the money to fight the South. Furthermore, the16th Amendment, signed into law in 1913, declares: "Congress shall have power to lay and collect taxes on incomes, from whatever source derived, without apportionment among the several States, and without regard to any census or enumeration."

Amendments to the US Constitution require the approval of 75 per cent of the States before they can become law. Officially,

79 per cent ratified the Amendment. Tax protestors, however, claim the ratification was invalid because the unhappily named Secretary, Philander Knox, ignored errors in the relevant documents, meaning the returns from these states were invalidated.

The documents do have errors; however, in the 1986 ruling on *US* v. *Thomas*, the Court ruled that the "deviations" were trivial and so "the [Solicitor of the Dept of State] authorized [Knox] to declare the amendment adopted".

Where the tax protestors have firmer ground under their feet is on the matter of subsequent revisions to the tax process. As one former IRS commissioner, Shirley Peterson, noted, "Eight decades of amendments ... to (the) code have produced a virtually impenetrable maze ... The rules are ... mysterious to many government employees who are charged with administering and enforcing the law."

Even the IRS cannot understand the IRS. Legitimate questions can also be raised about the IRS's behaviour and competence. In *Unbridled Power*, Shelley L. Davis, the IRS's first and last historian, laid bare a secretive organization which compiled lists of "enemies" and routinely destroyed records – a federal offence – which might prove incriminating or embarrassing. Before a Senate Finance Committee hearing, she testified that crucial IRS records, pertaining to government, states and individuals, "have been destroyed. Gone. Shredded. Tossed. They no longer exist ... No other agency of our government could get away with this ... Our fear of suffering a personal attack from the IRS generally keeps most of us in check ... This ensures that it can never be held accountable for its actions. How can you prove any wrongdoing when the evidence is already destroyed?"

How indeed? Fortunately, a few whistle-blowers, such as Davis herself, have done the right thing and spoken out. Some of the IRS's wrongdoing is staggering. At Nixon's request, it launched investigations of his opponents for his purely political purposes and no other reason at all. One such "enemy" was the Fund for Investigative Journalism, which funded Seymour Hersh's reporting on the My Lai massacre. In the words of Nixon's aide John Dean, the idea was to "use the available federal machinery to screw our political enemies".

> The IRS is engaged in a conspiracy against the American people to illegally gather income tax: ALERT LEVEL 4
>
> The IRS has conspired with Government in politically motivated attacks on US citizens and organizations: ALERT LEVEL 10

Further Reading
John A. Andrew III, *The Power to Destroy*, 2002
Shelley L. Davis, *Unbridled Power*, 1998
www.freedomclubusa.com/donald_duck_tax

ISRAELI BUBBLEGUM

In spring 1997, the Palestinian Authority reported on an Israeli plot fiendish in its machinations and consequences: to infiltrate into the West Bank and Gaza bubblegum laced with sex hormones to be sold at a discounted rate outside schools. The bubblegum aroused the sexual appetite of girls, but simultaneously sterilized them, suppressing Arab population growth. Worst of all, according to Palestinian Supply Minister Abdel Aziz Shaheen, it was capable of "completely destroying the genetic system of young boys".

According to Palestinian tests, the strawberry-flavoured gum was spiked with progesterone, one of the two hormones of femaleness. That Israel, an essentially Western society, should try to undermine Islamic morals with sex pills played on deep Palestinian fears.

The *Washington Post* commissioned tests on allegedly contaminated bubblegum. These tests were done by Dan Gibson, professor of pharmaceutical chemistry at Hebrew University and a member of the left-wing lobby group Peace Now (thus no Zionist). Using a mass spectrometer capable of detecting as little as a microgram of progesterone, he found no trace of the hormone in the gum.

In fairness, a story of adulterated food was not entirely implausible. Shady Israeli merchants, working in collaboration with Palestinian profiteers, had shipped canned baby food to Gaza which turned out to be soy formula past its sell by date. But weighing against the Palestinian bubblegum claim – aside from the *Washington Post*'s spectrometer test – was its timing: Israel and Palestine were in the middle of a propaganda war, with both sides making things up.

So, pop went the great Israeli bubblegum conspiracy. It blew up again in 2009 when Hamas charged Israeli intelligence operatives with distributing libido-increasing gum in the Gaza enclave. A Hamas police spokesman in the Gaza Strip, Islam Shahwan, announced: "The Israelis seek to destroy the Palestinians' social infrastructure with these products and to hurt the young generation by distributing drugs and sex stimulants."

Numerous teenage boys reportedly asked, "Where can I buy some of that gum?"

> Zionists plot to undermine Palestinian morals with spiked bubblegum: ALERT LEVEL 3

Further Reading
Barton Gellman, "Pop! Went the Tale of the Bubblegum Spiked with Sex Hormones", *Washington Post*, 28 July 1997

JACK THE RIPPER

Between August and November 1888, the Whitechapel district in the East End of London was the scene of five – possibly six – slayings by a serial killer, dubbed by the press "Jack the Ripper". The murdered were all female prostitutes, and all – except for Elizabeth Stride – were mutilated.

The first slaying, that of Polly Nicholls, took place on 31 August. Annie Chapman was murdered on 8 September. Elizabeth Stride and Catherine Eddowes were both killed on 30 September and Mary Jane Kelly on 9 November. These are the "canonical five" Ripper victims, although some "Ripperologists" consider that Martha Tabram, fatally stabbed on 6 August 1888, should also be included on the butcher's slate.

The identity of the perpetrator was, and is, a mystery. It is widely assumed that he (maybe she) had some medical training, based on the scalpel-like weapon used and the mutilations of the corpses, which showed a knowledge of anatomy. More than one hundred individuals have at some stage been proposed as the Ripper, but the most sensational suspect remains Prince Eddy, Duke of Clarence – the son of the Prince of Wales, third in line to the throne. Dr Thomas Stowell nominated Eddy as the Ripper in an article in *The Criminologist* in 1970, suggesting that Eddy's syphilis drove him insane, thus homicidal. Clearly a homicidal duke with a habit of mutilation was not good PR for the Royal Family, so they quickly bundled Eddy off to a private mental hospital, from which he briefly escaped to murder Mary Kelly, before being re-incarcerated. According to Stowell, Eddy died in the asylum of syphilitic "softening of the brain", and not of flu as the Palace claimed. The Duke of Clarence supposedly learned disembowelling techniques on hunting expeditions. The Prince Eddy accusation was substantially repeated by Frank Spiering in *Prince Jack*. Like Stowell, Spiering claims to have found the necessary proofs in the private papers of Sir William Withey Gull, the royal physician. Ripperologists, however, point out that royal court records show that Eddy was not in London on the dates of the murders.

As cause, rather than perpetrator, Prince Eddy figures in *Jack the Ripper: The Final Solution* by Stephen Knight, which posits a mass homicidal conspiracy instigated by the Royal Family to cover up Eddy's secret marriage to a commoner named Alice Mary Crook. And not just any old commoner, but a Catholic one, thus violating the 1701 Act of Settlement. In brief, Knight has Prince Eddy slumming it down the East End accompanied by artist Walter Sickert, where he meets, beds and marries Alice Crook. When Grandmama – who happens to be Queen Victoria – hears about the marriage and its issue, a baby girl, she is not only scandalized but fearful that the news that a Catholic is in line to the throne will cause riots in the streets of Britain. To keep the kingdom safe, Victoria orders Lord Salisbury to deal with the matter; in turn he enlists help of Sir William Gull (yes, him again) and Salisbury/Gull have Eddy and Alice kidnapped from their love nest on Cleveland Street, with Eddy hospitalized under Gull's care and Alice put in an asylum. Eddy dies from syphilis in 1892, and Alice dies insane in 1920. What about the Ripper murders? According to Knight, Eddy and Alice's daughter was being nannied by one Mary Kelly when the love nest was raided. She then committed the child to the care of nuns, before returning to the East End and falling into drink and prostitution. At the behest of her friends, Mary Kelly began blackmailing the Royal Family – their royal money for her silence over the Eddy and Alice tryst. To make absolutely certain Mary and her chums – Polly Nichols, Annie Chapman and Liz Stride – kept their mouths shut, Gull and his coachman, John Netley, murdered them all, plus Catherine Eddowes, whom they mistook for Kelly.

As a physician, Gull certainly had the knowledge to perform the spectacular dissection of Mary Kelly, who was skinned, her abdomen emptied, her womb placed at her feet. One of her

hands was placed in the evacuated abdominal cavity. Her intestines were placed over her left shoulder. Her heart was missing,
as was the foetus she was known to be carrying.

Gull, who died fifteen months after Kelly, escaped detection,
Knight believes, because the Assistant Commissioner of the
Metropolitan Police, Sir Robert Anderson, was a member of the
conspiracy. What bound the principal conspirators, aside from
their desire to carry out the royal will, was that they – Gull,
Salisbury, Anderson – were all Freemasons. Knight discloses
that the murders were actually re-enactments of the murder of
Mason Hirem Abiff in Solomon's Temple by Jubela, Jubelo and
Jubelum. The real evidence of the Masonic connection comes in
the placing of the victims in specific locations, most dramatically
that of Mitre Square, a "Mitre" and "Square" both being
Masonic tools.

Does Knight's book live up to its subtitle, *The Final Solution*?
Alas not. Knight's principal source of information was Joseph
Sickert, the artist's grandson. Joseph Sickert later recanted some
of his most sensational claims. William Gull was also six foot
tall, much taller than the eyewitness accounts of the Ripper. He
was also seventy years old at the time of the murders.

Additionally, there is nothing to suggest that Gull (or
Anderson) were Masons. It is also difficult to believe that the
Crown would have resorted to serial killing to protect itself when
invocation of the Royal Marriages Act would have set aside a
marriage between Eddy and Annie because it was illegal, Eddy
being underage and not having obtained the Queen's consent.
Lastly, almost all experts agree that the Ripper was insane. And
Dr Gull does not fit the profile.

> Members of the Royal Family committed/ instigated the
> Jack the Ripper murders: ALERT LEVEL 3

Further Reading
Stephen Knight, *Jack the Ripper: The Final Solution*, 1976
Donald Rumbelow, *The Complete Jack the Ripper*, 2004
www.casebook.org

MICHAEL JACKSON

Was Wacko Jacko whacked? The singer had not finished moon-walking off the mortal coil on 25 June 2009, before the w.w.w. went w-w-wild with rumours that he had been murdered. Iranian president Mahmoud Ahmadinejad took pole position in the suspect stakes, the reasoning being that the King of Pop's demise handily diverted media attention from his crackdown in Tehran to Bel Air. Ahmadinejad's rivals in responsibility for the deed were a criminal syndicate based in Russia, China, or was it Langley (HQ of the CIA), who controlled Jackson through his addiction to anaesthetics and raked in the moolah? Worried that Jackson was seeking to escape their nefarious clutches and go public, the gang/CIA had him bumped.

Theories that Jackson was murdered are rivalled only by the theories that Jackson is alive and well. Jacko is hanging out with Elvis south of the border, down Mexico way. The kings live! Why did Jackson fake his own death? Pressure of fame. Money. Or more precisely its lack. The hit-meister may have sold 61 million albums in the USA, but he was still in the red to the tune of $400 million. Aside from his habit of spending, spending, spending (the Neverland Ranch cost $14.6 million alone), his bank account had been sucked dry by lawsuits over his alleged child abuse. As conspiracists have it, by counterfeiting his death, Jacko could settle all his debts and still make money. Indeed, by demising, he would rekindle interest in his music, making it a very smart career move indeed. Death also had the advantage of being an inviolable excuse for cancelling his fifty-date comeback tour in the UK, which was shaping up to be Bad rather than a

Thriller due his ill health. To take Jackson's place on the mortuary slab, he and his accomplices (his family, chiefly) found a terminally ill double. To make sure nobody noticed the switch, the family therefore cancelled the announced lying in state at Neverland.

However, some think M. J. Jackson died of natural causes years before, and his body was rushed into a makeshift grave at Neverland. The police – who were afterwards paid handsomely to keep their lips sealed – had no difficulty in identifying the corpse because it was wearing a single glove. An impersonator then took over the singing duties. When he outlived his usefulness he was offed, and it is *his* body that was found on 25 June 2009.

Rewind to reality: Jackson died while in his bed at his rented mansion at 100 North Carolwood Drive in the Holmby Hills district of Los Angeles. The Los Angeles coroner's office – which is considered expert on these things – carried out a post-mortem and expressed no doubts that the body was a) Michael Jackson and b) dead. At time of writing, Jackson's physician, Conrad Murray, is on trial for involuntary manslaughter on the grounds that he had improperly supplied Jackson with the surgical anaesthetic propofol as a sedative. Jackson was reputedly addicted to the drug, which he called his "mother's milk". Jackson died of an acute overdose of propofol. Murray's crime was not malicious, neither was it part of a conspiracy. He breached medical standards by supplying the drug as a sleep aid and failing to monitor his patient.

This is it: Jackson's death was an accident.

The King of Pop was murdered: ALERT LEVEL 3

Further Reading
www.michaeljacksonsightings.com

DR DAVID KELLY

Those implicated in the 2003 demise of Dr David Kelly include the Iraqi secret service, the French secret service, and not least, Kelly himself. Whatever the truth about his death, he was as much a victim of the war in Iraq as any soldier or civilian killed on the battlefield.

The confusion, briefings and counter-briefings that surrounded the days running up to the invasion of Iraq in 2002 and early 2003 created a nervousness and state of tension which caused all parties involved to act in unpredictable ways. During this time the UK Government released two dossiers which set out evidence for its belief that Saddam Hussein's regime posed a real threat to world security: the September 2002 document which stated that Iraq possessed weapons of mass destruction (WMDs) and that, crucially, these weapons could be deployed within forty-five minutes; and a second, in February 2003, which detailed secret arms networks. A month later the UK had deployed troops in Iraq to secure Hussein's downfall in spite of vocal protests from the Government's own MPs and many other groups.

On 20 May 2003, BBC Radio's flagship current affairs programme *Today* featured a report from its defence correspondent, Andrew Gilligan, in which he revealed that a senior source at the Ministry of Defence accused a member of the Downing Street press office (later identified as Alastair Campbell) of having "sexed up" the September dossier by inserting the information about the 45-minute deployment. The BBC's *Newsnight* correspondent Susan Watts also reported that a "senior official" believed the intelligence services came under heavy political pressure to include the 45-minute claim in its dossier.

The Government, enraged by the leak, demanded that Gilligan reveal his source, and weeks of accusation and counter-accusation began, with the BBC defending Gilligan and the anonymity of his source and the Government's press machine attempting to discredit the story. Richard Sambrook, the BBC's director of news, described the attacks as "an unprecedented level of pressure from Downing Street". Both Gilligan and Campbell were asked to appear before the Foreign Affairs Select Committee (FAC) to explain their actions.

The media frenzy must have worried Dr Kelly, who wrote to his line manager at the ministry admitting he had met Gilligan on 22 May and could have been one of the sources for his story. After another ten days of increasing pressure to reveal the identity of the source, the MoD then identified Kelly indirectly by pointedly refusing to deny he was involved when a list of possible sources was read out at a press conference, although Kelly himself was not informed his name was being released to the press.

On 15 and 16 July Dr Kelly sat in front of the FAC facing allegations that it was he who had been the source of the Gilligan story. He appeared deeply uncomfortable at being the centre of so much public attention, and spoke so softly that air-conditioning fans had to be turned off so the committee members could hear what he was saying. Despite much probing, Kelly maintained that, although he had spoken to Gilligan, he had not been his primary source. Kelly said the controversial point about the 45-minute deployment claim being added by Alastair Campbell could not have come from him as he had no part in the actual compilation of the dossier, but had merely presented information for possible inclusion, and thus had not been party to the decisions by the Joint Intelligence Committee, who had produced the document.

At the end of the two days the FAC had concluded that Kelly was "most unlikely" to be the source of the "sexed-up" claim. Kelly, too, had relaxed, and was laughing and joking with the committee members.

The following day, 17 July, he left his home at 3.00 p.m., telling his wife he was going for his usual afternoon walk. He did not return. At 11.45 p.m. his family contacted the police and reported him missing. He was found at 9.20 the next morning by two search volunteers in woods on Harrowdown Hill, about a mile and a half (2.5 km) from his home. The police did not confirm the body as his until 19 July, and then stated that they believed he had committed suicide by taking the powerful pain-killer co-proxamol and then cutting his left wrist. A day later, after talking to his family, the BBC issued a statement naming Dr Kelly as the source of both Gilligan's and Watts's reports.

In the light of the previous train of events and unusual vigour with which the Government had pursued Andrew Gilligan and his source, it seems understandable that an independent inquiry into the whole affair was announced as the best way of uncover-ing the truth surrounding Kelly's death and the lingering accu-sation that Downing Street had tampered with intelligence reports. Lord Hutton was appointed to head the inquiry, and his inquiry heard several months' worth of evidence from experts, Kelly's friends and family, and members of the Cabinet, includ-ing Tony Blair. Five months later, after much hype and specula-tion, Hutton concluded that the Government had behaved properly, that the BBC should be heavily criticized for its actions, and that Kelly's death had been by his own hand.

There, it was presumably hoped, is where the whole unfortu-nate episode would end, but there were some who pointed to inconsistencies in the official version of events. Many people who had been close to Kelly, professionally and personally, did not believe the suicide story, and others believed his death bore all the hallmarks of a planned assassination.

The first to speak publicly of their misgivings were the two paramedics who had attended the scene of Dr Kelly's death, Paul Bartlett and Vanessa Hunt. Interviewed by Anthony Barnett in the *Observer* in December 2004, they said they found little or no evidence of the major bleeding that would have taken place if the severed wrist artery had been the cause of death, as stated by the pathologist. "When somebody cuts an artery, whether accidentally or intentionally, the blood pumps every-where. I just think it is incredibly unlikely that he died from the wrist wound we saw," said Hunt.

The paramedics' views were soon supported by a group of doctors who wrote to the *Guardian* newspaper, saying they too were deeply unhappy with the official cause of death. The severed ulnar artery, they argued, was too thin to have allowed a major haemorrhage, especially as, out in the open, the blood vessel would have been closed off by surrounding muscle long before Kelly bled to death. David Halpin, a trauma surgeon and one of the authors of the letter, maintains that even the deepest cut in the region of the ulnar artery would not have caused death: " ... a completed transacted artery retracts immediately and thus stops bleeding, even at a relatively high blood pressure". The artery itself lies deep in the wrist on the little finger side of the hand, under other nerves and tendons, and cannot be accidentally slashed like the more superficial radial artery. Following the suicide theory would mean believing Kelly had managed to cut down deep into his own wrist to locate and cut the ulnar artery ... with a blunt pruning knife.

The physicians also questioned the toxicology results, pointing out that the concentration of the drug co-proxamol in Kelly's blood was not high enough to have killed him, being only a third of a fatal dose. Kelly's stomach was virtually empty on examination, containing the equivalent of a fifth of one tablet, suggesting that, if he did swallow the cited twenty-nine tablets, he had regurgitated most of them before the drug could be absorbed.

As suicides go, this was a pretty amateurish affair, considering Kelly must have had an intimate knowledge of human biology in his work as a microbiologist and authority on biological weapons. He was the only person to die using these methods in the whole of 2003. Co-proxamol is often used in suicide attempts but most commonly in conjunction with alcohol. Severing the ulnar artery does not automatically lead to a fatal loss of blood. Kelly is known to have had an aversion to swallowing tablets. If his suicide was premeditated, why bring a small blunt concave-edged knife to do a tricky slicing job, along with the tablets? And if it was a spontaneous act, why did he bring thirty painkilling tablets with him on his daily constitutional?

As if there were not enough mystery surrounding the suicide, it became apparent during the Hutton Inquiry that there were other major discrepancies. The volunteers who found Dr Kelly's body said he was sitting or slumped against a tree when they discovered him, but in his evidence DC Coe of the Thames Valley Police stated Kelly was flat on his back and away from the tree. The volunteers swore that the knife, an opened bottle of Evian and a watch were not present when they were there, but these items had appeared next to the body by the time DC Coe left the scene.

As any viewer of TV crime will know, most solved cases are so because of the work of the forensics people, but in this case there was surprisingly little forensic evidence forthcoming. For instance, whose fingerprints were on the knife? Was any foreign DNA detected in the blood samples? Was the watch found beside Dr Kelly broken or intact, and, if broken, what time did it show? What were the last calls made to him on his mobile phone? None of these questions was asked during the inquiry, and no answers were volunteered.

In March 2005, Lib Dem MP Norman Baker resigned his front bench job expressly to investigate the circumstances surrounding Kelly's death. A year later he published his findings on his own website and contributed to a BBC TV programme, *Conspiracy Files*, which focused on Kelly. Baker voiced his serious doubts over the conclusion of the inquiry, not only on the basis of the medical evidence and the suicide verdict but also concerning the "irregularities in the actions of the coroner", the choice of the pathologist, the actions of the police at the beginning of the investigation, and why Lord Hutton, in particular, was picked to head the inquiry.

Baker questions why the Lord Chancellor, Lord Falconer, decided the inquiry should not be held under the usual rules, so that witnesses could not be subpoenaed, nor did they have to give evidence under oath, making the whole procedure less rigorous than a standard coroner inquest. Even more bizarrely, the Oxfordshire coroner, Nicholas Gardiner, pre-empted the findings of the inquiry by issuing a full death certificate on 18 August, while Hutton's investigation was still in its early stages, in spite of rules stating that at most only an interim certificate should be issued while an inquest is in adjournment. Baker doesn't think much of the appointed pathologist either, describing the medical evidence presented by him to the inquiry as "incomplete, inconsistent and inadequate".

As for the conduct of the police force, the most puzzling fact that has come to light has been that Operation Mason, as it was named, began at 2.30 p.m. on 17 July, about nine hours before Dr Kelly's family reported him missing and half an hour before he left his home to go for his walk. Quite how the police knew what was going to happen, they are not willing to divulge. Nor are they willing to say why they found it necessary to erect a 45-foot-high (15.7 m) antenna in the Kellys' garden, or turn Mrs Kelly out of her home in the middle of the night for some considerable time while a search dog was put through the house. According to Baker, one of the most senior police officers in the country, on being consulted, was at a loss as to why either action would have been required.

Norman Baker reserves particular scepticism for the choice of Lord Hutton to head the inquiry and the part Tony Blair played in the decision. In spite of being on a jet somewhere between Washington and Tokyo when formally advised of Dr Kelly's death, Blair decided on an inquiry and appointed Lord Brian Hutton as its head even before the journey was over. Parliament, perhaps rather conveniently, had adjourned for the summer, and the appointment was made on the advice of Lord Falconer and, Baker suspects, Peter Mandelson. The man they chose had no experience of chairing any other public inquiry but, during his distinguished career, plenty of history of upholding the views of the government of the day.

It was highly unlikely, therefore, that the Hutton Inquiry (see Document, p.226) was going to answer such sticky questions as why a highly respected scientist chose to take his life in quite such an unconventional way, days after being embroiled in a political scandal that was potentially deeply damaging to the Government. Kelly had been deeply upset by being thrust into the media spotlight and, no doubt, bewildered by the MoD's decision to leak his name to the press. However, he was also cheerful and joky with members of the Foreign Affairs Select Committee the day before his death, and had made plans to fly to Iraq the following week; one of his daughters was looking forward to her impending wedding day. Most importantly, perhaps, he was a practising member of the Baha'i faith, which forbids the act of suicide.

An email to a New York journalist, Judith Miller, on the morning of 17 July suggests that Dr Kelly realized that there was something worrying going on behind the soundbites and political posturing:

> David, I heard from another member of your fan club that things went well for you today. Hope it's true.
> (Original message sent by Judith Miller, 16 July 00.30)

> I will wait until the end of the week before judging – many dark actors playing games.
> Thanks for your support. I appreciate your friendship at this time.
> (Dr Kelly's reply, sent 17 July 11.18)

Conspiracy theorists believe Kelly had been labelled a loose cannon and as such a threat to the stability of the Government. If Britain lost Blair, Europe lost an important ally in its struggle for greater political and economic union. Michael Shrimpton, a barrister and intelligence services expert who also acted for the Kelly Investigation Group, claimed he was told Kelly had been assassinated. Speaking in an interview with Canadian broadcaster Alex Jones in 2004 he said: "Within forty-eight hours of the murder I was contacted by a British Intelligence officer who told me [Kelly had] been murdered ... now that source told me he'd done some digging and discovered that, he didn't name names, but he discovered that it had been known in Whitehall prior to 17 July that David Kelly was going to be taken down."

Shrimpton went on to explain that clever governments get the secret services of their allies to do their dirty work for them, and that Kelly's death bore all the hallmarks of a job by the DGSE (Direction Générale de la Sécurité Extérieure), the French equivalent of MI6. The tablets found in Kelly's pocket would have been a cover; he would actually have been killed by a lethal injection of dextropropoxythene, the active ingredient of co-proxamol, and the muscle relaxant succinylcholine, "a favourite method" of murder by intelligence services, with his wrist clumsily cut to disguise the needle's puncture mark. Shrimpton said the assassination team would most likely have been recruited from Iraqis living in Damascus, to disguise French involvement, and then its members killed after the event to ensure absolute secrecy.

There are others, such as UN weapons inspector Richard Spertzel, who claim it was the Iraqis themselves who killed Dr Kelly in revenge for all the trouble he'd brought upon Saddam Hussein's regime through his work. This seems far-fetched. Although Kelly had said he supported the invasion of Iraq, he had not been the author of the 45-minute claim that had precipitated military action. And he had only recently inspected trailers, claimed to be bio-weapons laboratories, and declared them to be no such thing. More hard-line conspiracy theorists maintain Dr Kelly's death was yet another in a suspicious pattern of untimely deaths among the world's leading microbiologists, who are being systematically bumped off for reasons that remain unclear.

However weird the theories, Kelly's death was not properly investigated. The glaring omissions and conflicts of evidence; the choice of an inquiry headed by a judge rather than a coroner, with terms drawn up at the outset by the Government; the continuing unease of expert doctors and political figures, willing to risk their own reputations to publicize their misgivings – all this suggests there is far more to this event than the Government is willing to be open about.

In 2009 a group of British doctors – including Michael Powers, who was also a former coroner – challenged Hutton's verdict in the press, stating instead that in their view the slash on the wrist was untenable as the cause of death, because the artery is small, difficult to access and would not have allowed sufficient loss. Another group of medics rallied to Hutton's defence in the *Guardian*, asserting that Kelly's heart disease meant only a small amount of blood loss would bring death.

Like the WMD case for war itself, theories and counter-theories about Kelly's death will run and run.

> WMD whistle-blower David Kelly was "suicided": ALERT LEVEL 8

DOCUMENT: LORD HUTTON, *REPORT OF THE INQUIRY INTO THE CIRCUMSTANCES SURROUNDING THE DEATH OF DR DAVID KELLY C.M.G.,* 2004 [EXTRACT]

CHAPTER 5

The search for Dr Kelly and the finding of his body
128. Dr Kelly did not return from his walk and Mrs Kelly, who was joined by two of her daughters during the course of the evening (her third daughter being in Scotland), became increasingly worried about him. Mrs Kelly's two daughters went out separately in their cars to look for their father on the roads and lanes along which he might have been walking, but when they had found no trace of him they rang the police about 12.20 a.m. on Friday 18 July.

129. The Thames Valley Police began an immediate search for Dr Kelly and the search operation was carried out with great efficiency. A police dog was used to assist in the search and a police helicopter with heat seeking equipment was called in. Assistant Chief Constable Michael Page was informed that Dr Kelly was missing at 3.09 a.m. and he arranged a meeting of key personnel at Abingdon Police Station at 5.15 a.m. By 7.30 a.m. 40 police officers were engaged in the search and Assistant Chief Constable Page was advised by two police specialists in the location of missing persons that Harrowdown Hill, which was an area where Dr Kelly had often walked, was an area to which particular attention should be given in the search. Assistant Chief Constable Page then directed that the area of Harrowdown Hill should be searched and members of the South East Berks Emergency Volunteers and the Lowland Search Dogs Association, who had joined the search, were deployed to Harrowdown Hill.

130. Two of the volunteers taking part in the search were Ms Louise Holmes, with her trained search dog, and Mr Paul

Chapman. They worked together as a team and began their search about 8.00 a.m. and after a time they went into the wood on Harrowdown Hill from the east side. The dog picked up a scent and Ms Holmes followed him. Ms Holmes saw the dog go to the bottom of a tree and he then ran back to her barking to indicate that he had found something. She then went in the direction from which the dog had come and she saw a body slumped against the bottom of a tree. She shouted to Mr Chapman, who was behind her, to ring control to tell them that something had been found and she went closer to see if there was any first aid which she could administer. She saw the body of a man at the base of the tree with his head and shoulders slumped back against it. His legs were straight in front of him, his right arm was at his side and his left arm had a lot of blood on it and was bent back in a strange position. It was apparent to her that the man was dead and there was nothing she could do to help him. The person matched the description of Dr Kelly which she had previously been given by the police. Ms Holmes then went back to Mr Chapman, retracing the route by which she had come into the wood although there was no definite path or track by which she had approached the tree.

131. Mr Chapman had been unable to contact control so he made a 999 call to speak to Abingdon Police Station and arranged to walk back to where he and Ms Holmes had parked their car in order to meet the police officers who were coming to meet them. On the way back to their car they met three other police officers who themselves had been engaged in searching the area and Mr Chapman told them that they had found the body. Mr Chapman then took one of the police officers, Detective Constable Coe, to show him where the body was. Mr Chapman showed Detective Constable Coe the body lying on its back and Detective Constable Coe said that the body was approximately 75 yards in from the edge of the wood. Detective Constable Coe saw that there was blood around the left wrist and he saw a knife, like a pruning knife, and a watch on the left side of the body. He also saw a small

water bottle. He remained about seven or eight feet away from the body and stayed in that position for about 25 or 30 minutes until two other police officers arrived who made a taped off common approach path to be used by everyone who came to the place where the body was lying. Two members of an ambulance crew, Ms Vanessa Hunt and Mr David Bartlett arrived at the scene about 9.55 a.m. They checked the body for signs of life and found none. They then placed four electrodes on the chest to verify that life was extinct and the monitor showed that there was no cardiac output and that life was extinct. They then disconnected the four electrodes from the heart monitor and left them on the chest and they themselves left the scene.

The investigations into the death of Dr Kelly

132. Assistant Chief Constable Page was informed at 9.20 a.m. that the body had been found. In his evidence he described the actions which he took and which were taken by others on his instructions as follows:

Q. What happened after that information had come to your attention?

A. Well, from my perspective I appointed a senior investigating officer, a man who would, if you like, carry out the technical issues around the investigation. I met fairly quickly with my Chief Constable and we decided what levels of resourcing and what levels of investigation we should apply to these circumstances.

Q. The fact that a body had been discovered, what sort of inquiry did you launch at the start?

A. We determined from the outset because of the attendant circumstances that we would apply the highest standards of investigation to this particular set of circumstances as was possible. I would not say I launched a murder investigation but the investigation was of that standard.

Q. We have heard how a common access path was established yesterday.

A. Yes.

Q. And the fingertip searching was carried out. Did forensic pathologists become involved?

A. Yes. We were very anxious, from the outset, to ensure the most thorough possible examination of the scene. I spoke to the Oxfordshire coroner, Mr Gardiner, and we agreed between us that we would use a Home Office pathologist, which is a very highly trained pathologist. It was also agreed with the senior investigating officer that we would use forensic biologists who are able to look at the scene and, in particular, blood splashes and make certain determinations from those in relation to what may have happened. As you say, a common approach path had been established; and it was determined that for that common approach path and for a distance of 10 metres either side and for a radius of 10 metres around Dr Kelly's body that we would carry out a fingertip search. It was also agreed that Dr Kelly's body would be left in situ so that the pathologist and the biologists could visit the scene with the body in situ to make their own assessment of the scene, which is not always the case but in this case we decided it would be wise to do so.

Q. Why was that, just to ensure—

A. Just to ensure that they could look at the environment and the surroundings and take in the full picture.

133. The detailed examinations which were carried out on the body at the place where it was found and of the area surrounding the body in the wood were as follows. Police search teams led by Police Constable Franklin and Police Constable Sawyer conducted a thorough fingertip search of the common approach path of the area surrounding the body and of the area on either side of the approach path. After the body had been moved they also conducted a fingertip search of the ground on which the body had been lying. This search lasted from 12.50 p.m. to 4.45 p.m. and the search of the ground on which the body had lain lasted from 7.24 p.m. to 7.45 p.m. Nothing of significance was found in the searches and Constable Sawyer said:

When I first saw Dr Kelly I was very aware of the serious nature of the search and I was looking for signs of perhaps a struggle; but all the vegetation that was surrounding Dr Kelly's body was standing upright and there were no signs of any form of struggle at all.

134. Dr Nicholas Hunt, a Home Office accredited forensic pathologist arrived at the place where the body was lying at 12.10 p.m. and at 12.35 p.m. he confirmed that the body was dead. He then waited whilst the police carried out a fingertip search of the common approach path and he then began a thorough investigation of the body at 2.10 p.m. After this examination of the body at the scene and after a post-mortem examination, Dr Hunt furnished a detailed post-mortem report dated 25 July 2003 to the Oxfordshire coroner and at the Inquiry he gave evidence in accordance with his findings set out in that report.

135. Dr Kelly was right handed. In a statement furnished to the Inquiry Police Constable Roberts stated:

On Saturday 19th July 2003, I was on duty performing the role of Family Liaison Officer for Thames Valley Police.
    On this date I spoke to Sian KELLY, the daughter of Dr David KELLY who confirmed that her father was right handed.

136. In the course of his evidence Dr Hunt gave (inter alia) the following evidence:
A. He was wearing a green Barbour type wax jacket and the zip and the buttons at the front had been undone. Within the bellows pocket on the lower part of the jacket there was a mobile telephone and a pair of bi-focal spectacles. There was a key fob and, perhaps more significantly, a total of three blister packs of a drug called Coproxamol. Each of those packs would originally have contained 10 tablets, a total of 30 potentially available.
Q. And how many tablets were left in those packs?

A. There was one left.

LORD HUTTON: Did you actually take those blister packs out? Did you discover them in the pocket yourself?

A. Yes, as part of the search, my Lord.

Q. Did you notice anything about the face?

A. His face appeared, firstly, rather pale but there was also what looked like vomit running from the right corner of the mouth and also from the left corner of the mouth and streaking the face.

Q. What would that appear to indicate?

A. It suggested that he had tried to vomit whilst he was lying on his back and it had trickled down.

Q. Did you investigate the scene next to the body?

A. Yes.

Q. And what did that show?

A. There was a Barbour flat-type cap with some blood on the lining and the peak near his left shoulder and upper arm. In the region of his left hand lying on the grass there was a black resin strapped wristwatch, a digital watch, which was also bloodstained.

Q. Was the watch face up or face down?

A. It was face down.

Q. What about next to the watch?

A. Lying next to that was a pruning knife or gardener's knife.

Q. Can you describe what type of pruning knife it was?

A. The make was a Sandvig knife. It was one with a little hook or lip towards the tip of the blade. It is a fairly standard gardener's type knife.

Q. Were there any bloodstains on that knife?

A. Yes, over both the handle and the blade.

Q. Was there any blood beneath the knife?

A. Yes, there was. There was blood around the area of the knife.

Q. How close to the knife was the blood?

A. It was around the knife and underneath it.

Q. Did you notice a bottle of water?

A. Yes, there was a bottle of Evian water, half a litre.

Q. Was there any water in that bottle?

A. Yes, there was some remaining water. I do not recall what volume exactly.

Q. Can you remember precisely where the bottle was in relation to the bottle? [sic]

A. Yes, it was lying propped against some broken branches to the left and about a foot away from his left elbow.

Q. And did you notice anything in particular about the bottle?

A. Yes, there was some smeared blood over both the bottle itself and the bottle top.

Q. Did that indicate anything to you?

A. It indicated that he had been bleeding whilst at least placing the bottle in its final position. He may already have been bleeding whilst he was drinking from it, but that is less certain.

Q. Was there any other bloodstaining that you noticed in the area?

A. There was. There was an area of bloodstaining to his left side running across the undergrowth and the soil and I estimated it was over an area of 2 to 3 feet in maximum length.

Q. Did you notice any signs of visible injury to the body while you were there?

A. Yes. At the scene I could see that there were at least five what I would call incised wounds or cuts to his left wrist over what is anatomically the front of the wrist, but that is the creased area of the wrist.

Q. Were there any other visible signs of injury to the body?

A. No, there was nothing at the scene.

137. At 7.19 p.m. Dr Hunt ended his examination of the body at the scene where it was found and the body was moved to the John Radcliffe Hospital in Oxford where Dr Hunt commenced a post-mortem examination at 9.20 p.m. The examination concluded at 12.15 a.m. on 19 July. In describing what he found on his post-mortem examination Dr Hunt gave (inter alia) the following evidence:

Q. On this further examination, did you find any signs of injury to the body that you have not already mentioned?

A. I did. I was able to note in detail the injuries over his left wrist in particular.

Q. You have made a report, a post-mortem examination report?

A. Yes.

Q. Would you just like to read from the significant parts of that in relation to the injuries you found?

A. Certainly. There was a series of incised wounds, cuts, of varying depth over the front of the left wrist and they extended in total over about 8 by 5 centimetres on the front of the wrist. The largest of the wounds and the deepest lay towards the top end or the elbow end of that complex of injuries and it showed a series of notches and some crushing of its edges. That wound had actually severed an artery on the little finger aspect of the front of the wrist, called the ulnar artery.

The other main artery on the wrist on the thumb aspect was intact. There were a number of other incisions of varying depth and many smaller scratch-like injuries over the wrist. The appearance that they gave was of what are called tentative or hesitation marks, which are commonly seen prior to a deep cut being made into somebody's skin if they are making the incision themselves.

Q. Did you see any signs of what are called defensive injuries?

A. No, there were no signs of defensive injuries; and by that I mean injuries that occur as a result of somebody trying to parry blows from a weapon or trying to grasp a weapon.

Q. What injuries would you normally expect to see of that type?

A. If somebody is being attacked with a bladed weapon, like a knife, then cuts on the palm of the hand or over the fingers where they are trying to grasp the knife, or cuts or even stabs on the outer part of the arm as they try to parry a blow.

138. In his evidence Dr Hunt stated that he had sent a sample of the stomach contents to a forensic toxicologist, Dr Alexander Allan, and he received a toxicology report back

from Dr Allan. He described what this report showed as
follows:

Q. In summary what did it show?
A. It showed the presence of two compounds in particular.
One of them is a drug called dextropropoxyphene. That is an
opiate-type drug, it is a mild painkiller, and that was present
at a concentration of one microgram per millilitre in the
blood.
Q. Did it show anything, this report, in summary?
A. Yes, it did. It showed the presence of paracetamol.
Q. The concentration of that?
A. 97 milligrams per millilitre.
Q. Where was that present in the body?
A. It was also present in the stomach contents, as well as the
blood.

139. With reference to the estimated time of death Dr Hunt's
evidence was as follows:

Q. Were you able to estimate the time of death?
A. Yes, within certain limits, using a particular technique
based upon the rectal temperature.
Q. What time of death did you estimate as a result of that?
A. The estimate is that death is likely to have occurred some
18 to 27 hours prior to taking the rectal temperature, and that
that time range was somewhere between quarter past 4 on
17th July and quarter past 1 on the morning of the 18th July.
Q. You took the rectal temperature at what time?
A. That was taken at quarter past 7 in the evening of the 18th.

140. In his evidence Dr Hunt summarised his conclusions as
a result of his examinations as follows:

I found that Dr Kelly was an apparently adequately nourished
man in whom there was no evidence of natural disease that
could of itself have caused death directly at the macroscopic or
naked eye level. He had evidence of a significant incised wound

to his left wrist, in the depths of which his left ulnar artery had been completely severed. That wound was in the context of multiple incised wounds over the front of his left wrist of varying length and depth. The arterial injury had resulted in the loss of a significant volume of blood as noted at the scene. The complex of incised wounds over the left wrist is entirely consistent with having been inflicted by a bladed weapon, most likely candidate for which would have been a knife. Furthermore, the knife present at the scene would be a suitable candidate for causing such injuries. The orientation and arrangement of the wounds over the left wrist are typical of self-inflicted injury. Also typical of this was the presence of small so-called tentative or hesitation marks. The fact that his watch appeared to have been removed deliberately in order to facilitate access to the wrist. The removal of the watch in that way and indeed the removal of the spectacles are features pointing towards this being an act of self harm.

Other features at the scene which would tend to support this impression include the relatively passive distribution of the blood, the neat way in which the water bottle and its top were placed, the lack of obvious signs of trampling of the under- growth or damage to the clothing. To my mind, the location of the death is also of interest in this respect because it was clearly a very pleasant and relatively private spot of the type that is sometimes chosen by people intent upon self harm.

Q. Is that something you have found from your past experience?

A. Yes, and knowledge of the literature. Many of the injuries over the left wrist show evidence of a well developed vital reaction which suggests that they had been inflicted over a reasonable period of time, minutes, though, rather than seconds or many hours before death.

LORD HUTTON: What do you mean by a "vital reaction"?

A. A vital reaction, my Lord, is the body's response to an area of damage. It manifests itself chiefly in the form of reddening and swelling around the area.

LORD HUTTON: I interrupted you. You were at 9 and you are coming on to 10, I think.

A. Thank you, my Lord. There is a total lack of classical defence wounds against sharp weapon attack. Such wounds are typically seen in the palm aspects of the hands or over the outer aspects of the forearms. It was noted that he has a significant degree of coronary artery disease and this may have played some small part in the rapidity of death but not the major part in the cause of death.

Given the finding of blister packs of Coproxamol tablets within the coat pocket and the vomitus around the ground, it is an entirely reasonable supposition that he may have consumed a quantity of these tablets either on the way to or at the scene itself.

Q. What did the toxicology report suggest?

A. That he had consumed a significant quantity of the tablets.

Q. I am not going to trouble you with the details of the toxicology report. Was there anything else in addition to the toxicology samples that you noticed?

A. (Pause). Really the only other thing in addition to that was the coronary artery disease that could have had a part in the rapidity of death in these circumstances.

Q. You have mentioned the minor injury to the inner aspect of the lip.

A. Yes.

Q. Moving on from that, you mentioned the abrasions to the head. Would you like to resume your summary at that point?

A. Yes. The minor injuries or abrasions over the head are entirely consistent with scraping against rough undergrowth such as small twigs, branches and stones which were present at the scene.

LORD HUTTON: Did you give any consideration or do anything in relation to the possibility of Dr Kelly having been overpowered by any substance?

A. Yes, indeed, my Lord. The substances which one thinks of, as a pathologist, in these terms are volatile chemicals. Perhaps chloroform is a classic example. So in order to investigate that—

LORD HUTTON: You need not go into the detail but if you state it in a general way.

A. I retained a lung and also blood samples until the toxicology was complete.

LORD HUTTON: And the purpose of that toxicology being?

A. To examine for any signs of a volatile chemical in the blood or, failing that, in the lungs.

LORD HUTTON: Yes, I see. Thank you.

Yes, Mr Knox.

MR KNOX: If you move on to conclusion 18.

A. Certainly. The minor reddened lesions on the lower limbs are typical of areas of minor hair follicle irritation or skin irritation, so they were not injuries in particular. They were not puncture wounds.

Q. Conclusion 19?

A. I had undertaken subcutaneous dissection of the arms and the legs and there is no positive evidence of restraint-type injury.

Q. Conclusion 20?

A. There is no positive pathological evidence that this man had been subjected to a sustained violent assault prior to his death.

LORD HUTTON: Just going back to your previous observation, a restraint-type injury of someone who has been held by the arms and the legs.

A. Yes, my Lord. Yes, particularly around the areas of the ankles and the wrists.

LORD HUTTON: Yes. Yes. Thank you.

MR KNOX: Conclusion 21?

A. There was no positive pathological evidence to indicate that he has been subjected to compression of the neck, such as by manual strangulation, ligature strangulation or the use of an arm hold.

Q. And next?

A. There is no evidence from the post-mortem examination or my observations at the scene to indicate that the deceased had been dragged or otherwise transported to the location where his body was found.

141. Dr Hunt summarised his opinion as to the major factor involved in Dr Kelly's death as follows:

Q. And in summary, what is your opinion as to the major factor involved in Dr Kelly's death?
A. It is the haemorrhage as a result of the incised wounds to his left wrist.
Q. If that had not occurred, would Dr Kelly have died?
A. He may not have done at this time, with that level of dextropropoxyphene.
Q. What role, if any, did the coronary disease play?
A. As with the drug dextropropoxyphene, it would have hastened death rather than caused it, as such.
Q. So how would you summarise, in brief, your conclusions as to the cause of death?
A. In the formulation, the cause of death is given as 1(a) haemorrhage due to 1(b) incised wounds of the left wrist. Under part 2 of the formulation of the medical cause of death, Coproxamol ingestion and coronary artery atherosclerosis.
Q. You have already dealt with this, I think, but could you confirm whether, as far as you could tell on the examination, there was any sign of third party involvement in Dr Kelly's death?
A. No, there was no pathological evidence to indicate the involvement of a third party in Dr Kelly's death. Rather, the features are quite typical, I would say, of self-inflicted injury if one ignores all the other features of the case.

142. A forensic biologist, Mr Roy Green, arrived at the scene where the body was lying at 2.00 p.m. on 18 July. He examined the scene with particular reference to the bloodstaining in the area. The relevant parts of his evidence are as follows:

Q. Did you examine the vegetation around the body?
A. Yes.
Q. Did you form any conclusions from that examination?
A. Well, the bloodstaining that was highest from the ground was approximately 50 centimetres above the ground. This

was above the position where Dr Kelly's left wrist was, but most of the stainings were 33 centimetres, which is approximately a foot above the ground. It was all fairly low level stuff.

Q. What does that mean?

A. It meant that because the injury – most of the injuries would have taken place while Dr Kelly was sitting down or lying down.

Q. Right. When you first saw the body, what position was it in?

A. He was on his back with the left wrist curled back in this sort of manner (Indicates).

Q. Did you make any other relevant discoveries while you were looking around the area?

A. There was an obvious large contact bloodstain on the knee of the jeans.

Q. What do you mean by a "contact bloodstain"?

A. A contact stain is what you will observe if an item has come into contact with a bloodstained surface, as opposed to blood spots and splashes when blood splashes on to an item.

Q. Which means at some stage his left wrist must have been in contact with his trousers?

A. No, what I am saying, at some stage he has knelt – I believe he has knelt in a pool of blood at some stage and this obviously is after he has been injured.

Q. Any other findings?

A. There were smears of blood on the Evian bottle and on the cap.

Q. And what did that indicate to you?

A. Well, that would indicate to me that Dr Kelly was already injured when he used the Evian bottle. As an explanation, my Lord—

LORD HUTTON: Yes.

A. —when people are injured and losing blood they will become thirsty.

MR DINGEMANS: They become?

A. Thirsty, as they are losing all that fluid.

Q. You thought he is likely to have had a drink then?

A. Yes.

Q. What else did you find?

A. There was a bloodstain on the right sleeve of the Barbour jacket. At the time that was a bit – slightly unusual, in that if someone is cutting their wrist you wonder how, if you are moving across like this, how you get blood sort of here (Indicates). But if the knife was held and it went like that, with the injury passing across the sleeve, that is a possible explanation. Another possible explanation is in leaning across to get the Evian bottle that the two areas may have crossed.

Q. Had crossed?

A. Yes.

Q. We know, in fact, the wrist which was cut was the left wrist, is that right?

A. That is correct.

Q. And we know that Dr Kelly was right handed.

A. I was not aware of that, but yes.

Q. Were those all your relevant findings?

A. The jeans, as I have talked about, with this large contact stain, did not appear to have any larger downward drops on them. There were a few stains and so forth but it did not have any staining that would suggest to me that his injuries, or his major injuries if you like, were caused while he was standing up, and there was not any – there did not appear to be any blood underneath where he was found, and the body was later moved which all suggested those injuries were caused while he was sat or lying down.

143. Dr Alexander Allan, a forensic toxicologist, was sent blood and urine samples and stomach contents taken from the body of Dr Kelly in the course of Dr Hunt's post-mortem examination which he then analysed. Dr Allan found paracetamol and dextropropoxyphene in the samples and stomach contents. He described paracetamol and dextropropoxyphene as follows:

The two components, paracetamol and dextropropoxyphene, are the active components of a substance called Coproxamol which is a prescription only medicine containing 325 milligrams of paracetamol and 32.5 milligrams of dextropropoxyphene.

Q. What sort of ailments would that be prescribed for?

A. Mild to moderate pain, typically a bad back or period pain, something like that. And the concentrations of both drugs represent quite a large overdose of Coproxamol.

Q. What does the dextropropoxyphene cause if it is taken in overdose?

A. Dextropropoxyphene is an opioid analgesic drug which causes effects typical of opiate drugs in overdose, effects such as drowsiness, sedation and ultimately coma, respiratory depression and heart failure and dextropropoxyphene is known particularly in certain circumstances to cause disruption of the rhythm of the heart and it can cause death by that process in some cases of overdose.

Q. And what about paracetamol, what does that do?

A. Paracetamol does not cause drowsiness or sedation in overdose, but if enough is taken it can cause damage to the liver.

Q. If enough? I think you mean if too much is taken.

A. If too much is taken. I beg your pardon.

Q. What about the concentrations you have mentioned that you found in the blood? What did that indicate?

A. They are much higher than therapeutic use. Typically therapeutic use would represent one tenth of these concentrations. They clearly represent an overdose. But they are somewhat lower than what I would normally expect to encounter in cases of death due to an overdose of Coproxamol.

Q. What would you expect to see in the usual case where dextropropoxyphene has resulted in death? What types of proportions or concentrations would you normally expect to see?

A. There are two surveys reported I am aware of. One reports a concentration of 2.8 micrograms per millilitre of blood of dextropropoxyphene in a series of fatal overdose cases. Another one reports an average concentration of 4.7 microgrammes per millilitre of blood. You can say that they are several-fold larger than the level I found of 1 [microgram].

Q. What about the paracetamol concentration you found?

A. Again, it is higher than would be expected for therapeutic use, approximately 5 or 10 times higher. But it is much lower or lower than would be expected for paracetamol fatalities normally unless there was other factors of drugs involved.

Q. What sort of level would you normal [sic] expect for paracetamol fatalities?

A. I think if you can get the blood reasonably shortly after the incident and the person does not die slowly in hospital due to liver failure, perhaps typically 3 to 400 micrograms per millilitre of blood.

Q. About four times as much in other words?

A. Yes.

Q. Putting it in short terms, you would expect there to be about four times as much paracetamol and two and a half to four times as much dextropropoxyphene?

A. Two, three, four times as much paracetamol and two, three, four times as much dextropropoxyphene in the average overdose case, which results in fatalities.

Q. You have mentioned that it seemed that a number of Coproxamol drugs were taken. Was it possible, from your examination, to estimate how many tablets must have been taken?

A. It is not possible to do that, because of the complex nature of the behaviour of the drugs in the body. I understand that Dr Kelly may have vomited so he would have lost some stomach contents then. There was still some left in the stomach and presumably still some left in the gastrointestinal tracts. What I can say is that it is consistent with say 29/30 tablets but it could be consistent with other scenarios as well.

144. Dr Allan also said in his evidence that the only way in which paracetamol and dextropropoxyphene could be found in Dr Kelly's blood was by him taking tablets containing them which he would have to ingest.

145. In relation to an examination of Dr Kelly's body Assistant Chief Constable Page said in evidence:

Q. We heard about investigations that have been carried out in the post-mortem and toxicology reports.

A. Yes.

Q. And the pathologist said that Dr Kelly's lung had been removed for tests. Have you discussed that matter with the toxicologist?

A. I have discussed that matter with the toxicologist. The lung was not subjected to tests, and the rationale given to my team by the toxicologist is that the blood was tested for an entire range of substances including volatile substances and stupefying substances. No trace whatsoever was found and therefore they considered that examining the lung would not be relevant because if it was not in the blood, it would not be in the lung.

146. Very understandably the police did not show the knife found beside Dr Kelly's body to his widow and daughters but the police showed them a photograph of that knife. It is clear that the knife found beside the body was a knife which Dr Kelly had owned since boyhood and which he kept in a desk in his study, but which was found to be missing from his desk after his death. In her evidence Mrs Kelly said:

Q. We have heard about the circumstances of Dr Kelly's death and the fact that a knife was used. Were you shown the knife at all?

A. We were not shown the knife; we were shown a photocopy of I presume the knife which we recognised as a knife he had had for many years and kept in his drawer.

Q. It was a knife he had had what, from childhood?

A. From childhood I believe. I think probably from the Boy Scouts.

And in a statement furnished to the Inquiry Police Constable Roberts stated: The knife found in possession of Dr David Kelly is a knife the twins, Rachel and Ellen recognise (from pictures shown by Family Liaison Officers). It would not be unusual to be in his possession as a walker. They have seen it on their walks with him. He would have kept it in his study drawer with a collection of small pocket knives (he did like gadgets) and the space in the study drawer where a knife was clearly missing from the neat row of knives is where they believe it would [have] lived and been removed from.

147. It also appears probable that the Coproxamol tablets which Dr Kelly took just before his death came from a store of those tablets which Mrs Kelly, who suffered from arthritis, kept in their home. In a statement furnished to the Inquiry Detective Constable Eldridge stated:

At 1000hrs on Thursday 7th AUGUST 2003 I was on duty at Long Hanborough Incident Room when I removed from secure storage the following items for examination: –
1. Exhibit SK/2 CO-PROXAMOL BOX AND STRIP OF TEN TABLETS taken from Janice KELLY
2. Exhibit NCH/17/2 CO-PROXAMOL BLISTER PACKETS FRONT BOTTOM BELLOWS POCKET these had been removed from Dr KELLY'S coat pocket by the Pathologist.
   On examining both items I saw that they were identical. They were marked M & A Pharmacy Ltd and had the wording CO-PROXAMOL PL/4077/0174 written on the foil side of each of the blister type packs.
   I can say that enquiries have been made with M & A PHARMACHEM who are the manufacturers of CO-PROXAMOL. The batch number shown on the tablets in our possession was checked with a view to tracing the chemist that these tablets had been purchased from. I can say that this batch number relates to approximately 1.6 million packets of tablets that will have been distributed to various chemists throughout the country.

148. In relation to the question whether Dr Kelly took his own life the opinion of Dr Hunt was as follows:

[16 September, page 23, line 14]
The orientation and arrangement of the wounds over the left wrist are typical of self-inflicted injury. Also typical of this was

the presence of small so-called tentative or hesitation marks. The fact that his watch appeared to have been removed whilst blood was already flowing suggest that it had been removed deliberately in order to facilitate access to the wrist. The removal of the watch in that way and indeed the removal of the spectacles are features pointing towards this being an act of self harm.

Other features at the scene which would tend to support this impression include the relatively passive distribution of the blood, the neat way in which the water bottle and its top were placed, the lack of obvious signs of trampling of the under-growth or damage to the clothing. To my mind, the location of the death is also of interest in this respect because it was clearly a very pleasant and relatively private spot of the type that is sometimes chosen by people intent upon self harm.

Q. Is that something you have found from your past experience?

A. Yes, and knowledge of the literature.

149. Professor Keith Hawton was requested by the Inquiry to give evidence in relation to the death of Dr Kelly. Professor Hawton is an eminent expert on the subject of suicide and is the Professor of Psychiatry at Oxford University and is the Director of the Centre for Suicide Research in the University Department of Psychiatry in Oxford. He stated in his evi-dence that the majority of those who commit suicide do not leave a suicide note or message. He further stated:

Q. Did you form any assessment of whether Dr Kelly's death was consistent with suicide?

A. I think all the information we have about his death and the circumstances of his death strongly point to his death having been by suicide.

Q. And what would you say drives you to that conclusion?

A. Well, the first thing is the site in which the death occurred. We have heard that it occurred in an isolated spot on Harrowdown Hill. In fact it was, as I think you have been told, in woodland about 40 or 50 yards off the track taken by ramblers. The site is well protected from the view of other people.

Q. Have you been to the site?

A. I have visited the site, yes.

Q. And what did you notice there then?

A. Well, I noticed, first of all – what struck me was it is a very peaceful spot, a rather beautiful spot and we know that it was a favourite – it was in the area of a favourite walk of Dr Kelly with his family.

Q. What other factors have you considered relevant?

A. The nature of his injuries is very consistent with an act of self cutting. The doctor – I have read Dr Hunt's report , who is the Home Office forensic pathologist. I have also seen the photographs of the injuries to Dr Kelly's body; and the nature of the injuries to his wrist are very consistent with suicide.

Q. Why do you say that? We have heard from some of the ambulance personnel who did not themselves see very much blood. We have heard from others who did see more blood. What is relevant here?

A. Well I am referring here particularly to the nature of the cutting which perhaps I would prefer not to describe in detail.

Q. Right.

A. But it—

Q. Perhaps you can just explain why you do not want to describe these matters in detail.

A. Well, one of the concerns I have is that there is now good evidence that reporting and portrayal of detailed methods of suicide in the media can actually sometimes facilitate suicide in other people.

Q. So it is perfectly obvious there are lots of members of the press here. If you had to say anything to them about the reporting of your evidence today, what would it be?

A. I think with regard to the specific method of suicide, I would prefer that that was kept as general as possible.

Q. For those reasons?

A. Yes.

Q. You have talked about the cutting. What else do you consider to have been consistent with suicide?

A. Well, the situation or the circumstances in which Dr
Kelly's body was found are consistent, in that he had apparently removed – his glasses were found by his body in a way
– in a manner suggesting that they had been taken off by him,
as was his cap; his watch had been taken off, was removed
from the body.

Q. What does that indicate?

A. It suggests that he removed the watch to give him better
access to be able to carry out the cutting.

Q. And was there anything else that you saw from the pathologist's report that assisted you in your conclusion?

A. Well, the instrument that was used, which I have seen a
photograph of, and the family, as you know, I think, have
been shown a copy of a similar instrument, a large penknife
– I will call it a penknife, but it is a rather primitive style of
penknife – is very similar to one that he had in his drawer in
his study, and it was one I think you heard yesterday he had
had since his childhood.

Q. Yes.

A. When considering something like this, one obviously has
to think about whether there could have been some other
person or persons involved in the act, and the circumstances
suggest that this was not the case.

Q. What, whether some third parties were involved in Dr
Kelly's death?

A. Yes.

Q. And what circumstances do you consider show that there
were not?

A. Well, there were no signs of violence on his body other
than the obvious injury to his wrist that would be in keeping
with his having been involved in some sort of struggle or a
violent act. There was no sign I understand of trampling
down of vegetation and undergrowth in the area around his
body. So that makes it highly unlikely that others could have
been or were involved.

Q. We are going to hear from a toxicologist. Have you had a
chance to read that report?

A. I have.

Q. Does that assist you in your determinations?

A. Well, we know that evidence was found in Dr Kelly's body and also on his person of him having consumed some particular medication.

Q. Right. And what medication was that?

A. That is Coproxamol.

Q. And why does that assist in your determination?

A. Well, it in itself is quite a dangerous medication taken in overdose because it can have particular effects on both breathing and also on the heart rhythm.

LORDHUTTON: Just going back to the knife, Professor Hawton, you said it was very similar to one in his drawer. Now, we have been told, for very understandable reasons, that Mrs Kelly was not shown the knife. But when you say "very similar", are you drawing the inference that in fact it was probably a knife that had been in his drawer, is that why you say "very similar"?

A. Yes, I am my Lord.

LORD HUTTON: Yes, quite. Thank you very much. Yes.

MR DINGEMANS: We were dealing with the toxicologist's report. What do you understand the position to be in relation to that Coproxamol?

A. Well, I understand that the evidence found from blood levels and from the contents of Dr Kelly's – in Dr Kelly's stomach suggests that he had absorbed – he had taken approximately 30 tablets – I am sorry, the number of tablets is based on the number that were missing from the sheets he had with him.

Q. Right.

A. But that he had consumed well in excess of a therapeutic dose of Coproxamol and given the blood levels and the relatively small amounts in his stomach, although he had vomited, I believe you have heard evidence he has vomited, but this would suggest he had consumed Coproxamol some time before death.

Q. Does that assist you in determining whether or not any third party was involved?

A. Well, for a third party to have been involved in the taking of the Coproxamol would, I imagine, have involved a struggle. I mean if somebody was forced to take a substantial number of tablets, it is difficult to believe there would not have been signs of a struggle.

Q. That is a factor you have borne in mind?

A. Yes.

Q. Did you come, then, to any overall conclusion about whether or not Dr Kelly had committed suicide?

A. I think that taking all the evidence together, it is well nigh certain that he committed suicide.

150. In his evidence Assistant Chief Constable Page stated:

Q. Can you just briefly outline to his Lordship the lines of inquiry that you set out when confronted with the discovery of Dr Kelly's body?

A. Yes, certainly. Very early on in the inquiry one sets up a series of hypotheses which one tries then to knock down. For the sake of completeness the first of these would be: was the death natural or accidental? In this case it is fairly obvious that was not the case. The next question is: was it murder? I think as I pointed out in my last evidence, the examination of the scene and the supporting forensic evidence made me confident that actually there was no third party involved at the scene of the crime and therefore, to all intents and purposes, murder can be ruled out. One is then left with the option that Dr Kelly killed himself.

LORD HUTTON: Sorry, may I just ask you, Mr Page, you say no third party was involved at the scene of the crime. Did you consider the possibility that Dr Kelly might have been overpowered and killed elsewhere and his body then taken to the wooded area where it was found?

A. Yes, my Lord; and I think, again, upon examination of the pathologist's evidence and of the biologist's evidence, it is pretty clear to me that Dr Kelly died at the scene.

LORD HUTTON: Yes. Thank you.

MR DINGEMANS: You were going on to say having ruled out natural causes, having ruled out murder.

A. One is left with the fact that Dr Kelly killed himself. My duty in that respect is to establish to the best of my satisfaction that there was no criminal dimension to Dr Kelly's death.

Q. Have you found any evidence suggesting that there was a criminal element?

A. Based on the extensive inquiries that we have undertaken thus far, I can find no evidence to suggest any criminal dimension to Dr Kelly's death.

Q. Can you give his Lordship, and everyone else, some idea of how many people you have interviewed in the course of your inquiries?

A. Yes, certainly. We have made contact with somewhere in the region of 500 individuals during the course of our inquiry.

Q. How many statements have you taken?

A. We have taken 300 statements and we have seized in excess of 700 documents in addition to the computer files I referred to when I gave evidence last time.

LORD HUTTON: Mr Page, could you just elaborate just a little on what you mean by no criminal dimension?

A. Well, again, my Lord, I would– I suppose being a police officer and I am inherently suspicious and I would look at the circumstances and ask myself a range of questions as to why Dr Kelly would have taken his own life.

LORD HUTTON: Yes.

A. And very early on in the inquiry, based on early discussions with the inquiry it seemed entirely out of character for Dr Kelly to take that move. Therefore, my view of whether there was a criminal dimension to this would centre around: was he being blackmailed? Was he being put under some other criminal behaviour that would have prompted him to take this action?

LORD HUTTON: Thank you for that, I just wanted you to elaborate that. And you have excluded that in your inquiries?

A. We have carried out extensive inquiries and based on those inquiries, I can find no evidence that he was being blackmailed or indeed any other evidence of any other criminal dimension.

151. Those who try cases relating to a death or injury (whether caused by crime or accident) know that entirely honest witnesses often give evidence as to what they saw at the scene which differs as to details. In the evidence which I heard from those who saw Dr Kelly's body in the wood there were differences as to points of detail, such as the number of police officers at the scene and whether they were all in uniform, the amount of blood at the scene, and whether the body was lying on the ground or slumped against the tree. I have seen a photograph of Dr Kelly's body in the wood which shows that most of his body was lying on the ground but that his head was slumped against the base of the tree – therefore a witness could say either that the body was lying on the ground or slumped against the tree. These differences do not cause me to doubt that no third party was involved in Dr Kelly's death.

The evidence of Mr David Broucher
152. Mr David Broucher, a member of the Diplomatic Service, gave evidence that in February 2003 he was the United Kingdom's Permanent Representative to the Conference on Disarmament in Geneva. He said that he had met Dr Kelly once in connection with his duties. He had not made a minute of the meeting or recorded it in his diary and doing the best that he could he thought that the meeting was in February 2003 in Geneva. He said that he wanted to pick Dr Kelly's brains because he knew that he was a considerable expert on compliance with the biological weapons convention in relation to Iraq. He had a meeting with Dr Kelly for about an hour.

They talked about the history of Iraq's biological weapons capability, about Dr Kelly's activities with UNSCOM, about what he thought might be the current state of affairs, and they also talked about Iraq and the biological weapons convention.

153. Mr Broucher was asked:

Q. Did you then go on to discuss the possible use of force in Iraq?

A. We did.

Q. Can you tell us, in your own words, what was said?

A. I said to Dr Kelly that I could not understand why the. Iraqis were courting disaster and why they did not cooperate with the weapons inspectors and give up whatever weapons might remain in their arsenal. He said that he had personally urged – he was still in contact with senior Iraqis and he had urged this point on them. Their response had been that if they revealed too much about their state of readiness this might increase the risk that they would be attacked.

Q. Did Dr Kelly say how he was in contact or not?

A. He did not give any details of names or places or times; and I did not ask him that.

Q. Did he say what he had said to those persons that he had contacted?

A. He said that he had tried to reassure them that if they cooperated with the weapons inspectors then they had nothing to fear.

Q. Which, as I understand it, was the position adopted by the United Nations.

A. So I understand, yes.

Q. And did he disclose how he felt about the situation?

A. My impression was that he felt that he was in some personal difficulty or embarrassment over this, because he believed that the invasion might go ahead anyway and that somehow this put him in a morally ambiguous position.

Q. Did he say anything further to you?

A. I drew some inferences from what he said, but I cannot recall the precise words that he used.

Q. What inferences did you draw?

A. Well, I drew the inference that he might be concerned that he would be thought to have lied to some of his contacts in Iraq.

Q. Did you discuss the dossier at all in this conversation?

A. We did discuss the dossier. I raised it because I had had to – it was part of my duties to sell the dossier, if you like, within the United Nations to senior United Nations officials; and I told Dr Kelly that this had not been easy and that they did not find it convincing. He said to me that there had been a lot of pressure to make the dossier as robust as possible; that every judgment in it had been closely fought over; and that it was the best that the JIC could do. I believe that it may have been in this connection that he then went on to explain the point about the readiness of Iraq's biological weapons, the fact they could not use them quickly, and that this was relevant to the point about 45 minutes.

Q. Did you discuss Dr Kelly's position in the Ministry of Defence?

A. He gave me to understand that he – it was only with some reluctance that he was working in the Ministry of Defence. He would have preferred to go back to Porton Down. He felt that when he transferred into the Ministry of Defence they had transferred him at the wrong grade, and so he was concerned that he had been downgraded.

Q. Right. Did you have any other conversation with Dr Kelly that day?

A. As Dr Kelly was leaving I said to him: what will happen if Iraq is invaded? And his reply was, which I took at the time to be a throwaway remark – he said: I will probably be found dead in the woods.

Q. You understood it to be a throwaway remark. Did you report that remark at the time to anyone?

A. I did not report it at the time to anyone because I did not attribute any particular significance to it. I thought he might have meant that he was at risk of being attacked by the Iraqis in some way.

Q. And you, at the time, considered it to be a sort of general comment one might make at the end of a conversation?

A. Indeed.

Q. Where were you in July this year on about 17th/18th July?

A. I was on leave in Geneva.

Q. And did you hear of Dr Kelly's death at all?

A. I believe I heard about it on the television news.

Q. Right. And did you see a picture of Dr Kelly on the news?

A. Yes.

Q. What was your reaction to that?

A. I recognised him, I realised that I knew him.

Q. And as a result of that what happened?

A. Nothing happened immediately because I was aware that I knew him but it was not until later that I became aware of the circumstances of his death and realised the significance of this remark that he had made to me, seemingly as a throw-away line, when we met in February.

Q. Did you contact anyone about your recollection?

A. Yes, I did, not immediately but when the Inquiry began on 1st August it seemed to me that I needed to make known this fact.

Q. Can I take you to CAB/10/9? How did you make this fact known?

A. I sent an e-mail to my colleague, the press officer for biological weapons in the Foreign Office, Patrick Lamb.

Q. And you say to Patrick Lamb: "Is the FCO preparing evidence for the Hutton Inquiry?" We have heard from Mr Lamb: "If so, I may have something relevant to contribute that I have been straining to recover from a very deep memory hole." Is that right, that at the time your impression was that it was a throwaway remark, and is it also fair to say that it was deeply buried within your memory?

A. Yes, that is fair to say, and the other facts of the meeting took sometime for me to remember; and it took a long time to establish when the meeting took place because it was not noted in my diary.

154. Mr Broucher was clear in his evidence that he had only met Dr Kelly on one occasion. After he had given evidence Dr Kelly's daughter, Miss Rachel Kelly, looked at her father's diary and found that it contained an entry that he had met Mr Broucher in Geneva on 18th February 2002. In her evidence Miss Kelly said:

Q. We have heard from your mother this morning. She has given us some of the background. Can I ask you to look at a diary entry for 2002? Before I ask you to look at that, can you just tell me where you found the diary?

A. Yes. The diary was in my father's study—

Q. It is FAM/1/1. If we look at the entry for February, what does it tell us?

A. It mentions specifically a meeting with David Broucher on 18th February 2002, and the interesting thing with my father's diaries is he tended to write entries in them after the event and this would have been a meeting that he actually had because it is in his diary.

Q. It does not look like we have been able to get the diary on the screen, but if I look at the diary that I have in front of me, it says: "Monday 18th February 2002, 9.30, David Broucher, USmis."

A. Yes, US mission.

Q. It gives details of his flights into Geneva the day before.

A. Yes, the day before.

Q. And out of Geneva on 20th February; is that right?

A. Yes, that is correct, on the 20th.

Q. And that is February 2002?

A. It is a year earlier than the date that David Broucher gave as being this year, the conversation he had with my father.

Q. And I think Mr Broucher told us he had only had one meeting with your father.

A. Yes, that is what made me look at it. I actually thought that was the case.

Therefore it appears to be clear that Dr Kelly's one meeting with Mr Broucher was in February 2002 and not in February 2003.

155. In his evidence Professor Hawton said:

Q. We have heard evidence from a Mr Broucher, who relayed a comment about Dr Kelly being found "dead in the woods" and he had at the time thought it was a throwaway remark. He had attributed it, if he attributed it at all, to Iraqi agents. Then after hearing of Dr Kelly's suicide he thought perhaps it was something else. Can you assist with that at all?

A. Well, I gained the impression talking to family members about that particular alleged statement that it was not a typical – not that he would say that particularly – communicate that, but it was the sort of throwaway comment he might make. I have also gathered that it is quite possible that it was not made at the time that was initially alleged but possibly a year beforehand.

Q. We have seen now diaries. Mr Broucher thought it was February 2003. He did say it was a deep memory pocket. We have seen diaries which suggest that he has met Mr Broucher in February 2002 and Mr Broucher has said they only met once. So that may mean it is February 2002. Does that assist?

A. I think it is pure coincidence. I do not think it is relevant to understanding Dr Kelly's death.

156. It is a strange coincidence that Dr Kelly was found dead in the woods, but for the reasons which I give in paragraph 157 I am satisfied that Dr Kelly took his own life and that there was no third party involvement in his death.

The cause of the death of Dr Kelly

157. In the light of the evidence which I have heard I am satisfied that Dr Kelly took his own life in the wood at Harrowdown Hill at a time between 4.15 p.m. on 17 July and 1.15 a.m. on 18 July 2003 and that the principal cause of death was bleeding from incised wounds to the left wrist which Dr Kelly inflicted on himself with the knife found beside his body. It is probable that the ingestion of an excess amount of Coproxamol tablets coupled with apparently clinically silent coronary artery disease would both have played a part in bringing about death more certainly and more rapidly than would have otherwise been the case. Accordingly the causes of death are:

1a Haemorrhage

1b Incised wounds to the left wrist

2 Coproxamol ingestion and coronary artery atherosclerosis

I am satisfied that no other person was involved in the death of Dr Kelly for the following reasons:

1) A very careful and lengthy examination of the area where his body was found by police officers and by a forensic biologist found no traces whatever of a struggle or of any involvement by a third party or third parties and a very careful and detailed post-mortem examination by Dr Hunt, together with the examination of specimens from the body by a forensic toxicologist, Dr Allan, found no traces or indications whatever of violence or force inflicted on Dr Kelly by a third party or third parties either at the place where his body was found or elsewhere.

2) The wounds to his wrist were inflicted by a knife which came from Dr Kelly's desk in his study in his home, and which had belonged to him from boyhood.

3) It is highly unlikely that a third party or third parties could have forced Dr Kelly to swallow a large number of Coproxamol tablets.

These conclusions are strongly supported by the evidence of Professor Hawton, Dr Hunt and Assistant Chief Constable Page.

158. I am further satisfied from the evidence of Professor Hawton that Dr Kelly was not suffering from any significant mental illness at the time he took his own life.

The statement issued by the BBC after Dr Kelly's death
159. On Sunday 20 July the BBC issued the following statement:

The BBC deeply regrets the death of Dr David Kelly. We had the greatest respect for his achievements in Iraq and elsewhere over many years and wish once again to express our condolences to his family.

There has been much speculation about whether Dr Kelly was the source for the *Today* programme report by Andrew Gilligan on May 29th. Having now informed Dr Kelly's family, we can confirm that Dr Kelly was the principal source for both Andrew Gilligan's report and for Susan Watts' reports on Newsnight on June 2nd and 4th.

The BBC believes we accurately interpreted and reported the factual information obtained by us during interviews with Dr Kelly.

Over the past few weeks we have been at pains to protect Dr Kelly being identified as the source of these reports. We clearly owed him a duty of confidentiality. Following his death, we now believe, in order to end the continuing speculation, it is important to release this information as swiftly as possible. We did not release it until this morning at the request of Dr Kelly's family.

The BBC will fully cooperate with the Government's inquiry. We will make a full and frank submission to Lord Hutton and will provide full details of all the contacts between Dr Kelly and the two BBC journalists including contemporaneous notes and other materials made by both journalists, independently.

We continue to believe we were right to place Dr Kelly's views in the public domain. However, the BBC is profoundly sorry that his involvement as our source has ended so tragically.

JOHN F. KENNEDY

Since the assassination of the thirty-fifth President of the US in Dealey Plaza, Dallas, in 1963, an average of forty books a year have sought to explain – even explain away – his murder. It is the Big One. The Mother of All Mysteries, the Daddy of all Conspiracy Theories.

Nearly fifty years on, the images still loop from that fateful November day:

Kennedy in the back of the open-top Lincoln, next to Jackie, all smiles and waves in the sun ...

Kennedy, his head slumped sideways ...

Jackie leaning over to her husband ...

Jackie trying to climb up the back of the car ...

A blur of speeding cars and motorbike outriders ...

Lyndon B. Johnson inside Air Force One taking the oath of presidency, Jackie statue-like by his side ...

Elected to the White House in 1960 aged forty-six, Democrat John F. Kennedy was supposedly the bringer of a fresh new dawn. Handsome, charismatic and liberal, JFK promised hope for an entire generation. That hope was snuffed out at 12.30 p.m. on 22 November 1963 in Dealey Plaza.

Kennedy had chosen to visit Dallas to boost the Democratic cause in Texas, a marginal state, and to generate funds for the upcoming November 1964 presidential election. Both Kennedy and his staff had expressed concerns about security because, only a month earlier, US Ambassador to the UN Adlai Stevenson had been jostled and spat upon during a visit to Dallas. Nevertheless, the route the president's motorcade would take through Dallas was published in Dallas newspapers on the eve of the visit, 21 November 1963. The next day, a little before 12.30 p.m. CST, his Lincoln limousine entered Dealey Plaza and slowly approached the Texas School Book Depository. It then turned 120 degrees left, directly in front of the Depository, just 65 feet away.

As the presidential Lincoln passed the Depository and continued down Elm Street, shots were fired at Kennedy, who was waving to the crowds on his right. One shot entered his upper back, penetrated his neck, and exited his throat. He raised his clenched fists up to his neck and leaned to his left as Jacqueline Kennedy put her arms round him. Texas Governor John Connally, sitting with his wife in front of the Kennedys in the limousine, was hit in the back and yelled out, "Oh, no, no, no ... My God, they're going to kill us all!"

The final shot occurred as the presidential limo passed in front of the John Neely Bryan pergola. As the shot sounded, President Kennedy's head exploded, covering the interior of the Lincoln with blood and tissue.

Secret Service agent Clint Hill was riding on the running board of the car behind the limousine. After the first shot struck the president, Hill jumped off and ran to overtake it. By then the president had been hit in the head and Mrs Kennedy was climbing onto the boot of the car. Hill jumped on the back of the limousine, pushed Mrs Kennedy back into her seat, and clung to the car as it sped to Parkland Memorial Hospital. At 1.00 p.m. President John F. Kennedy was pronounced dead by hospital staff. A formality. The president was certainly dead before the limo reached the doors of the emergency department.

Meanwhile, back in Dealey Plaza, the first witnesses were talking to police. Howard Brennan, across from the Texas School Book Depository, distinctly heard gunshots from that building. So did Harold Norman, James Jarman Jr and Bonnie Ray Williams, employees of the Depository who had watched the motorcade from a window at the south-east corner of the fifth floor; they heard three shots from directly over their heads. (Of the eye and ear witnesses who would eventually give testimony as to the direction from which the fatal shots came, 56 [53.8 per cent] believed they came from the direction of the

Depository, 35 [33.7 per cent] thought they came from a "grassy knoll" on the north side of the Plaza, and 8 [7.7 per cent] thought the shots came from other locations. Only 5 [4.8 per cent] thought they heard shots from two separate locations.) A police search of the Book Depository revealed that one employee, Lee Harvey Oswald, was missing, having left the building immediately after the shooting. After eighty minutes of frantic manhunt Oswald was spotted on a sidewalk by Dallas police officer J. D. Tippit, who on approaching Oswald was shot dead. One hour later, Oswald was cornered in a movie house and arrested. The next day he was charged with the murders of Kennedy and Tippit. He denied shooting anyone and claimed he'd been set up as a "patsy".

On 24 November at 11.21 a.m., as Oswald was being transferred from Dallas Police Headquarters to the county jail, a local strip-club owner, Jack Ruby, stepped out of the crowd and fatally gunned him down. Ruby was convicted of Oswald's murder in 1964, but the conviction was overturned. Ruby died in jail awaiting retrial.

A week after Kennedy's assassination, President Lyndon Baines Johnson ("LBJ") set up a commission under Chief Justice Earl Warren to investigate the killing. The Warren Commission published its findings in September 1964. According to the Commission, Lee Harvey Oswald had shot Kennedy from the sixth floor of the Texas Book Depository, where an Italian Mannlicher-Carcano M91/38 bolt-action rifle had been found with his fingerprints on it. A bullet on Governor Connally's stretcher matched this rifle. Oswald, a misfit with Marxist leanings, had been instrumental in setting up the New Orleans branch of the pro-Castro Fair Play for Cuba Committee. He had, concluded the Commission, "an overriding hostility to his environment ... [a] hatred for American Society" and had sought "a place in history". The Commission "could not find any persuasive evidence of a domestic or foreign conspiracy involving any other person(s), group(s), or country(ies), and [believed] that Lee Harvey Oswald acted alone".

In a US still traumatized by the event, the Warren Commission report was initially met with a sense of relief and acceptance. The mood, however, gradually passed to unease and then outright distrust, as it became clear that LBJ had ordered an embargo on huge swathes of the report for thirty years to come. Moreover, the bits and pieces of the report that had been released contained as many questions as they did answers. Why hadn't the Commission interviewed Ruby, especially as he had informed them he would "come clean"? Then there was the matter of the murder weapon: could a bolt-action relic of the Second World War really deliver three accurate shots, at range, in six to seven seconds?

With the manifest inadequacy of the official investigation into Kennedy's death, numerous independent investigations tried to get at the truth. Among the keenest-eyed readers of the Warren Report's selected extracts was New Orleans District Attorney Jim Garrison, who spotted a passing reference to one Clay Bertrand, whom Garrison identified as homosexual New Orleans businessman Clay Shaw. In 1969, Garrison prosecuted Shaw for conspiring to murder the president; unfortunately for Garrison, two of his key witnesses, David Ferrie and Guy Bannister, died in suspicious circumstances before they could testify. (Aside from Oswald, Ruby, Ferrie and Bannister, anything up to forty witnesses in the JFK case have mysteriously died or been murdered.) Shaw was acquitted after less than an hour of deliberation by the jury, yet Garrison's quest was not in vain; Ferrie would later be identified as a possible co-conspirator by the 1976 House of Representatives Select Committee on Assassinations (HSCA). Also, Garrison forced the first public showing of the 486-frame, 8 mm movie shot by Abraham Zapruder of Kennedy's killing, which shows a backwards blast of brains and blood from Kennedy's head. On the Zapruder film, it looks as though the president has been shot from in front; Oswald was high up, to the president's right, at the time of the shooting. If the fatal bullet came from the front, there must have been another gunman. In its 1979 report, the HSCA concluded that there was "a high probability that two gunmen" fired at Kennedy, and that he was "probably assassinated as a result of a conspiracy". In evidence, the HSCA heard a Dictabelt recording from a Dallas police motorcyclist's radio, on which four gunshots could be heard, one more than Oswald supposedly fired. Among the other evidence supporting the two-gunmen theory was the testimony of Dr McClelland, a physician in the Portland emergency room, that the back right-hand part of President Kennedy's head had been blown out. Top rifle experts of the FBI could not make the Mannlicher rifle used by Oswald fire two shots in the 2.3-second time frame that Oswald allegedly fired off his first two rounds. Neither could Gunnery Sergeant Carlos Hathcock, the senior instructor for the US Marine Corps Sniper Instructor School at Quantico, Virginia. "We reconstructed the whole thing," said Hathcock, "the angle, the range, the moving target, the time limit, the obstacles, everything. I don't know how many times we tried it, but we couldn't duplicate what the Warren Commission said Oswald did. Now if I can't do it, how in the world could a guy who as a non-qual on the rifle range and later only qualified 'marksman' do it?"

Disregarding the truly lunatic theories that John F. Kennedy was murdered by Martin Bormann (who, like Elvis Presley never dies) or time-travelling aliens, the finger of suspicion points at five possible culprits:

CIA and Anti-Castro Cuban Exile Conspiracy

Something very bad is going on within the CIA and I want to know what it is. I want to shred the CIA into a thousand pieces and scatter them to the four winds.

President John F. Kennedy

Kennedy despised the CIA for bungling the Bay of Pigs invasion of Cuba in April 1961, and afterwards accepted the resignation of the CIA chief Allen Dulles. The Agency reciprocated Kennedy's feeling because, aside from his stinging criticism, he was intending to withdraw from Vietnam and seek detente with the Communists. According to *Crime and Cover-Up* (1977) by Peter Dale Scott, Kennedy's initiatives would have caused the scaling down of the CIA empire, as well as the curbing of its lucrative narcotics-trafficking business. The Military-Industrial Complex financed the hit, since it had a vested interest in continuing the war in 'Nam, from which it was making billions. Assassination was the CIA's stock-in-trade. It had participated in the successful murders of two (at least) heads of state, Ngo

Dinh Diem of Vietnam and Rafael Trujillo of the Dominican Republic. Why not murder its own head of state? It had the expertise, after all.

HSCA reviewed these theories and concluded that, although Oswald assassinated Kennedy in a conspiracy with others, the conspiracy did not include any US Intelligence agencies. HSCA did believe, however, that anti-Castro Cuban exiles might have participated in Kennedy's murder. These exiles had worked closely with CIA operatives in covert operations against Castro's Cuba.

> Cuban exiles/CIA offed the president: ALERT LEVEL 5

The Commies

Early JFK conspiracy theories centred on the USSR and its stooges. Kennedy had, of course, gone toe-to-toe with the USSR during the Cuban Missile Crisis. In *Plot and Counterplot*, Edward J. Epstein suggested that Dallas was payback time by a smarting Moscow. Oswald, who had once defected to the USSR but returned to the US, was according to this hypothesis a KGB agent. A variant of the Reds dunnit is that the Communist leader of Cuba, Fidel Castro, organized the assassination. During its investigation, HSCA visited Cuba and interviewed Castro about Cuban complicity in Kennedy's assassination. He replied: "That [the Cuban Government might have been involved in Kennedy's death] was insane. From the ideological point of view it was insane. And from the political point of view, it was a tremendous insanity."

Obviously Castro might have been lying to HSCA, but his point is good: why give the US a 22-carat pretext to invade Cuba by assassinating its leader?

> Castro/USSR assassinated JFK: ALERT LEVEL 3

The Military-Industrial Complex

In his farewell speech to the nation, Kennedy's predecessor Dwight Eisenhower – a former soldier and Republican, so no pinko – railed against the US arms industry: "This conjunction of an immense military establishment and a large arms industry is new in the American experience. The total influence – economic, political, even spiritual – is felt in every city, every State house, every office of the Federal government ... We must guard against the acquisition of unwarranted influence, whether sought or unsought, by the military-industrial complex."

A year later the new White House incumbent, JFK, blamed the military-industrial complex for fanning fears about the "bomber" and "missile" gaps, which pushed military spending to levels beyond those Eisenhower already thought intolerable. Kennedy's call for cuts and stated intention of withdrawing troops from 'Nam was hardly likely to win him friends in boardrooms and messes. So, the military-industrial complex wanted him out of the White House, and a more amenable president in his place.

Since the military-industrial complex is a phenomenon or concept, not a corporeal body, it would have been incapable of pulling a trigger. That is not to say that elements of the military-industrial complex were not delighted with, and maybe even helped, the accession of Lyndon B. Johnson.

> Military-Industrial Complex killed Kennedy: ALERT LEVEL 5

LBJ

One of the most vociferous blamers of Cuba was VP LBJ, whose oft-repeated mantra was: "Kennedy was trying to kill Castro. Castro got him first."

A smokescreen? After all, on the basis of "who profits?" LBJ wins out as Barr McClellan noted in 2003's *Blood, Money and Power: How LBJ Killed JFK*. Here Kennedy's successor Lyndon

B. Johnson, together with an accomplice, Edward Clark, planned and covered up the assassination in Dallas. LBJ certainly had a motive: aside from the intrinsic attraction of succeeding to the most important job in the world, Johnson was the subject of four major criminal investigations involving government contract violations, misappropriation of funds, money-laundering and bribery at the time of Kennedy's murder. All these investigations were terminated upon LBJ's assumption of the presidency. Worse, LBJ knew Malcolm "Mac" Wallace, a convicted murderer, because Wallace was the on-off boyfriend of LBJ's sister Josefa; in 1998 JFK assassination researcher Walt Brown announced that he had identified a fingerprint in the "sniper's nest" in the Book Depository as belonging to Wallace. Former CIA officer and Watergate agent E. Howard Hunt also implicated LBJ in a deathbed confession, along with CIA agents Bill Harvey, Cord Meyer and David Sanchez Morales; in Hunt's confession the shooter was named Lucien Sarti and shot Kennedy from the grassy knoll.

LBJ apparently had no shortage of willing helpers. Mark North's *Act of Treason* (1991) posits that LBJ was helped by FBI head J. Edgar Hoover, who was known to loathe JFK and his brother Bobby, the Attorney General.

In a taped interview with historian Arthur Schlesinger, Jackie Kennedy is reported to have put her name to the list of those who believe LBJ was behind JFK's murder.

LBJ killed JFK: ALERT LEVEL 5

The Mob

The HSCA investigation also identified the Mafia as possible conspirators in the plot to assassinate Kennedy. The Mob, so the theory runs, murdered JFK in retaliation for the heat put upon them by Attorney General Robert Kennedy (who had increased by twelve times the number of mob prosecutions Eisenhower had managed). What HSCA was too discreet to mention was that the Kennedys had long been in bed with the

Mob (literally in the case of JFK, who had an affair with Sam Giancana's girlfriend Judith Campbell Exner) and had used Mafia money in the campaign to secure the White House. The Mob didn't like the campaign against them, and even less did it like the Kennedys' hypocrisy. Mafia bosses Carlos Marcello, Sam Giancana and Santo Trafficante Jr topped the list of HSCA gangster suspects.

In their turn, David E. Scheim in *The Mafia Killed President Kennedy*, and Lamar Waldron/Thom Hartmann in *Legacy of Secrecy* squarely accuse Marcello as being the man who whacked the president, with a little help from his friends Santos Trafficante and Johnny Roselli. Marcello, whose Mob territory embraced New Orleans and Texas, had once been hustled out of the USA by immigration agents directed by Robert Kennedy to be dumped in Guatemala. Slipping secretly back into New Orleans, he vowed revenge against the Kennedys. According to a memo quoted in the Waldron/Hartmann book by an FBI informant who met with Marcello in 1985: "Carlos Marcello discussed his intense dislike of former President John Kennedy as he often did. Unlike other such tirades against Kennedy, however, on this occasion Carlos Marcello said, referring to President Kennedy, 'Yeah, I had the son of a bitch killed. I'm glad I did it. I'm sorry I couldn't have done it myself.'"

HSCA, Scheim and Waldron/Hartmann all found ties between Oswald, Jack Ruby and the Marcello mob of New Orleans. Ruby, a sometime foot soldier for Capone in Chicago, was tasked with "offing" Oswald before he could squeal. Scheim highlights telephone records showing that, as the assassination date approached, Ruby made numerous calls to relatively high Mob figures in Chicago, New Orleans and Los Angeles, as well as to two associates of Jimmy Hoffa, the Mob-friendly teamster boss. Ruby later told the FBI that the calls were made to get help in stopping rival Dallas clubs from using amateur strippers. Would the Mr Bigs of crime really trouble their unpretty heads with dime-undercutting strippers?

An argument against Mafia culpability is that the JFK assassination did not bear the hallmark of Mafia hits, which tend to be up close and personal; if the Mob did kill Kennedy then it must have hired a trained military marksman, possibly someone in or on the dissident fringes of the CIA, with whom the Mob had cooperated in attempted assassinations of Castro. Someone like Oswald. *Legacy of Secrecy*'s contention is that Oswald probably thought he was part of the coup plan against Castro but he was actually being set up by Marcello's goons to be the fall guy when the hit on the president went down in Dallas. When Oswald said he was a patsy he meant it.

An added twist to the Mob theory is given by Mark North in *Act of Treason*, in which he claims that Marcello tipped off J. Edgar Hoover of the FBI in 1962 that the assassination was being planned. Hoover, who despised Kennedy's civil rights agenda, intentionally sat on the information and let JFK die.

Da Mob whacked Kennedy: ALERT LEVEL 7

There is no shortage of other possible, within reason, culprits. The Freemasons (antipathetic to JFK's Catholicism), Jackie Kennedy (embarrassed and ashamed by her husband's affairs), Richard Nixon (desiring revenge for his defeat in the 1960 presidential election) and the Israelis (in anger at JFK's use of **Project Paperclip** Nazi scientists in his nuclear programme and his opposition to theirs) have all had their fifteen minutes of infamy as the suspected sponsors of the hit. A remarkable number – more than thirty – hoodlums, policemen and government agents have all stepped into the limelight to claim that *they* pulled the trigger on 22 November 1963, and for a while the diary entry of Dallas policeman Roscoe White, in which he detailed the murder, had many convinced – until it was proven to be a forgery.

In all the JFK confessions and babel, voices do occasionally break through in support of the Warren Commission's "lone gunman" theory, headed by Gerald Posner's *Case Closed* (1994) and Mark Fuhrman's *A Simple Act of Murder* (2006). In their scenarios Oswald, an ex-Marine, was a good shot (the calvacade was moving slowly, and a single bullet might have hit both JFK and Governor Connally, meaning that Oswald had to fire only two shots in the time frame, not three).

The lone gunman arguments fall on disbelieving ears. An ABC News poll in 2003 found that 70 per cent of American respondents "suspect a plot" in the assassination of President Kennedy. Jack Leon Ruby is the weak link in the lone gunman, anti-conspiracy case. Why did Ruby step out of the crowd and gun down Oswald? Because he was so morally or politically outraged by Oswald's murder of JFK that he had to take revenge? Hardly. Ruby was a hood of no fixed moral views. For the fame of it? Possibly, but the HSCA found no evidence that 56-year-old Ruby was psychologically flawed to the degree that he wished to make his mark in history as a shootist. And, when Ruby informed the Warren Commission that he would "come clean" what was he about to divulge? On balance, it must be assumed that Ruby stepped forward with his gun because he was either paid or pressurized by others to silence Oswald permanently. If someone needed to silence Lee Harvey Oswald, then there was a conspiracy

Kennedy was killed by a conspiracy, not a lone gunman:
ALERT LEVEL 7

Further Reading
Mark Fuhrman, *A Simple Act of Murder*, 2006
Jim Marrs, *Crossfire: The Plot that Killed Kennedy*, 1989
Barr McClellan, *Blood, Money and Power: How LBJ Killed JFK*, 2003
Mark North, *Act of Treason*, 1991
Gerald Posner, *Case Closed*, 1994
Robin Ramsay, *Who Shot JFK?*, 2000
David E. Scheim, *The Mafia Killed President Kennedy*, 1988
Peter Dale Scott, *Crime and Cover-Up: the CIA, the Mafia, and the Dallas-Watergate Connection*, 1977
Lamar Waldron and Thom Hartmann, *Legacy of Secrecy*, 2009
www.jfk-online.com/jfk100menu

DOCUMENT: EXTRACTS FROM THE REPORT OF THE SELECT COMMITTEE ON ASSASSINATIONS OF THE US HOUSE OF REPRESENTATIVES: PRESIDENT JOHN F. KENNEDY

The Involvement of organized crime. In contrast to the Warren Commission, the committee's investigation of the possible involvement of organized crime in the assassination was not limited to an examination of Jack Ruby. The committee also directed its attention to organized crime itself.

Organized crime is a term of many meanings. It can be used to refer to the crimes committed by organized criminal groups – gambling, narcotics, loan-sharking, theft and fencing, and the like. It can also be used to refer to the criminal group that commit those crimes. Here, a distinction may be drawn between an organized crime enterprise that engages in providing illicit goods and services and an organized crime syndicate that regulates relations between individual enterprises – allocating territory, settling personal disputes, establishing gambling payoffs, etc. Syndicates, too, are of different types. They may be metropolitan, regional, national or international in scope; they may be limited to one field of endeavor – for example, narcotics – or they may cover a broad range of illicit activities.

Often, but not always, the term organized crime refers to a particular organized crime syndicate, variously known as the Mafia or La Cosa Nostra and it is in this sense that the committee has used the phrase. This organized crime syndicate was the principal target of the committee investigation.

The committee found that by 1964 the fundamental structure and operations of organized crime in America had changed little since the early 1950s, when, after conducting what was then the most extensive investigation of organized crime in history, the Kefauver committee concluded:

1) There is a nationwide crime syndicate known as the Mafia, whose tentacles are found in many large cities. It

has international ramifications which appear most clearly in connection with the narcotics traffic.

2) Its leaders are usually found in control of the most lucrative rackets in their cities.

3) There are indications of a centralized direction and control of these rackets, but leadership appears to be in a group rather than in a single individual.

4) The Mafia is the cement that helps to bind the ... syndicate of New York and the ... syndicate of Chicago as well as smaller criminal gangs and individual criminals through the country.

5) The domination of the Mafia is based fundamentally on "muscle" and "murder." The Mafia is a secret conspiracy against law and order which will ruthlessly eliminate anyone who stands in the way of its success in any criminal enterprise in which it is interested. It will destroy anyone who betrays its secrets. It will use any means available – political influence, bribery, intimidation, et cetera, to defeat any attempt on the part of law enforcement to touch its top figures ...

The committee reviewed the evolution of the national crime syndicate in the years after the Kefauver committee and found continuing vitality, even more sophisticated techniques, and an increased concern for the awareness by law enforcement authorities of the danger it posed to the Nation. In 1967, after having conducted a lengthy examination of organized crime in the United States, the President's Crime Commission offered another description of the power and influence of the American underworld in the 1960s:

Organized crime is a society that seeks to operate outside the control of the American people and their governments. It involves thousands of criminals, working within structures as complex as those of any large corporation, subject to laws more rigidly enforced than those of legitimate governments. Its actions are not impulsive but rather the result of intricate conspiracies, carried on over many years and aimed at gaining control over whole fields of activity in order to amass huge profits.

An analysis by the committee revealed that the Kennedy administration brought about the strongest effort against organized crime that had ever been coordinated by the Federal Government. John and Robert Kennedy brought to their respective positions as President and Attorney General an unprecedented familiarity with the threat of organized crime – and a commitment to prosecute its leaders – based on their service as member and chief counsel respectively of the McClellan Committee during its extensive investigation of labor racketeering in the late 1950s. A review of the electronic surveillance conducted by the FBI from 1961 to 1964 demonstrated that members of La Cosa Nostra, as well as other organized crime figures, were quite cognizant of the stepped-up effort against them, and they placed responsibility for it directly upon President Kennedy and Attorney General Kennedy.

During this period, the FBI had comprehensive electronic coverage of the major underworld figures, particularly those who comprised the commission. The committee had access to and analyzed the product of this electronic coverage; it reviewed literally thousands of pages of electronic surveillance logs that revealed the innermost workings of organized crime in the United States. The committee saw in stark terms a record of murder, violence, bribery, corruption, and an untold variety of other crimes. Uniquely among congressional committees, and in contrast to the Warren Commission, the committee became familiar with the nature and scope of organized crime in the years before and after the Kennedy assassination, using as its evidence the words of the participants themselves.

An analysis of the work of the Justice Department before and after the tenure of Robert Kennedy as Attorney General also led to the conclusion that organized crime directly benefited substantially from the changes in Government policy that occurred after the assassination. That organized crime had the motive, opportunity and means to kill the President cannot be questioned. Whether it did so is another matter.

In its investigation of the decision making process and dynamics of organized crime murders and intrasyndicate assassinations during the early 1960s, the committee noted the extraordinary web of insulation, secrecy, and complex machinations that frequently surrounded organized crime leaders who ordered such acts. In testimony before the Senate on 25 September 1963, 2 months before his brother's assassination, Attorney General Kennedy spoke of the Government's continuing difficulty in solving murders carried out by organized crime elements, particularly those ordered by members of the La Cosa Nostra commission. Attorney General Kennedy testified that:

> ... because the members of the Commission, the top members, or even their chief lieutenants, have insulated themselves from the crime itself, if they want to have somebody knocked off, for instance, the top man will speak to somebody who will speak to somebody else who will speak to somebody else and order it. The man who actually does the gun work, who might get paid $250 or $500, depending on how important it is, perhaps nothing at all, he does not know who ordered it. To trace that back is virtually impossible.

The committee studied the Kennedy assassination in terms of the traditional forms of violence used by organized crime and the historic pattern of underworld slayings. While the murder of the President's accused assassin did in fact fit the traditional pattern – a shadowy man with demonstrable organized crime connections shoots down a crucial witness – the method of the President's assassination did not resemble the standard syndicate killing. A person like Oswald – young, active in controversial political causes, apparently not subject to the internal discipline of a criminal organization – would appear to be the least likely candidate for the role of Mafia hit man, especially in such an important murder. Gunmen used in organized crime killings have traditionally been selected with utmost deliberation and care, the most important considerations being loyalty and a willingness to remain silent if apprehended. These are qualities best guaranteed by past participation in criminal activities.

There are, however, other factors to be weighed in evaluating the method of possible operation in the assassination of President Kennedy. While the involvement of a gunman like Oswald does not readily suggest organized crime involvement, any underworld attempt to assassinate the President would in all likelihood have dictated the use of some kind of cover, a shielding or disguise. The committee made the reasonable assumption that an assassination of a President by organized crime could not be allowed to appear to be what it was.

Traditional organized crime murders are generally committed through the use of killers who make no effort to hide the fact that organized crime was responsible for such murders or "hits." While syndicate-authorized hits are usually executed in such a way that identification of the killers is not at all likely, the slayings are nonetheless committed in what is commonly referred to as the "gangland style." Indeed, an intrinsic characteristic of the typical mob execution is that it serves as a self-apparent message, with the authorities and the public readily perceiving the nature of the crime as well as the general identity of the group or gang that carried it out.

The execution of a political leader – most particularly a President would hardly be a typical mob execution and might well necessitate a different method of operation. The overriding consideration in such an extraordinary crime would be the avoidance of any appearance of organized crime complicity.

In its investigation, the committee noted three cases, for the purposes of illustration, in which the methodology employed by syndicate figures was designed to insulate and disguise the involvement of organized crime. These did not fit the typical pattern of mob killings, as the assassination of a President would not. While the typical cases did not involve political leaders, two of the three were attacks on figures in the public eye.

In the first case, the acid blinding of investigative reporter Victor Riesel in April 1956, organized crime figures in New York used a complex series of go-betweens to hire a petty thief and burglar to commit the act. Thus, the assailant did not know who had actually authorized the crime for which he had been recruited. The use of such an individual was regarded as unprecedented, as he had not been associated with the syndicate, was a known drug user, and outwardly appeared to be unreliable. Weeks later, Riesel's assailant was slain by individuals who had recruited him in the plot.

The second case, the fatal shooting of a well-known businessman, Sol Landie, in Kansas City, Mo., on 22 November 1970, involved the recruitment, through several intermediaries, of four young Black men by members of the local La Cosa Nostra family. Landie had served as a witness in a Federal investigation of gambling activities directed by Kansas City organized crime leader Nicholas Civella. The men recruited for the murder did not know who had ultimately ordered the killing, were not part of the Kansas City syndicate, and had received instructions through intermediaries to make it appear that robbery was the motive for the murder. All of the assailants and two of the intermediaries were ultimately convicted.

The third case, the shooting of New York underworld leader Joseph Columbo before a crowd of 65,000 people in June 1971, was carried out by a young Black man with a petty criminal record, a nondescript loner who appeared to be alien to the organized crime group that had recruited him through various go-betweens. The gunman was shot to death immediately after the shooting of Columbo, a murder still designated as unsolved. (Seriously wounded by a shot to the head, Columbo lingered for years in a semiconscious state before he died in 1978.)

The committee found that these three cases, each of which is an exception to the general rule of organized crime executions, had identifiable similarities. Each case was solved, in that the identity of the perpetrator of the immediate act became known. In two of the cases, the assailant was himself murdered soon after the crime. In each case, the person who wanted the crime accomplished recruited the person or persons who made the attack through more than one intermediary. In each case, the person suspected of inspiring the violence was a member of, or connected to, La Cosa Nostra. In each case, the person or persons hired were not professional killers, and they were not part of organized criminal groups. In each case, the persons recruited to carry out the acts could be characterized as dupes or tools who were being used in a conspiracy they were not fully aware of. In each case, the intent was to insulate the organized crime connection, with a particular requirement for disguising the true identity of the conspirators, and to place the blame on generally nondescript individuals. These exceptions to the general rule of organized crime violence made it impossible for the committee to preclude, on the basis of an analysis of the method of the assassination, that President Kennedy was killed by elements of organized crime.

In its investigation into the possibility that organized crime elements were involved in the President's murder, the committee examined various internal and external factors that bear on whether organized crime leaders would have considered, planned and executed an assassination conspiracy. The committee examined the decision-making process that would have been involved in such a conspiracy, and two primary propositions emerged. The first related to whether the national crime syndicate would have authorized and formulated a conspiracy with the formal consent of the commission, the ruling council of Mafia leaders. The second related to whether an individual organized crime leader, or possibly a small combination of leaders, might have conspired to assassinate the President through unilateral action, that is, without the involvement of the leadership of the national syndicate.

The most significant evidence that organized crime as an institution or group was not involved in the assassination of President Kennedy was contained in the electronic surveillance of syndicate leaders conducted by the FBI in the early 1960s. As the President's Crime Commission noted in 1967, and as this committee found through its review of the FBI surveillance, there was a distinct hierarchy and structure to organized crime. Decisions of national importance were generally made by the national commission, or at least they depended on the approval of the commission members. In 1963, the following syndicate leaders served as members of the commission: Vito Genovese, Joseph Bonanno, Carlo Gambino, and Thomas Lucchese of New York City; Stefano Magaddino of Buffalo; Sam Giancana of Chicago; Joseph Zerilli of Detroit; Angelo Bruno of Philadelphia and Raymond Patriarca of Providence. The committee's review of the surveillance transcripts and logs, detailing the private conversations of the commission members and their associates, revealed that there were extensive and heated discussions about the serious difficulties the Kennedy administration's crackdown on organized crime was causing.

The bitterness and anger with which organized crime leaders viewed the Kennedy administration are readily apparent in the electronic surveillance transcripts, with such remarks being repeatedly made by commission members Genovese, Giancana, Bruno, Zerilli, Patriarca and Magaddino. In one such conversation in May 1962, a New York Mafia member noted the intense Federal pressure upon the mob, and remarked, "Bob Kennedy won't stop today until he puts us all in jail all over the country. Until the commission meets and puts its foot down, things will be at a standstill." Into 1963, the pressure was continuing to mount, as evidenced by a conversation in which commission member Magaddino bitterly cursed Attorney General Kennedy and commented on the Justice Department's increasing knowledge of the crime syndicates inner workings, stating, "They know everything under the sun. They know who's back of it – they know there is a commission. We got to watch right now – and stay as quiet as possible."

While the committee's examination of the electronic surveillance program revealed no shortage of such conversations during that period, the committee found no evidence in the conversations of the formulation of any specific plan to assassinate the President. Nevertheless, that organized crime figures did discuss possible violent courses of action against either the President or his brother, Attorney General Robert F. Kennedy – as well as the possible repercussions of such action – can be starkly seen in the transcripts.

One such discussion bears quoting at length. It is a conversation between commission member Angelo Bruno of Philadelphia and an associate Willie Weisburg, on 8 February 1962. In the discussion, in response to Weisburg's heated suggestion that Attorney General Kennedy should be murdered, Bruno cautioned that Kennedy might be followed by an even worse Attorney General:

WEISBURG. See what Kennedy done. With Kennedy, a guy should take a knife, like all them other guys, and stab and kill the [obscenity], where he is now. Somebody should kill the [obscenity], I mean it. This is true. Honest to God. It's about time to go. But I tell you something. I hope I git a week's notice, I'll kill. Right in the [obscenity] in the White House. Somebody's got to rid of this [obscenity].

BRUNO. Look, Willie, do you see there was a king, do you understand. And he found out that everybody was saying that he was a bad king. This is an old Italian story. So, he figured. Let me go talk to the old woman. She knows everything. So he went to the old wise woman. So he says to her: "I came here because I want your opinion." He says: "Do you think I'm a bad king?" She says: "No, I think you are a good king." He says: "Well how come everybody says I'm a bad king?" She says: "Because they are stupid. They don't know." He says: "Well how come, why do you say I'm a good king?" "Well," she said, "I knew your great-grandfather. He was a bad king. I knew your grandfather. He was worse. I knew your father. He was worse than them. You, you are worse than them, but your son, if you die, your son is going to be worse than

you. So it's better to be with you." [All laugh.] So Brownell
– former Attorney General – was bad. He was no [obscen-
ity] good. He was this and that.

WEISBURG. Do you know what this man is going to do?
He ain't going to leave nobody alone.

BRUNO. I know he ain't. But you see, everybody in there
was bad. The other guy was good because the other guy
was worse. Do you understand? Brownell came. He was
no good. He was worse than the guy before.

WEISBURG. Not like this one.

BRUNO. Not like this one. This one is worse, right? If
something happens to this guy … [laughs].

While Angelo Bruno had hoped to wait out his troubles,
believing that things might get better for him as time went by,
such was not to be the case during the Kennedy administration. The electronic surveillance transcripts disclosed that by
mid 1963, Bruno was privately making plans to shut down his
syndicate operations and leave America, an unprecedented
response by a commission member to Federal law enforcement pressure.

Another member of the mob commission, Stefano Magaddino, voiced similar anger toward the President during that
same period. In October 1963, in response to a Mafia family
member's remark that President Kennedy "should drop dead,"
Magaddino exploded, "They should kill the whole family, the
mother and father too. When he talks he talks like a mad dog,
he says, my brother the Attorney General."

The committee concluded that had the national crime syndicate, as a group, been involved in a conspiracy to kill the
President, some trace of the plot would have been picked up
by the FBI surveillance of the commission. Consequently,
finding no evidence in the electronic surveillance transcripts
of a specific intention or actual plan by commission members
to have the President assassinated, the committee believed it
was unlikely that it existed. The electronic surveillance transcripts included extensive conversations during secret meetings of various syndicate leaders, set forth many of their most

closely guarded thoughts and actions, and detailed their
involvement in a variety of other criminal acts, including
murder. Given the far-reaching possible consequences of an
assassination plot by the commission, the committee found
that such a conspiracy would have been the subject of serious
discussion by members of the commission, and that no matter
how guarded such discussions might have been, some trace of
them would have emerged from the surveillance coverage. It
was possible to conclude, therefore, that it is unlikely that the
national crime syndicate as a group, acting under the leadership of the commission, participated in the assassination of
President Kennedy.

While there was an absence of evidence in the electronic
surveillance materials of commission participation in the
President's murder, there was no shortage of evidence of the
elation and relief of various commission members over his
death. The surveillance transcripts contain numerous crude
and obscene comments by organized crime leaders, their lieutenants, associates and families regarding the assassination of
President Kennedy. The transcripts also reveal an awareness
by some mob leaders that the authorities might be watching
their reactions. On 25 November 1963, in response to a lieutenant's remark that Oswald "was an anarchist ... a Marxist
Communist," Giancana exclaimed, "He was a marksman
who knew how to shoot." On 29 November 1963, Magaddino
cautioned his associates not to joke openly about the
President's murder, stating, "You can be sure that the police
spies will be watching carefully to see what we think and say
about this." Several weeks later, during a discussion between
Bruno and his lieutenants, one participant remarked of the
late President, "It is too bad his brother Bobby was not in that
car too."

While the committee found it unlikely that the national
crime syndicate was involved in the assassination, it recognized the possibility that a particular organized crime leader
or a small combination of leaders, acting unilaterally, might
have formulated an assassination conspiracy without the
consent of the commission.

In its investigation of the national crime syndicate, the committee noted factors that could have led an organized crime leader who was considering an assassination to withhold it from the national commission. The committee's analysis of the national commission disclosed that it was splintered by dissension and enmity in 1963. Rivalry between two blocks of syndicate families had resulted in a partial paralysis of the commission's functions.

One significant reason for the disarray was, of course, the pressure being exerted by Federal law enforcement agencies. In the fall of 1963, Attorney General Kennedy noted, " ... in the past 2 years, at least three carefully planned commission meetings had to be called off because the leaders learned that we had uncovered their well-concealed plans and meeting places."

The Government's effort got an unprecedented boost from the willingness of Joseph Valachi, a member of the "family" of commission member Vito Genovese of New York, to testify about the internal structure and activities of the crime syndicate, a development described by Attorney General Kennedy as "the greatest intelligence breakthrough" in the history of the Federal program against organized crime. While it was not until August 1963 that Valachi's identity as a Federal witness became public, the surveillance transcripts disclose that syndicate leaders were aware as early as the spring of 1963 that Valachi was cooperating with the Justice Department. The transcripts disclose that the discovery that Valachi had become a Federal informant aroused widespread suspicion and fear over the possibility of other leaks and informants within the upper echelons of the syndicate. The televised Senate testimony by Valachi led to considerable doubt by syndicate leaders in other parts of the country as to the security of commission proceedings, with Genovese rapidly losing influence as a result of Valachi's actions.

The greatest source of internal disruption within the commission related to the discovery in early 1963 of a secret plan by commission member Joseph Bonanno to assassinate fellow members Carlo Gambino and Thomas Lucchese. Bonanno's assassination plan, aimed at an eventual takeover of the commission leadership, was discovered after one of the gunmen Bonanno had enlisted, Joseph Columbo, informed on him to the commission. The Bonanno conspiracy, an unheard-of violation of commission rules, led to a long series of acrimonious deliberations that lasted until early 1964. Bonanno refused to submit to the judgment of the commission, and his colleagues were sharply divided over how to deal with his betrayal, Gambino recommending that Bonanno be handled with caution, and Giancana urging that he be murdered.

The committee concluded, based on the state of disruption within the commission and the questions that had arisen as to the sanctity of commission proceedings, that an individual organized crime leader who was planning an assassination conspiracy against President Kennedy might well have avoided making the plan known to the commission or seeking approval for it from commission members. Such a course of unilateral action seemed to the committee to have been particularly possible in the case of powerful organized crime leaders who were well established, with firm control over their jurisdictions.

The committee noted a significant precedent for such a unilateral course of action. In 1957, Vito Genovese engineered the assassination of Albert Anastasia, then perhaps the most feared Mafia boss in the country. Six months earlier, Genovese's men had shot and wounded Frank Costello, who once was regarded as the single most influential organized crime leader. Both the Anastasia assassination and the Costello assault were carried out without the knowledge or consent of the national commission. Genovese did, however, obtain approval for the crimes after the fact. It was an extraordinary sequence of events that Attorney General Kennedy noted in September 1963, when he stated that Genovese "... wanted Commission approval for these acts – which he has received." The Genovese plot against Anastasia and Costello and the ex post facto commission approval were integral events in the rise to dominance of organized crime figures for the years that followed. It directly led to the assemblage of national syndicate leaders at the Apalachin conference three weeks after the Anastasia murder, and to the rise of Carlo Gambino to a position of pre-eminence in La Costa Nostra.

- *Analysis of the 1963–64 investigation.* In its investigation, the committee learned that fears of the possibility that organized crime was behind the assassination were more common among Government officials at the time than has been generally recognized. Both Attorney General Kennedy and President Johnson privately voiced suspicion about underworld complicity. The Attorney General requested that any relevant information be forwarded directly to him, and there was expectation at the time that the recently created Warren Commission would actively investigate the possibility of underworld involvement.

The committee found, however, that the Warren Commission conducted only a limited pursuit of the possibility of organized crime complicity. As has been noted, moreover, the Warren Commission's interest in organized crime was directed exclusively at Jack Ruby, and it did not involve any investigation of the national crime syndicate in general, or individual leaders in particular. This was confirmed to the committee by J. Lee Rankin, the Commission's general counsel, and by Burt W. Griffin, the staff counsel who conducted the Ruby investigation. Griffin testified before the committee that "… the possibility that someone associated with the underworld would have wanted to assassinate the President … [was] not seriously explored" by the Warren Commission.

The committee similarly learned from testimony and documentation that the FBI's investigation of the President's assassination was also severely limited in the area of possible organized crime involvement. While the committee found that the Bureau was uniquely equipped, with the Special Investigative Division having been formed two years earlier specifically to investigate organized crime, the specialists and agents of that Division did not play a significant role in the assassination investigation. Former Assistant FBI Director

Courtney Evans, who headed the Special Investigative Division, told the committee that the officials who directed the investigation never consulted him or asked for any participation by his Division. Evans recalled, "I know they sure didn't come to me. We had no part in that that I can recall." Al Staffeld, a former FBI official who supervised the day-to-day operations of the Special Investigative Division, told the committee that if the FBI's organized crime specialists had been asked to participate, "We would have gone at it in every damn way possible."

Ironically, the Bureau's own electronic surveillance transcripts revealed to the committee a conversation between Sam Giancana and a lieutenant, Charles English, regarding the FBI's role in investigating President Kennedy's assassination. In the 3 December 1963 conversation, English told Giancana: "I will tell you something, in another 2 months from now, the FBI will be like it was 5 years ago. They won't be around no more. They say the FBI will get it (the investigation of the President's assassination). They're gonna start running down Fair Play for Cuba, Fair Play for Matsu. They call that more detrimental to the country than us guys."

The committee found that the quality and scope of the investigation into the possibility of an organized crime conspiracy in the President's assassination by the Warren Commission and the FBI was not sufficient to uncover one had it existed. The committee also found that it was possible, based on an analysis of motive, means and opportunity, that an individual organized crime leader, or a small combination of leaders, might have participated in a conspiracy to assassinate President Kennedy. The committee's extensive investigation led it to conclude that the most likely family bosses of organized crime to have participated in such a unilateral assassination plan were Carlos Marcello and Santos Trafficante. While other family bosses on the commission were subjected to considerable coverage in the electronic surveillance program, such coverage was never applied to Marcello and almost never to Trafficante.

● *Carlos Marcello.* The committee found that Marcello had the motive, means and opportunity to have President John F. Kennedy assassinated, though it was unable to establish direct evidence of Marcello's complicity.

In its investigation of Marcello, the committee identified the presence of one critical evidentiary element that was lacking with the other organized crime figures examined by the committee: credible associations relating both Lee Harvey Oswald and Jack Ruby to figures having a relationship, albeit tenuous, with Marcello's crime family or organization. At the same time, the committee explicitly cautioned: association is the first step in conspiracy; it is not identical to it, and while associations may legitimately give rise to suspicions, a careful distinction must always be drawn between suspicions suspected and facts found.

As the long-time La Cosa Nostra leader in an area that is based in New Orleans but extends throughout Louisiana and Texas, Marcello was one of the prime targets of Justice Department efforts during the Kennedy administration. He had, in fact, been temporarily removed from the country for a time in 1961 through deportation proceedings personally expedited by Attorney General Kennedy. In his appearance before the committee in executive session, Marcello exhibited an intense dislike for Robert Kennedy because of these actions, claiming that he had been illegally "kidnapped" by Government agents during the deportation.

While the Warren Commission devoted extensive attention to Oswald's background and activities, the committee uncovered significant details of his exposure to and contacts with figures associated with the underworld of New Orleans that apparently had escaped the Commission. One such relationship actually extended into Oswald's own family through his uncle, Charles "Dutz" Murret, a minor underworld gambling figure. The committee discovered that Murret, who served as a surrogate father of sorts throughout much of Oswald's life in New Orleans, was in the 1940s and 1950s and possibly until his death in 1964, an associate of significant organized crime figures affiliated with the Marcello organization.

The committee established that Oswald was familiar with his uncle's underworld activities and had discussed them with his wife, Marina, in 1963. Additionally, the committee found that Oswald's mother, Marguerite Oswald, was acquainted with several men associated with lieutenants in the Marcello organization. One such acquaintance, who was also an associate of Dutz Murret, reportedly served as a personal aide or driver to Marcello at one time. In another instance, the committee found that an individual connected to Dutz Murret, the person who arranged bail for Oswald following his arrest in August 1963 for a street disturbance, was an associate of two of Marcello's syndicate deputies. (One of the two, Nofio Pecora, as noted, also received a telephone call from Ruby on 30 October 1963, according to the committee's computer analysis of Ruby's phone records.)

During the course of its investigation, the committee developed several areas of credible evidence and testimony indicating a possible association in New Orleans and elsewhere between Lee Harvey Oswald and David W. Ferrie, a private investigator and even, perhaps, a pilot for Marcello before and during 1963. From the evidence available to the committee, the nature of the Oswald–Ferrie association remained largely a mystery. The committee established that Oswald and Ferrie apparently first came into contact with each other during Oswald's participation as a teenager in a Civil Air Patrol unit for which Ferrie served as an instructor, although Ferrie, when he was interviewed by the FBI after his detainment as a suspect in the assassination, denied any past association with Oswald.

In interviews following the assassination, Ferrie stated that he may have spoken in an offhand manner of the desirability of having President Kennedy shot, but he denied wanting such a deed actually to be done. Ferrie also admitted his association with Marcello and stated that he had been in personal contact with the syndicate leader in the fall of 1963. He noted that on the morning of the day of the President's death he was present with Marcello at a courthouse in New Orleans. In his executive session testimony before the committee, Marcello acknowledged that Ferrie did work for his lawyer, G. Wray Gill, on his case, but Marcello denied that Ferrie worked for him or that their relationship was close. Ferrie died in 1967 of a ruptured blood vessel at the base of the brain, shortly after he was named in the assassination investigation of New Orleans District Attorney Jim Garrison.

The committee also confirmed that the address 544 Camp Street, that Oswald had printed on some Fair Play for Cuba Committee handouts in New Orleans, was the address of a small office building where Ferrie was working on at least a part-time basis in 1963. The Warren Commission stated in its report that despite the Commission's probe into why Oswald used this return address on his literature, "investigation has indicated that neither the Fair Play for Cuba Committee nor Lee Oswald ever maintained an office at that address."

The committee also established associations between Jack Ruby and several individuals affiliated with the underworld activities of Carlos Marcello. Ruby was a personal acquaintance of Joseph Civello, the Marcello associate, who allegedly headed organized crime activities in Dallas; he also knew other individuals who have been linked with organized crime, including a New Orleans nightclub figure, Harold Tannenbaum, with whom Ruby was considering going into partnership in the fall of 1963.

The committee examined a widely circulated published account that Marcello made some kind of threat on the life of President Kennedy in September 1962 at a meeting at his Churchill Farms estate outside New Orleans. It was alleged that Marcello shouted an old Sicilian threat, *"Livarsi na petra di la scarpa!"* "Take the stone out of my shoe!" against the Kennedy brothers, stating that the President was going to be assassinated. He spoke of using a "nut" to carry out the murder.

The committee established the origin of the story and identified the informant who claimed to have been present at the meeting during which Marcello made the threat. The committee also learned that even though the FBI was aware of the informant's allegations over a year and half before they were published in 1969, and possessed additional information indicating that the informant may in fact have met with Marcello in the fall of 1962, a substantive investigation of the information was never conducted. Director Hoover and other senior FBI officials were aware that FBI agents were initiating action to "discredit" the informant, without having conducted a significant investigation of his allegations. Further, the committee discovered that the originating office relied on derogatory information from a prominent underworld figure in the ongoing effort to discredit the informant. An internal memorandum to Hoover noted that another FBI source was taking action to discredit the informant, "in order that the Carlos Marcello incident would be deleted from the book that first recounted the information."

The committee determined that the informant who gave the account of the Marcello threat was in fact associated with various underworld figures, including at least one person well-acquainted with the Marcello organization. The committee noted, however, that as a consequence of his underworld involvement, the informant had a questionable reputation for honesty and may not be a credible source of information.

The committee noted further that it is unlikely that an organized crime leader personally involved in an assassination plot would discuss it with anyone other than his closest lieutenants, although he might be willing to discuss it more freely prior to a serious decision to undertake such an act. In his executive session appearance before the committee, Marcello categorically denied any involvement in organized crime or the assassination of President Kennedy. Marcello also denied ever making any kind of threat against the President's life.

As noted, Marcello was never the subject of electronic surveillance coverage by the FBI. The committee found that the Bureau did make two attempts to effect such surveillance during the early 1960s, but both attempts were unsuccessful. Marcello's sophisticated security system and close-knit organizational structure may have been a factor in preventing such surveillance. A former FBI official knowledgeable about the surveillance program told the committee, "That was our biggest gap ... With Marcello, you've got the one big exception in our work back then. There was just no way of penetrating that area. He was too smart."

Any evaluation of Marcello's possible role in the assassination must take into consideration his unique stature within La Cosa Nostra. The FBI determined in the 1960s that because of Marcello's position as head of the New Orleans Mafia family (the oldest in the United States, having first entered the country in the 1880s), the Louisiana organized crime leader had been endowed with special powers and privileges not accorded to any other La Cosa Nostra members. As the leader of "the first family" of the Mafia in America, according to FBI information, Marcello has been the recipient of the extraordinary privilege of conducting syndicate operations without having to seek the approval of the national commission.

Finally, a caveat, Marcello's uniquely successful career in organized crime has been based to a large extent on a policy of prudence; he is not reckless. As with the case of the Soviet and Cuban Governments, a risk analysis indicated that he would be unlikely to undertake so dangerous a course of action as a Presidential assassination. Considering that record of prudence, and in the absence of direct evidence of involvement, it may be said that it is unlikely that Marcello was in fact involved in the assassination of the President. On the basis of the evidence available to it, and in the context of its duty to be cautious in its evaluation of the evidence, there is no other conclusion that the committee could reach. On the other hand, the evidence that he had the motive and the evidence of links through associates to both Oswald and Ruby, coupled with the failure of the 1963–64 investigation to explore adequately possible conspiratorial activity in the assassination, precluded a judgment by the committee that Marcello and his associates were not involved.

● *Santos Trafficante*. The committee also concentrated its attention on Santos Trafficante, the La Cosa Nostra leader in Florida. The committee found that Trafficante, like Marcello, had the motive, means, and opportunity to assassinate President Kennedy.

Trafficante was a key subject of the Justice Department crackdown on organized crime during the Kennedy administration, with his name being added to a list of the top ten syndicate leaders targeted for investigation. Ironically, Attorney General Kennedy's strong interest in having Trafficante prosecuted occurred during the same period in which CIA officials, unbeknownst to the Attorney General, were using Trafficante's services in assassination plots against the Cuban chief of state, Fidel Castro.

The committee found that Santos Trafficante's stature in the national syndicate of organized crime, notably the violent narcotics trade, and his role as the mob's chief liaison to criminal figures within the Cuban exile community, provided him with the capability of formulating an assassination conspiracy against President Kennedy. Trafficante had recruited Cuban nationals to help plan and execute the CIA's assignment to assassinate Castro. (The CIA gave the assignment to former FBI Agent Robert Maheu, who passed the contract along to Mafia figures Sam Giancana and John Roselli. They, in turn, enlisted Trafficante to have the intended assassination carried out.)

In his testimony before the committee, Trafficante admitted participating in the unsuccessful CIA conspiracy to assassinate Castro, an admission indicating his willingness to participate in political murder. Trafficante testified that he worked with the CIA out of a patriotic feeling for his country, an explanation the committee did not accept, at least not as his sole motivation.

As noted, the committee established a possible connection between Trafficante and Jack Ruby in Cuba in 1959. It determined there had been a close friendship between Ruby and Lewis McWillie, who, as a Havana gambler, worked in an area subject to the control of the Trafficante Mafia family.

Further, it assembled documentary evidence that Ruby made at least two, if not three or more, trips to Havana in 1959 when McWillie was involved in underworld gambling operations there. Ruby may in fact have been serving as a courier for underworld gambling interests in Havana, probably for the purpose of transporting funds to a bank in Miami.

The committee also found that Ruby had been connected with other Trafficante associates – R. D. Matthews, Jack Todd, and James Dolan – all of Dallas.

Finally, the committee developed corroborating evidence that Ruby may have met with Trafficante at Trescornia prison in Cuba during one of his visits to Havana in 1959, as the CIA had learned but had discounted in 1964. While the committee was not able to determine the purpose of the meeting, there was considerable evidence that it did take place.

During the course of its investigation of Santos Trafficante, the committee examined an allegation that Trafficante had told a prominent Cuban exile, Jose Aleman, that President Kennedy was going to be assassinated. According to Aleman, Trafficante made the statement in a private conversation with him that took place sometime in September 1962. In an account of the alleged conversation published by the *Washington Post* in 1976, Aleman was quoted as stating that Trafficante had told him that President Kennedy was "going to be hit." Aleman further stated, however, that it was his impression that Trafficante was not the specific individual who was allegedly planning the murder. Aleman was quoted as having noted that Trafficante had spoken of Teamsters Union President James Hoffa during the same conversation, indicating that the President would "get what is coming to him" as a result of his administration's intense efforts to prosecute Hoffa.

During an interview with the committee in March 1977, Aleman provided further details of his alleged discussion with Trafficante in September 1962. Aleman stated that during the course of the discussion, Trafficante had made clear to him that he was not guessing that the President was going to be killed. Rather he did in fact know that such a crime was being planned. In his committee interview, Aleman further stated that Trafficante had given him the distinct impression that Hoffa was to be principally involved in planning the Presidential murder.

In September 1978, prior to his appearance before the committee in public session, Aleman reaffirmed his earlier account of the alleged September 1962 meeting with Trafficante. Nevertheless, shortly before his appearance in public session, Aleman informed the committee staff that he feared for his physical safety and was afraid of possible reprisal from Trafficante or his organization. In this testimony, Aleman changed his professed understanding of Trafficante's comments. Aleman repeated under oath that Trafficante had said Kennedy was "going to be hit," but he then stated it was his impression that Trafficante may have only meant the President was going to be hit by "a lot of Republican votes" in the 1964 election, not that he was going to be assassinated.

Appearing before the committee in public session on 28 September 1978, Trafficante categorically denied ever having discussed any plan to assassinate President Kennedy. Trafficante denied any foreknowledge of or participation in the President's murder. While stating that he did in fact know Aleman and that he had met with him on more than one occasion in 1962, Trafficante denied Aleman's account of their alleged conversation about President Kennedy, and he denied ever having made a threatening remark against the President.

The committee found it difficult to understand how Aleman could have misunderstood Trafficante during such a conversation, or why he would have fabricated such an account. Aleman appeared to be a reputable person, who did not seek to publicize his allegations, and he was well aware of the potential danger of making such allegations against a leader of La Costa Nostra. The committee noted, however, that Aleman's prior allegations and testimony before the committee had made him understandably fearful for his life.

The committee also did not fully understand why Aleman waited so many years before publicly disclosing the alleged incident. While he stated in 1976 that he had reported Trafficante's alleged remarks about the President to FBI agents in 1962 and 1963, the committee's review of Bureau reports on his contacts with FBI agents did not reveal a record of any such disclosure or comments at the time. Additionally, the FBI agent who served as Aleman's contact during that period denied ever being told such information by Aleman.

Further, the committee found it difficult to comprehend why Trafficante, if he was planning or had personal knowledge of an assassination plot, would have revealed or hinted at such a sensitive matter to Aleman. It is possible that Trafficante may have been expressing a personal opinion, "The President ought to be hit," but it is unlikely in the context of their relationship that Trafficante would have revealed to Aleman the existence of a current plot to kill the President. As previously noted with respect to Carlos Marcello, to have attained his stature as the recognized organized crime leader of Florida for a number of years, Trafficante necessarily had to operate in a characteristically calculating and discreet manner. The relationship between Trafficante and Aleman, a business acquaintance, does not seem to have been close enough for Trafficante to have mentioned or alluded to such a murder plot. The committee thus doubted that Trafficante would have inadvertently mentioned such a plot. In sum, the committee believed there were substantial factors that called into question the validity of Aleman's account.

Nonetheless, as the electronic surveillance transcripts of Angelo Bruno, Stefano Magaddino and other top organized crime leaders make clear, there were in fact various underworld conversations in which the desirability of having the President assassinated was discussed. There were private conversations in which assassination was mentioned, although not in a context that indicated such a crime had been specifically planned. With this in mind, and in the absence of additional evidence with which to evaluate the Aleman account of Trafficante's alleged 1962 remarks, the committee concluded that the conversation, if it did occur as Aleman testified, probably occurred in such a circumscribed context.

As noted earlier, the committee's examination of the FBI's electronic surveillance program of the early 1960s disclosed that Santos Trafficante was the subject of minimal, in fact almost nonexistent, surveillance coverage. During one conversation in 1963, overheard in a Miami restaurant, Trafficante had bitterly attacked the Kennedy administration's efforts against organized crime, making obscene comments about "Kennedy's right-hand man" who had recently coordinated various raids on Trafficante gambling establishments. In the conversation, Trafficante stated that he was under immense pressure from Federal investigators, commenting "I know when I'm beat, you understand?" Nevertheless, it was not possible to draw conclusions about Trafficante actions based on the electronic surveillance program since the coverage was so limited. Finally, as with Marcello, the committee noted that Trafficante's cautious character is inconsistent with his taking the risk of being involved in an assassination plot against the President. The committee found, in the context of its duty to be cautious in its evaluation of the evidence, that it is unlikely that Trafficante plotted to kill the President, although it could not rule out the possibility of such participation on the basis of available evidence.

KISSINGER ASSOCIATES

According to the **Bible Code** conspiracy, the Good Book contains hundreds of secret predictions. In *Death in the Air*, Bible code-breaker Dr Leonard G. Horowitz cracks the beast of all cryptograms, the identity of the Devil. "Among the names of leading suspects," Dr Horowitz advises, "[Henry] KISSINGER is the only name that decodes to 666."

Mind you, you don't have to be a Bible Code basher to believe that Dr Henry Kissinger, former US Secretary of State and National Security Advisor, is evil. British-American journalist Christopher Hitchens, in *The Trial of Henry Kissinger*, calls for Kissinger to be prosecuted "for war crimes, for crimes against humanity, and for offences against common or customary or international law, including conspiracy to commit murder, kidnap, and torture". Hitchens believes Kissinger's identifiable crimes include "The deliberate mass killing of civilian populations in Indochina and the personal suborning and planning of murder of a senior constitutional officer in a democratic nation – Chile – with which the United States was not at war ... this criminal habit of mind extends to Bangladesh, Cyprus, East Timor, and even to Washington, DC."

The "senior constitutional officer" Hitchens referred to was General Rene Schneider, former Commander-in-Chief of the Chilean Army; it is asserted that Kissinger ordered Schneider's assassination because he refused to back plans for a military overthrow of Chilean president Salvador Allende. Schneider's family tried to sue Kissinger in a Washington, DC, federal court; the case was dismissed, not on its merits, but because the political question doctrine made it non-justiciable. In connection with Kissinger's alleged role in the disappearance of citizens in South America during Operation Condor, a cross-national scheme by which right-wing dictatorships "disappeared" opponents, Kissinger had had to sidestep legal summons from investigators in Spain, Chile, Argentina and France.

When Henry Kissinger won the Nobel Peace Prize in 1973, the musical satirist Tom Lehrer quipped, "It was at that moment that satire died. There was nothing more to say after that." Kissinger had only recently instigated the mass carpet bombing of Cambodia to cut off North Vietnamese supply routes. Neither did Kissinger's thesis that a limited atomic war was winnable, as advanced in his *Nuclear War and Foreign Policy*, immediately seem the stuff of which Nobel Peace Prize winners are made. Reputedly, the discourse led to Kissinger becoming the inspiration for Kubrick's film, *Dr Strangelove*. And Among Kissinger's hawkish bon mots are the classics: "It is an act of insanity and national humiliation to have a law forbidding the President from ordering assassination," and, "I don't see why we need to stand by and watch a country go Communist due to the irresponsibility of its own people."

After Kissinger left office, his musings were still in demand on the international power circuit. He also knew anybody who was anybody. In 1982, Henry Kissinger – born Heinz Kissinger, in Germany in 1923, by the by – founded a private New York-based international consulting agency. In the words of Hitchens, the said Kissinger Associates "exists to facilitate contact between multinational corporations and foreign governments". Kissinger co-opted a number of big names, such as former National Security Advisor Brent Scowcroft and NATO chief Lord Carrington, and with such luminaries, collective know-how and connections, Kissinger Associates could hardly fail. And it didn't. Within five years, the company had paid off its foundation loans, and was turning over $5 million per annum. Kissinger Associates does not disclose its clients' identities, and when Kissinger himself was asked to head the **9/11** inquiry he stood down rather than reveal the company's client list as asked to do by Democrats concerned about conflicts of interest. Still, some information leaks out – or is burbled out by CEOs only to anxious to boast their connection to Dr Kissinger – and Kissinger Associates' known clients include such mega-players as Union Carbide, Coca-Cola, HSBC, American Express, Fiat and Heinz.

Given Kissinger's track record, it hardly comes as a surprise that pertinent questions have been raised about the activity of Kissinger Associates in, inter alia, the BCCI banking scandal, the ecological catastrophe in Indonesia caused by mining client Freeport McMoran, loans and exports to Hussein's Iraq, and undue influence on Capitol Hill on behalf of clients, even client states. (Despite Henry Kissinger's avowed anti-Communism, he is big in China, and has lobbied on China's behalf; he was an almost lone Western voice supporting the Communist dictatorship's crackdown on democratic protesters in Tiananmen Square.) Kissinger Associates' staff also have the useful habit of dropping in and out of government – Brent Scowcroft and Laurence Eagleburger both served in the regime of George H. W. Bush, for example – which, it is suggested, gives the Associates unparalleled access to power, plus inside information which can be turned to unfair commercial advantage.

Kissinger Associates goes from strength to strength. So, inevitably, do suspicions about its influence.

Watch this space.

Consultancy run by former secretary of state wields undue power in US and world: ALERT LEVEL 8

Further Reading
Christopher Hitchens, *The Trial of Henry Kissinger*, 2001
www.tetrahedron.org

KKK

To accuse the Ku Klux Klan of conspiracy is a little like accusing **Osama bin Laden** of fanaticism, or the Pope of Catholicism. It is plain obvious. After all, running around in bed sheets (to hide identity, rather than to pretend to be a ghost at a fancy dress party) in the execution of sticksville plots to lynch uppity "Niggas" squares precisely with the dictionary definition of conspiracy as "a secret plan or agreement to carry out an illegal or harmful act, esp. with political motivation". What is less recognized, however, is that the Klan from the 1960s has been a terrorist organization, of which three pertinent questions can be asked:

- Did the Klan sponsor the assassination of Martin Luther King?
- Was the Klan behind the Oklahoma City bombings in 1995?
- Did the Klan, as some believe, inject popular foods and drinks to make black men impotent?

Deriving its name from "*kyklos*" the Greek for "circle", the Ku Klux Klan was founded by six Confederate soldiers in Pulaski, Tennessee in 1865. Initially the Ku Klux Klan – invariably called the "Klan" or the "KKK" – was a high-spirited quasi charity which looked after Civil War veterans, but it soon turned into a violent network opposed to Reconstruction and for Segregation. The KKK costume of an all-white robe, mask and pointed hood became a symbol of fear and loathing across the ex-Confederacy.

By the end of the decade, the KKK had tens of thousands of members in the South, prominent among them the former Reb cavalry general, Nathan Bedford Forrest. Under Forrest's headship, the Klan evolved a whole set of Masonic-like names and rituals, with the South becoming the "Invisible Empire", and the leader the "Grand Wizard". Each state was titled a "Realm", headed by a "Grand Dragon". Forrest, however, was unable to stop the KKK's hood-long lurch towards terrorism, and in 1869 ordered the Klan to disband. The membership ignored him, and if anything ramped up its night attacks on the black community in the Southern states. With the South burning, President Ulysses Grant passed laws in 1870 and 1871 to outlaw and suppress the organization. Thousands of Klansmen went to the pen. Within a decade the Klan was merely a bad memory.

Bizarrely, the Klan was reborn by a movie, *Birth of a Nation*, D. W. Griffith's 1919 epic but racist masterpiece in which an heroic South stands proud against Northern no-gooders and lascivious blacks. After watching the movie, a certain failed preacher by the name of William J. Simmons determined to resurrect the Klan. Astutely, Simmons got on board the project the savvy Indiana businessman David Curtiss Stephenson. The new Klan grew exponentially; by 1924, the KKK had four million members nationwide; in Indiana one in four adult males was a Klansman. The key to Simmons's/Stephenson's success was to widen the hate-base of the Klan: Catholics, Jews and union activists joined blacks in the KKK's gallery of loathing. Underneath the public political campaign of legitimate voting drives, hustings and boycotts, the Klan widely indulged in violent intimidation in the old-style white hoods with the dramatic addition of flaming crosses.

Then, in 1925, the Klan II's bubble burst as quickly as it had inflated. Stephenson, who was by now the Grand Dragon of twenty-two states (and a rich man on Klan membership dues), was found guilty of the rape and murder of his secretary; one of the causes of her death was from septicaemia, caused by Stephenson's multiple bites to her body. Embarrassed Klan members could not rip up their membership cards quickly enough; by 1930, Klan membership, hit by the double whammy of the Stephenson scandal and the moneyless Depression, had sunk to 30,000. To absolutely ensure its own demise, the Klan then allied itself with Nazi groups in the USA, such as the German-American Bund, leading to accusations of disloyalty. Thirty years later, KKK membership was estimated at 3,000.

This truncated Klan turned to outright terrorism. During the Civil Rights era the Klan was implicated in a string of outrages: the assassination of NAACP member Medgar Evers in Alabama; the bombing of the 16th Street Baptist Church in Birmingham; the shooting of Detroit civil rights activist Viola Gregg Liuzzo; the murder of black Army veteran Lt Colonel Lemuel Penn; the shooting of Civil Rights workers James Chaney, Andrew Goodman and Michael Schwerner in Mississippi in 1964.

Then there was the assassination of Martin Luther King. Dr Martin Luther King had a dream of racial harmony, but King's dream was a nightmare for racists. At 6.11 p.m. on 4 April 1968, as he lounged on the balcony of the Lorraine Motel in Memphis, King was fatally shot. The shot which killed him was traced to a flophouse opposite, where a rifle was retrieved bearing the fingerprints of James Earl Ray. Two months later, after a massive manhunt, Ray was captured in London travelling under a false passport. He was extradited to Tennessee, where he was sentenced to a 99-year prison term.

Days after his sentencing, Ray began protesting his innocence, claiming he had only made an earlier confession of guilt on the advice of his lawyer, so he would avoid the possibility of execution. Numerous other observers of the case weighed in on Ray's behalf, because aspects of the conviction did not stack up:

- Ray was a two-bit petty criminal, who somehow funded an escape to England with a false passport.
- He was not a trained sniper, but pulled off a difficult single shot to assassinate King. And the bullet from King's body was never matched to the supposedly responsible rifle.
- The drunk who identified Ray as a denizen of the flophouse recanted when sober.

Although the 1977 House Select Committee on Assassinations disbelieved Ray's claim that he was a guiltless patsy, it did allow

the "likelihood" that Ray did not act alone. The Select
Committee noted further that FBI files "revealed approximately
25 Klan-related leads" in the King assassination, but that the
passage of time, conflicting testimonies, and a lack of cooperation from witnesses meant that the leads should be discounted.
But two of these leads were always suggestive. First, was the
evidence of diner waitress Myrtis Hendricks. The Select
Committee recorded:

2. In an interview with an agent of the Dallas FBI field office
on April 22, 1968, Myrtis Ruth Hendricks, accompanied by
Thomas McGee, maintained she had overheard discussions of
a conspiracy to kill Dr. King. Hendricks said that while working
as a waitress at John's Restaurant in Laurel, Miss., on April 2,
1968, she heard the owner, Deavours Nix, say he "had gotten
a call on King". Nix was then head of intelligence and the
grand director of the Klan Bureau of Investigation for the
White Knights of Ku Klux Klan of Mississippi (WKKKKOM)
the most violent Klan organization during 1967 and 1968.
Hendricks said that on April 3, 1968, she saw in Nix's office a
rifle with a telescopic sight in a case, which two men put in a
long box in the back of a 1964 maroon Dodge. Hendricks
alleged that on the following day Nix received a phone call
announcing Dr. King's death before the news was broadcast
on the radio. Hendricks left Laurel shortly after Dr. King's
death to join her boyfriend, Thomas McGee, in Texas.

The Bureau had independently confirmed that John's
Restaurant was a gathering place for known Klan members
and that members had been there on April 3 and 4, 1968.
Nevertheless, it found no corroboration of the Hendricks rifle
story. The committee's review of FBI files concerning the
White Knights' activities uncovered informant information
similar to the Hendricks' allegation. In addition, statements
attributed to Samuel H. Bowers, the imperial wizard of the
WKKKKOM, in John's Restaurant on April 5, 1968, raised
the possibility of his involvement in the assassination. As a
result of this information and an indication that it was not
developed further in the FBI investigation, the committee
pursued the lead.

Myrtis Hendricks denied the substance of her allegation when contacted by the committee. While admitting that she had worked for Nix, she said she was afraid of her former boyfriend, Thomas McGee, but refused to elaborate further. The committee's attempt to interview FBI informants who had furnished relevant information was unsuccessful. The informants were either unavailable or uncooperative.

The Committee did note, however, that "Laurel, Miss., the scene of the alleged activities, lies between New Orleans and Birmingham. James Earl Ray traveled between these two cities in March 1968."

More recently, two other pieces of information have surfaced to tie the KKK to MLK's death. According to a 1993 report in the Memphis Commercial Appeal, rogue government agents in the South recruited KKK members for local ops during the sixties – and some of these Klan stooges were in Memphis on the day of King's assassination. And, FBI records turned up by researchers Larry J. Hancock and Stuart Wexler show that Ray knew of a $100,000 bounty being offered by the White Knights of the Ku Klux Klan in Mississippi to kill Martin Luther King Jr before Ray escaped from a Missouri prison prior to reaching Memphis.

In his definitive book of the King assassination, *Killing the Dream*, historian Gerald Posner speculates that "there was a conspiracy [to kill King], but on a very low level. Someone, I'd guess part of a racist group, probably agreed to pay him [Ray] maybe $25,000 or $50,000." Posner, it should be said, is no paranoid conspiracy loon. He thinks JFK *was* murdered by a lone nut.

The KKK's connection to Timothy McVeigh, the bomber who brought down the Alfred P. Murrah building in downtown Oklahoma City on 19 April 1995 is straightforward. When the FBI raided McVeigh's house they found overwhelming evidence that he was a member of the KKK, which he probably joined in 1992. That said, he seems to have been a disaffected, inactive member who was more committed to other far right organizations, specifically the Aryan Republican Army, a group of Midwest bank robbers and racists, whose explosive kit he seems to have borrowed. Or been supplied with.

The Klan's own take on McVeigh and the Oklahoma City bombing is a convoluted scheme whereby the Feds committed the outrage to blacken the Klan. Why, the FBI would go to such efforts to discredit such small political fry is unclear. Following paramilitarization in the 1970s, the Klan had split into some one hundred autonomous or semi-autonomous fragments, and declined until its main variant had no more than 2,000 members. The Klan's place on the racist right of the US has long been taken by the militias and neo-Nazi groups.

As for the KKK running major companies with a view to lacing their products with drugs to make black men impotent, this is a plain and simple urban myth. Kentucky Fried Chicken is the favourite target of the legend, with the Colonel reputed to put saltpetre in with the spices, and have 10 per cent of profits put in the Klan coffers. Actually, the Colonel is long dead, and 10 per cent of KFC's profits, even 10 per cent of the Colonel's will – if it did a have a pro-Klan clause, which it didn't – would leave a public paper trail wider than a four-lane black top. Marlboro (you get three K shapes from the chevrons on the packet!), Kools and Coors have all been the target of similar rumours that they are tools of the Klan. They are not.

Indisputably, the Klan has been involved in numerous local terrorist conspiracies over the years. As for the MLK assassination, there is no evidence to tie the Klan as an organization to the crime, but it is not beyond possibility that Klan individuals were involved.

> KKK sponsored the assassination of Martin Luther King: ALERT LEVEL 3
>
> Individual KKK members aided and abetted the MLK assassination: ALERT LEVEL 6

Further Reading
Wyn Wade, *The Fiery Cross: The Ku Klux Klan in America*, 1987
Worth H. Weller and Brad Thompson, *Under the Hood: Unmasking the Modern Ku Klux Klan*, 1998
www.snopes.com/business/alliance/sanders.asp

KNIGHTS OF COLUMBUS

The Knights of Columbus society was founded by Father Michael McGivney, an Irish Catholic priest, in Connecticut in 1882. Catholics in America were excluded from many labour unions and fraternal benefit societies, and McGivney hoped his society would be a mutual help society based on the Church of Rome's teachings. Like other clubs of the time, it adopted arcane rituals and promises, but ensured these not so onerous that they conflicted with the Papal ban on secret orders. Only Catholics were, and are, allowed.

The KoC is invariably and robustly right wing, and in the 1950s supported Joe McCarthy's anti-Red witch-hunts. Nonetheless, it is lauded for its charitable works, funded through such exciting means as pasta nights. So popular has the KoC become, that it has spread throughout the USA and to Canada and Mexico. An Irish facsimile, the Knights of St Columbanus was founded in Eire in 1915, and remains active.

It may come as a surprise to the KoC members and their families attending the pasta night, but the KoC is actually nothing but a front for the **Society of Jesus**/the **Bavarian Illuminati** (take your pick) and is conspiring to overthrow the Protestant faith. Aside from swearing the Bloody Oath, which is the same one the Jesuits promise to obey (allegedly; see p. 492), members of the KoC, like the Jesuits, perform their initiation under the symbol INRI. According to www.biblebelievers.org.au, INRI stands for "*Iustum, Necar, Reges, Impious*", meaning "It is just to exterminate or annihilate impious or heretical Kings, Governments, or Rulers".

Er, actually INRI is the abbreviation for the Latin "*Iesvs Nazarenvs Rex Ivdaeorvm*". This means "Jesus of Nazareth, King of the Jews".

Still, never let the facts get in the way of a good conspiracy. Or indeed let logic be a bar. One internet site seeking to expose the Knights of Columbus reaches the exemplar in non sequiturs: "The capital of the United States is Washington D.C. which stands for 'District of Columbia'. America was discovered by a man named Columbus. The Fraternal order Knights of Columbus have been exposed aided [sic] the drug trade in Colombia the country."

KoC members have brought successful libel actions against parties proclaiming they uphold the Bloody Oath.

Catholic charity doubles as secret army fighting for Catholic theocracy: ALERT LEVEL 2

Further Reading
Christopher Kauffman, *Faith and Fraternalism: The History of the Knights of Columbus*, 1982

KNIGHTS OF THE GOLDEN CIRCLE

Founded in 1854 by Dr George W. L. Bickley, the Knights were initially a ginger group for an expansion of the US southwards by which it would make a "Golden Circle" around the Gulf of Mexico. Bickley's project had a particular lure for southerners, because the acquired lands were deemed wholly suitable for slave-worked plantations. And in this newly expanded US the South would dominate the abolitionist North.

When the geographical Golden Circle failed to materialize, the Knights turned to cheerleading for Southern independence. With the coming of the Civil War in 1861, the Knights thickened the plot by working behind enemy lines (i.e. in the North), where their castles (lodges) tried to sabotage the Union military effort. Especially active in the Midwest, the Knights opposed the draft, spread anti-war propaganda, organized politically to stymie the Republican party of Lincoln, ran contraband goods to Confederate capital Richmond, ran escaped Confederate POWs home, and assisted Confederate spies. Joseph Holt, United States Judge Advocate General, warned in a report to Congress that the KGC was involved in the "Northwest Conspiracy" to remove this part of the Union from Washington's control.

But the KGC's real claim to infamy came with the assassination of **Abraham Lincoln**. Northern politicians immediately rushed into ink to damn the Knights for their role in Lincoln's murder. They had lots of suspicions, but little evidence. However, a century later, in 1966, the Northern accusation was retrospectively aided by the publication of a diary by John H.

Surratt, one of those implicated in the plot to kill the president. A Confederate spy, Surratt was also a member of the KGC. Aside from an intoxicating account of the Masonic-like initiation ceremony of the KGC (see Document, p.308), Surratt drops tantalizing mentions of another KGC member throughout his diary – one John Wilkes Booth, Lincoln's undisputed assassin. Although Surratt was quite happy to claim a role in a plot to kidnap Lincoln, he was at pains to proclaim his innocence in Lincoln's murder most foul. Thus he writes:

> November 8, 1864. – The election returns are in, at least enough to decide that McClellan is defeated. To save the South, Lincoln must be removed before the 4th of March. He shall never again be inaugurated. Booth wants his life, but I shall oppose anything like murder. It would serve our turn quite as well to capture the despot, and keep him for a while in Libby Prison. I reckon the South would then gain the day.

Surratt's diary is not as damning as it seems; it was largely authored by its editor Dion Haco, who was not beyond exaggeration in the interests of a good sell. Which is not to say that the "Fifth Columnist" Knights of the Golden Circle did not aid John Wilkes Booth; it is merely to note that the "proof" is not beyond reasonable doubt. The KGC certainly had the appetite for bumping off Lincoln. When Clement Vallandigham, the Knights' titular head, ran a failed campaign for the governorship of Ohio, large numbers of despairing Knights departed for the Order of American Knights (OAK) – and *they* advocated the plain and simple armed overthrow of the North. Vallandigham himself took the office of Supreme Commander of the OAK.

Like numerous other political secret societies, the Knights went under a bewildering number of pseudonyms, all intended to put Fed agents off their trail. They were known as the Knights of the Mighty Host, the Circle of Honor, the Circle (not to be confused with *Le Cercle*), the Peace Organization, and the Mutual Protection Society. Northerners dismissively nicknamed them "Copperheads", after the poisonous snake. Although the Knights – however named – ceased to be an active potent force after the surrender of the Confederate armies at Appomattox in

1865, they are reputed to have lingered on until 1916, by which time they were old or dead men, and the bitter torch of anti-black politics had passed to the Ku Klux Klan.

> South-sympathizing secret society had a hand in the murder of President Lincoln: ALERT LEVEL 8

Further Reading

Dion Haco, *The Private Journal and Diary of John H. Surratt, The Conspirator*, 1966

Joseph Holt, *Report of the Judge Advocate General on "The Order of American Knights", alias "The Sons of Liberty". A Western Conspiracy in aid of the Southern Rebellion*, Washington, DC: Union Congressional Committee, 1864

DOCUMENT: INITIATION INTO THE KNIGHTS OF THE GOLDEN CIRCLE: JOHN H. SURRATT, c. 1860

It might have been an hour, or only twenty minutes, that I had waited alone in that room; but, as I took no account of the time, it seemed almost an age. Every feature of the apartment had been examined, and I could have described every color therein, from the paper on the walls, and the hangings of the windows to the uniforms of the revolutionary heroes, and the background of the portraits. Still no one came, and the solitude became painful.

"Can this have been a deception?" thought I; "and has the trip from Washington to this place been made only to play a trick upon me ?"

Patience is a virtue, but still it may at times be overtested; and, certainly, on this occasion, it required a great deal of it to reconcile me to remain (alone so long.) Young and impetuous, I wished to know the secret; but, at the same, I had no desire to be kept there in that manner – especially, as it might after all only prove a trick, a practical joke of my friends playing. This thought first excited me, then vexed, and finally made me mad; and, in an instant, starting to my feet, I rushed to the door by which I had entered the room. Useless – it was fastened.

"There is no help for it," thought I; "therefore the best thing to do, is to wait and abide the result."

The longer I had to wait, the more nervous I became; until at last my patience was entirely exhausted, and a nameless dread took its place. The salutations in the dark rushed to my memory; and the thought of facing fire and steel, to find out a secret that might in the end only prove worthless, was not entirely pleasant, even to me who never flinched from any known or open danger.

While in this state of mind I heard a voice, from some invisible form, say: "Arise, and follow, if you would be made acquainted with the secrets of the Knights of the Golden Circle."

Without delay I sprang to my feet, but my guide was still not to be seen – at least, I had not yet observed him, although certain that the speaker must have been in the room when giving me the order to get up from my seat.

Suddenly the room grew dark, and I became aware of the fact that, by some unaccountable means, the heavy curtains had dropped before the windows, and had thus excluded the light. The next moment my hands were seized on either side, each by a strong and gauntleted grasp, and an unknown and unseen person next placed a bandage over my eyes. Then my clothing was torn from my breast, which was thus barer; and held and blinded, I was led from the room – whither, I knew not, and have not since divined. There seemed to be no end to the long path, if path it was; and the doors that were opened and closed were so numerous that all attempt at counting their numbers was soon given up by me.

At length we stopped before a door – at least, such I judged it to be, from the signal given upon it and returned from the other side – and the following question was asked in a military tone of voice: "Who comes here?"

"One who is true to our cause," was the reply of one near me.

"How is he known to be true?" was the question next uttered by the first voice.

"By the recommendation of a tried knight," replied my supposed guide, for the voice was strange to my ears, as indeed were they all.

"He can then be trusted?" were the next words uttered.

"Such is our belief," was the reply.

"But should he fail, and betray us – what then?"

"He will learn the penalty soon enough."

"Advance."

We moved onward a few steps, when the same cold contact with steel, and the same sharp but slight puncture of the breast, was felt, as on a former occasion.

This time I did not flinch, although the sharp pain was as unexpected as before. Again I heard a solemn voice utter, in a slow and measured tone, the ominous words: "Those who would pass here must face both fire and steel."

"Are you willing to do so?" asked another, addressing me.

Having, after a few moments' consideration, answered in the affirmative, I was again told to advance, and commanded to kneel, on what seemed to be a cushion, as it yielded slightly to the pressure of my knee.

While in this position, an oath, terrible, horrible and appalling, was administered by the same solemn voice, and, while kneeling, I had to repeat the words after him in a slow and distinct tone, one hand resting on something cold as ice, the other on a book which appeared to be open.

The obligations taken, I was then informed that it would be necessary to remember every word I had uttered – can I ever forget them? – and not to forget the penalty of a disclosure of what I should learn, or a betrayal of the names of any one with whom I should be brought into companionship, no matter when, where, or under what pain, peril or promise. I was also admonished never to allude, either publicly or privately, to what I might then or hereafter learn; always to be ready to assist a brother-knight, even unto death; to abide by and follow all the directions of the order with which I had become connected; to carry out the objects which should be subsequently communicated to me, if found worthy of confidence; to bear witness and even to swear falsely in order to save a brother's life or liberty, if arrested for anything appertaining to the directions of the order; never to give a verdict against a brother, if on a jury to try him for any offense arising from directions emanating from the order, or any of its officers; and, in every way, to make the business of the new body, to which I had become allied, pre-eminent before religion, political feeling, parental or fraternal duty, or even before love of country. It was to be first and foremost in everything, at daylight or midnight, at home or abroad, before the law of the land or the affection for a wife, mother or child; to be all and everything.

"Are you willing to abide by this obligation?" asked the voice.

What could I do, or say? Refuse, I dare not; for I had felt the sharp point of the sword at my breast, and the words of that horrible oath still rang in my ears and vibrated through my aching brain. I was powerless to refuse, and therefore answered – faintly, it is true – in the affirmative.

"You remember the penalty?" asked the voice.

Could I have ever forgotten it? Remember it? Yes, indeed, did I remember it; perhaps, too vividly for the calm reflection of my mind at that moment. The very question, calling up, as it did, the remembrance, made me silent for the time, and I could not give a reply.

"Brother Knights!" exclaimed the voice, in a solemn tone. "Recall to the mind of him who now kneels here, the penalty of betrayal, either by sign, word or deed."

A sound like thunder rang around me; the clanging of arms broke the former almost death-like silence, and a hundred or more voices murmured, hissed, whispered or groaned out, three times, the single word,

"Death! Death!! DEATH!!!"

The first sound was horrible in its solemnity; the second utterance was terrible in its significance; the third and last was appalling in the repetition and the grave-like silence which followed it. My senses almost reeled under the influence of the fearful warning; my tongue appeared to swell until it filled my mouth and nearly choked me; I felt the hot blood rush over my brain and burn as it pursued its rapid course; it seemed as if the tortures of all the infernal regions had come upon me in a moment; I thought madness would be the result, unless the trial was soon to be ended, and yet I could not speak. And all this time my eyes were bandaged and my limbs bound. It was not the fear of death that caused within such terror – for I was willing to face any danger that could be seen; it was not the binding obligation I had taken – for I had firmly resolved to be true; but the nameless, unknown and unseen perils of that place and from those around me, appeared to call up to my imagination a thousand fears, indistinct and shadowy, yet plain enough to my mental vision. I had longed, craved for and earnestly desired to obtain a secret; but would, at that moment, have given up all I then possessed, or ever hoped to gain, could I have safely withdrawn from the "Circle" within which I found myself so inextricably enclosed. Shall I, can I ever forget that time, those few, long moments of agony?

Never; no not while life remains within this body, or until my senses become benumbed with the frosts of age or imbecility. Never!

How long the silence lasted, I know not; but the same solemn voice – it seemed miles away, and yet was plainly distinct – again addressed me in a slow manner, first repeating the awful word that had been repeated by so many voices, then admonishing me never to forget it, and finally inquiring whether I was ready to proceed with my initiation. I could return no verbal answer – my tongue refused its office – and I merely bowed my head, more mechanical than otherwise, for, to my present remembrance, it does not appear that I had any voluntary power left within my body.

"It is well," said the voice. "Proceed!"

A movement of feet was next heard by me, followed by a low murmur of voices; the words uttered were drowned by the one single sound that burned through my brain, rang in my ears, appeared in letters of blood before my blinded eyes, and was present to me in every possible shape. That word was, "Death."

The movements and sounds all ceased, and the solemn silence again ensued, which after a short interval was broken by the voice I had before heard, saying, "Show him all."

A chorus of voices repeated the words, and the next instant the bandage was quickly taken from my eyes.

For a few seconds my vision was blinded by the light, the dazzling light that fell upon me at that moment; and, before I could recover from the strain thus inflicted upon those organs of sight, I felt a number of sharp points pierce my breast, back and sides. My right hand had become almost frozen with the cold object upon which it rested, while the remainder of my body was in a perfect fever. I gave one glance around me, and, amid what appeared to be a cloud of fire, stood a number of armed men, clothed in coats of mail, their helmeted heads surmounted by red and white feathers, and their faces covered with barred vizors of metallic plates. Each had a sword in his hand, and every one of the points were directed at my almost paralyzed body, puncturing the flesh, and causing the smarts I had so recently felt.

Gradually my sight became restored, and, one by one, the objects before and around me were visible.

The mailed knights stood as still as statues, and any movement of mine might have caused a serious if not a deadly wound from one or the other of their weapons, which shone with a bright, glaring and flashing brilliancy on every side. Had I desired it ever so much, movement or escape was an impossibility.

The light next appeared to become, through some invisible agency, slowly, very slowly of a dimmer character, and to burn with less radiance and dazzling glare; but whether this was actually the case, or some optical illusion, I am now at a loss to determine. I then perceived for the first time that I was kneeling before an altar on which burned a dull blue flame; that my left hand had rested on an open Bible, and my right – horror of horrors – on the face of a corpse.

"Death!"

How the word rang in my ears. With a horrifying glance I looked down towards the floor, and beheld another corpse, upon whose breast I had been compelled to kneel.

"Death!!"

Again the word rang in my ears. I raised my eyes to those around, saw no glance of encouragement beyond those helmeted faces, and could comprehend nothing but the bright, polished swords, presented at me on every side.

"DEATH!!!"

Still that pitiless word was present. A mailed knight stood beyond the altar, in the direction from which I had heard that solemn voice, and with his unsheathed sword he pointed silently to the ghastly object on which my right hand rested. Not a word emanated from his lips, but his sword's point echoed the appalling, terrible word, "DEATH!"

Darkness appeared to spread itself before my vision. I felt my senses leaving me, and a nameless horror took possession of my whole soul!

ABRAHAM LINCOLN

Abraham Lincoln, helmsman of the Union in the Civil War and emancipator of the slaves, was the first US president to be assassinated. That "Honest Abe" died at the hand of conspiracy is sure-fire certain; the only debate is over the size and motive of the plot.

Lincoln was mortally shot by a single bullet to the head from a Derringer .44 pistol while watching the play *Our American Cousins* from the state box at Ford's Theater, Washington DC, on the evening of 14 April 1865. The killer, after administering the fatal lead injection, leaped eleven feet from the box down to the stage, landed badly, but raised himself to shout dramatically, "*Sic semper tyrannis!*" to the audience. The Latin tag, which means "Thus ever to tyrants!", is also the state motto of Virginia.

Since the killer was an actor – indeed a familiar face at Ford's – and the crowd was 1,000-strong, he was not difficult to identify. Pausing only to have his injured leg fixed by Dr Mudd, John Wilkes Booth – for it was he – lit out for the South. Federal authorities caught up with him a fortnight later at a barn at Garrett's Farm, Virginia, where he was shot dead before he could surrender by an itchy-fingered Sergeant Boston Corbett.

A memo book was found on Booth's body, which left no doubt of his guilt. Neither did the Federal investigators have much trouble in rounding up Booth's co-plotters, John Surratt, Mary Surratt, Lewis Powell, George Atzerodt, David Herold, Michael O'Laughlen, Dr Samuel Mudd and Samuel Arnold. After facing a military tribunal, Herold, Atzerodt, Powell and Mary Surratt were all hanged on 7 July 1865; the remainder were imprisoned, with the exception of John Surratt who escaped to Canada.

Such are the basic facts of the case. In orthodox histories, Booth is a Confederate "nut" who was motivated by racist indignation at Lincoln's plan to extend the voting franchise to blacks and who sweet-talked a motley collection of acquaintances and Southern-sympathizers into helping him. However, for a century and a half, conspiracists have suggested that Booth et al were merely "trigger men" for vast dark forces, the conspiracists' suspicions fuelled by the actions of some of the central characters. The behaviour of Sergeant Boston Corbett – who is the Jack Ruby of the Lincoln murder – is a case in point. Why did he not let Booth surrender? Was it because Booth might implicate someone high up the chain of the plot? Corbett was a religious lunatic, who had castrated himself to help his concentration on higher things, and was later locked up in an asylum. From which he then escaped and vanished without trace. Good going for a mad man, no?

If John Wilkes Booth and Boston Corbett were pawns in the assassination of Lincoln, there is no shortage of contenders for the title of the "Arch-Conspirator", the cabal or the individual who masterminded the deed:

- In the febrile days after Lincoln's death, Northern politicians loudly blamed Jefferson Davis, the President of the Confederacy for the murder. Even accounting for Northern prejudice against the South, this theory has legs. Although General Robert E. Lee had recently surrendered the main Confederate army at Appomattox Courthouse, Davis was unwilling to haul up the white flag. Killing Lincoln was a means of keeping the Civil War going.

  Booth *did* have incriminating connections to the Southern top table around Davis. Ideologically Booth was a die-hard "Rebel" of the Davis stripe. More: Booth was almost certainly a Confederate spy. Six months before the assassination Booth travelled to Montreal in Canada, where he conferred with Jacob Thompson, chief of the Confederacy's secret service. Booth also made an unexplained deposit of $20,000 into his bank account on his return. And what better cover for a spy than the itinerant profession of thespianism?

- On the other hand, the First Lady, Mary Todd Lincoln, pointed the finger of blame at someone *inside* the Lincoln camp – at no less than Andrew Johnson, the Vice President. Her evidence? Aside from being a Southerner – admittedly almost enough in itself to guarantee guilt in the paranoid aftermath of Abe's death – he did know Booth socially. Booth had even called on Johnson on the afternoon of the assassination and left his card.

  Yet the VeePee does not quite fit the frame as Mister Big, for one overwhelming reason: he was on the list of figures to be killed by the conspiracy on that April night. Luckily for Johnson, George Atzerodt, slated for the homicide, developed cold feet and went on a drinking bender instead. Why did Booth call on Johnson in the afternoon of that bloody Good Friday? Probably to determine his whereabouts so he could be butchered.

- In Otto Eisenschiml's 1937 book *Why Lincoln Was Murdered*, another of the president's men is outed as the master of the conspiracy. Secretary of War Edwin Stanton certainly had a motive, because he was wholly opposed to Lincoln's soft, liberal Reconstruction policies for the South. Also Stanton, curiously, refused Lincoln's request that Stanton's Atlas-like aide, Major Eckert, accompany the party to the Ford Theater. Instead Abe got a buffoon as a bodyguard, who was in the pub at the fateful moment. Rather than taking a bullet for the president, John Parker was taking a shot of rye.

  Another circumstantial piece of evidence against Stanton is Booth's memo book, which the Secretary of War stashed away in his safe; when the memo book was later made public, at least eighteen pages were found to be missing. Chief of the National Detective Police, Lafayette C. Baker, testified that the journal had been complete when his men handed it over to Stanton …

- But then Baker himself is under suspicion. Three years after the assassination, the venal cop wrote what appears to be a rhyming confession: "In New Rome there walked three men, a Judas, a Brutus, and a spy. Each planned that he should be the kink [sic] when Abraham should die … As the fallen man lay dying, Judas came and paid respects to one he hated, and when at last he saw him die, he said 'Now the ages have him, and the nation now have I.'"

Stanton is obviously Judas, but who Baker meant by Brutus is uncertain. Possibly it was Ward H. Lamon, Lincoln's buddy and US marshal for Washington DC, who just happened to be elsewhere on the evening in question. As to the identity of the spy, Baker answered that himself: "But lest one is left to wonder what has happened to the spy, I can safely tell you this, it was I. Lafayette C. Baker 2-5-68."

Shortly after composing his cryptogram, the previously healthy 44-year-old Baker died. His wife believed he was poisoned by government agents.

Of course, there is always someone who sees Jewish bankers behind every evil deed, and sure enough the Rothschilds have been nominated as the hands that steered Booth. Their reason? Because Lincoln had issued "greenbacks", government notes to fund the war, thus robbing the Rothschilds of easy high-interest shekels. Equally, no conspiracy is complete without putting a secret society in its sights, and as soon as Lincoln's heart stopped beating at 7.22 on the morning after he was shot, rumours began to circulate that the **Knights of the Golden Circle**, a circle of pro-South Northern Democrats, were up to their elegant necks in the deed. And there is always the super-ambitious alternative history in which plural plotters come together for one epoch shaping moment; in *The Lincoln Conspiracy*, David Balsiger and Charles E. Sellier Jr propose a heady, swirling scenario whereby Secretary of War Stanton linked up with Confederate spymaster Jacob Thompson, plus Northern speculators who wanted to keep the money-making war going and good ol' Maryland boys who wanted to keep Negroes in their place, viz. down on the slave plantation. Just in case you thought that Booth was treated a little harshly for his part in delivering a bullet to Lincoln's brain, he did not die staggering from a bullet in a blazing barn. No, no, no. In this left field conspiracy scenario, the body in the barn belonged to a James William Boyd, a Confederate fugitive, who unfortunately for him looked like Booth, the latter having been smuggled by Stanton out of the country. Some said to California, England and India. Yes, exotic India, not humdrum Indiana.

Like the controversy over the assassination of **John F. Kennedy**, that over the assassination of Lincoln shows no sign of slowing up. Unfortunately, the death of Lincoln is now so far in the past that any new evidence is unlikely to be unearthed. The truth lies buried with the bodies of the main actors in the drama.

President Abe Lincoln was assassinated by a Jefferson Davis inspired Confederate-conspiracy: ALERT LEVEL 8

President Abe Lincoln was murdered by one of his own inner circle: ALERT LEVEL 7

Further Reading
David Balsiger and Charles E Sellier, *The Lincoln Conspiracy*, 1977
Otto Eisenschiml, *Why Lincoln was Murdered*, 1937
Theodore Roscoe, *The Web of Conspiracy: The Complete Story of the Men Who Murdered Abraham Lincoln*, 1960

LUSITANIA

On 7 May 1915 the British passenger liner *Lusitania*, under the command of Captain Turner, was sunk by a U-boat off the south coast of Ireland.

The loss of life was terrible. Since the ship was lying on its side, the starboard lifeboats could not be used, and 1,201 people died. Of these, 128 were citizens of neutral America.

Firing at a passenger liner was outside the accepted rules of war, and anti-German riots occurred in many countries. The President of the USA, Woodrow Wilson, wrote to the German government demanding "reparation so far as reparation is possible". At the fourth time of writing, the Germans caved in, accepted responsibility and agreed to stop the sinking of passenger ships.

In the short term, German capitulation to Wilson's demands was enough to prevent the USA entering the war on the Allied side. However, anti-German sentiment had been so effectively stoked by the sinking, that when Germany resumed unrestricted submarine warfare in 1917 it was inevitable that the US would side with Britain, France and Russia.

Over time, military historians have come to suspect that the sinking was a set-up in which the Germans were deliberately encouraged by the British to sink the liner in the expectation that the negative publicity would lure the Americans onto the British side.

The suspicions were brought together in 1972 by Colin Simpson in *The Lusitania*. As Simpson detailed, the British failed to provide the *Lusitania* with any form of escort, although the Germans had placed advertisements in the newspapers of New York (from where *Lusitania* sailed) warning "that any travellers sailing in the war zone on ships of Great Britain or her allies do so at their own risk". More, the *Lusitania* appeared to make no effort to avoid a U-boat attack although it was travelling through a zone where U-boats lurked. No less than twenty-three merchantmen had already gone to Davy Jones's locker in the area.

A letter written by Winston Churchill, First Lord of Admiralty, to Walter Runciman, the president of Britain's Board of Trade, seems damning evidence of the conspiracy: "It is most important to attract neutral shipping to our shores in the hope especially of embroiling the United States with Germany ... For our part we want the traffic – the more the better; and if some of it gets into trouble, better still."

Furthermore, the radio exchanges between the *Lusitania* and the Admiralty from early May remain classified to this day.

Conspiracy or cock-up? The *Lusitania* was not "neutral shipping" and the fact that Churchill hoped that a ship got into useful trouble is not proof he planned the *Lusitania* sinking. In 1915, the minds of the Admiralty were concentrated on the Dardenelles campaign, and the sailing of one liner was a minor matter. Also, the ship was famously fast and well built, and the brass at the Admiralty likely presumed she was uncatchable at best, unsinkable at worst.

A foul-up would also explain the cover-up and locking-up of the radio traffic between the Admiralty and *Lusitania*: if the blunder had been made public, it would have been an embarrassment in front of the world.

> The *Lusitania* was sunk in a set-up to lure the US into the First World War: ALERT LEVEL 3

Further Reading
Colin Simpson, *The Lusitania*, 1972

PAUL McCARTNEY

The Beatles, a.k.a. the Fab Four. John, Paul, George and Ringo.

Actually, make that the Terrific Three plus an imposter. According to a rumour broadcast in October 1969 by Detroit disc jockey Russ Gibb, Paul McCartney had died in a car crash in 1966, having been distracted by a lovely meter maid. As this would have destroyed The Beatles, Paul was replaced by a lookalike, William Campbell. (Or was it Billy Shears?) With a little plastic surgery here, a handy growth of facial hair there, William/Billy made a passable Paul and The Beatles kept on making money, money, money.

The Paul is Dead rumour swept the world. The evidence for Gibb's proposition? Nothing less than The Beatles' own lyrics and album covers. Racked by guilt, the remaining mop-tops could not stop themselves inadvertently hinting at Paul's demise, in a sort of mass outbreak of Freudian slips. Thus on the sleeve of *Sergeant Pepper* Paul is standing next to a grave, while the hand of the statue of the Hindu god Shiva, "The Destroyer", points *directly* at Paul. Then there's the BEATLES wreath, and the doll in the red-lined dress, to symbolize Jane Asher, who died in the car with him. Inside, the sleeve depicts Paul wearing an arm patch with the letters OPD, standing for "Officially Pronounced Dead". The lyrics are the clincher. In "She's Leaving Home" the accident is revealed to have been on "Wednesday morning at five o'clock", while "Good Morning Good Morning" confirms there was "nothing to do to save his life" and the climactic "A Day in the Life" acknowledges he "blew his mind out in a car".

If the track "I'm so Tired" on *The White Album* is played backwards, the words become "Paul is dead, man, miss him, miss him".

But it is The Beatles' 1969 *Abbey Road* that provides the mother lode of clues to Paul's death. On the LP cover the four Beatles are pictured crossing the road in a funeral procession. Lennon is the priest (he's wearing white), Harrison is the gravedigger (wearing denim), Starr is the funeral director (dressed formally). McCartney is the corpse: he's out of step with the others, has bare feet, and is smoking a cigarette – the symbol of death in Sicilian culture. More, the licence plate on the car reads "LMW 281F", which stands for "Linda McCartney Weeps".

In 1993, Paul McCartney played sly homage to the long-running conspiracy theory about his premature death by titling his live album – *Paul is Live!*

On this album, as on all the other records made by Paul McCartney post-1966, Billy Shears/William Campbell sounded exactly like the pre-1966 Paul McCartney.

Funny that.

> Paul McCartney, distracted by Lovely Rita, crashed his car in 1966, killing himself and Jane Asher, after which the remaining Beatles hired a lookalike to replace him: ALERT LEVEL 1

MARY MAGDALENE

She only had a walk-on part in the drama of the New Testament, but Mary Magdalene has become the star turn of modern conspiracy theory.

In the gospel accounts of Jesus's life, Mary (a.k.a. Miriam of Magdala) is the woman from Galilee who watches his crucifixion, and is the first person to see him after the resurrection. But lo! in the modern alternative theory Mary is Jesus's wife and the mother of his children, whose descendants then walked the face of the Earth, specifically France, where they ruled as the Merovingian dynasty. The Holy Grail of legend is no longer the platter used by Jesus at the Last Supper, but Christ's bloodline, which has extended down over the years to reach, inter alia, the Sinclairs in Scotland, Italian nobility and Princess Diana. Safeguarding the Holy Grail are two ancient orders: the Knights Templar and the Priory of Sion. Although sworn to secrecy, Templars and Priory members have been unable to resist leaving clues to the existence of Mary's marriage and motherhood, notably in Leonardo da Vinci's *Last Supper* painting, where it is not the apostle John that is depicted to the right of Jesus but Mary, while the V shape formed between the two acknowledges the symbol for femininity.

Obviously, all of the above contradicts the theology of the Catholic Church. To cover up Jesus's intimacy with Mary – and so maintain its own power – the Catholic Church, it is suggested, cast Mary as a harlot and excised gospels featuring her. The Church also deliberately misinterpreted in medieval times "Sangreal" as "Saint Grail" rather than the correct *"sang real"*, meaning royal blood.

If Dan Brown's novel *The Da Vinci Code* takes the laurels for most popular exposition of the Mary Magdalene conspiracy, the vade mecum is the 1982 "non-fiction" bestseller *Holy Blood, Holy Grail* by Henry Lincoln, Michael Baigent and Richard Leigh. And this in turn owes something to Hugh Schonfield's *The Passover Plot* (1965), while the British poet Robert Graves had speculated that Mary was Jesus's wife as early as 1946 in *King Jesus*.

The Priory of Sion, Christ's children ruling Gaul, the mistranslation of "Sangreal", the discovery by Father Berenger Sauniere of the Holy Grail at Rennes-le-Chateau is ... all humbug, set afoot by a hoaxing minor French aristocrat, Pierre Plantard de Saint-Clair, who wanted to give himself regal glory by planting "evidence" that he was the rightful king of France. (He would have done a more persuasive job if the key Middle Ages documents "found" at the Bibliothèque Nationale had been written in medieval and not modern Latin.) Even so, aspects of the Mary Magdalene conspiracy hold up. The early Catholic Church did ban and burn gospels not in accordance with its views. Courtesy of the discovery in 1948 by an Egyptian peasant called Muhammad Ali al-Samman of a buried collection of "Gnostic" texts at Nag Hammadi the content of some of these banned gospels is now known. The role they assign to Mary is controversial. In the Gospel of Philip, Jesus is declared to be "the partner of Mary Magdalene, [and he] loved her more than all the disciples and often kissed her on the mouth". In Greek, the language of the Gnostic texts, "partner" can also mean "companion"; but whether "bride" or "close friend", it is abundantly obvious that in this early strain of Christianity Mary was regarded as being a crucial figure in Christ's ministry. There is even a Gospel of Mary Magdalene in the Nag Hammadi haul. A key incident in this gospel is a confrontation between Mary and the apostle Peter, in which Peter tries to humiliate Mary on the grounds that she is a woman, but is roundly told off by Jesus.

Even if Mary was the literal bride of Christ – and it is a big if – there is no guarantee that children came from the union. But it is a matter of historical record that various early Church dignitaries, from St Peter to St Paul (whose Letter to Timothy is an unintentional classic of misogyny) to Pope Gregory the Great, suppressed pro-Mary Magdalene currents in early Christianity and denigrated her role in Christ's ministry. They would not have seen themselves as conspirators, but fighters for "orthodoxy" in what was effectively a theological battle.

> Mary Magdalene was the mother of Christ's children: ALERT LEVEL 3

Further Reading
Michael Baigent, Richard Leigh and Henry Lincoln, *Holy Blood, Holy Grail*, 1982
Dan Brown, *The Da Vinci Code*, 2003
Elaine Pagels, *The Gnostic Gospels*, 1980

MANCHURIAN CANDIDATE

What do Robert F. Kennedy, John Lennon, Martin Luther King and Israeli Premier Yitschak Rabin have in common? All four are alleged to have been assassinated by remote-controlled, hypnotized killers or "Manchurian candidates".

The expression "Manchurian candidate" comes from Richard Condon's 1959 bestselling novel of that name, which features a brainwashed killer under the control of Chinese and Soviet intelligence located in Manchuria during the Korean War. The assassin is an American POW repatriated to the US, where he is programmed to kill the president.

Condon did not pluck the scenario out of thin air. During the Korean War, the Communists were understood to have achieved conspicuous success in brainwashing US POWs into confessing to war crimes they could not possibly have committed. Although a 1953 investigation by Drs Harold Wolff and Lawrence Hinkle of Cornell Medical College found that the Chinese had not used hypnosis or drugs to "re-educate" POWs (relying rather on violence to produce "confessions"), this did not stop the Agency heading pell-mell into a secret project to create a programmed assassin using hypnosis and drugs. Set up by CIA head Allen Dulles in 1953, Project MK-ULTRA experimented with LSD, electronic brain implants, mescaline, psilocybin, radiation, barbiturates, amphetamines and sensory deprivation on hapless subjects as it sought the Holy Grail of mind control. Probably the most grotesque of the MK-ULTRA experiments was subcontracted to Montreal psychiatrist D. Ewen Cameron, which involved the "breaking down of ongoing pattern of the patient's behaviour by means of particularly intensive electroshocks" while LSD was simultaneously applied. Some of Cameron's subjects received electro-convulsive therapy at thirty to forty times the normal rate, this followed by weeks of LSD-induced coma in which they were played an endless loop of noise or speech.

At one stage, MK-ULTRA consumed 6 per cent of the CIA's entire budget. Whether the CIA succeeded in programming a Manchurian candidate is unknown. The Agency has always claimed that its attempt to produce a real life Raymond Shaw – Condon's assassin character – was fruitless, and this was also the conclusion of a Senate Committee headed by Ted Kennedy when the MK-ULTRA programme was finally dragged out into the light by the *New York Times* in 1974.

The cynics are legion, however. By 1974, CIA director Richard Helms had destroyed the bulk of the MK-ULTRA files because of a "burgeoning paper problem". Suspicious? Almost as suspicious as the 1953 defenestration suicide of Dr Frank Olsen, a CIA researcher, who had voiced opposition to the MK-ULTRA project. On later exhumation Olsen's body was found to have marks on the skull consistent with a repeated attack. Suspicious? Almost as suspicious as the accidental death by drowning of ex-CIA director William Colby in 1993 days after being subpoenaed to testify about Olsen.

Cults like the Scientologists are widely held to achieve brainwashing. Is it really plausible that the CIA with millions of dollars and legions of scientists failed where L. Ron Hubbard succeeded?

Then there is the assassination of Robert Kennedy in the Ambassador Hotel in Los Angeles on 4 June 1968. Dozens of witnesses saw "lone nut" Sirhan Sirhan pull the trigger on Kennedy. But Sirhan himself could never recall the shooting, and to this day protests his innocence. William Turner and John Christian in *The Assassination of Robert F. Kennedy* and Philip Melanson in *The Robert F. Kennedy Assassination* all suggest that Sirhan was programmed by hypnosis to kill Kennedy. One leading expert, Dr Herbert Spiegal, estimates that Sirhan is among the 10 per cent of the population most susceptible to hypnosis. Under hypnosis by prosecution psychiatrist Dr

Seymour Pollack, Sirhan answered the question, "Who was with you when you shot Kennedy?" as follows: "Girl the girl, the girl ..." A girl in a polka-dot dress was seen running from the Ambassador shouting "We shot him!" If Sirhan was a Manchurian candidate, then the girl was his handler. According to a BBC *Newsnight* investigation in 2006, several CIA operatives were also in the Ambassador on the fateful night, although they had no reason to be there, since the CIA has no domestic jurisdiction.

The CIA had a plausible motive to kill RFK: if RFK had succeeded to the White House he might have uncovered evidence of the CIA's complicity in the killing of his brother. The CIA also had the immoral appetite to kill an American politician: a 1954 CIA memo specifically proposed using a hypno-programmed killer to assassinate "a prominent [deleted] politician or, if necessary, against an American official".

The official version remains that Sirhan alone killed RFK. Few believe it.

CIA developed programmed remote-controlled killers a la *The Manchurian Candidate*: ALERT LEVEL 10

Further reading

John Marks, *The Search for the Manchurian Candidate: The CIA and Mind Control*, 1989

Philip H. Melanson, *The Robert F. Kennedy Assassination: New Revelations on the Conspiracy and Cover Up*, 1991

Gordon Thomas, *Journey into Madness: The True Story of Secret CIA Mind Control and Medical Abuse*, 1989

William Turner and John G. Christian, *The Assassination of Robert F. Kennedy*, 1978

DOCUMENT: DECLASSIFIED MKULTRA MEMOS

I) *The CIA memo below was written on April 18, 1958 by Dr. Sidney Gottlieb, chief of the Chemical Division of the Agency's Technical Services Staff.*

DRAFT/
18 April 1958

MEMORANDUM FOR: THE RECORD

SUBJECT: MKULTRA, Subproject No. 83

1. The purpose of Subproject No. 83 will be to support the editorial and technical survey activities of [deleted] assigned to the [deleted] and is covered as an employee of the [deleted]. During the past six months, his activities have been to make technical surveys of social and behavioral science matters of interest to TSS/CD/Branch III. During this period he has been carried on the budget of the [deletion]. However, it was originally proposed that as soon as he demonstrated his ability, he would be established as an independent project and his activities widened.

2. [Deleted] has completed a detailed survey of handwriting analysis. He has prepared a review of current attitudes towards handwriting analyses as reflected by scientific researchers in the technique; fringe or pseudo-scientific developments in the field; general attitudes of psychiatrists, psychologists and other behavioral scientists to the techniques; and attitudes of document analysts and law enforcement agencies to the method. He has isolated the various "schools" of handwriting analysis, both American and European, and has prepared a readable, accurate and informative document that can be made available to potential consumers of handwriting analyses. More important, however, he has assembled data making it possible to design relevant

and meaningful research into the usefulness and applicability of handwriting analyses to intelligence activities.

3. On the basis of the many contacts developed by [deleted] it is now possible to undertake systematic research. During the next year, [deleted] will be responsible for the development of a research project on handwriting analysis. The recommendations for the design of this project, as developed by [deleted] are included as Attachment No. 2.

4. In addition [deleted] will begin to develop similar technical surveys on other controversial and misunderstood areas. These will include, though not necessarily in the next year:

   a) a revision and adaptation of material already developed on deception techniques (magic, sleight of hand, signals, etc.)
   b) psychic phenomena and extrasensory perception
   c) subliminal perception
   d) hypnosis
   e) "truth serums"
   f) expressive movements (body type, facial characteristics, etc.)

He will also assist the [deleted] in editing the material they develop including annual reports, project summaries, and conference notes.

5. [Deleted] will be under the supervision of the Executive Secretary of the [deleted] and will continue to work out of the [deleted] offices. Additional space for his activity is necessary and is included in the summary budget attached. Accounting for money spent will be included in the regular [deleted] audit.

6. The total cost of this subproject will be $25,000.00 for a period of one year beginning 1 May 1958. Charges should be made against Allotment 8-2502-10-001.

7. [Deleted] has been cleared for access to Top Secret material by the Agency.

II) *This memo, again from Sidney Gottlieb, records his approval of a test on "the biochemical, neurophysiological, sociological, and clinical psychiatric aspects of L.S.D."*

DRAFT – [deleted] 9 June 1953

MEMORANDUM FOR THE RECORD

SUBJECT: Project MKULTRA, Subproject 8

1. Subproject 8 is being set up as a means to continue the present work in the general field of L.S.D. at [deleted] until 11 September 1954.

2. This project will include a continuation of a study of the biochemical, neurophysiological, sociological, and clinical psychiatric aspects of L.S.D., and also a study of L.S.D. antagonists and drugs related to L.S.D., such as L.A.E. A detailed proposal is attached. The principal investigators will continue to be [deleted] all or [deleted].

3. The estimated budget of the project at [deleted] is $39,500.00. The [deleted] will serve as a cut-out and cover the project for this project and will furnish the above funds to the [deleted] as a philanthropic grant for medical research. A service charge of $790.00 (2% of the estimated) is to be paid to the [deleted] for this service.

4. Thus the total charges for this project will not exceed $40, 290.00 for a period ending September 11, 1954.

5. [deleted] (Director of the hospital) are cleared through TOP SECRET and are aware of the true purpose of the project.

[deleted]
Chemical Division/TSS

APPROVED:

[signature of Sidney Gottlieb]
Chief, Chemical Division/TSS

III) *A memo from Gottlieb of the CIA on the Agency's early experiments with hypnosis.*

DRAFT-SG/111 11 May 1953

MEMORANDUM FOR THE RECORD

SUBJECT: Visit to Project [deleted]

1. On this day the writer spent the day observing experiments with Mr. [deleted] on project [deleted] and in planning next year's work on the project (Mr. [deleted] has already submitted his proposal to the [deleted]).

2. The general picture of the present status of the project is one of a carefully planned series of five major experiments. Most of the year has been spent in screening and standardizing a large group of subjects (approximately 100) and the months between now and September 1 should yield much data, so that these five experiments should be completed by September 1. The five experiments are: (N stands for the total number of subjects involved in the experiment).

Experiment 1 – N-18 Hypnotically induced anxieties to be completed by September 1.

Experiment 2 – N-24 Hypnotically increasing the ability to learn and recall complex written matter, to be completed by September 1.

Experiment 3 – N-30 Polygraph response under Hypnosis, to be completed by June 15.

Experiment 4 – N-24 Hypnotically increasing ability to observe and recall a complex arrangement of physical objects.

Experiment 5 – N-100 Relationship of personality to susceptibility to hypnosis.

3. The work for next year (September 1, 1953 to June 1, 1954) will concentrate on:

Experiment 6 – The morse code problem, with the emphasis on relatively loser I.Q. subjects than found on University volunteers.

Experiment 7 – Recall of hypnotically acquired information by very specific signals.

[deleted] will submit detailed research plans on all experiments not yet submitted.

4. A system of reports was decided upon, receivable in June, September and December 1953, and in March and June 1954. These reports, besides giving a summary of progress on each of the seven experiments, will also include the raw data obtained in each experiment. At the completion of any of the experiments a complete, organized final report will be sent to us.

5. After June 1, [deleted] new address will be:

[deleted]

6. A new journal was observed in [deleted] office:

Journal of Clinical and Experimental Hypnosis published quarterly by the Society for C. F. & E. H., publisher is Woodrow

Press, Inc., 227 E. 45th Street, New York 17, N.Y. Price is $6.00

To date two numbers issued, Vol. 1 #1 January 1953, and Vol. 1 #2 April 1953.

7. A very favorable impression was made on the writer by the group. The experimental design of each experiment is very carefully done, and the standards of detail and instrumentation seems to be very high.

Sidney Gottlieb
Chief
Chemical Division, TSS

IV) *A 1955 CIA document reviewing the Agency's research and development of mind-altering substances and methods, including materials which will render the indication of hypnosis easier or otherwise enhance its usefulness.*

DRAFT
[deleted]

5 May 1955

A portion of the Research and Development Program of TSS/ Chemical Division is devoted to the discovery of the following materials and methods:

1. Substances which will promote illogical thinking and impulsiveness to the point where the recipient would be discredited in public.

2. Substances which increase the efficiency of mentation and perception.

3. Materials which will prevent or counteract the intoxicating effect of alcohol.

4. Materials which will promote the intoxicating effect of alcohol.

5. Materials which will produce the signs and symptoms of recognized diseases in a reversible way so that they may be used for malingering, etc.

6. Materials which will render the indication of hypnosis easier or otherwise enhance its usefulness.

7. Substances which will enhance the ability of individuals to withstand privation, torture and coercion during interrogation and so-called "brainwashing".

8. Materials and physical methods which will produce amnesia for events preceding and during their use.

9. Physical methods of producing shock and confusion over extended periods of time and capable of surreptitious use.

10. Substances which produce physical disablement such as paralysis of the legs, acute anaemia, etc.

11. Substances which will produce "pure" euphoria with no subsequent let-down.

12. Substances which alter personality structure in such a way that the tendency of the recipient to become dependent upon another person is enhanced.

13. A material which will cause mental confusion of such a type that the individual under its influence will find it difficult to maintain a fabrication under questioning.

14. Substances which will lower the ambition and general working efficiency of men when administered in undetectable amounts.

15. Substances which will promote weakness or distortion of the eyesight or hearing faculties, preferably without permanent effects.

16. A knockout pill which can surreptitiously be administered in drinks, food, cigarettes, as an aerosol, etc., which will be safe to use, provide a maximum of amnesia, and be suitable for use by agent types on an ad hoc basis.

17. A material which can be surreptitiously administered by the above routes and which in very small amounts will make it impossible for a man to perform any physical activity whatever.

The development of materials of this type follows the standard practice of such ethical drug houses as [deleted]. It is a relatively routine procedure to develop a drug to the point of human testing. Ordinarily, the drug houses depend upon the services of private physicians for the final clinical testing. The physicians are willing to assume the responsibility of such tests in order to advance the science of medicine. It is difficult and sometimes impossible for TSS/CD to offer such an inducement with respect to its products. In practice, it has been possible to use the outside cleared contractors for the preliminary phases of this work. However, that part which involves human testing at effective dose levels presents security problems which cannot be handled by the ordinary contractor.

The proposed facility [deleted] offers a unique opportunity for the secure handling of such clinical testing in addition to the many advantages outline in the project proposal. The security problems mentioned above are eliminated by the fact that the responsibility for the testing will rest completely with the physician and the hospital. [deleted] will allow TSS/CD personnel to supervise the work very closely to make sure that all tests are conducted according to the recognized practices and embody adequate safeguards.

MANTELL INCIDENT

On 4 June 1947, veteran pilot Kenneth Arnold was cruising in his private plane over Washington State's Cascade Mountains when he saw strange batwing craft in the distance. Afterwards, Mr Arnold likened the sight and motion of the craft to "saucers skipping on the water".

On that day, in that place, the "flying saucer" phenomenon was born. The Air Force said that Arnold had been chasing a mirage. The newspapers talked glibly of little green men. The public, brought up on pulp sci-fi stories, went out at night UFO-spotting for a lark.

Seven months later, on 7 January 1948, the UFO phenomenon went serious. Servicemen at Godman Army Airfield at Fort Knox in Kentucky began reporting an unusual aerial object in the vicinity (see Document, p.339). P-51 Mustangs of C Flight, 165th Fighter Squadron Kentucky Air National Guard, already in the air on a routine patrol, were requested to approach the object. Piloting one of the Mustangs was Captain Thomas F. Mantell, a 25-year-old flyer with combat experience from World War II

One of the Mustangs turned back low on fuel. The other two pilots accompanied Mantell as he ascended almost vertically in pursuit of the object, which air traffic control reportedly heard him describe as "metallic, and of tremendous size". Only one of Mantell's wingmen had an oxygen mask; since he was low on oxygen, and the other wingman had none, they called off the chase at 22,500 feet, leaving Mantell to go it alone.

Minutes later, Mantell's Mustang crashed in a fiery ball at a farm near Franklin, Kentucky. His watch, stopped by the force of the crash read, 3.18. Half an hour later, the UFO was no longer visible to personnel at Godman Field.

An American had died. A UFO had been sighted. Sensational rumours swept the nation, the biggest of all being that Mantell had been gunned down (rayed-down?) by a UFO. The Mantell Incident, along with the Godman encounter, fixed UFOs in the civilian mind as absolutely, 100 per cent real. As for the military's new research group for the study of UFOs, Project Sign, it never came to a conclusion on Mantell's demise.

What happened to Mantell? He *may* have taken a broadside from a UFO phaser. A more likely explanation is that he blacked out from lack of oxygen as he climbed. And the mysterious object in the sky? Some experts propose Venus, others nominate a skyhook weather balloon, noting that the balloons at 30 metres diameter are indeed "metallic, and of tremendous size". At the time skyhook balloons were a top-secret US Navy project, and according to UFO doubter Philip Klass skyhooks were in the air over Kentucky that fateful day. Truth to tell, the skies of America at the beginning of the Cold War buzzed with top-secret craft, and the Air Force deliberately pumped-up UFO sightings to distract the public – and the pesky Russkies – from what they were really up to.

> Captain Thomas Mantell dog-fought a UFO: ALERT LEVEL 3

DOCUMENT: EYEWITNESS REPORTS OF THE "MANTELL INCIDENT" BY USAF PERSONNEL

HEADQUARTERS   A/GFH/hmg
315Th AF BASE UNIT
OFFICE OF THE AIR INSPECTOR
GODMAN FIELD, FORT KNOX, KENTUCKY

9 January 1948

SUBJECT: Report of Observation of Unidentified Object in Skies Above Godman Field

TO: Commanding General, Eleventh Air Force
ATTENTION: Lt Col Chandler PIO Section

1. The inclosed certifications are of personnel from Godman
Field who witnessed the object in the southwestern sky from
Godman Field on 8 January 1948. With additional informa-
tion concerning the loss of a P-51 (NG869).

2. Standiford Tower, Standiford Field, Louisville, Ky.,
reported that two aircraft of an unspecified type were taking
off from Standiford at approximately 1500 hrs and could be
directed to proceed to Godman to assist in determining a
definite status of the reported object. These aircraft did not
appear. Another flight composed of four P-51's flew directly
over Godman Tower at approximately 1500 hrs, at which
time they were asked their identification. Upon being
informed that they were National Guard aircraft from
Standiford Field, and upon their replying in the affirmative
that sufficient gas was available, they were asked if they would
deviate from their course to assist in determining the nature
of the object. Their ETA for the flight to Standiford was
changed at that time.

3. The object, as it appeared to the undersigned was circular
in shape and, if it was a great distance away, was 1/10th the
size of a full moon. If it was an earthly object, the size, as
compared to the diminishing size of the P-51's flying toward
it, seemed to be at least several hundred feet in diameter.

E. GARRISON WOOD
Lt Colonel USAF
6 Incl Air Inspector

1. Statement: Pfc. Stanley Oliver

2. Statement: T. Sgt Q. A. Blackwell

3. Statement: Capt. Cary W. Carter

4. Statement: Capt. James F. Duesler, Jr.

5. Statement: Col Guy F. Hix, Commanding Officer

6. Statement: Lt Orner

USAF-SIGN1-374
1. Pfc. Stanley Oliver statement

UNITED STATES AIR FORCE
AIRWAYS AND AIR COMMUNICATIONS SERVICE, ATC
DETACHMENT 733-5 AF BASE UNIT (103D AACS SQ)
Godman Field, Fort Knox, Ky

9 January 1948

STATEMENT OF PFC STANLEY OLIVER
I, Pfc Stanley Oliver, was on duty in the Control Tower at Godman Field on the afternoon of 7 January 1948. When first heard of the object in the sky about 1320 CST, we received a phone call from Colonel Hix's office that a large object was sighted at Mansville, Kentucky, the supposed object was supposed to be about 250 feet to 300 feet in diameter at 1330 CST or more.

Sgt Blackwell sighted an object to the southwest of Godman Field and he asked me if I saw it. I saw the object but thought I was imagining I saw it and Sgt Blackwell told me to look again. This time I was really sure I saw an object and then we called Lt Orner, who came to the Control Tower and he too saw the object. Lt Orner then called Captain Carter who, after coming to the Control Tower, also saw this object. Captain Carter called Colonel Hix who came to the Control Tower and he too saw the object. We all then attempted to figure out just what it could be and to me it had the resemblance of an ice cream cone topped with red.

At or about 1445 CST we sighted five (5) P-51 aircraft coming on from the southwest and as they came over the

Control Tower someone suggested contacting the aircraft. Sgt Blackwell contacted them on "B" channel (VHF) and aircraft acknowledged his call. Someone suggested they try to overtake the object and we requested the planes to try and the flight leader stated he would. The call sign of this ship was NG869. They turned around and stared toward the southwest again. One pilot in the formation told the flight leader that he would like to continue on to Louisville with the flight leader giving his permission to do so. We kept in contact with the flight leader for about twenty-five (25) minutes. The last contact we had with the flight leader was when one of his wingmen called and said, "What the hell are we looking for?" Flight leader stated had the object in sight and he was going up to see what it was. He said at present he was at 15,000 feet and was still climbing. Those were the last words I believe we heard from him. Other pilots in the formation tried to contact him but to no avail.

In about another ten or fifteen minutes another P-51 took off from Standiford Field to look for the object. He gave me a call and asked if we still had the object in sight. He was told that at present the object was behind a cloud formation but he said he would try and locate it and in the meantime he tried contacting his flight leader but was unable to do so. He then reported he was unable to see the object and was coming back in when he came over the Control Tower.

I received a call from Standiford Operations that the plane had crashed and the pilot was killed at Franklin, Kentucky. He then saw the object again and to my belief the object was a great distance from Godman Field and it was so far I couldn't tell if it was moving or not.

NARA-PBB2-860
2. T. Sgt Q. A. Blackwell statement

UNITED STATES AIR FORCE
AIRWAYS AND AIR COMMUNICATIONS SERVICE, ATC

DETACHMENT 733-5 AF BASE UNIT (103D AACS SQ)
Godman Field, Fort Knox, Ky

9 January 1948

STATEMENT OF T. SGT QUINTON A. BLACKWELL
I, T. Sgt Quinton A. Blackwell, AF18162475, was on duty as chief operator in the Control Tower at Godman Field, Ky. on the afternoon of 7 January 1948. Up until 1315 or 1320 matters were routine. At approximately that time I received a telephone call from Sgt Cook, Col Hix's office, stating that according to Ft Knox Military Police and "E" Town state police, a large circular object from 250 to 300 ft in diameter over Mansville, Ky. and requested I check with Army Flight Service to see if any unusual type aircraft was in the vicinity. Flight Service advised negative on the aircraft and took the other info, requesting our CO verify the story. Shortly afterward Flight Service gave Godman Tower positions on the object over Irvington, Ky. then Owensboro, Ky. of about the same size and description. About 1345 or 1350 I sighted an object in the sky to the South of Godman Field. As I wanted verification, I called my Detachment Commander, 1st Lt Orner, to the Tower. After he had sighted the object, he called for the Operations Officer, Capt. Carter, over the tele-talk box from the Traffic Desk. He came upstairs immediately, and looked at the object through the field glasses in the Tower. He then called for the CO, Col Hix. He came to the tower about 1420 (appx) and sighted the object immediately. About 1430 to 1440 a flight of four P-51s approached Goldman Field from the South, en route from Marietta, Ga. to Standiford Field, Ky. As they passed over the tower I called them on "B" channel, VHF and asked the flight leader, NG 869, if he had enough gas and if so, would he mind trying to identify an object in the sky to the South of Godman Field. He replied in the affirmative and made a right turn around with two planes and proceeded South from Godman Field. The fourth plane proceeded on to Standiford Field alone.

The three ship formation proceeded South on a heading of 210°, climbing steadily. About 1445 the flight leader, NG 869, reported seeing the object "ahead and above, I'm still climbing". To which a wingman retorted, "What the hell are we looking for?" The leader reported at 15,000 ft that "The object is directly ahead of and above me now, moving about half my speed." When asked for a description he replied, "It appears metallic object of tremendous size." At 15,000 ft, the flight leader reported, "I'm still climbing, the object is above and ahead of me moving at about my speed or faster, I'm trying to close in for a better look." This last contact was at about 1515. About 5 min. afterward, the other two ships in the flight turned back. As they passed over Godman NG 800 reported, "It appears like the reflection of sunlight on an airplane canopy." Shortly afterward, the same pilot and plane took off from Standiford and resumed the search. He went to 33,000 ft. one hundred miles South and did not sight anything. I left the Control Tower shortly afterward.

The foregoing statement is true and correct to the best of my knowledge.

/a/Quinton A. Blackwell

MAXW-PBB3-718

3. Capt. Cary Carter statement

HEADQUARTERS
315 AF BASE UNIT (RES TNG)   A/hmg

GODMAN FIELD, FORT KNOX, KENTUCKY

9 January 1948

The undersigned was on duty at Godman Field 7 Jan 48 as Operations Officer.

At approximately 1400 hours and 7 minutes, 7 Jan '48 I received a call from Lt Orner, AACS Detachment Commander, that the tower had spotted an unidentified object and requested that I take a look. Lt Orner pointed out the object to the southwest, which was easily discernible with the naked eye. The object appeared round and white (whiter than the clouds that passed in front of it) and could be seen through cirrus clouds. After looking through field glasses for approximately 3 or 4 minutes I called Co. Hix's office, advising that office of the object's presence. Lt Col Wood and Capt. Duesler came to the tower immediately. Col Hix followed them.

About this time a flight of four P-51 aircraft were noticed approaching from the south. I asked Tec. Sgt Blackwell, Tower Operator, to contact the planes and see if they would take a look at the object for us. The planes were contacted and stated they had sufficient gas to take a look. One of the planes proceeded on to Standiford, the other planes were given a heading of 230°. One of the planes said he spotted the object at 1200 o'clock and was climbing toward it. One of the planes then said, "This is 15,000 ft, let's level out." One of the planes, at this point (apparently the plane who saw the object) estimated its speed (the object's) at 180 M.P.H. A few seconds later he stated the object was going up and forward as fast as he was. He stated that he was going to 20,000 feet, and if no closer was going to abandon the chase. This was the last radio contact I heard. It was impossible to identify which plane was doing the talking in the above report. Later we heard that one plane had landed at Standiford to get fuel and oxygen to resume the search.

The undersigned reported to Flight Service a description, position of the object while the planes searched for it.

/a/Cary W. Carter
CARY W. CARTER
Captain, USAF

MAXW-PBB3-719, 832,833

4. Captain James Duesler statement

HEADQUARTERS
315 AF BASE UNIT (RES TNG)   A/hmg
GODMAN FIELD, FORT KNOX, KENTUCKY

9 January 1948

At approx 1420, 7 Jan 48, I accompanied Lt Col E. G. Wood to the Godman Field Control Tower to observe "an object hanging high in the sky south of Godman".

Shortly after reaching the tower, Col Guy F. Hix, the Commanding Officer, was summoned; it was at that time that I first sighted the bright silver object.

Approximately five minutes after Col. Hix came into the tower, a flight of four P-51's flew over Godman. An officer in the tower requested that the Tower Operator call this flight and ask the Flight Leader to investigate this object if he had sufficient fuel. The Flight Leader (Capt. Thomas F. Mantell) answered that he would, and requested a bearing to this object. At that time one member of the flight informed the leader that it was time for him to land and broke off from the formation. This A/C was heard requesting landing instructions from his home field, Standiford, in Louisville.

In the meantime the remaining three P-51's were climbing on the course given to them by Godman Tower towards this object that still appeared stationary. The Tower then advised the Flight Leader to correct his course 5 degrees to the left; the Flight Leader acknowledged this correction and also reported his position at 7,500 feet and climbing. Immediately following the Flight Leader's transmission, another member of the flight asked "Where in the hell are we going?" In a few minutes the Flight Leader called out an object "twelve o'clock high". Asked to describe this object, he said that it was bright and that it was climbing away from him. When asked about its speed, the Flight Leader stated it was going about half his speed, approximately 180 M.P.H.

Those of us in the Tower lost sight of the flight, but could still see this object. Shortly after the last transmission, the Flight Leader said he was at 15,000 ft, and still climbing after "it", but that he judged its speed to be the same as his. At that time a member of the Flight called to the leader and requested that he "level off", but we heard no reply from the leader. That was the last message received from any member of the flight by Godman.

/a/James F. Duesler, Jr
JAMES F. DUESLER, JR
Captain, USAF

MAXW-PBB3-720

5. Col Guy F. Hix statement

HEADQUARTERS
315TH AF BASE UNIT (RES TNG)   A/hmg
GODMAN FIELD, FORT KNOX, KENTUCKY

9 January 1948

At approximately 1300 hours a call came to this Headquarters from State Police, reporting a flying object near Elizabethtown. Another report came in from Madisonville about ten minutes later. A third call came in from Lexington, Kentucky. (All towns are south of Godman Field.)

We alerted the Tower to be on the lookout for flying objects. At 1445 hrs the Tower notified me that an object had been sighted at about 215°. I went to the Tower and observed the object until 1550 hrs., when it disappeared behind the clouds.

The object observed could be plainly seen with the naked eye, and appeared to be about one-quarter the size of a full moon, white in color. Through eight-power binoculars, the object seemed to have a red border at the bottom, at times, and a red border at the top at times. It remained stationary for 1½ hours.

When I arrived at the Tower, Tech. Sgt Quinton Blackwell had contacted the P-51 airplanes over the field and suggested that they have a look if they had sufficient fuel. When I arrived they were within sight of the Tower, heading on a course of 215°.

I heard one of the pilots report that he saw the object straight ahead and estimated the speed of 180 M.P.H. The pilot stated that the object was very large and very bright.

/a/ Guy F. Hix
GUY F. HIX
Colonel, USAF Commanding

NARA-PBB2-865

6. Lt Paul Orner statement

UNITED STATES AIR FORCE
AIRWAYS AND AIR COMMUNICATIONS SERVICE, ATC
DETACHMENT 733-5 AF BASE UNIT (103D AACS SQ)
Godman Field, Fort Knox, Ky

9 January 1948

STATEMENT OF LT PAUL I. ORNER
Following is an account of the sighting of unknown objects from the Control Tower on 7 January 48 at Godman Field.

On the above date at approximately 1400 CST a report came in to the Control Tower through M Sgt. Cook of a report of an unidentified object flying at terrific speed in the vicinity of Maysville. This call was cancelled minutes later by the Military Police at Fort Knox who had instructions from the Kentucky State Police.

Very soon thereafter several reports of the same nature came from Flight Service saying this object was over Irvington and Owensboro, Kentucky. At the same time an object was reported by T. Sgt Blackwell, Chief Control Tower operator on duty. I was in the office of the Commanding Officer checking the call from the Fort Knox Military Police at this time. When the call was cancelled I was returning to the Control Tower to see the object sighted by them. I immediately went to the Control Tower and saw a small white object in the southwest sky. This object appeared stationary. I was unable to tell if it was an object radiating its own light or giving off reflected light. Through binoculars it partially appeared as a parachute does with bright sun shining on the top of the silk but there also seemed to be some red light around the lower of it.

The Commanding Officer, Operations Officer, S-2 and Executive Officer were called immediately. Several minutes after the object was sighted a flight of four (4) P-51's came over the field from the south. I instructed T. Sgt Blackwell to call the flight leader and ask if they had seen any evidence of this object. The flight leader answered negative and I suggested to the Operations Officer that we ask them if they had enough gas to go look for this object. The Tower operator was instructed to call the flight leader and he answered "yes" to this question. One (1) P-51 had permission from the flight leader to break formation and continue where he landed several minutes later on their original flight plan. The flight leader and two (2) other planes flew a course of 210° and in about five (5) minutes sighted the object. At first the flight leader reported it high and about one-half his speed at "12 o'clock". Shortly thereafter the flight leader reported it at about his speed and later said he was closing in to take a good look. This was the last message from NG869, the flight leader. NG800 shortly thereafter reported NG869 disappeared. From pilots reports in the formation NG869 was high and ahead of the wing man at about 1515 CST to 1530 CST when he disappeared. NG800 said he was breaking off with other wingman to return to Standiford Field due to lack of gas. This was about 1523 CST to 1530 CST. From messages transmitted by the formation it is estimated the flight leader was at 18 to 20 thousand feet and the wingman at approximately 15 thousand feet wide formation when the flight leader NG869 disappeared. NG800 and other wing man returned to Standiford Field.

NG800 gassed up and got more oxygen and flew a second mission on the same heading of 210° to a position of about 100 miles south of Godman Field to an altitude of 33 thousand feet and did not sight the object. At about 1645 CST when NG800 reported not seeing the object I left the Control Tower.

At about 1735 CST I returned to the Control Tower and a bright light different than a star at a position of about 240° azimuth and 8° elevation from the Control Tower. This was a round object. It seemed to have a dark spot in the center and the object moved north and disappeared from the horizon at a point 250° from the Tower. The unusual fact about this object was the fact that it remained visible and glowed through the haze near the Earth when no other stars were visible and did not disappear until it went below the level of the earth in a manner similar to the sun or moon setting. This object was viewed and tracked with the Weather Station theodolite from the hangar roof.

MAYAN CALENDAR

If you are reading this in 2013 or beyond, then the Mayan Calendar was wrong and the world has not disappeared in a catastrophe.

The medieval Central American civilization of the Maya used three intersecting calendar cycles, the *haab* (civil year, 365 days), the *tzolkin* (religious year, 260 days) and the Long Count. The Long Count gives the total number of days which have passed since a fixed point in the past which, for we users of the Gregorian calendar, is 11 August 3114 BC. Since the Long Count or "Great Cycle" lasts for 5,125.36 years, this means that time runs out on 21 December 2012 .

Did the Maya know something we didn't? Forgotten after the invasion of Yucatan by the Spanish, the Mayan Calendar was revived in the late twentieth century from information preserved in the study *Relación de las cosas de Yucatán* by Fray Diego de Landa, a Franciscan monk, accompanying the conquistadors. Soberingly for the apocalyptically minded, numerous other native myths based on the sun cycle also end with the end of days.

How the catastrophe will arrive is open to conjecture. Some claim that 2012 is the year the Earth will experience a polar shift, others moot the final triumph of the **New World Order**. The End Game scenario with the most scientific substance is that 2012 will see massive solar activity on the scale of the 1859 supercharged sun strike known as the Carrington Event. Most worrying of all, the Earth's magnetic shield ain't what it used to be in 1859, meaning that solar activity has a large hole through which to enter and zap the globe's electrical and electronic systems. Human cost, with no communications, refrigerated medicines, heat, financial services could be extreme. Some scientists postulate that full recovery could take a decade.

2012 is the year of Armageddon: ALERT LEVEL 3

Further Reading
John Jenkins, *Tzolkin: Visionary Perspectives and Calendar Studies*, 1994

NAZCA LINES

Ever since the first explorers stumbled on the Nazca Lines, high in the Peruvian Andes, they have exercised the Western imagination. The artificial lines, cut into the red desert floor rock, range from animal shapes to complex geometric patterns. By carbon-dating the hundreds of giant geoglyphs, as the shapes are properly known, archaeologists have determined that the Nazca Lines are at least 1,500 years old. After that, it is open season on who made the lines and why.

Noting that some of the lines are only intelligible from the air, many theorists have reached for the stars for the answers. Frenchmen Louis Pauwels and Jacques Bergier proposed in *The Morning of the Magicians* that the lines had an alien origin, and that said ETs helped hairy lumbering proto-humans to stand up, count and take over the planet from other earthly life forms. The doyen of alternative history, Erich Von Daniken, climbed on the alien-wagon and mooted in his 1969 classic *Chariots of the Gods?: Unsolved Mysteries of the Past* that the Nazca Plateau was an airfield for ET-craft. The lines were markers for the runway, and the figures enticers by humans for the aliens to drop in (a sort of ancient take on the cargo cult). Going one better, a current troop of UFO-centric conspiracists maintain that the Nazca Lines are still a landing ground for alien astronauts, with members of the **New World Order** making up the reception committee. Quite how the ETs and the NWO manage to avoid the gaze of the hundreds of tourists to the Nazca Desert, an UNESCO World Heritage site, is left deafeningly silent. Neither do the "runway" theories explain how a spacecraft can land on the soft desert without getting stuck in the mud.

Closer to planet Earth, but still edging towards the wacky, is the notion of Jim Woodman of the International Explorers Society that the ancient Nazca Indians who inhabited the region fabricated hot-air balloons for "ceremonial flights" during which they could "appreciate the great ground drawings on the *pampas*". Full marks to Mr Woodman for effort: using cloth, reeds and rope, Woodman and his colleagues made a balloon and basket, in which he and British balloonist Julian Nott made a shaky 300 feet high flight over the Nazca plain. When the balloon took a dive downwards, Woodman and Nott were lucky to escape with their lives, jumping clear of the craft ten feet off the desert floor. Woodman's thesis flies about as well as his balloon: there is no evidence whatsoever that balloons existed 1,500 years back.

With her feet planted firmly on the Earth, Dr Maria Reiche spent nearly fifty years mapping and studying the Nazca geoglyphs, starting as the assistant to American archaeologist Paul Kosok. Like Kosok, who called the Nazca Lines, "the largest astronomy book in the world", Reiche maintained that the geoglyphs comprised a sun calendar for the ancient Nazca peoples. Her magnum opus *The Mystery on the Desert*, however, attracted as many brickbats as bouquets, because numerous of the geoglyphs have no astronomical significance. The likelihood is that lines that do not align with the stars have a religious purpose, these drawings being a form of worship to their sky gods. Who, after all, would be in a position to see them.

Any Von Danikenesque belief that only alien astronauts could have ordered up the Nazca Lines was convincingly ended in a muddy field in Kentucky by researcher Joe Nickell in 1982. Using simple tools and technology available to Nazca Indians – such as wooden stakes, numbers of which archaeologists have found next to the Nazca designs – Nickell and a small team was able to recreate the geoglyphs within a week without any aerial assistance at all.

Nazca Lines in Peru are runway for alien craft: ALERT
LEVEL 2

Further Reading
Erich von Daniken, *Chariots of the Gods?*, 1960
Louis Pauwels and Jacques Bergier, *Le Matin des magiciens*, 1960
Maria Reiche, *The Mystery on the Desert*, 1949

NAZI GOLD

Treasure hunters have flocked to Lake Toplitz in the picturesque Austrian Alps ever since a group of diehard Nazis retreated to the area in the final days of the Second World War. With US troops closing in, the Nazis transported metal boxes to the edge of the lake, by lorry and by horse-drawn wagon, then chucked them into the icy depths.

What was in the boxes? A rumour soon swept around that the said crates contained gold looted by German troops throughout Europe and carried back to Germany. Or gold stolen from the Nazis' German victims.

In searching for the fabled lost gold of the Nazis many have died, causing the Austrian authorities to ban diving without express approval.

The tragedy is that the Nazis' stolen gold was not dumped in Lake Toplitz – from which it would have been all but impossible to recover it, short of hauling a U-boat there – but in the altogether drier environment of the Merkers mine, 200 miles southwest of Berlin, and in the mountains above Oberbayern. And in the cool vaults of Swiss banks.

Following a B-17 raid on 3 February 1945 which hit the Berlin Reichsbank, $238 millions' worth of the Third Reich's gold reserves was taken by German Alpine troops under the command of Colonel Franz Pfeiffer and hidden in the Merker mine. Three months later the mine and mountain hoards were captured by Patton's US Third Army and placed under safe military control.

Well, not quite. Even by the estimates of the US Army, 2 per cent of the closing balance of the Reichsbank went missing, amounting to several million dollars (at 1945 values). *The Guinness Book of Records* called the disappearance of the Merkers and Oberbayern gold "the largest robbery on record". Some conspiracy researchers suggest that the missing gold was appropriated by SS clandestine escape network **ODESSA**, then shipped to Spain to fund various ex-Nazi organizations such as **Paladin**.

Ian Sayer and Douglas Botting, authors of *Nazi Gold*, have a less convoluted explanation for the gold missing from Merkers and Oberbayern; it was heisted in bits by just about every GI and *soldat* who could get their mitts on it.

The story of the rest of the Third Reich's missing gold is more sordid still.

In 1997, the World Jewish Congress and the US Senate Banking Committee uncovered a tainted tale of Swiss-based financial institutions accepting gold from Nazi Germany without any proper scrutiny. The deposits included gold stolen from Jewish bank deposits, jewellery and even dental work from the millions of Jews exterminated in the death camps, all of which was smelted down into bullion bars, and stamped with pre-war dates to make it appear genuine. The sums involved were vast – more than $400 million went into Basel's Bank for International Settlements alone – and the "laundered" bullion was afterwards diverted into the central banks of Sweden, Argentina, Turkey, Portugal and Spain as payments for trade. The Swiss, despite their avowed neutrality, were aiding the Nazi war effort. Post-1945 the Swiss banks vigorously denied accepting looted gold – until the 1997 report from the WJC and US Senate obliged them to admit that the nation's banks had made no discernible effort to check the provenance of gold deposited by the Third Reich until late in the war. And that the said banks still held as much as $20 billion in "Nazi gold". Swiss banks also denied, then admitted, keeping for themselves the contents of "heirless accounts" – the accounts of Holocaust victims. With the threat of class actions by US beneficiaries, the Swiss Government set up a $5 billion annual compensation fund for the victims of the Holocaust *and other* human catastrophes – a weasel formulation that allowed the Swiss to pretend to be beneficent humanitarians.

Alas, it was not only the Swiss that had bloodstained Nazi gold in their coffers. The governments of the US, Britain and France set up the Tripartite Gold Commission after the war to return seized gold. Only about 70 per cent of the gold, however, was reimbursed, and two tons remains in the Federal Reserve in the US and three and half tons in the Bank of England. A document discovered in the US Embassy in Paris asserted that one shipment of 8,307 gold bars taken by the Allies from a German salt mine might "represent melted down gold teeth fillings". Quite possibly some of this remodelled gold is held in the Fed or the Bank of England.

Then there is the Vatican. In 1997 a declassified US intelligence report from 1946 indicated that the Vatican was holding $170 million Nazi gold "for safe keeping". The gold, mainly in coins, was stolen from gypsies, Serbs and Jews exterminated by the Nazis' puppet Ustasha Government in Yugoslavia. Holocaust research groups, notably the Simon Wiesenthal Centre, accused the Vatican of using the gold in the years after the war to smuggle Nazi war criminals out of Europe down the "ratlines" run by **ODESSA**.

The accusations were rejected by the Vatican, which opened its World War II archives in 2003 to researchers in an attempt to prove its innocence. Such "transparency" did little to mollify Holocaust groups and conspiracy theorists, because it seemed entirely plausible that any damning documents had already been destroyed.

The Vatican was far from being a monolith during World War II. Certainly, some factions were pro-Nazi and provided material aid to SS on the run in the conflict's aftermath; on the other hand, there were Vatican factions that were resolutely anti-Nazi. Lest it be forgotten, agencies in the Vatican helped thousands of Jews flee persecution.

What then, you might wonder, did the Nazis dump in Lake Toplitz? In 1959, a team financed by the German magazine *Stern* retrieved £72 million in forged sterling currency hidden in boxes, and a printing press.

The currency was part of a secret counterfeiting operation, Operation Bernhard, personally authorized by Adolf Hitler to weaken the British economy.

Swiss banks handled Nazi gold: ALERT LEVEL 10

Further Reading
Ian Sayer and Douglas Botting, *Nazi Gold: The Story of the World's Greatest Robbery – and Its Aftermath*, 1984

NEW COKE

Meet the new Coke. Same as the old Coke?

Back in the rock 'n' roll fifties, Coca-Cola (popularly called "Coke") had the American soft drinks market sewn up, with a 60 per cent share. Thirty years later, Coke's share of the beverage business was down to 24 per cent due to competition from arch-rival Pepsi.

The big bubbles at Coke decided to fight back in 1985 by changing the formula of Coke. Alas, "New Coke" was loathed by pretty much everyone in the USA (with the exception of Angelinos) and consequent public clamour forced Coke bosses to hastily reintroduce the original drink formulation, now rebranded as Coca-Cola Classic.

Pepsi executives laughed themselves silly at Coke's marketing disaster and fast U-turn, gave their staff a day's holiday and declared that they had won the "Coke wars".

They laughed too soon. Coca-Cola Classic put on sales galore and Coke gained itself the rep as "the company that listens to its customers" – leading to speculation that the "New Coke" venture had been nothing but a clever marketing ploy. Or conspiracy.

There are almost as many versions of the New Coke conspiracy as there are bubbles in a can of New Coke/Classic Coke. The main trio are:

Version one maintains that there was no actual difference between Classic Coke and New Coke save what was on the outside of the tin, and the introduction of New Coke was designed to fail and make Joe Public clamour for the real stuff.

A certain fact is suggestive here: in numerous blind taste trials punters could not tell the two drinks apart. Also, the speed with which Coke reintroduced the classic brand – within three months, with cans enough for everyone – led to speculation that the company had a stockpile of the classic stuff ready waiting in the wings.

In version two people believe the switch back – planned all along – to "classic" Coke allowed the company to subtly change the drink's formula, substituting inexpensive high fructose corn syrup for sugar. Working against this conspiracy is the fact that Classic Coke everywhere outside the US is made with sugar.

By the lights of version three, the New Coke–Classic Coke manoeuvre was cover for the company to remove all traces of cocoa plant from the drink at the behest of the Drug Enforcement Agency. Actually the new version *was* cocoa free, but there is zero evidence to suggest that the DEA laid down the law to Coke's executives.

Although sly, black-hearted, power-mad capitalist execs are stock characters in conspiracy theories, in real life the suits are more prone to cock-up than conspire. When one Coke exec said of the New Coke venture, "We're not that dumb, and we're not that smart," he likely spoke the truth. Coke underestimated the affection of the American people for the iconic drink (the dumb bit) but when the New Coke deal started to go wrong, the company smartly responded by bringing back the real thing (the smart bit). And, hey, even capitalists can get lucky.

> Coca-Cola introduced New Coke as a coy marketing ploy to boost sales of Classic Coke/cover up changes to the drink's formula: ALERT LEVEL 3

NEW WORLD ORDER

During the Persian Gulf War, 1991, as USAF aircraft and ships launched their opening missile salvoes against Baghdad, President George H.W. Bush gave a speech to Congress proclaiming, "a big idea – a new world order, where diverse nations are drawn together in common cause to achieve the universal aspirations of Mankind: peace and security, freedom and the rule of law".

Whoa. In one fell speech Poppy Bush confirmed the worst fears of the John Birch Society (JBS), the patriotic militias, the fundamentalist Christian right and pale computer buffs who need to get out more: George Bush was bent on the introduction of one-world government controlled by a micro clique of capitalists. Within weeks the world of conspiracists went mad for the New World Order (NWO) conspiracy.

The phrase "New World Order" had been common currency in the Birch Society, almost since its foundation in 1958 by Robert Welch. A fervent anti-Red, Welch initially identified Communism as the primary force pushing a globalist agenda. (Not unreasonably: one of the first proponents of the concept "New World Order" was British socialist and writer H. G. Wells in his 1940 book of that title, (see Document, p.364) which envisioned a technocratic global order with a planned economy.) Looking at the US Republican right, Welch saw an equally criminal desire to construct a global power system run by the "Insiders" and one, given the inherent weaknesses of the USSR, the main power-base of Communism, with a better chance of realization. Welch was heavily influenced by his readings of eighteenth-century scribes on the **Bavarian Illuminati**, Augustin de Barruel and John Robison, while the theory was honed by John Birch Society's pet intellectual Gary Allen in *None Dare Call It Conspiracy* (1971), which described a "world supra-government" headed by international bankers and controlled by NY-based, Rockefeller-funded think tank the Council on Foreign Relations (CFR).

If Gary Allen put the wheels on the NWO conspiracy, others promptly climbed aboard. Christian fundamentalist Pat Robertson was one of the first to take a seat with *The New World Order* (1991), which detailed the long roots of the NWO plot beyond the CFR, beyond Adam Weishaupt and the Bavarian Illuminati to … Satan. In Robertson's millennarian vision, the NWO is paving the way for the coming of the Anti-Christ. At least if the NWO do make Hell on Earth the alien **Reptilian Humanoids**, which David Icke believes head up the conspiracy, will find the heat to their liking. Aliens also make their bow in the US patriotic militia's take on the NWO, whereby the Black Helicopters supposedly used to monitor them are powered by "back-engineered" ET technology. A subterranean base at **Denver International Airport** is NWO/alien HQ. Reputedly. Invariably, in NWO conspiriology the fronts by which the cabal will instigate its final coup in the USA are the United Nations and **FEMA**.

Truth to tell, the NWO theory, with its apocalyptic scenarios and instrumentalist politics, has long left the orbit of history and entered the realm of paranoid mythology.

> NWO cabal of capitalists/Satanists/Aliens seeks global power: ALERT LEVEL 2

Further Reading

Gary Allen, *None Dare Call It Conspiracy*, 1971
William Guy Carr, *Pawns in the Game*, 1954
William Cooper, *Behold a Pale Horse*, 1989
Jim Keith, *Black Helicopters Over America: Strike Force for the New World Order*, 1995
Pat Robertson, *The New World Order*, 1991

DOCUMENT: H. G. WELLS, *THE NEW WORLD ORDER*, 1940 [EXTRACT]

There will be no day of days then when a new world order comes into being. Step by step and here and there it will arrive, and even as it comes into being it will develop fresh perspectives, discover unsuspected problems and go on to new adventures. No man, no group of men, will ever be singled out as its father or founder. For its maker will be not this man nor that man nor any man but Man, that being who is in some measure in every one of us. World order will be, like science, like most inventions, a social product, an innumerable number of personalities will have lived fine lives, pouring their best into the collective achievement.

We can find a small-scale parallel to the probable development of a new world order in the history of flying. Less than a third of a century ago, ninety-nine people out of a hundred would have told you that flying was impossible; kites and balloons and possibly even a navigable balloon, they could imagine; they had known of such things for a hundred years; but a heavier than air machine, flying in defiance of wind and gravity! that they KNEW was nonsense. The would-be aviator was the typical comic inventor. Any fool could laugh at him. Now consider how completely the air is conquered.

And who did it? Nobody and everybody. Twenty thousand brains or so, each contributing a notion, a device, an amplification. They stimulated one another; they took off from one another. They were like excited ganglia in a larger brain sending their impulses to and fro. They were people of the most diverse race and colour. You can write down perhaps a hundred people or so who have figured conspicuously in the air, and when you examine the rôle they have played, you will find for the most part that they are mere notorieties of the Lindbergh type who have put themselves modestly but firmly in the limelight and can lay no valid claim to any effective contribution whatever. You will find many disputes about records and priority in making this or that particular step, but the lines of suggestion, the growth and elaboration of the idea, have been an altogether untraceable process. It has been going on for not more than a third of a century, under our very eyes, and no one can say precisely how it came about. One man said "Why not this?" and tried it, and another said "Why not that?" A vast miscellany of people had one idea in common, an idea as old as Dædalus, the idea that "Man can fly". Suddenly, swiftly, it GOT ABOUT – that is the only phrase you can use – that flying was attainable. And man, man as a social being, turned his mind to it seriously, and flew.

So it will certainly be with the new world order, if ever it is attained. A growing miscellany of people are saying – it is GETTING ABOUT – that "World Pax is possible", a World Pax in which men will be both united and free and creative. It is of no importance at all that nearly every man of fifty and over receives the idea with a pitying smile. Its chief dangers are the dogmatist and the would-be "leader" who will try to suppress every collateral line of work which does not minister to his supremacy. This movement must be, and it must remain, many-headed. Suppose the world had decided that Santos Dumont or Hiram Maxim was the heaven-sent Master of the Air, had given him the right to appoint a successor and subjected all experiments to his inspired control. We should probably have the Air Master now, with an applauding retinue of yes-men, following the hops of some clumsy, useless and extremely dangerous apparatus across country with the utmost dignity and self-satisfaction ...

Yet that is precisely how we still set about our political and social problems.

Bearing this essential fact in mind that the Peace of Man can only be attained, if it is attained at all, by an advance upon a long and various front, at varying speed and with diverse equipment, keeping direction only by a common faith in the triple need for collectivism, law and research, we realise the impossibility of drawing any picture of the new order as though it was as settled and stable as the old order imagined itself to be. The new order will be incessant; things will never stop happening, and so it defies any Utopian description. But we may nevertheless assemble a number of possibilities that will be increasingly realisable as the tide of disintegration ebbs and the new order is revealed.

To begin with we have to realise certain peculiarities of human behaviour that are all too disregarded in general political speculation. We have considered the very important rôle that may be played in our contemporary difficulties by a clear statement of the Rights of Man, and we have sketched such a Declaration. There is not an item in that Declaration, I believe, which a man will not consider to be a reasonable demand – so far as he himself is concerned. He will subscribe to it in that spirit very readily. But when he is asked not only to subscribe to it as something he has to concede by that same gesture to everybody else in the world, but as something for which he has to make all the sacrifices necessary for its practical realisation, he will discover a reluctance to "go so far as that". He will find a serious resistance welling up from his sub-conscious and trying to justify itself in his thoughts.

The things he will tell you will be very variable; but the word "premature" will play a large part in it. He will display a tremendous tenderness and consideration with which you have never credited him before, for servants, for workers, for aliens and particularly for aliens of a different colour from himself. They will hurt themselves with all this dangerous liberty. Are they FIT, he will ask you, for all this freedom? "Candidly, are they fit for it?" He will be slightly offended if you will say, "As fit as you are". He will say in a slightly amused tone, "But how CAN you say that?" and then going off rather at a tangent, "I am afraid you idealise your fellow-creatures."

As you press him, you will find this kindliness evaporating from his resistance altogether. He is now concerned about the general beauty and loveliness of the world. He will protest that this new Magna Carta will reduce all the world to "a dead level of uniformity". You will ask him why must a world of free-men be uniform and at a dead level? You will get no adequate reply. It is an assumption of vital importance to him and he must cling to it. He has been accustomed to associate "free" and "equal", and has never been bright-minded enough to take these two words apart and have a good look at them separately. He is likely to fall back at this stage upon that Bible of the impotent genteel, Huxley's Brave New World, and implore you to read it. You brush that disagreeable fantasy aside and continue to press him. He says that nature has made men unequal, and you reply that that is no reason for exaggerating the fact. The more unequal and various their gifts, the greater is the necessity for a Magna Carta to protect them from one another. Then he will talk of robbing life of the picturesque and the romantic and you will have some difficulty in getting these words defined. Sooner or later it will grow clear that he finds the prospect of a world in which "Jack's as good as his Master" unpleasant to the last degree.

If you still probe him with questions and leading suggestions, you will begin to realise how large a part the NEED FOR GLORY OVER HIS FELLOWS plays in his composition (and incidentally you will note, please, your own secret satisfaction in carrying the argument against him). It will become clear to you, if you collate the specimen under examination with the behaviour of children, yourself and the people about you, under what urgent necessity they are for the sense of triumph, of being better and doing better than their fellows, and having it felt and recognised by someone. It is a deeper, steadier impulse than sexual lust; it is a hunger. It is the clue to the unlovingness of so much sexual life, to sadistic impulses, to avarice, hoarding and endless ungainful cheating and treachery which gives men the sense of getting the better of someone even if they do not get the upper hand.

In the last resort this is why we must have law, and why Magna Carta and all its kindred documents set out to defeat human nature in defence of the general happiness. Law is essentially an adjustment of that craving to glory over other living things, to the needs of social life, and it is more necessary in a collectivist society than in any other. It is a bargain, it is a social contract, to do as we would be done by and to repress our extravagant egotisms in return for reciprocal concessions. And in the face of these considerations we have advanced about the true nature of the beast we have to deal with, it is plain that the politics of the sane man as we have reasoned them out, must anticipate a strenuous opposition to this primary vital implement for bringing about the new world order.

I have suggested that the current discussion of "War Aims" may very effectively be transformed into the propaganda of this new Declaration of the Rights of Man. The opposition to it and the attempts that will be made to postpone, mitigate, stifle and evade it, need to be watched, denounced and combatted persistently throughout the world. I do not know how far this Declaration I have sketched can be accepted by a good Catholic, but the Totalitarian pseudo-philosophy insists upon inequality of treatment for "non-Aryans" as a glorious duty. How Communists would respond to its clauses would, I suppose, depend upon their orders from Moscow. But what are called the "democracies" are supposed to be different, and it would be possible now to make that Declaration a searching test of the honesty and spirit of the leaders and rulers in whom they trust. These rulers can be brought to the point by it, with a precision unattainable in any other fashion.

But the types and characters and authorities and officials and arrogant and aggressive individuals who will boggle at this Declaration and dispute and defy it, do not exhaust the resistances of our unregenerate natures to this implement for the establishment of elementary justice in the world. For a far larger proportion of people among the "democracies" will be found, who will pay it lip service and then set about discovering how, in their innate craving for that sense of superiority and advantage which lies so near the core of our individual wills, they may unobtrusively sabotage it and cheat it. Even if they only cheat it just a little. I am inclined to think this disingenuousness is a universal weakness. I have a real passion for serving the world, but I have a pretty keen disposition to get more pay for my service, more recognition and so on than I deserve. I do not trust myself. I want to be under just laws. We want law because we are all potential law-breakers.

This is a considerable digression into psychology, and I will do no more than glance at how large a part this craving for superiority and mastery has played in the sexual practices of mankind. There we have the ready means for a considerable relief of this egotistical tension in mutual boasting and re-assurance. But the motive for this digression here is to emphasise the fact that the generalisation of our "War Aims" into a Declaration of Rights, though it will enormously simplify the issue of the war, will eliminate neither open and heartfelt opposition nor endless possibilities of betrayal and sabotage.

Nor does it alter the fact that even when the struggle seems to be drifting definitely towards a world social democracy, there may still be very great delays and disappointments before it becomes an efficient and beneficent world system. Countless people, from maharajas to millionaires and from pukkha sahibs to pretty ladies, will hate the new world order, be rendered unhappy by the frustration of their passions and ambitions through its advent and will die protesting against it. When we attempt to estimate its promise we have to bear in mind the distress of a generation or so of malcontents, many of them quite gallant and graceful-looking people.

And it will be no light matter to minimise the loss of efficiency in the process of changing the spirit and pride of administrative work from that of an investing, high-salaried man with a handsome display of expenditure and a socially ambitious wife, into a relatively less highly-salaried man with a higher standard of self-criticism, aware that he will be esteemed rather by what he puts into his work than by what he gets out of it. There will be a lot of social spill, tragi-comedy and loss of efficiency during the period of the change over, and it is better to be prepared for that.

Yet after making allowances for these transitional stresses we may still look forward with some confidence to certain phases in the onset of World Order. War or war fear will have led everywhere to the concentration of vast numbers of workers upon munition work and the construction of offen-sive and defensive structures of all sorts, upon shipping, inter-nal communications, replacement structures, fortifications.

There will be both a great accumulation and control of material and constructive machinery and also of hands already growing accustomed to handling it. As the possibility of conclusive victory fades and this war muddle passes out of its distinctively military phase towards revolution, and as some sort of Peace Congress assembles, it will be not only desirable but necessary for governments to turn over these resources and activities to social reconstruction. It will be too obviously dangerous and wasteful to put them out of employment. They must surely have learnt now what unemployment means in terms of social disorganisation. Governments will have to lay out the world, plan and build for peace whether they like it or not.

But it will be asked, "Where will you find the credit to do that?" and to answer this question we must reiterate the fact that money is an expedient and not an end. The world will have the material and the hands needed for a reconditioning of its life everywhere. They are all about you now crying out to be used. It is, or at any rate it has been, the function of the contemporary money-credit system to bring worker and material together and stimulate their union. That system always justified its activities on that ground, that is its claim to exist, and if it does not exist for that purpose then for what purpose does it exist and what further need is there for it? If now the financial mechanism will not work, if it confronts us with a non possumus, then clearly it resigns its function.

Then it has to get out of the way. It will declare the world has stopped when the truth will be that the City has stopped. It is the counting-house that has gone bankrupt. For a long time now an increasing number of people have been asking questions about the world counting-house, getting down at last to such fundamental questions as "What is money?" and "WHY are Banks?" It is disconcerting but stimulating to find that no lucid answer is forthcoming.

One might have imagined that long before this one of the many great bankers and financial experts in our world would have come forward with a clear and simple justification for the monetary practices of today. He would have shown how completely reasonable and trustworthy this money-credit system was. He would have shown what was temporarily wrong with it and how to set it working again, as the electrician does when the lights go out. He would have released us from our deepening distress about our money in the Bank, our little squirrel hoard of securities, the deflating lifebelt of property that was to assure our independence to the end. No one of that quality comes forward. There is not so much as a latter-day Bagehot. It dawns upon more and more of us that it is not a system at all and never has been a system, that it is an accumulation of conventions, usages, collateral developments and compensatory expedients, which creaks now and sways more and more and gives every sign of a complete and horrifying social collapse.

Most of us have believed up to the last moment that somewhere distributed among the banks and city offices in a sort of world counting-house, there were books of accounts, multitudinous perhaps and intricate, but ultimately proper accounts. Only now is it dawning upon comfortable decent people that the counting-house is in a desperate mess, that codes seem to have been lost, entries made wrong, additions gone astray down the column, records kept in vanishing ink ...

For years there has been a great and growing literature about money. It is very various but it has one general characteristic. First there is a swift exposure of the existing system as wrong. Then there is a glib demonstration of a new system which is right. Let this be done or that be done, "let the nation own its own money", says one radio prophet earnestly, repeatedly, simply, and all will be well. These various systems of doctrine run periodicals, organise movements (with coloured shirt complete), meet, demonstrate. They disregard each other completely and contradict each other flatly. And without exception all these monetary reformers betray signs of extreme mental strain.

The secret trouble in their minds is a gnawing doubt that their own proper "plan", the panacea, is in some subtle and treacherous way likely to fail them if it is put to the test. The internal fight against this intolerable shadow betrays itself in their outer behaviour. Their letters and pamphlets, with scarcely an exception, have this much in common with the letters one gets from lunatics, that there is a continual resort to capital letters and abusive terms. They shout out at the slightest provocation or none. They are not so much shouting at the exasperating reader who remains so obstinate when they have been so clear, so clear, as at the sceptical whisper within.

Because there is no perfect money system by itself and there never can be. It is a dream like the elixir vitæ or perpetual motion. It is in the same order of thought.

Attention has already been drawn, in our examination of Mr Streit's proposals for Union Now, to the fact that money varies in its nature and operations with the theory of property and distribution on which society is based, that in a complete collectivism for example it becomes little more than the check handed to the worker to enable him to purchase whatever he likes from the resources of the community. Every detachment of production or enterprise from collective control (national or cosmopolitan) increases the possible functions of money and so makes a different thing of it. Thus there can be endless species of money – as many types of money as there are types and varieties of social order. Money in Soviet Russia is a different organ from money in Nazi Germany, and that again is different from French or American money. The difference can be as wide as that between lungs and swimming bladders and gills. It is not simply a quantitative difference, as so many people seem to imagine, which can be adjusted by varying the rate of exchange or any such contrivance, it goes deeper, it is a difference in quality and kind. The bare thought of that makes our business and financial people feel uncomfortable and confused and menaced, and they go on moving their bars of gold about from this vault to that, hoping almost beyond hope that no one will say anything more about it. It worked very well for a time, to go on as though money was the same thing all the world over. They will not admit how that assumption is failing to work now.

Clever people reaped a certain advantage from a more or less definite apprehension of the variable nature of money, but since one could not be a financier or business director without an underlying faith in one's right to profit by one's superior cleverness, there did not seem to be any reason for them to make a public fuss about it. They got their profits and the flats got left.

Directly we grasp this not very obscure truth that there can be, and are, different sorts of money dependent on the economic usages or system in operation, which are not really interchangeable, then it becomes plain that a collectivist world order, whose fundamental law is such a Declaration of Rights as we have sketched, will have to carry on its main, its primary operations at least with a new world money, a specially contrived money, differing in its nature from any sort of money conventions that have hitherto served human needs. It will be issued against the total purchasable output of the community in return for the workers' services to the community. There will be no more reason for going to the City for a loan than for going to the oracle at Delphi for advice about it.

In the phase of social stress and emergency socialisation into which we are certainly passing, such a new money may begin to appear quite soon. Governments finding it impossible to resort to the tangled expedients of the financial counting-house, may take a short cut to recuperation, requisition the national resources within their reach and set their unemployed hands to work by means of these new checks. They may carry out international barter arrangements upon an increasing scale. The fact that the counting-house is in a hopeless mess because of its desperate attempts to ignore the protean nature of money, will become more manifest as it becomes less important.

The Stock Exchange and Bank credit and all the arts of loaning and usury and forestalling will certainly dwindle away together as the World Order establishes itself. If and when World Order establishes itself. They will be superseded, like egg-shells and foetal membranes. There is no reason for denouncing those who devised and worked those methods and institutions as scoundrels and villains. They did honestly according to their lights. They were a necessary part of the process of getting Homo sapiens out of his cave and down from his tree. And gold, that lovely heavy stuff, will be released from its vaults and hiding-places for the use of the artist and technician – probably at a price considerably below the present quotations.

Our attempt to forecast the coming World Order is framed then in an immense and increasing spectacle of constructive activity. We can anticipate a rapid transfiguration of the face of the earth as its population is distributed and re-distributed in accordance with the shifting requirements of economic production.

It is not only that there is what is called a housing shortage in nearly every region of the earth, but most of the existing accommodation, by modern standards, is unfit for human occupation. There is scarcely a city in the world, the new world as well as the old, which does not need to have half its dwelling-places destroyed. Perhaps Stockholm, reconditioned under a Socialist regime, may claim to be an exception; Vienna was doing hopefully until its spirit was broken by Dollfuss and the Catholic reaction. For the rest, behind a few hundred main avenues and prospects, sea and river fronts, capitols, castles and the like, filthy slums and rookeries cripple childhood and degrade and devitalise its dulled elders. You can hardly say people are born into such surroundings; they are only half born.

With the cooperation of the press and the cinema it would be easy to engender a worldwide public interest and enthusiasm for the new types of home and fitment that are now attainable by everyone. Here would be an outlet for urban and regional patriotism, for local shame and pride and effort. Here would be stuff to argue about. Wherever men and women have been rich enough, powerful enough and free enough, their thoughts have turned to architecture and gardening. Here would be a new incentive to travel, to see what other towns and countrysides were doing. The common man on his holidays would do what the English milord of the seventeenth century did; he would make his Grand Tour and come back from his journeys with architectural drawings and notions for home application. And this building and rebuilding would be a continuing process, a sustained employment, going on from good to better, as the economic forces shifted and changed with new discoveries and men's ideas expanded.

It is doubtful in a world of rising needs and standards if many people would want to live in manifestly old houses, any more than they would want to live in old clothes. Except in a few country places where ancient buildings have wedded themselves happily to some local loveliness and become quasi-natural things, or where some great city has shown a brave façade to the world, I doubt if there will be much to preserve. In such large open countries as the United States there has been a considerable development of the mobile home in recent years. People haul a trailer-home behind their cars and become seasonal nomads ... But there is no need to expatiate further on a limitless wealth of possibilities. Thousands of those who have been assisting in the monstrous clumsy evacuations and shiftings of population that have been going on recently, must have had their imaginations stirred by dim realisation of how much better all this might be done, if it were done in a new spirit and with a different intention. There must be a multitude of young and youngish people quite ripe for infection by this idea of cleaning up and resettling the world. Young men who are now poring over war maps and planning annexations and strategic boundaries, fresh Maginot lines, new Gibraltars and Dardanelles, may presently be scheming the happy and healthy distribution of routes and residential districts in relation to this or that important region of world supply for oil or wheat or water-power. It is essentially the same type of cerebration, better employed.

Considerations of this sort are sufficient to supply a background of hopeful activities to our prospective world order. But we are not all architects and gardeners; there are many types of minds and many of those who are training or being trained for the skilled cooperations of warfare and the development of a combatant morale, may be more disposed to go on with definitely educational work. In that way they can most easily gratify the craving for power and honourable service. They will face a world in extreme need of more teachers and fresh-minded and inspiring teachers at that. At every level of educational work from the kindergarten to the research laboratory, and in every part of the world from Capricornia to Alaska and from the Gold Coast to Japan, there will be need of active workers to bring minds into harmony with the new order and to work out, with all the labour saving and multiplying apparatus available, cinema, radio, cheap books and pictures and all the rest of it, the endless new problems of human liaison that will arise. There we have a second line of work along which millions of young people may escape the stagnation and frustration which closed in upon their predecessors as the old order drew to its end.

A sturdy and assertive variety of the new young will be needed for the police work of the world. They will be more disposed for authority and less for teaching or creative activities than their fellows. The old proverb will still hold for the new order that it takes all sorts to make a world, and the alternative to driving this type of temperament into conspiracy and fighting it and, if you can, suppressing it, is to employ it, win it over, trust it, and give it law behind it to respect and enforce. They want a loyalty and this loyalty will find its best use and satisfaction in the service of world order. I have remarked in the course of such air travel as I have done, that the airmen of all nations have a common resemblance to each other and that the patriotic virus in their blood is largely corrected by a wider professionalism. At present the outlook before a young airman is to perish in a spectacular dog-fight before he is five and twenty. I wonder how many of them really rejoice in that prospect.

It is not unreasonable to anticipate the development of an ad hoc disarmament police which will have its greatest strength in the air. How easily the spirit of an air police can be denationalised is shown by the instance of the air patrols on the United States–Canadian border, to which President Roosevelt drew my attention. There is a lot of smuggling along that border and the planes now play an important part in its suppression. At first the United States and Canada had each their own planes. Then in a wave of common sense, the two services were pooled. Each plane now carries a United States and a Canadian customs officer. When contraband is spotted the plane comes down on it and which officer acts is determined by the destination of the smuggled goods. There we have a pattern for a world struggling through federation to collective unity. An ad hoc disarmament police with its main strength in the air would necessarily fall into close coopera-tion with the various other world police activities. In a world where criminals can fly anywhere, the police must be able to fly anywhere too. Already we have a world-wide network of competent men fighting the white-slave traffic, the drug traffic and so forth. The thing begins already.

All this I write to provide imaginative material for those who see the coming order as a mere blank interrogation. People talk much nonsense about the disappearance of incen-tive under socialism. The exact opposite is the truth. It is the obstructive appropriation of natural resources by private ownership that robs the prosperous of incentive and the poor of hope. Our Declaration of Human Rights assures a man the proper satisfaction of all his elementary needs IN KIND, and nothing more. If he wants more than that he will have to work for it, and the healthier he is and the better he is fed and housed, the more bored he will be by inactivity and the more he will want something to do. I am suggesting what he is likely to do in general terms, and that is as much as one can do now. We can talk about the broad principles upon which these matters will be handled in a consolidating world social-ism, but we can scarcely venture to anticipate the detailed forms, the immense richness and variety of expression, an ever-increasing number of intelligent people will impose upon these primary ideas.

But there is one more structural suggestion that it may be necessary to bring into our picture. So far as I know it was first broached by that very bold and subtle thinker, Professor William James, in a small book entitled The Moral Equivalent of War. He pointed out the need there might be for a conception of duty, side by side with the idea of rights, that there should be something in the life of every citizen, man or woman alike, that should give him at once a sense of personal obligation to the World State and personal ownership in the World State. He brought that into relation with the fact that there will remain in any social order we can conceive, a multitude of necessary services which by no sort of device can be made attractive as normal life-long occupations. He was not thinking so much of the fast-vanishing problem of mechanical toil as of such irksome tasks as the prison warder's, the asylum attendant's; the care of the aged and infirm, nursing generally, health and sanitary services, a certain residuum of clerical routine, dangerous exploration and experiment. No doubt human goodness is sufficient to supply volunteers for many of these things, but are the rest of us entitled to profit by their devotion? His solution is universal conscription for a certain period of the adult life. The young will have to do so much service and take so much risk for the general welfare as the world commonwealth requires. They will be able to do these jobs with the freshness and vigour of those who know they will presently be released, and who find their honour in a thorough performance; they will not be subjected to that deadening temptation to self-protective slacking and mechanical insensitiveness, which assails all who are thrust by economic necessity into these callings for good and all.

It is quite possible that a certain percentage of these conscripts may be caught by the interest of what they are doing; the asylum attendant may decide to specialise in psychotherapeutic work; the hospital nurse succumb to that curiosity which underlies the great physiologist; the Arctic worker may fall in love with his snowy wilderness....

One other leading probability of a collectivist world order has to be noted here, and that is an enormous increase in the pace and amount of research and discovery. I write research, but by that I mean that double-barrelled attack upon ignorance, the biological attack and the physical attack, that is generally known as "Science". "Science" comes to us from those academic Dark Ages when men had to console themselves for their ignorance by pretending that there was a limited amount of knowledge in the world, and little chaps in caps and gowns strutted about, bachelors who knew a passable lot, masters who knew a tremendous lot and doctors in crimson gowns who knew all that there was to be known. Now it is manifest that none of us know very much, and the more we look into what we think we know, the more hitherto undetected things we shall find lurking in our assumptions.

Hitherto this business of research, which we call the "scientific world", has been in the hands of very few workers indeed. I throw out the suggestion that in our present-day world, of all the brains capable of great and masterful contributions to "scientific" thought and achievement, brains of the quality of Lord Rutherford's, or Darwin's or Mendel's or Freud's or Leonardo's or Galileo's, not one in a thousand, not one in a score of thousands, ever gets born into such conditions as to realise its opportunities. The rest never learn a civilised language, never get near a library, never have the faintest chance of self-realisation, never hear the call. They are undernourished, they die young, they are misused. And of the millions who would make good, useful, eager secondary research workers and explorers, not one in a million is utilised.

But now consider how things will be if we had a stirring education ventilating the whole world, and if we had a systematic and continually more competent search for exceptional mental quality and a continually more extensive net of opportunity for it. Suppose a quickening public mind implies an atmosphere of increasing respect for intellectual achievement and a livelier criticism of imposture. What we call scientific progress today would seem a poor, hesitating, uncertain advance in comparison with what would be happening under these happier conditions.

The progress of research and discovery has produced such brilliant and startling results in the past century and a half that few of us are aware of the small number of outstanding men who have been concerned in it, and how the minor figures behind these leaders trail off into a following of timid and ill-provided specialists who dare scarcely stand up to a public official on their own ground. This little army, this "scientific world" of today, numbering I suppose from head to tail, down to the last bottle-washer, not a couple of hundred thousand men, will certainly be represented in the new world order by a force of millions, better equipped, amply coordinated, free to question, able to demand opportunity. Its best will be no better than our best, who could not be better, but they will be far more numerous, and its rank and file, explorers, prospectors, experimental team workers and an encyclopædic host of classifiers and coordinators and interpreters, will have a vigour, a pride and confidence that will make the laboratories of today seem half-way back to the alchemist's den.

Can one doubt that the "scientific world" will break out in this way when the revolution is achieved, and that the development of man's power over nature and over his own nature and over this still unexplored planet, will undergo a continual acceleration as the years pass? No man can guess beforehand what doors will open then nor upon what wonderlands.

These are some fragmentary intimations of the quality of that wider life a new world order can open to mankind. I will not speculate further about them because I would not have it said that this book is Utopian or "Imaginative" or anything of that sort. I have set down nothing that is not strictly reasonable and practicable. It is the soberest of books and the least original of books. I think I have written enough to show that it is impossible for world affairs to remain at their present level. Either mankind collapses or our species struggles up by the hard yet fairly obvious routes I have collated in this book, to reach a new level of social organisation. There can be little question of the abundance, excitement and vigour of living that awaits our children upon that upland. If it is attained. There is no doubting their degradation and misery if it is not.

There is nothing really novel about this book. But there has been a certain temerity in bringing together facts that many people have avoided bringing together for fear they might form an explosive mixture. Maybe they will. They may blast through some obstinate mental barriers. In spite of that explosive possibility, that explosive necessity, it may be, this remains essentially an assemblage, digest and encouragement of now prevalent but still hesitating ideas. It is a plain statement of the revolution to which reason points an increasing number of minds, but which they still lack resolution to undertake. In The Fate of Homo sapiens I have stressed the urgency of the case. Here I have assembled the things they can and need to do. They had better summon up their resolution.

9/11

Tuesday 11 September 2001. A day of infamy. At 8.35 a.m., a hijacked passenger plane crashed into the north tower of New York City's World Trade Center. Thirty minutes later, a second plane hit the south tower. Over in Washington DC, a third airliner crashed into the Pentagon.

Nearly 3,000 people died as a result of these attacks. The US had just suffered its worst terrorist incident in history. Kjalid Sheikh Mohammed, the head of the military committee of Islamic terrorist organization al-Qaeda, accepted responsibility: "Yes, we did it," he told al-Jazeera TV. According to intelligence received, the White House of George W. Bush agreed that al-Qaeda had committed the attack.

Case closed? Not quite.

9/11 was a tragedy for all except paranoid conspiracy theorists, to whom every cloud of explosive smoke has a silver lining. Within weeks of 9/11, the internet was humming with alternative versions of whodunnit and why. By mid-2007 the 9/11 internet conspiracy documentary *Loose Change* had been downloaded over four million times.

For all the multiplicity of post-9/11 conspiracy theories, they boil down to two main hypotheses: that George W. Bush either staged the 9/11 attacks or purposely allowed them to occur because the attacks would generate public support for an invasion of Afghanistan, Iraq and other fuel-rich countries. With American oil running out, such invasions were a strategic necessity.

Proponents of the theories – who include Hollywood luminaries Charlie Sheen and David Lynch – point accusingly at the

Project for the New American Century, the right-wing think tank that campaigns for increased American global leadership. Former PNAC members include 9/11-era Secretary of Defense Donald Rumsfeld and Vice-President Dick Cheney. An internal PNAC document, *Rebuilding America's Defenses*, allegedly claims that "some catastrophic and catalyzing event – like a new Pearl Harbor" would be needed to move public opinion in their favour. Proponents of this theory also note the Bush–bin Laden Connection, the long ties between the two families, together with the administration's initial opposition to an investigation into the attacks. Could the US Government willingly allow an attack on its own people?

Proponents answer "Pearl Harbor". Even commit a false-flag attack on its own people? Answer: **Operation Northwoods**. This latter plan, proposed by the Joint Chiefs of Staff in 1962, proposed a stage-managed "terrorist" attack on US soil; Castro would get the blame, thus providing the justification for an invasion of Cuba.

So far as the false-flag case goes, theorists find quite a lot of evidence that the Government put its rampant political desires into practice.

First there's the sheer amount of incriminating evidence the plotters left around. Oddly, amidst 1.6 million tons of debris, investigators found the intact passport of Mohammed Atta, the man alleged to be the ringleader of the 9/11 attacks. So fortuitous was this find, conspiracy researchers suggest, that it must have been a plant. In fact, a number of other laminated passports were found in the debris. Atta also left flight-simulation manuals behind in a car, and apparently a will. However, he cannot have minded their discovery since he was intent on suicide. In fact, he may have wished them to be discovered to let the world know his martyrdom.

Second, what befell the towers of the World Trade Center bears examination. To most observers what happened to the WTC towers on 9/11 is straightforward: two planes hit the towers, then the towers fell down. This "reality" was soon challenged by conspiracy theorists, together with a covey of scientific experts.

Before 9/11 no steel-framed skyscraper had collapsed because of fire, yet WTC buildings 1, 2 and 7 collapsed like pancakes.

Particularly unusual was the death of WTC 7, which was not hit by an aircraft. Additionally, according to at least one demolition expert, the billows of dust coming out of the towers were more indicative of explosion than fire. Steel wreckage recovered from the site shows that it became molten; fire is not usually able to effect this change in steel. But a bomb is.

The "controlled demolition hypothesis" is a central plank of 9/11 conspiracy theory, featuring heavily in David Ray Griffin's *The New Pearl Harbor* (2005), and most cogently argued by Steven Jones, a physicist at Brigham Young University. Jones asserts that without demolition charges a "gravity-driven collapse" of the sort that happened to the WTC buildings would defy the laws of physics.

By the laws of the "controlled demolition hypothesis" the WTC was rigged with explosive devices, probably containing thermite. The strange comment by Larry Silverstein, owner of WTC 7, on a PBS documentary that he told the fire department to "pull it" makes sense in this scenario: "pull it" is demolition industry slang for setting off demolition charges. (Silverstein's spokesman said later that Silverstein meant "pull it" as in "pull outta there".) The bottom-to-top style collapse of WTC buildings 1, 2 and 7 is said to be typical of controlled demolitions. Fuelling conspiracy theory is the fact that building 7 housed offices of the CIA and the FBI, plus New York City's emergency command bunker.

In counterpoint to the controlled demolition hypothesis is the finding of the US Department of Commerce's National Institute of Standards and Technology (NIST) report into 9/11. According to this report the fireproofing on the Twin Towers' steel infrastructures was blown off by the impact of the planes, thus opening them to fire damage. Fires weakened the trusses supporting the floors, which made the floors sag. Sagging floors pulled on the exterior steel columns, making them bow inwards. Buckled columns could not support the building. Thus the buildings collapsed. NIST's findings are supported by a whole range of independent researchers.

What the controlled-demolition hypothesis fails to take into account is the aviation fuel carried by the planes. Skyscrapers were never made to withstand the effects of having thousands of gallons of ignited aviation fuel swilling around inside them.

Demolition experts have also weighed in on NIST's side. To place enough lethal charges around three skyscrapers would require weeks of work and tons of explosive. Security at the WTC was among the tightest in the US, following a terrorist attack there in 1993. Wouldn't *somebody* have noticed men carrying in bags of explosives for days on end or heard the drilling work needed to secure the devices to the steel frames?

Over to Washington DC. Like the WTC, the Pentagon was hit by a hijacked plane ... well, no, the 9/11 "Truthers" say. Whereas in NY the dramatic extent of the damage done by the hijacked planes arouses suspicion, in Washington it is the *limited* extent of the damage done that incurs disbelief. In 2002, French writer Thierry Meyssan published *9/11: The Big Lie*, which noted that the hole in the outer wall of the west wing was too small to have been caused by an incoming Boeing 747 and that the interior of the Pentagon was suspiciously undamaged.

Specifically, the holes punched in the interior walls of the Pentagon were 16 feet in diameter, too small to be made by a 757. According to Meyssan, the hole was caused by a cruise missile. (A more realistic weapon, some commentators feel, than the **HAARP**-like energy beam nominated by Assistant Professor Judy Woods as the doomslayer-of-the-day on 9/11.) Why did the Pentagon fire a missile at itself? Conspiracist Jesse Ventura, sometime wrestler and Minnesota governor, posited on his TV show that the Pentagon was trying to bury bad news. Literally. The Defense Department had lost $2.3 trillion. As it happens, the portion of the building destroyed by "Flight 77" was the precise office that housed the computers recording the DoD's accounting irregularity.

Something else about the Pentagon attack raises the Truthers' doubts. There were about eighty-five security cameras trained on the Pentagon, but all the Pentagon would show (after five years of petitioning by Truthers) was five frames of CCTV footage which showed an indefinable blur and an explosion.

To release just five frames prompted an obvious question: what might the other frames reveal? The Pentagon "bomb" conspiracy theory grew wings, especially when it was discovered that the section of the Pentagon which the plane crashed into was nearly empty at the time.

All this is taken by the 9/11 Truth Campaign as definite evidence that 9/11 was stage-managed or known about.

The clincher for the Truthers is the footage of George W. Bush's infamous response when his reading of a story to a Florida kindergarten was interrupted by an aide to tell him of the attacks. Bush continued reading. He could only have carried on being so calm, the theory goes, if he knew about the attacks in advance.

The fact is that the Pentagon was designed to withstand an air attack. The limestone layers shattered with the impact of the Boeing but the reinforced steel internal cage remained intact, hence the apparent lack of internal damage. Bush's response can be explained in a multitude of ways: he wanted to give the appearance of calm, he was shocked into immobility, he was too unintelligent to grasp what had occurred. Of all the claims of the Truthers, the Pentagon "missile" is the most ludicrous. Hundreds of drivers stuck in the morning rush hour traffic saw a plane hit the side of the military administration building.

What about Flight 93? Flight 93 was the fourth airliner hijacked by terrorists that morning. Unlike the others, it failed to find its target, instead plummeting into a Pennsylvania field. It is commonly considered that Flight 93 came down because its passengers heroically fought back against the hijackers and, in the melee, the plane went out of control or perhaps a terrorist aboard pulled the pin on a bomb.

In 9/11 conspiracy theory, Flight 93 was shot down on the orders of the White House before it could reach its target – which was the White House. Welcome to the world of Alice in the Looking Glass, because conspiracists complain that it is suspicious that "Flight 77" plane/cruise missile was *not* shot down as it crossed US airspace.

Admittedly, on Flight 93 alone of the events of 9/11 the evidence is unclear. By 8.52 the White House had ordered fighters into the air to seek out any hijacked airliners. Around 10.00 a.m. CBS TV reported that F-16 fighters were tailing Flight 93. Several witnesses to the Flight 93 crash report seeing a white plane nearby. The wide spread of debris from the plane, it is alleged, points to a mid-air crash. In 2004, Donald Rumsfeld seemed to say that Flight 93 had been shot down, though the White House later maintained he'd made a slip of the tongue.

Whatever, shooting down a hijacked plane – if it did happen – to stop its potential use as dive-bomber is not in the same moral league as a false-flag operation. Or a terrorist attack.

The weight of evidence is that al-Qaeda, and al-Qaeda alone, carried out the 9/11 attacks. Elements of the assault were planned and directed by al-Qaeda in Afghanistan, but the donkey work was done by a self-supporting al-Qaeda cell in Hamburg, led by Mohammed Atta. After receiving training in Afghanistan, the cell moved to the US by summer 2000; in Florida Atta opened an account at the SunTrust bank into which $109,000 was transferred from Dubai, seemingly to finance the upcoming operation. In the following year, al-Qaeda sent a number of Saudi volunteers to join Atta. On the morning of 9/11 a total of nineteen terrorists hijacked four aircraft from East Coast airports ...

The rest is history, not conspiracy theory.

Oh, and the smallness of the hole in the interior wall of the Pentagon? Sixteen feet is the width of a 757 fuselage. The wings had been ripped off by the outside walls, where the plane had smashed in a 90-feet wide section.

The true problem with the 9/11 "Truth" campaign is that it is barking up the wrong tree. Bush did not deliberately plan 9/11 or allow it to happen, but it is pertinent to ask whether, when he was shown the CIA daily briefing paper headed "bin Laden determined to strike in US", he failed to push for an adequate investigation because the bin Ladens were family friends and oil industry partners. (The Bushes and the bin Ladens go way back, to the 1970s, when George H. W. Bush's Arbusto company received a $1 million investment from Salem bin Laden, Osama's older brother.) The Bush White House consistently refused to release a copy of the briefing, even to the Congressional 9/11 inquiry.

As for the CIA, as far back as 1995, they were informed by the Phillipines police that Khalid Sheikh Mohammed was planning to use planes as flying bombs. The French and Russian secret services warned of the attack, and the Egyptians passed on the crucial detail that twenty Al-Qaeda members had slipped into the US for flight training.

Despite this epic dereliction of duty not a single CIA official has been disciplined.

9/11 was a false-flag, "inside job" operation: ALERT
LEVEL 3

Further Reading
David Ray Griffin, *The New Pearl Harbor*, 2005
Jim Marrs, *Inside Job: Unmasking the Conspiracies of 9/11*, 2005
National Commission on Terrorist Attacks, *The 9/11 Commission
    Report*, 2004
Anthony Summers and Robbyn Swan, *The Eleventh Day: The
    Full Story of 9/11 and Osama Bin Laden*, 2011
Conspiracy Theory with Jesse Ventura: Pentagon, 17/12/2010
www.Loosechange911.com
www.911truth.org

NORTH AMERICAN UNION

The notion that there are powerful forces seeking the integration of Canada, the USA and Mexico into a political union on the model of the European Union is one of the most subtly persuasive of conspiracy theories.

The main elements of the North American Union (NAU) conspiracy feature:

- the construction of a twelve-lane super highway, from Yukon to Yucatan, complete with railtrack and fibre optic cables
- cancellation of the peso, and the Canadian and US dollars in favour of a single currency, the amero
- promotion of Spanish over English

"Follow the money" is as good a rule in conspiriology as it is in journalism or police work. A clique of industrialists – who would benefit from a barrier-free market – are said to be behind the NAU. These industrialists have promoted their continental dream through the North American Free Trade Agreement (NAFTA), the Council on Foreign Relations (CFR), the Security and Prosperity Partnership, the North American SuperCorridor Coalition, the Independent Task Force on North America (a joint post-9/11 venture by the CFR, the Mexican Council on Foreign Relations, and the Canadian Council of Chief Executives) which are all designed to bring about the North American Union.

There demonstrably *are* industrialists, academics and lobbyists seeking closer economic and political ties between the three nations of North America. The Council on Foreign Relations has produced a report entitled "Building a North American Community", while the amero received fulsome support in 1999 from Canadian economist Herbert Grubel, senior fellow of the Fraser Institute think tank, in *The Case for the Amero*, and in 2001 from Robert Pastor, vice-chairman of the Independent Task Force on North America, in *Toward a North American Community*. Making no bones about it, Pastor stated: "In the long term, the amero is in the best interests of all three countries."

Doubtless, some of the lobbying and organizing for the NAU is done behind doors. Less obvious, is whether there is one cabal of string-pullers behind the NAU, rather than a loose, amorphous movement of like-minded people. Or whether the NAU project seriously proposes a political union. According to www.stopthenorthamericanunion.com:

> The formation of the European Union (EU) is the "blueprint" being used to construct the North American Union (NAU). In multiple acts of treason, our government is illegally creating the NAU by using secret meetings and deceptive double-speak to hide their **"INCREMENTAL STEALTH"**. They are making MASSIVE changes to our bureaucratic-administrative-regulatory laws by calling them **"HARMONIZATIONS"**. What they are doing is rewriting our legal regulatory law to the benefit of, by, and for the corporate elite, which is ... classic fascism.

On the other hand, the CFR's "Building a North American Community" monograph actually rules out any sort of EU lash-up:

> North America is different from other regions of the world and must find its own cooperative route forward. A new North American community should rely more on the market and less on bureaucracy, more on pragmatic solutions to shared problems than on grand schemes of confederation or union, such as those in Europe. We must maintain respect for each other's national sovereignty.

Of course, those clever policy wonks in the CFR could be dealing a double bluff. Pretending not to want something but organizing for it behind doors anyway ...

Cabal seeks to covertly install Mex–US–Canadian super union: ALERT LEVEL 5

Further Reading
Jerome Corsi, *The Late Great USA: The Coming Merger with Mexico and Canada*, 2007
Herbert Grubel, *The Case for the Amero*, 1991
www.stopthenorthamericanunion.com

DOCUMENT: COUNCIL ON FOREIGN RELATIONS, PRESS RELEASE "TASK FORCE URGES MEASURES TO STRENGTHEN NORTH AMERICAN COMPETITIVENESS, EXPAND TRADE, ENSURE BORDER SECURITY".

May 17, 2005 – North America is vulnerable on several fronts: the region faces terrorist and criminal security threats, increased economic competition from abroad, and uneven economic development at home. In response to these challenges, a trinational, **Independent Task Force on the Future of North America** has developed a roadmap to promote North American security and advance the well-being of citizens of all three countries.

When the leaders of Canada, Mexico, and the United States met in Texas recently they underscored the deep ties and shared principles of the three countries. The Council-sponsored Task Force applauds the announced "Security and Prosperity Partnership of North America," but proposes a more ambitious vision of a new community by 2010 and specific recommendations on how to achieve it.

Pointing to increased competition from the European Union and rising economic powers such as India and China in the eleven years since NAFTA took effect, co-chair **Pedro C. Aspe**, former Finance Minister of Mexico, said, "We need a vision for North America to address the new challenges." The Task Force establishes a blueprint for a powerhouse North American trading area that allows for the **seamless movement of goods, increased labor mobility**, and **energy security**.

"We are asking the leaders of the United States, Mexico, and Canada to be bold and adopt a vision of the future that is bigger than, and beyond, the immediate problems of the present," said co-chair John P. Manley, Former Canadian Deputy Prime Minister and Minister of Finance. "They could be the architects of a new community of North America, not mere custodians of the status quo."

At a time of political transition in Canada and Mexico, the Task Force proposes new ideas to cope with continental challenges that should be the focus of debate in those two countries as well as the United States. To ensure a free, secure, just, and prosperous North America, the Task Force proposes a number of specific measures:

Make North America safer:

- Establish a common security perimeter by 2010.
- Develop a North American Border Pass with biometric identifiers.
- Develop a unified border action plan and expand border customs facilities.

Create a single economic space:

- Adopt a common external tariff.
- Allow for the seamless movement of goods within North America.
- Move to full labor mobility between Canada and the U.S.
- Develop a North American energy strategy that gives greater emphasis to reducing emissions of greenhouse gases – a regional alternative to Kyoto.

- Review those sectors of NAFTA that were excluded.
- Develop and implement a North American regulatory plan that would include "open skies and open roads" and a unified approach for protecting consumers on food, health, and the environment.
- Expand temporary worker programs and create a "North American preference" for immigration for citizens of North America.

Spread benefits more evenly:

- Establish a North American Investment Fund to build infrastructure to connect Mexico's poorer regions in the south to the market towards the north.
- Restructure and reform Mexico's public finances.
- Fully develop Mexican energy resources to make greater use of international technology and capital.

Institutionalize the partnership:

- Establish a permanent tribunal for trade and investment disputes.
- Convene an annual North American summit meeting.
- Establish a Tri-national Competition Commission to develop a common approach to trade remedies.
- Expand scholarships to study in the three countries and develop a network of Centers for North American Studies.

Co-chair **William F. Weld**, former Governor of Massachusetts and U.S. Assistant Attorney General, said, "We are three liberal democracies; we are adjacent; we are already intertwined economically; we have a great deal in common historically; culturally, we have a lot to learn from one another."

Organized in association with the Consejo Mexicano de Asuntos Internacionales and the Canadian Council of Chief Executives, the Task Force includes prominent former officials, businessmen, and academic experts from all three countries. A Chairmen's Statement was released in March in advance of the trinational summit; the full report represents the consensus of the entire Task Force membership and leadership.

Chief Executive of the Canadian Council of Chief Executives **Thomas d'Aquino**, President of the Consejo Mexicano de Asuntos Internacionales **Andrés Rozental**, and Director of the Center for North American Studies at American University **Robert A. Pastor** serve as vice chairs. **Chappell H. Lawson**, Associate Professor of political science at the Massachusetts Institute of Technology, is director.

Building a North American Community: Report of the Independent Task Force on the Future of North America is available on the Council website.

Founded in 1921, the **Council on Foreign Relations** is an independent, national membership organization and a non-partisan center for scholars dedicated to producing and disseminating ideas so that individual and corporate members, as well as policymakers, journalists, students, and interested citizens in the United States and other countries, can better understand the world and the foreign policy choices facing the United States and other governments.

The **Mexican Council on Foreign Relations** (COMEXI) is the only multi-disciplinary organization committed to fostering sophisticated, broadly inclusive political discourse and analysis on the nature of Mexico's participation in the international arena and the relative influence of Mexico's increasingly global orientation on domestic priorities. The Council is an independent, non-profit, pluralistic forum, with no government or institutional ties that is financed exclusively by membership dues and corporate support. The main objectives of COMEXI are to provide information and analysis of interest to our associates, as well as to create a solid institutional framework for the exchange of ideas concerning pressing world issues that affect our country.

Founded in 1976, the **Canadian Council of Chief Executives** is Canada's premier business association, with an outstanding record of achievement in matching entrepreneurial initiative with sound public policy choices. A not-for-profit, non-partisan organization composed of the chief executives of 150 leading Canadian enterprises, the CCCE was the Canadian private sector leader in the development and promotion of the Canada–United States Free Trade Agreement during the 1980s and of the subsequent trilateral North American Free Trade Agreement.

Members of the Independent Task Force on North America

Minister Pedro Aspe
(Mexican co-chair)
Protego
Mr. Thomas S. Axworthy
Queen's University
Ms. Heidi S. Cruz
Merrill Lynch & Co., Inc.
Mr. Nelson W. Cunningham
Kissinger McLarty Associates
Mr. Thomas P. d'Aquino
(Canadian co-vice chair)
Canadian Council of Chief Executives
Mr. Alfonso de Angoitia
Grupo Televisa, S.A.
Dr. Luis de La Calle Pardo
De la Calle, Madrazo, Mancera, S.C.
Professor Wendy K. Dobson
University of Toronto
Dr. Robert A. Pastor (U.S. co-vice chair)
American University
Mr. Andrés Rozental
(Mexican co-vice chair)
Consejo Mexicano de Asuntos Internacionales
Dr. Richard A. Falkenrath
The Brookings Institution
Dr. Rafael Fernandez de Castro
Instituto Tecnológico Autónomo de México

Mr. Ramón Alberto Garza
Montemedia
The Honorable Gordon D. Giffin
McKenna Long & Aldridge LLP
Mr. Allan Gotlieb
Donner Canadian Foundation
Mr. Michael Hart
Norman Paterson School of International Affairs
Mr. Carlos Heredia
Consejo Mexicano de Asuntos Internacionales
The Honorable Carla A. Hills
Hills & Company
Dr. Gary C. Hufbauer
Institute for International Economics
Dr. Luis Rubio
CIDAC
Dr. Jeffrey J. Schott
Institute for International Economics
Mr. Pierre Marc Johnson
Heenan Blaikie
The Honorable James R. Jones
Manatt Jones Global Strategies
Dr. Chappell H. Lawson (Task Force Director)
Massachusetts Institute of Technology
The Honourable John P. Manley (Canadian co-chair)
McCarthy Tetrault
Mr. David McD. Mann
Cox Hanson O'Reilly Matheson
Ms. Doris M. Meissner
Migration Policy Institute
The Honorable Thomas M.T. Niles
Institute for International Economics
The Honorable William F. Weld (U.S. co-chair)
Leeds Weld & Co.
Mr. Raul H. Yzaguirre
Arizona State University

NOSTRADAMUS

Michael de Nostradame was born in Saint-Rémy, France, in 1503, to a prosperous grain trader. The family had originally been Jewish but had converted to Christianity, which may explain Nostradame's lifelong interest in Kabbala, the mystical branch of Judaism and inspiration for the **Bible Code**. After an early grounding in Latin, Greek, Hebrew, maths, science and astrology, Nostradame left home in 1522 to study medicine at Montpellier. For nearly two decades he practised as an apothe-cary, reputedly formulating a pill that warded off the plague, but in the late 1540s moved to Salon-de-Provenance where he began writing prophecies, usually late at night through meditation, with help from astrology, hallucinogens, and an "angelic spirit". The prophecies, later collected in a work known as "The Centuries", were deliberately couched in a cryptic style to prevent the religious authorities from understanding them. He maintained that people in a more enlightened, rational future age would interpret their true meaning.

Could the seer Nostradamus see into the future? His followers insist that Nostradamus foretold Napoleon and Hitler, both of which he labelled the anti-Christ. An anagram "Pau, Nay, Loron" almost spells Napoleon, who was indeed "an Emperor … born near Italy. Who shall cost the Empire dear." Century 2 Quatrain 24, meanwhile, predicted that:

Beasts ferocious with hunger will cross the rivers
The greater part of the battlefield will be against Hister
Into a cage of iron will the great one be drawn,

When the child of Germany observes nothing.

Give or take a consonant, Nostradamus has Hitler to a T.

Actually, Nostradamus prophesied that three anti-Christs would beguile the world. Post-**9/11** speculation that the French seer had predicted the destruction of the World Trade Center and identified **Osama bin Laden** as Lucifer number *trois* was rife. After all, in Century 5 Quatrain 55 Nostradamus wrote:

Out of the country of Greater Arabia
Shall be born a strong master of Mohammed ...
He will enter Europe wearing a blue turban.
He will be the terror of mankind.
Never more horror.

And in Century 6, Quatrain 97:

At forty-five degrees the sky will burn,
Fire to approach the great new city:
In an instant a great scattered flame will leap up,
When one will want to demand proof of the Normans.

The "Normans" are a bit inconvenient, but references to fire and terror from the sky fit with the aerial attack, argue Nostradamus's followers, and New York city is around 40° 5' N latitude (relatively close to "forty-five degrees").

As with the earlier prophecies, Nostradamus purportedly hid the name of the last antichrist in an anagram. This was "Mabus", which can be arranged as "Usamb", a single letter off Usama. Which is quite like Osama. To put the fear of the devil into everyone, students of Nostradamus point out that the "Mabus" prophecy rounds off with global destruction courtesy of a comet crashing into Earth. Funnily enough comet Elenin *is* expected to pass close to Earth in October 2011, and doomsayers suggest its gravitational effect will cause tidal waves, while its magnetic pull will topple the Earth off its axis.

The sceptics' argument against Nostradamus is that his writings are so voluminous – there are about a thousand four-line quatrains, many of which contain more than one prophecy

– and so ambiguous that some actual events are bound to appear to align with the predictions simply through chance. Misinterpretations and mistranslations are also frequent; "Hister" might resemble "Hitler" but was actually a place near the Danube; "great new city" is a massacring of Villeneuve, outside Paris.

Sixteenth-century French astrologer could foretell the future: ALERT LEVEL 2

Further Reading
Henry C. Roberts, *The Complete Prophecies of Nostradamus*, 1947

BARACK OBAMA

Some people, you get the feeling, do not want Barack Obama as President of the USA.

Whispers that Obama was not a US citizen first began to circulate during his run-off with Hillary Clinton for the Democratic nomination. If Obama was not born on American soil he would be ineligible to be President under Article Two of the Constitution. When Obama beat Hillary for the Democratic ticket, the "birthers" – as those who doubt Obama's credentials are called – started to roar. As many level-headed commentators noted, the closer Obama – a black – got to the White House the louder the din about his citizenship ineligibility became.

In an attempt to end the birthers' speculations, Obama pre-election released his short-form birth certificate, which clearly showed that he was born in Hawaii on 4 August 1961. Hawaii is a state of the union, and the short form is accepted by the US Department as conclusive proof of citizenship. Obama's aides also pointed out that the child's birth had been announced in Hawaiian newspapers the *Honolulu Advertiser* and the *Honolulu Star-Bulletin* in August 1961.

Unpersuaded, some birthers even tried to file (unsuccessfully) lawsuits seeking to disqualify Obama from running for the presidency, and when he won anyway they tried to re-file the suits to stop him being sworn in. To no avail. Although the most stubborn birthers belonged to the baying dog wing of the American right, they had a mass, sympathetic audience; one poll taken after Obama became the forty-fourth President of the United States found that 47 per cent of Republican voters believed that

Mr Obama was not born in the US. Another 22 per cent said they were unsure.

If anything, Obama's release of his short-form certificate in 2008 led to more questions than answers. Leading birther Jerome Corsi – he of the book *The Obama Nation: Leftist Politics and the Cult of Personality* – informed any TV outlet that would listen that the birth certificate was 'a fake ... it's been shown to have marks from Photoshop.' Meanwhile, health officials in Hawaii were bombarded with requests to view the original certificate. This could only be released to someone with a tangible interest, but for clarification the departmental head man released a statement:

I, Dr. Chiyome Fukino, director of the Hawai'i State Department of Health, have seen the original vital records maintained on file by the Hawai'i State Department of Health verifying Barack Hussein Obama was born in Hawai'i and is a natural-born American citizen. I have nothing further to add to this statement or my original statement issued in October 2008, over eight months ago.

Undaunted, the birthers covered hoardings around America with a poster asking: "WHERE'S THE BIRTH CERTIFICATE?"

Property tycoon Donald Trump upped the ante by announcing to a TV interviewer that he had doubts over Mr Obama's account of his birth, adding that Obama's paternal grandmother had said she witnessed his birth in Kenya (no she hadn't) and that false birth notices could have been placed by Obama's grandparents to secure his citizenship (no they couldn't: the notices were sent to the newspapers by the Hawaiian health department).

In April 2011 President Obama bowed to the inevitable, and released the full-length version of his birth certificate. This confirmed the details of the short certificate released in 2008 that Barack Hussein Obama was indeed born in Hawaii.

The reaction of the birthers? The Drudge Report proclaimed the certificate a fake concocted with image-editing software. And a stubborn whole quarter of the US population still believed that he was a foreigner.

Shoosh. They don't know the half of it. According to www.davidicke.com Obama ain't only from abroad, he's from another universe, being a **Reptilian Humanoid** from a planet far, far away. Mind you, Obama once did a very good job of catching a fly in a TV studio.

When the president calls his press conference to protest that he is not actually a lizard in human form, he may wish to take the opportunity to knock on the head all the other paranoid anti-Obama conspiracies. In no particular order of unimportance, these include the theory that Obama is the love child of Malcolm X, that Obama killed his gay lover, is a covert Muslim intent on turning the Land of the Free into a theocratic dictatorship (check out the pres's speeches backwards), is an Illuminati, is the anti-Christ, is the puppet of the **New World Order** ...

All the Obama conspiracies have one thing in common. They are ways of saying that they don't want a black in the White House without actually saying it.

Barack Obama is not a genuine US citizen and is therefore not eligible to be President: ALERT LEVEL 1

OCTOBER SURPRISE

In January 1979, the Shah of Iran was forced to flee the country after mass streets protests. His place as ruler was taken by the Islamic opposition leader Ayatollah Khomeini, returned from exile in Paris.

The Shah had been America's Man, the Ayatollah was most certainly not. Neither were his followers who in the following November seized the US embassy in Tehran, took more than sixty staff hostage and announced that they would only be released when the Shah was returned for trial and the US unfroze $12 billion in Iranian assets held in Stateside banks.

The plight of the hostages exercised the American public – but not as much as it exercised American politicians. The year 1980 was presidential election year, and the hostage crisis went to the top of the political agenda. White House incumbent Jimmy Carter faced a strong challenge from Republican candidate Ronald Reagan, and his VP running mate, George Bush, former head of the CIA. Polls put Reagan and Carter neck and neck, and Bush went on record that he feared an "October Surprise" whereby the Democrats suddenly achieved the release of the hostages and got a poll boost.

Alas for the hapless Carter he did not secure the hostages release. The spectacle of Uncle Sam looking powerless against an uppity country difficult to find on a map did not play well with the American electorate, so Governor Reagan took the prize of the White House.

In his inauguration speech on January 20, 1981, Reagan promised a patriotic new birth for America: "Let us begin an era of national renewal. Can we solve the problems confronting us? Well, the answer is an unequivocal and emphatic 'yes'."

The Great Communicator was not joking. Minutes later, it was announced that the hostages had been freed.

Reagan was clearly a more efficient, ass-kicking Pres than Carter ... or had there been skulduggery? The "October Surprise" conspiracy theory alleges that it was the Republicans – *contra* George Bush – and not the Democrats who had done a deal with Iran to win the presidential election. Confused? You won't be.

The conspiracy theory states that in October 1980, Bush and Reagan's campaign manager, William Casey, held negotiations with Iranian officials in Paris and Madrid to *delay* the release of the fifty-two hostages still held (some had been previously released on health and humanitarian grounds). Thus Carter was unable to profit from their release, and had to skulk off to a peanut farm in Georgia, while former B-movie actor Reagan saddled up for Washington DC. What did the Iranians get out of the deal? The handsome reward of arms for their war against Iraq.

What proof, your honour, for the October Surprise conspiracy? It is tantalizing but circumstantial. A congressional probe in 1983 declared that Honest Ron Reagan's campaign had set up a network to spy on Carter and his negotiations with the Iranian regime. And there are witnesses for the prosecution, the most eminent being former Iranian president Abol-Hassan Bani-Sadr, who claimed to have received a message from the Iranian foreign ministry about the direction of discussions with the Reagan camp. A host of arms dealers and private spooks over the years have stepped forward to state they organized the discussions between the Reaganites and the Iranians, including Jamshid and Cyrus Hashemi, Ari Ben-Menashe and Ahran Moshell.

It should also be noted on the rap sheet that during the Iran–Contra scandal Reagan grudgingly admitted that the US had ransomed hostages by illegally selling arms to Iran (using the profits to fund Nicaraguan right-wing rebels). If Team Reagan could do a dodgy deal in office why not out of office?

That said, any fair-minded judge would find the spook and gun-runner "witnesses" for the October Surprise theory as suspect a bunch as you could wave a gavel at. Ari Ben-Menashe will serve to damn the lot; this supposed former Mossad agent Ben-Menashe claims to have fitted Saddam Hussein's nuclear reactor at Osirak with a homing beacon – an espionage stunt that would have tested Tom Cruise in *Mission Impossible* mode. A number of the gunrunners on the list are popular with various police forces. And claiming to be the guy that set up one of the arms deals of the century is clearly a good business card.

By 1992, the October Surprise brouhaha had reached such a crescendo that the House of Representatives investigated the charges. The subsequent report, "The 'October Surprise' Allegations and the Circumstances Surrounding the Release of the American Hostages Held in Iran", found that "the credible evidence now known falls far short of supporting the allegation of an agreement between the Reagan campaign and Iran to delay the release of the hostages". The House investigation did find that William Casey, an ex-OSS/CIA bigwig, had been fishing in very murky waters. There was no "credible" evidence that Casey had been in Madrid when the meeting with Iranians was alleged to have taken place – but then the key pages from his desk diary had been torn out.

The phrase "now known" is the rub. One suggestive piece of evidence was forwarded too late for conclusion. It was sent from Moscow – and disclosed that the Kremlin's spooks had monitored the October Surprise deal between Reagan's team and the Iranians.

The stink of conspiracy still hovers over the timing of the release of the US hostages from Tehran.

> Reagan campaign did deal with Iranians to delay release of hostages for electoral advantage: ALERT LEVEL 8

Further Reading
Robert Parry, *Trick or Treason*, 1993
Gary Sick, *October Surprise: America's Hostages in Iran and the Election of Ronald Reagan*, 1992

THE OCTOPUS

A "unified field theory" is the Higgs boson of conspiriology, the presumption that there is one entity holds everything together. Danny Casolaro a 44-year-old freelance journalist from Virginia believed that he had found the omnipotent underground cabal that ran the planet. Casolaro called the transnational master conspiracy "the Octopus".

In the early afternoon of 10 August 1991, a nude male body was found in the bath of room 517 in the Sheraton Inn in Martinsburg, West Virginia. There were a dozen slashes to his wrists, and the blood had sprayed over the walls. Near the corpse was a note that read "Please forgive me for the worst possible thing I could have done."

The cadaver was that of Danny Casolaro. Martinsburg's boys in blue immediately concluded that it was a routine suicide, and so the county coroner decided against an inquest and released the body to a mortician. Casolaro's body was embalmed that evening, before the next of kin had been notified. This was illegal. It was certainly unfortunate, because had Danny Casolaro's family been notified they would certainly have asked for an autopsy. When eventually informed of his brother's death, Anthony Casolaro, a medical doctor, announced that Danny had gone to Martinsburg to interview a "Deep Throat" who would give him the final proof of the Octopus's existence. Danny had also told his brother, "If anything happens to me, don't believe it was accidental."

Danny Casolaro had named the Octopus well. He had, he claimed, first discovered its existence whilst researching **October**

Surprise, the alleged deal between Reagan and Iran to hold the fifty-two US hostages in Tehran until after the 1980 presidential election so as to embarrass Jimmy Carter, but gradually realized that the mega-cabal had tentacles in the BCCI banking scandal, the Inslaw/PROMIS theft of surveillance software, the Medallin drug cartel, Iran–Contra – to name just a few of its long-reaching arms. In a draft of a book on the Octopus, Casolaro portrayed the Octopus as "a web of thugs and thieves who roam the earth with their weapons and their murders, trading dope and dirty money for the secrets of the temple".

Casolaro's overwrought, overexcited manuscript does little to advance his case for the Octopus's existence. A grandiose, over-arching stream of consciousness, the manuscript redefines every event of the twentieth century without a back-up fact. Also, any suggestion that Casolaro was "offed" by the Octopus because he was getting too close to the truth, was damned by the belated autopsy done by the state medical examiner, who concluded that the wounds of Casolaro's wrists appeared to be self-inflicted. Meanwhile, local officials determined that the suicide note found in room 517 was written by Casolaro himself.

The national media had long dismissed Casolaro as a flake. His suicide was simply proof of his craziness. The fact that the autopsy revealed traces of antidepressant only confirmed his mental fragility.

Not everyone, however, was convinced that Casolaro died by his own hand. There was suggestive evidence to suggest the contrary:

- According to a review of the autopsy by a pathologist at George Washington University, the gashes on Casolaro's wrists did not have the usual "hesitation marks" of the suicide. One cut went so deep as to sever a tendon making it impossible to hold the razor responsible.
- The assistant head housekeeper at the Sheraton discovered two bloody towels under the sink. "It looked like someone threw the towels on the floor," she told investigative reporter John Connolly. This was *before* the arrival of the emergency crews.
- The accordion file containing Casolaro's latest researches was missing.

There were other oddities in the case. A waitress in the Sheraton's cocktail lounge recalled that Casolaro had been drinking there with an "Arab or Iranian" man. He was never located. And at Casolaro's funeral two unknown figures appeared, one of whom placed a medal on Casolaro's casket and saluted. Casolaro had never served in the military.

Undoubtedly Casolaro had been mixing with some shady characters towards the end of his life. One of his "informants" was Michael Riconoscuito, a self-professed intelligence operative cum science genius. Riconoscuito claimed to have developed gene warfare for the CIA, along with Gerald Bull's supergun for Iraq, plus the modifications of the Department of Justice PROMIS software, believed by many conspiracists to be implicated in **October Surprise**. Riconoscuito *was* up to his neck in the PROMIS controversy, because he had been assisting Inslaw, Inc., who were alleging that the DoJ had pilfered the PROMIS software from them. In his notes, Casolaro identified Riconoscuito as "Danger Man". He lived down to his nickname: aside from being a narcotics trafficker – a little misdemeanour he went to the penitentiary for – he was involved with the Wackenhut Corporation, a CIA subcontractor based at the semi-autonomous Cabazon tribal homeland. Another Wackenhut associate, the smooth Robert Booth Nichols, also provided Casolaro with "intelligence". Three days before his death, Nichols warned Casolaro, "If you continue this investigation, you will die." But Casolaro wasn't sure whether Nichols was threatening him or warning him. Or which investigation he was referring to; Casolaro had recently discovered that Robert Booth Nichols himself was tied to the Gambino mob and, for good measure, the Yakuza. Worst still, Casolaro reputedly knew from the DoJ that Nichols had offered to snitch on the Gambinos – and that was very dangerous information to know.

For the record, Nichols claimed to be out of the country when Casolaro committed suicide, or was suicided.

Although the Octopus as an omnipotent conspiracy theory is more the stuff of thriller than of history, Casolaro was wading in a murky swamp with some dark-hearted creatures. The list of why and who had cause to off Casolaro is almost endless. To all the above can be added: he may have stumbled across information on a Wackenhut–CIA "dirty job" that no one wanted aired; a Judiciary Committee's Investigative Report on Inslaw/PROMIS declared "As long as the possibility exists that Danny Casolaro died as a result of his investigation into the Inslaw matter ... it is imperative that further investigations be conducted."

While a subsequent report by DoJ Special Counsel Nicholas Bua released in 1993 on the PROMIS case declared Casolaro's death to be suicide, conspiracists noted that Bua was not the independent counsel requested by the Judiciary Committee.

If Casolaro was "suicided" his death is a grim stop sign to other conspiracy researchers. A point perhaps underlined by the fate of Jim Keith, who wrote (with Kenn Thomas) an exhaustive study of the Casolaro case. In 2004, Keith went into the Washoe Medical Hospital for a mundane knee operation. He died "in mysterious circumstances" from a blood clot on his lung.

> Conspiracy investigator Danny Casolaro was murdered because he was about to divulge details of the mega-cabal: ALERT LEVEL 2
>
> Danny Casolaro was murdered to stop his investigations into the Mob/CIA/PROMIS: ALERT LEVEL 7

Further Reading
John Connolly, "Dead Right", *SPY*, January 1993
Ken Thomas and Jim Keith, *The Octopus: The Secret Government and the Death of Danny Casolaro*, 2003
"The Inslaw Affair: Investigative Report by the Committee on the Judiciary", 1992

DOCUMENT: HOUSE REPORT 102-85, "THE INSLAW AFFAIR: INVESTIGATIVE REPORT BY THE COMMITTEE ON THE JUDICIARY", 1992 [EXTRACTS]

1. THE DEATH OF DANIEL CASOLARO

On August 10, 1991, the lifeless body of Mr. Daniel Casolaro, an investigative reporter investigating the INSLAW matter, was discovered in a hotel room in Martinsburg, WV. Mr. Casolaro's body was found in the bathtub with both of his wrists slashed several times. There was no sign of forced entry into the hotel room nor of a struggle. A short suicide note was found.

Following a brief preliminary investigation by the local authorities, the death was ruled a suicide. The investigation was reopened following numerous inquiries by Mr. Casolaro's brother and others into the suspicious circumstances surrounding his death. On January 25, 1992, after expending over 1,000 man-hours investigating his death, the local authorities again ruled Mr. Casolaro's death a suicide.

The committee did not include the death of Daniel Casolaro as part of its formal investigation of the INSLAW matter. Nevertheless, it is a fair statement to observe that the controversy surrounding the death continues to be discussed in the press and to other figures connected to the INSLAW litigation. These questions appear to be fostered by the suspicious circumstances surrounding his death and the criticism of the Martinsburg Police Department's investigation.

Other sources have been quoted in the media indicating that Mr. Casolaro did not commit suicide, and that his death was linked to his investigation of INSLAW, Bank of Credit and Commerce International (BCCI), and other matters such as the Iran/Contra affair. It has been reported that Mr. Casolaro had confided to several people that he was receiving death threats because he was getting close to concluding his investigation. Furthermore, he told family and friends not to believe that, if he died, it was by accident. According to his brother, Mr. Casolaro's investigation began to come together during the summer of 1991. Several people indicated he was upbeat and that on the weekend of August 10, 1991, he was in Martinsburg, WV, to receive significant information for his project from a source.

Mr. Casolaro died on August 10, 1991, and his death was officially ruled a suicide on January 25, 1992, over 5 months later. The criticism of the investigation of Casolaro's death by the Martinsburg, WV, police center on the following areas: Prior to any coroner's investigation and before his family was notified, Mr. Casolaro's body was embalmed, which may have limited the effectiveness of autopsies or toxicological examinations. Some evidence has also surfaced indicating that immediately following the discovery of the body, the room was not sealed by the Martinsburg authorities, potentially allowing for the contamination of the possible crime scene. Additionally, it was reported that the room in which Mr. Casolaro was found was cleaned before a thorough criminal investigation could be conducted.

Information received from other sources reveal other curious circumstances surrounding Mr. Casolaro's death that may or may not have been considered by Martinsburg authorities. In a sworn statement to the committee, Richard Stavin (a former Department of Justice Organized Crime Strike Force prosecutor) stated:

> I received a call from Danny Casolaro approximately one week before he was found dead.... He spoke to me about INSLAW. He spoke to me about a group he called, the Octopus. I believe he mentioned Robert Nichols, and possibly also John Phillip Nichols, in this conversation, and was extremely interested, intrigued and frustrated in his inability to get a grasp on what he called the Octopus.
>
> He had indicated that he had met with again I believe it was Robert Nichols on several occasions, that Robert Nichols was extremely talkative to a point, but when Mr. Casolaro would ask specific questions, he (Nichols) would become somewhat evasive.

William Hamilton and Michael Riconosciuto both told committee investigators that Robert Booth Nichols was Danny Casolaro's primary source of information in his investigation into the theft of the PROMIS software system. In a later telephone interview, Mr. Nichols told committee investigators that he was acting as a sounding board for Mr. Casolaro and providing direction and insight for his investigation into the INSLAW matter. **Mr. Nichols would not provide a sworn statement to committee investigators.**

In addition, the committee was informed by three separate individuals Mr. Riconosciuto's attorney, a private investigator and a FBI agent that a current FBI field agent, Thomas Gates, likely had information relating to Danny Casolaro's efforts to investigate the INSLAW matter. At the request of the committee, Director Sessions agreed to allow Special Agent Gates to provide the committee a sworn statement. Though Special Agent Gates' statement covered a broad range of subject matter areas, some speculative and some reflecting first person accounts, he indicated under oath that he had received several calls from Mr. Casolaro, beginning approximately four weeks before his death.

Special Agent Gates stated that he was very suspicious about Mr. Casolaro's death for several reasons, including:

In his conversations with Casolaro, even days before the reporter's death, Gates had felt that Casolaro sounded very "upbeat" and not like a person contemplating suicide.

Mr. Casolaro had a phone book which contained his (Special Agent Gates) telephone number. Special Agent Gates said that the phone book had not been located during the police investigation.

The Martinsburg Police Department told him that the wounds to Mr. Casolaro's arms were "hacking" wounds. Special Agent Gates felt that the amount of injury to the arms of Mr. Casolaro were not consistent with injuries inflicted by an individual who had slit his own wrists. Special Agent Gates said he was told by Martinsburg Police investigators that: "... he (Mr. Casolaro) hacked his wrists ... the wrists were cut,

but they were cut almost in a slashing or hacking motion ...''

An open bottle of wine was allegedly found in the room, but the contents had not been tested at the time of Special Agent Gates' conversation with Martinsburg authorities.

Special Agent Gates said that he made his suspicions known to Martinsburg authorities, and that he called the local FBI office and suggested that they investigate because it was possibly related to criminal activity which falls within the jurisdiction of the FBI.

In his sworn statement, Special Agent Gates concluded that: "... based upon my prior testimony concerning my contacts with Casolaro and also with the Captain of the Martinsburg Police Department, there is cause for suspicions to be raised... .''

2. POSSIBLE CONNECTION BETWEEN EARL BRIAN, MICHAEL RICONOSCIUTO, ROBERT BOOTH NICHOLS AND THE CABAZON INDIAN RESERVATION

Mr. Riconosciuto has alleged in a sworn statement to the committee that Dr. Brian and Mr. Peter Videnieks secretly delivered INSLAW's PROMIS software to the Cabazon Indian Reservation, located in California, for "refitting" for use by intelligence agencies in the United States and abroad. Mr. Riconosciuto could not provide evidence other than his eyewitness account that Dr. Brian was involved in the PROMIS conversion at the reservation. Dr. Brian flatly contradicts Riconosciuto's claims in his own sworn statement to committee investigators. In addition, in a sworn affidavit provided on April 2, 1991, in connection with the INSLAW bankruptcy case, Dr. Brian stated that he had never heard of, or was associated with, the so-called Wackenhut/Cabazon Indian joint venture, nor had he ever met, or had conversations with Peter Videnieks all in direct opposition to the Riconosciuto deposition as well as to certain law enforcement information on file at the committee. In light of these disputed versions of events, the committee is not in a position to

make findings of fact on Dr. Brian's role, but would strongly
recommend that further investigation be given to ascertaining
the role, if any, of Dr. Brian in INSLAW-related matters
including, but not limited to, questions surrounding the
Department of Justice's alleged conversion of the PROMIS
software and its possible dissemination to other customers
beyond the intended usage of the public domain version.

ODESSA/THE ORG

Truth, they say, is stranger than fiction.

It most definitely is in the case of *The Odessa File*, a 1972 thriller by Frederick Forsyth, which follows the adventures of a young German reporter who stumbles across an international Nazi organization dedicated to protecting former SS members after 1945. The Nazi network was called "ODESSA", this being an acronym for the German "Organization der Ehemaligen SS-Angehoerigen", which translates as "Organization of Former SS Members".

ODESSA existed in fact, as well as Forsyth's fertile imagination. Forsyth had been tipped off to ODESSA's existence by the Nazi-hunter Simon Wiesenthal, who acted as consultant to Forsyth on *The Odessa File*.

Otto Skorzeny, Hitler's former SS Special Forces chief, is generally credited with setting up ODESSA, which was principally an escape committee, funded by looted millions, to enable ex-Nazis to flee Europe between 1947 and 1952. In organizing his "ratlines", Skorzeny found a friend in the Vatican. In the belief that fascists on the run were "freedom fighters", the Vatican hid them in its churches and monasteries before helping spirit them out of Europe to places where they could take up the struggle against the atheistic Communist menace. The Vatican end of the scheme was overseen by Pope Pius XII and Cardinal Giovanni Montini (later Pope Paul VI), but run mainly by Bishop Alois Hudal of the German College of Santa Maria dell'Anima in Rome. Hudal's Nazi-sympathizing credentials were impeccable; he was a former spy for Abwehr [German military intelligence organization] during World War II. In 1946 the Vatican and ODESSA managed to send an entire Ukrainian Waffen SS Division, plus their families, down the ratlines, many of them exiting Italy on Red Cross passports provided by Hudal. Some of those proceeding along the ODESSA–Vatican ratlines were much bigger fry, and included Martin Bormann, Adolf Eichmann and Treblinka commandant Franz Stangl. The Vatican's dubiously pro-Nazi activities extended to channelling looted **Nazi Gold** and treasures into safe Swiss banks, as well as war criminals to safe havens.

ODESSA found Peron's notoriously pro-Nazi Argentine an especially happy home for its members, but many other far right-wing regimes provided a welcome. Nazis with military expertise were highly sought after – who knew better, after all, how to run a totalitarian state? Hitler's former henchmen ended up organizing everything from the bodyguard corps of Middle Eastern potentates' to Latin American death squads. ODESSA helped run the secret service in Syria, and probably took a hand in the 1953 coup in Iran, which saw the installation of the pro-Nazi Pahlevi family. Egypt, meanwhile, was virtually controlled by ex-Nazis. Joachim Daumling, the former Gestapo chief in Dusseldorf, explicitly founded the Egyptian secret service on the lines of Himmler's Reich Security Main Officer, and at least sixty former members of the Waffen-SS were employed as advisers in the Egyptian army. Then there were the 200 German and Austrian Nazi technicians who were deployed at the aircraft and missile centre at Helwan, Egypt, where the staff doctor was none other than Dr Hans Eisele, SS captain and sometime torturer at Buchenwald death camp. That Egypt under President Gamal Abdel Nasser was well disposed to the Nazis was hardly surprising: he wanted the destruction of the Jewish state of Israel. Nor, indeed, was Nasser averse to persecuting Jews inside Egypt. Unsurprisingly, Egypt's Jews fled. From a population of 75,000 Jews in 1948, by 1974 only 350 remained, after being deprived of citizenship, forced to renounce all property rights and dismissed from official positions.

ODESSA's circle of influential friends was not limited to the Vatican, Peron and Nasser's Egypt. It allegedly had close links with the "the Org" of Reinhard Gehlen.

Gehlen was Hitler's former chief of Eastern Intelligence, who had deftly avoided a Russian noose by offering his collection of intelligence on the Soviet Union (safely stored in Austrian Alps) to the American Counter-Intelligence-Corps (CIC) in return for immunity from prosecution for war crimes. So impressed was the CIC by Gehlen that they had flown him to Fort Hunt Maryland, the HQ of the OSS (the forerunner of the CIA), wined and dined him, then offered him the chance to run his own former spy-ring in countries now Soviet-dominated. Known as "the Org", Gehlen's Bavarian-based intelligence operation was funded by the CIA to the tune of a cool $200 million.

So successful was the Org in tapping into networks of Nazi sympathizers in Eastern Europe that it became NATO's main source of intelligence there. (Although, in retrospect, this was not an exactly miraculous achievement, given that Romania, Bulgaria and Hungary had all been fascist before the war.)

The CIA under Allen Dulles was so wholly keen on using ODESSA and the Org to fight the Cold War against the Soviet Bloc that it was quite prepared to payroll indicted war criminals as "intelligence operatives". Said Dulles of Gehlen, "He's on our side, and that's all that matters," in what effectively was the CIA's motto concerning erstwhile Nazis. Thus Klaus Barbie, the infamous SS "Butcher of Lyon", happily worked for Gehlen after the war. Neither was the usefulness of former fascists limited to spying in the Cold War. Under **Project Paperclip** the War Department secretly imported Nazi scientists into the US to work in the weapons industry.

Employing ex-Nazi Gehlen as NATO's master spy may well have been a pact with the devil. In his book *Blowback: The First Full Account of America's Recruitment of Nazis*, Christopher Simpson suggests that Gehlen deliberately exaggerated the Red threat: "Gehlen provided US Army Intelligence and later the CIA with many of the dire reports that were used to justify increased US military budgets and intensified US/USSR hostilities," Simpson wrote. According to Simpson and other espionage historians, Gehlen's alarmist report about an imminent Soviet invasion of the West in 1948 almost touched off a new world war. He also fed the Pentagon the specious claim that the Soviets had outstripped the US in weapons ("the missile gap"), which led to waves of anti-Commie paranoia. Plus an eye-watering national bill for military hardware.

It gets dodgier. The Org was so penetrated by Soviet agents that the CIA and Western intelligence was hampered for years. Effectively, Reinhard Gehlen had sabotaged the very security of the free West he had sought to defend.

Which raises the interesting question: was Gehlen's Org playing a double game? Conspiracy theorist Carl Oglesby asserts that Gehlen's Org was actually the cover for ODESSA, which was rather more than a shadowy escape outfit, but a full-blown underground movement headed by Martin Bormann with the intention of preserving the Third Reich. Oglesby's prime piece of evidence is a declassified CIA document which reports that while Gehlen was waiting in a POW camp in Wiesbaden, Germany, he sought permission to do his deal with the Americans from Admiral Karl Donitz. The admiral was Hitler's appointed successor. "The German chain of command was still in effect," Oglesby concludes, "and it approved of what Gehlen was doing with the Americans."

What can be said for sure is that the Nazis once again found themselves in a position of power in Germany. Gehlen's Org was officially incorporated into West Germany's state intelligence department, the *Bundesnachrichtendienst*, in 1955.

A secret Nazi underground sought to revive the Third Reich: ALERT LEVEL 8

Further Reading

Carl Oglesby, "Reinhard Gehlen: The Secret Treaty of Fort Hunt", *Covert Action Information Bulletin*, No. 35, Autumn 1990

Christopher Simpson, *Blowback*, 1988

OPERATION BLACK DOG

On his DeepBlackLies website, conspiracist David Guyatt claims to have "The Gulf War story that no one would publish". This is Operation Black Dog, by which a US Navy Viking plane was flown off a carrier in the Red Sea on 25 February 1991 and hit an Iraqi chemical and biological weapons plant with a bio-warfare bomb of its own ("numerous deaths resulted"). On the homeward flight, the Viking was shot down, and a bio bomb on board split and spilled its bacteriological agent. Near the downed craft, later recovered by the Americans, were a number of dead Iraqis, who had presumably inhaled the bio agent leading to death by internal drowning. While the op was done in Navy colours, it was actually a CIA project.

Guyatt's source for the story was "B", about whom Guyatt mentions zilch, save for their meeting in a "seamy pub" in England. (Handy, that. No one challenges the story of a man with no name and no background.) After nine months of research, Guyatt took his info on Black Dog to a member of the House of Lords, Countess Mar who, with former Foreign Secretary Geoffrey Howe, met with the MoD in 1997. In Guyatt's account, "The meeting was acrimonious. The result was that the MOD official could neither confirm nor deny the operation ..."

Black Dog, if Guyatt is to be believed, was the CIA's successor attack to Black Cat, the dropping of a chemical XV nerve bomb from a B52 on the Republican Guard. To hide this under-hand, immoral, illegal action – which would put the American military in the same evil bracket as Saddam Hussein – the US

Air Force then dropped fuel air bombs, which rid the ground of incriminating traces. Handy, that.

Without corroborating evidence, Black Dog looks like a Black Lie.

US launched bio and chemical weapons attacks during Gulf War I: ALERT LEVEL 3

Further Reading
www.deepblacklies.co.uk/operation_black_dog.htm

OPERATION NORTHWOODS

After the failure of the CIA to get **Fidel Castro,** the US military decided it was their turn to remove the bearded being from the face of the earth. Not for Army officer Lyman Lemnitzer such penny ante stuff as exploding cigars and "invasions" by half-trained exiles. No. Lemnitzer thought big. His idea was to manipulate public opinion into supporting a full-scale war against Cuba by organizing a fake Cuban attack on American people or territory. Among the "false-flag" scenarios Lemnitzer conjured were blowing up a US ship in Guantanamo Bay, attacks on the Cuban exile community in Florida, the shooting down of passenger planes by "Cuban" fighters, the planting of bombs in Miami and Washington and, if anything should go accidentally wrong with John Glenn's Apollo space mission, fabricating electronic interference from Cuba to prove Castro guilty. As a further refinement, Lyman Lemnitzer suggested committing an outrage against one of the Commonwealth states in the Caribbean, such as Jamaica or Trinidad and Tobago, so Great Britain could be persuaded to join in.

Lemnitzer was no maverick soldier. He was chairman of the Joint Chiefs of Staff. All the above proposals were official plots outlined in the Operation Northwoods memo sent by General Lemnitzer and his fellow top brass to Secretary of Defense Robert McNamara and President Kennedy in March 1962. McNamara and Kennedy vetoed the idea.

The existence of Operation Northwoods was confirmed after author James Bamford sued the National Security Agency for documents on the Cuban missile crisis.

Only two words are necessary to say to those who do not believe in government conspiracies: Operation Northwoods.

> US military plotted "false-flag" attacks on American citizens to promote war on Cuba: ALERT LEVEL 10

Further Reading
James Bamford, *Body of Secrets*, 2001

DOCUMENT: "JUSTIFICATION FOR U.S. MILITARY INVOLVEMENT IN CUBA" FROM THE JOINT CHIEFS OF STAFF TO SECRETARY OF DEFENSE MCNAMARA, 13 JUNE 1962

The document was declassified in 2000. The original is stored at US National Security Archives, George Washington University, Washington DC,

TOP SECRET SPECIAL HANDLING NOFORN

The Joint Chiefs of Staff
Washington 23, DC

13 March 1962

Memorandum for the Secretary of Defense
Subject: Justification for U.S. Military Intervention in Cuba (TS)

1. The Joint Chiefs of Staff have considered the attached memorandum for the chief of Operations, Cuba Project, which responds to a request by that office for brief but precise description of pretexts which would provide justification for US military intervention in Cuba.

2. The Joint Chiefs of Staff recommend that the proposed memorandum be forwarded as a preliminary submission suitable for planning purposes. It is assumed that there will be similar submissions from other agencies and that these inputs will be used as a basis for developing a time-phased plan. Individual projects can then be considered on a case-by-case basis.

3. Further, it is assumed that a single agency will be given the primary responsibility for developing military and para-military [terrorist] aspects of the basic plan. It is recommended that this responsibility for both overt and covert military operations be assigned to the Joint Chiefs of Staff.

For the Joint Chiefs of Staff
signed: General L.L. Limnitzer
Chairman, Joint Chiefs of Staff

NOTE BY THE SECRETARIES TO THE JOINT CHIEFS OF STAFF ON NORTHWOODS

[...]

RECOMMENDATIONS:

This paper NOT be forwarded to commanders of specified or unified commands.

This paper NOT be forwarded to US officers assigned to NATO activities.

This paper NOT be forwarded to the Chairman, US Delegation, United Nations Military Staff Committee.

ANNEX TO APPENDIX TO ENCLOSURE A: PRETEXTS TO JUSTIFY US MILITARY INTERVENTION IN CUBA

1) Since it would seem desirable to use legitimate provocation as the basis for US military intervention in Cuba a cover and deception plan, to include requisite preliminary actions such as has been developed in response to Task 33c, could be executed as an initial effort to provoke Cuban reactions. Harrassment plus deceptive actions to convince the Cubans of imminent invasion would be emphasized. Our military posture throughout execution of the plan will allow a rapid change from exercise to invention if Cuban response justifies.

2) A series of well-coordinated incidents will be planned to take place to give genuine appearance of being done by hostile Cuban forces.

Incidents to establish a credible attack:

1) Start rumors (many). Use clandestine radio.
2) Land friendly Cubans in uniform "over-the-fence" to stage attack on the base.
3) Capture Cuban (friendly) saboteurs inside the base.
4) Start riots near the entrance to the base (friendly Cubans).
5) Blow up ammunition inside the base; start fires.
6) Burn aircraft on airbase (sabotage).
7) Lob mortar shells from outside the base to inside the base. Some damage to installation.
8) Capture assault teams.
9) Capture militia group which storms the base.
10) Sabotage ship in harbor; large fires – napthalene [napalm].
11) Sink ship near harbor entrance. Conduct funerals for mock-victims.

(b) United States would respond by executing offensive operations.

3) A "Remember the Maine" incident could be arranged in several forms:

a. We could blow up a US ship and blame Cuba.

b. We could blow up a drone (unmanned) vessel anywhere in the Cuban waters. The presence of Cuban planes or ships merely investigating the intent of the vessel could be fairly compelling evidence that the ship was taken under attack. The US could follow with an air/sea rescue operation covered by US fighters to "evacuate" remaining members of the non-existent crew. Casualty lists in US newspapers would cause a helpful wave of national indignation.

4) We could develop a Communist Cuba terror campaign in the Miami area, in other Flordia cities and even in Washington. The terror campaign could be pointed at Cuban refugees seeking haven in the United States. We could sink a boatload of Cubans en route to Florida (real or simulated). We could foster attempts on lives of Cubans in the United States even to the extent of wounding in instances to be widely publicized. Exploding a few bombs in carefully chosen spots. The arrest of Cuban agents and the release of prepared documents substantiating Cuban involvement also would be helpful in projecting the idea of an irresponsible government.

5) A "Cuban-based, Castro-supported" filibuster could be simulated against a neighboring Caribbean nation. These efforts can be magnified with additional ones contrived for exposure. "Cuban" B-26 or C-46 type aircraft could make cane-burning raids at night. Soviet Bloc incidiaries could be found. This could be coupled with "Cuban" messages to the Communist underground and "Cuban" shipments of arms which would be found, or intercepted, on the beach.

6) Use of MIG-type aircraft by US pilots could provide additional provocation. Harassment of civil air, attacks on surface shipping, and destruction of US military drone aircraft by MIG type planes would be useful. An F-86 properly painted would convince air passengers that they saw a Cuban MIG, especially if the pilot of the transport were to announce that fact.

7) Hijacking attampts against US civil air and surface craft should be encouraged.

8) It is possible to create an incident which would demonstrate convincingly that a Cuban aircraft has attacked and shot down a chartered civilian airliner from the United States.

   a. An aircraft at Eglin AFB [10 separate landing strips on one giant base in the jungle] would be painted and numbered as an exact duplicate for a civil registered aircraft belonging to a CIA proprietary organization in the Miami area. At a designated time the duplicate would be substituted for the actual civil aircraft and the passengers, all boarded under carefully prepared aliases. The actual registered aircraft would be converted to a drone.

   b. Take off times of the drone aircraft and the actual aircraft will be scheduled to allow a rendezvous. From the rendezvous point the passenger-carrying aircraft will descend to minimum altitude and go directly to an auxiliary airfield at Eglin AFB where arrangements will have been made to evacuate the passengers and return the aircraft to its original status. Meanwhile the drone aircraft will continue to fly the filed flight plan. The drone will be transmitting on the international distress frequency "MAY DAY" message stating it is under attack by Cuban MIG aircraft. The transmission will be interrupted by the destruction of aircraft which will be triggered by radio signal. This will allow IACO radio stations to tell the US what has happened to the aircraft instead of the US trying to "sell" the incident.

9) a. It is possible to create an incident that will make it appear that Communist Cuban MIGs have destroyed a USAF aircraft over international waters in an unprovoked attack. [...]

   b. On one such flight, a pre-briefed pilot would fly Tail-end Charlie. While near the Cuban island this pilot would broadcast that he had been jumped by MIGs and was going down. This pilot would then fly at extremely low altitude and land at a secure base, an Eglin auxiliary. The aircraft would be met by the proper people, quickly stored and given a new tail number. The pilot who performed the mission under an alias would resume his proper identity. The pilot and aircraft would then have disappeared.

c. A submarine or small craft would distribute F-101 parts, parachute, etc. The pilots retuning to Homestead would have a true story as far as they knew. Search ships and aircraft could be dispatched and parts of aircraft found.

3. It is understood that the Department of State is also preparing suggested courses of action to develop justification for US military intervention in Cuba.

THE PALADIN GROUP

In more ways than one, Otto Skorzeny was a big figure in the post-War conspiracy world. The scar-faced former SS commando was a hulking six feet seven inches tall; he was also a main player in, inter alia, the Werwolf stay-behind Nazi guerrilla movement, the **ODESSA** network, the Spider ratline, Reinhard Gehlen's the Org, and the International Fascista terrorist-organization, a sub-contractor for both CIA and the Org in the war against Communism.

Skorzeny was also the founder in 1970 of the Paladin Group, "an international directorship of strategic assault personnel [that would] straddle the watershed between paramilitary operations carried out by troops in uniform and the political warfare which is conducted by civilian agents". Put more plainly, Paladin claimed to train guerrillas for anybody who would pay, from the South African Bureau of State Security to Gaddafi's Libya. What Paladin advertised less widely, was that it operated a contract-killing facility on behalf of the Spanish intelligence agency SCOE. During the Franco-era, Paladin operated out of the offices of Skorzeny's Madrid-based import-export firm MC Inc., which just happened to share an address with a front for SCOE, plus a local branch of the CIA. Paladin's mercenary killers were former members of the French OAS, Portugal's PIDE as well as the SS, and carried out abductions and executions of Basque ETA members in the mid seventies. Paladin was also rumoured to be the organization that carried out the "false-flag" bombing of Rome's Fiumicino airport (thirty-two people died) for which Italian Communists were blamed. After

Skorzeny's death in 1975, Dr Gerhard von Schubert took over the reins of Paladin. Von Schubert's CV included a stint in Goebbels' propaganda ministry.

Mercenary outfit run by ex-Nazis undertook contract killings on behalf of Western intelligence agencies: ALERT LEVEL 9

PEAK OIL

It's the oil, stupid.

While black gold may not have been the only reason for the invasion of Iraq in 2003, it would be a fool who maintained that securing the oil locked in the ground there was not at least a fleeting thought in the mind of President Bush – who was, after all, a former oil man himself, the director of Harken Energy Corporation. (And let's not forget that Vice-President Dick Cheney was ex-chief executive of Halliburton Energy, and Condolezza Rice sat on the board of Chevron.) There was an awful lot of oil in Iraq; it had proven reserves of 112 billion barrels. Before the Iraq War, most Iraqi oil contracts were done with the French and Russians ... after the war, Uncle Sam was the partner of choice.

"Peak oil" refers to the time when worldwide oil production reaches its maximum level, after which the supply of oil – a finite natural resource made a million years ago – enters a downward curve until the global tank is empty. The peak oil theory is based on the findings of geoscientist M. King Hubbert who in 1956 suggested that America's oil would begin to run out in the 1970s. US society is particularly exposed to oil consumption; with about 6 per cent of the world's population, it guzzles 25 per cent of the world's oil supply, 19.4 million barrels of oil a day.

Or is peak oil a myth, a scare story fabricated by an elite group of politicians and oilmen to create a state of artificial scarcity? And thus keep the price of a barrel of crude nice and high. Those who allege the falsity of peak oil invariably agree with Russian geologist Nikolai Kudryavtsev that petroleum does not come from dead dinosaurs and Pleistoscene plants but has abiotic origins and is in constant production in the bowels of the planet. Since how else can the curious history of production at Eugene Island 330 oilfield in the Gulf of Mexico be explained?

In 1973, the Eugene Island rigs yielded 15,000 barrels a day, before slowing to 4,000 barrels a day in 1989. A few years later, oil gushed at 13,000 barrels a day. An analysis of the oil field with seismic imaging seemed to show the pool being replenished by a migration of upwards oil of a different geological age. Mobil, Chevron, Texaco and others are all accused of controlling the supply of oil to inflate prices. A Chevron memo purportedly warned of the effect on profits of high levels of extraction. Oil-friendly governments are also implicated in the suppression of alternative technologies.

The verdict: it would be amazing if oil producers did not collaborate to push up the price of crude. In fact, that collaboration is a cartel called OPEC. As British entrepreneur Richard Branson once remarked, "OPEC is effectively an illegal cartel that can meet happily, nobody takes them to court. They collude to keep prices high."

While hard scientific evidence for abiotic production of oil is scarce, the steady discovery of major oil fields around the globe, from the Gulf of Mexico to Uganda to Iran, suggests that peak oil is not the truth, the whole truth, so help us petrolheads dear God. At the very least, according to the International Energy Agency, the world has until 2030 before demand overwhelms supply.

Oil industry honchos invented peak oil theory to drive up prices: ALERT LEVEL 7

Further Reading
Colin J. Campbell, *The Coming Oil Crisis*, 1997
David Goodstein, *Out of Gas: The End of the Age of Oil*, 2005
Kenneth D. Worth, *Peak Oil and the Second Great Depression*, 2010

PLUM ISLAND

In 1896, H. G. Wells penned a nightmare sci-fi novel in which mad-but-brilliant scientist Doctor Moreau conducted hideous experiments on animals.

Plum Island is *The Island of Doctor Moreau* come to real life.

An elongated blob of land in the dark waters of Long Island Sound off the coast of Connecticut, Plum Island hosts a US Government scientific facility studying animal-borne diseases. For decades after the facility's foundation at the end of WWII, the White House blithely informed all that asked that everything at Plum Island Animal Disease Center (PIADC) was above board and in no way connected with biowarfare.

So why was an early director at Plum Island Erich Traub? Traub was a Third Reich researcher on cancer – in the Hitler era a code for biowarfare – who was spirited out of the defeated Deutschland to the US under **Project Paperclip**. As files held in the National Archives reveal, Traub's research on Plum Island in the 1950s concerned the use of ticks as "vectors" to carry pathogens which could destroy Russia's livestock/grain harvest.

In 1971, a mysterious disease, marked by lassitude, psychosis and organ degeneration, broke out in the town of Old Lyme, Connecticut. The syndrome was given the name Lyme disease. Medical researchers determined that Lyme disease had one carrier: deer ticks. A decade later, an Austrian scientist isolated and identified the responsible bacteria carried by the deer ticks, which was named *Borellia burgdorferi* after him. When gene researchers later cracked the code of *Borellia burgdorferi* they received a mighty surprise: it was the most complex bacterium ever put under a microscope.

What has all this to do with Herr Traub? It seemed unlikely that Lyme disease would arise spontaneously in the sticks of Connecticut. Looking slightly further afield, some researchers believe they found antique traces of *Borellia* in preserved fauna samples taken from Shelter Island and Long Island. The samples were from the 1940s, when Herr Traub was busy at nearby Plum Island. The latter has numerous birds that frequent it, so the disease may have been borne away from there. Michael Carroll, an attorney and no wild-eyed conspirator, also posits in *Lab 257* that mainland US outbreaks of West Nile disease and Dutch duck plague can be trailed back to Plum Island. The Cuban Government directly accused the PIADC of being the manufacturer of bioweapons which destroyed Cuban pigs and sugar cane in the 1970s. Under the weight of evidence, the White House admitted in 1992 that, surprise surprise, biowarfare research had been, and was being, conducted at Plum Island.

Thereafter the White House went largely schtum on the strange happenings around Plum Island. Some of which were very strange indeed.

On a summer's day in 2008 a holidaymaker on Montauk, Long Island, noticed the washed-up body of a large animal on the beach. On closer investigation, the animal had patches of uneven hair and an elongated skull. Its fingers were matchstick thin.

Plum Island is ten miles from Montauk. No official gave an explanation, and Plum Island – now under the aegis of Homeland Security – issued a denial of responsibility. In spring of 2009, a second hideous corpse came ashore at Montauk. This one was almost identical – same elongated skull, same weird clawlike fingers. The carcass was quickly spirited away and, to anyone's knowledge, was never examined by an independent zoologist. Meanwhile, back on the island itself, the body of a white male with, according to the police record, oddly elongated fingers was discovered on the foreshore.

The Montauk and Plum Island "monsters" might be fakes, misidentifications, the products of hysterical imaginations. What is beyond doubt is that the historical safety record of PIADC's seventy buildings – full of deadly diseases – is atrocious. According to one maintenance worker on the island, James McCoy, lab staff at the island's super-secret Building 257 once resorted to sticking duct tape around doors to keep their test microbes in. McCoy got fired for his whistle-blowing.

The Department of Homeland Security (DHS) announced in 2008 that Plum Island is to be closed, and the germ labs and research facilities moved to Kansas State University.

Unlucky Kansas.

> Plum Island is home to US biowarfare centre: ALERT LEVEL 10

Further Reading
Michael C. Carroll, *Lab 257: The Disturbing Story of the Government's Secret Plum Island Germ Laboratory*, 2004
John Loftus, *The Belarus Secret*, 1982

POPE JOHN PAUL II

On Wednesday, 13 May 1981, Pope John Paul II was shot as his popemobile entered St Peter's Square in the Vatican City. The shootist, who used a Browning Hi-Power semi-automatic pistol, was grabbed by the Vatican security chief and promptly identified as one Mehmet Ali Ağca, a Turkish national. The Pope, despite being wounded by four bullets, survived. A miracle claimed the faithful.

Altogether less miraculous were cogent explanations for Ağca's attempted whacking of His Holiness.

Ağca was a member of the Grey Wolves, a vitriolic neo-fascist Turkish group. He had form for murder (of a liberal journalist) and had previously sent letters threatening Pope John Paul's life. So, the classic right-wing "lone nut"? Unfortunately for any straightforward explanation of why he peppered the pontiff with 9 mm slugs, Ağca suddenly remembered after a year in his prison cell that it was a trio of Bulgarians living in Rome who had put him up to the job. With the Cold War still a going concern, Ağca's "confession" was manna from heaven for anti-Communists such as veteran Yankee hackette Claire Sterling who stuck her sharpened pen into Bulgarian intelligence *and* the KGB. Sterling's *The Time of the Assassins*, co-authored with CIA-veteran and Cold War warrior Paul Henze, lucidly implicated the KGB as the directors of Bulgarian spookery, who in turn manipulated wires that made Ağca move. The KGB's motive for offing the Polish pope? He supported the free trade union Solidarity in Communist Poland. As to why the Bulgarians/

KGB needed a Turkish nazi to do their dirty work, that was easily accounted for: it allowed the KGB "deniability".

The Bulgarian connection looked oh, oh so promising when Bulgarian airline worker Sergei Antonov was arrested on Ağca's say-so, as being his controller. However, a fair trial of Antonov in Italy failed to find him guilty of so much as stealing sweets. (It did reveal Ağca to be mad, or a liar, or both. He claimed to be Christ.) As several pundits wisely noted, Ağca did not mention the Bulgarian connection until visited in jail by agents of the Italian intelligence bureau, the SISMI, whose incompetence was only matched by their corruption. Fancying a spot of Red-baiting, the SISMI had already tried to implicate the USSR in the papal misfortune with a "document" that proved that Ağca had been trained in Moscow. It was later proved to be a forgery.

Just when the Bulgarian connection looked like the Bulgarian concoction, the Italian Mitrokhin Commission came to the conclusion that Bulgarian intelligence *was* implicated in the plot to kill the pope, *and* that "leaders of the former Soviet Union were behind the assassination attempt". After a moment's reflection the sane recalled that the impressive sounding Mitrokhin Commission had been set up by the perma-tanned Silvio Berlusconi, was fronted by one of his favourite right-wing *Forza* stooges and was the same bunch of buffoons who had slander-ously accused Romano Prodi, sometime Italian PM (and fre-quent Berlusconi opponent), of being the KGB's man in Italy.

So much SISMI/CIA effort went into pinning the blame for the attempted offing of the pope that it looked suspicious in itself. Indeed, the Bulgarian secret services argued that Ağca's "Bulgarian connection" story was an anti-Commie plant placed by SISMI, the CIA and the Grey Wolves. They would say that, wouldn't they? Yes, but an intriguing piece of support on behalf of the secret service boys from Bulgaria came from no less than Abdullah Catli, a Grey Wolves leader (top dog?), who told a Rome judge that German intelligence asked him to implicate the Bulgarians/Soviets in return for a nice lump of money.

Ah yes, the Grey Wolves. One John Paul II conspiracy has the Grey Wolves down as the bedfellows of neo-Italian fascists in their "strategy of tension" by which they terrorized Italy (e.g. the bombing of Bologna rail station), put the blame on the Reds and theoretically built popular support for themselves. In this scenario, the quasi-Masonic **P2** lodge and Ordine Nuova, also got under the black sheets. Far-fetched? Actually, no. One P2 big cheese, Francesco Pazienza (who also happened to be an ex-SISMI agent), informed US authorities of a meeting held in Miami a month before the attack on the pope attended by the Grey Wolves and Italy's most wanted fascist terrorist, Stefano della Chiaie.

It's worth pointing out for the record that during a May 2002 visit to Bulgaria, Pope John Paul II told Bulgarian president Georgi Parvanov that he never believed allegations that there was a Bulgarian connection. The pope also credited the Madonna of Fátima with saving his life, and in 2000 the Vatican disclosed that the long suppressed **Third Secret of Fátima** had been an assassination attempt on a pope.

The Bulgarian secret service was behind the attempted assassination of Pope John Paul II: ALERT LEVEL 5

Pope John Paul's would-be assassins were an unholy alliance of Turkish nationalists and Italian neo-fascists: ALERT LEVEL 8

Further Reading
Edward S. Herman and Frank Brodhead, *The Rise and Fall of the Bulgarian Connection*, 1986
Claire Sterling and Paul Henze, *The Time of the Assassins*, 1984

PRINCESS DIANA

It was news that shocked the world. In the early hours (GMT) of Sunday 31 August 1997, reports started coming from Paris that Diana, Princess of Wales, had been injured in a car accident. Then came updates reporting she was dead. Also killed in the car crash in the tunnel beneath Pont de l'Alma were Diana's lover, Dodi Al-Fayed, and the driver, Henri Paul. Dodi's bodyguard, Trevor Rees-Jones, was seriously injured.

The cause of the crash seemed clear. Chased by paparazzi on motorcycles, Paul had driven too fast – 75 mph (120 kph) according to one French police estimate – into the tunnel, clipped a white Fiat Uno and, in overcorrecting, had swerved the Mercedes S280 into the thirteenth pillar. There were also reports that he had been drinking. None of the occupants had been wearing seat belts.

Autumn seemed to come early to Britain that year, as a stunned nation shed tears for "the Queen of Hearts". As the sorrow subsided, people began to wonder how the female icon of the latter half of the twentieth century, the most famous and photographed woman on the planet, could have died in something so mundane as a car crash.

Perhaps, people began to say, it wasn't an accident. The loudest voice of suspicion belonged to Dodi's father, Mohamed Al-Fayed, the owner of Harrods department store. According to Al-Fayed, Diana and his son were assassinated. Al-Fayed even named the guilty party: Prince Philip of the British Royal Family. Naturally, Philip didn't dirty his hands personally – he ordered the security service MI6 to carry out the hit on his 36-year-old daughter-in-law. There are legion other Diana conspiracies (it was the IRA whatdunnit, it was *Le Cercle* who sponsored her death because of her opposition to wealth-generating landmines, she was a ritual sacrifice by Satanists, she faked her death to live a paparazzi-free life ...) but Al-Fayed's retains the pole position.

In his view, the British Royal Family needed Diana eliminated because she had become pregnant by Dodi and intended to marry him. Their child would be a Muslim half-brother to the second and third in line to the throne, an impossible embarrassment to the white, Anglican Windsors. Al-Fayed claims that Diana told him personally that her life had been threatened. "The person who is spearheading these threats," she said, "is Prince Philip." Diana also told a number of other people that she feared for her life. In his account of life as Diana's butler, *A Royal Duty* (2003), Paul Burrell recorded that ten months before her death she wrote to him claiming that "XXXX is planning an 'accident' in my car, brake failure and serious head injury in order to make the path clear for Charles to marry." She also told her voice coach Peter Settelen that she thought that her former lover, bodyguard Barry Mannakee, had been murdered in a faked motorcycle crash. Evidently, Diana had concerns over safety. And the Windsors had a motive of sorts.

Suddenly, it wasn't only Al-Fayed raising questions about the crash in the tunnel under Pont de l'Alma. Why had the lights and security cameras in the tunnel been turned off just before the crash? Why did the ambulance take forty-three minutes to get Diana to Pitie-Salpêtrière hospital? Why had her body been embalmed before a proper autopsy could be undertaken? Why had the crash site been cleansed and disinfected before a forensic examination could be carried out? And where was the driver of the white Fiat Uno? Wasn't it too convenient that Rees-Jones had "no memory" of the crash?

Then a former MI6 agent, Richard Tomlinson, revealed that MI6 had been planning an assassination at the time of Diana's death. In a sworn affidavit Tomlinson stated that MI6's Balkans operations officer had shown him the service's plan to assassinate Slobodan Milosevic, the Serbian president, in a car crash ... in a tunnel. Tomlinson stated that MI6's planned assassination of Milosevic showed "remarkable similarities to the

circumstances and witness accounts of the crash that killed the
Princess of Wales, Dodi Al-Fayed, and Henri Paul". How had
MI6 caused the car to crash? Possibly, suggested Tomlinson,
with a disorientating strobe light held by an operative in the
tunnel, or by another car forcing the Mercedes into the pillar.
There were rumours that Henri Paul was a CIA/DGSE/MI6
agent and had deliberately taken the roundabout Pont de l'Alma
route to the Al-Fayeds' Paris flat to get Diana into the killing
zone. (If Paul was a spook this might explain, people said, the
series of 40,000-franc deposits in his bank account.) A more far-
fetched suggestion was that Rees-Jones, a former paratrooper,
wrenched the wheel from Paul's grasp. Suspicions of a cover-up
mushroomed when the body of James Andanson was found in a
burnt-out car in 2000. Andanson, a paparazzo, had owned a
white Fiat Uno three years before and had been investigated by
the French police. There was a final oddity: just after Andanson's
death his office was burgled. Meanwhile, an investigation by
French forensic specialists found no significant mechanical
faults in the Mercedes S280, ruling out the possibility that the
crash had been caused by some internal failure.

So far, so bad for the Windsors. Yet Al-Fayed's case has a
number of weaknesses:

- The only source for the story that Dodi and Diana were to be
  married, and that an engagement ring had been bought from
  Repossi in Paris, is Al-Fayed himself.
- Despite a multi-million pound personal investigation,
  Al-Fayed has been unable to establish any link between
  Prince Philip and MI6.
- Although Diana reportedly told Frederic Mailliez, the off-
  duty doctor who first attended her in the Pont de l'Alma
  tunnel, that she was pregnant, the only other evidence of
  pregnancy came from an anonymous French policeman who
  said he had the papers to prove this but to date has not made
  these public. By contrast, scientific tests carried out on
  Diana's pre-transfusion blood have shown no evidence of
  pregnancy. Myriah Daniels, a holistic healer who travelled
  with Dodi and Diana on their cruise aboard the Jonikal yacht
  at the end of August 1997, stated: "I can say with one

hundred per cent certainty that she was not pregnant. I will explain how I can be so sure of this fact. Firstly, she told me herself that she was not pregnant. Secondly ... It is incomprehensible to me that Diana would have allowed me to carry out such an invasive treatment [massage] on her stomach and intestines if she thought she was pregnant.

- The Operation Paget Inquiry was given access to MI6 to investigate Tomlinson's claims. The inquiry tracked down the assassination plan he referred to and found the target to be not Slobodan Milosevic but another Serbian figure. Since it is against British Government policy to carry out assassinations, the memo's author was disciplined. Tomlinson admitted this memo was the one he was referring to in his claim.
- Given the long-standing antipathy between France and Britain, why would the French police/security services collude in the conspiracy to kill Diana?
- In December 2006 the *Independent* newspaper stated there were at least fourteen CCTV cameras in the Pont de l'Alma tunnel, yet none recorded footage of the fatal collision. Mohamed Al-Fayed raised the absence of CCTV images of the Mercedes' journey on the fateful night as evidence of conspiracy. A Brigade Criminelle investigation, however, found only ten CCTV cameras along the route, and it was for a quite simple reason that none had relevant images: they were security cameras on buildings and were pointed at those buildings' exits and entrances. Inside the Alma underpass there was one camera, which was under the control of the Compagnie de Circulation Urbaines de Paris (Paris Urban Traffic Unit). The CCUP closed down at 11.00 p.m. and made no recordings after that time.
- The lengthy "43-minute" ambulance journey of Diana from the Pont de l'Alma tunnel to hospital was no such thing, taking from 1.41 a.m. to 2.06 a.m. The SAMU ambulance did admittedly stop en route for ten minutes, but that was because the accompanying doctor needed the ambulance to be stationary while he gave Diana blood-pressure treatment. The ambulance did not go to the Hotel Dieu, the nearest hospital to the crash scene, because Pitié-Salpêtrière was the main centre for multiple trauma cases.

- Fayed challenged the French investigators' conclusion that Henri Paul was drunk (with an alcohol level three times the legal limit) on the evening of the tragedy; his bearing, as captured on the Ritz Hotel CCTV that evening, showed a man apparently sober. There were also suggestions that the blood samples tested belonged not to Henri but to another subject. There certainly seem to have been irregularities in the report of French forensic pathologist Dominique Lecomte, but in December 2006 DNA testing confirmed that the blood samples showing a level of alcohol in excess of legal limits did indeed belong to Paul.

Al-Fayed nonetheless maintained that his son and Diana died as the result of a vast conspiracy by the Royal Family and MI6. In response, the coroner of the royal household requested Lord Stevens, a former chief of the Metropolitan Police, to head an investigation into the deaths. The subsequent Operation Paget agreed that some questions asked by Al-Fayed were "right to be raised" and confirmed that Paul had been a low-level informer for the French domestic secret service, DST. The Operation Paget report also pointed out that hotel security staff the world over act as low-grade informers for their national spy organizations.

Essentially, the Operation Paget report came to the same conclusion as had the French inquiry into the tragedy. Mme Coujard, the prosecutor heading the French inquiry, determined: "The direct cause of the accident is the presence, at the wheel of the Mercedes S280, of a driver who had consumed a considerable amount of alcohol, combined with ... medication, driving at a speed ... faster than the maximum speed-limit in built-up areas."

In 2007, Mohamed Al-Fayed forced a coroner's inquest into the deaths of Dodi and Diana, which was held at the Royal Courts of Justice, London, and headed by Lord Justice Scott Baker. On 7 April 2008, the jury released its verdict (see Document, p.443), stating that Diana and Dodi were unlawfully killed by the grossly negligent driving of chauffeur Henri Paul and the pursuing paparazzi. The jury also named the intoxication of the driver, the victims' decisions to not wear seat belts and the speed of the Mercedes as contributing factors in the deaths.

There may be an innocuous reason for the serially identical conclusions of the French inquiry, Operation Paget and the Scott Baker inquest: they are correct and the goddess-like Diana suffered the fate of many poor mortals. She was killed by a drunk driver.

Princess Diana was assassinated: ALERT LEVEL 3

Further Reading
Noel Botham, *The Assassination of Princess Diana*, 2004
Peter Hounam and Derek McAdam, *Who Killed Diana?*, 1998
Trevor Rees-Jones and Moira Johnston, *The Bodyguard's Story: Diana, the Crash, and the Sole Survivor*, 2000

DOCUMENT: CORONER'S INQUESTS INTO THE DEATHS OF DIANA, PRINCESS OF WALES AND MR DODI AL FAYED: RULING ON VERDICTS [EXTRACTS] AND JURY'S VERDICT

Ruling on Verdicts [Extracts]

Introduction

1) I propose to leave the following verdicts to the jury:-
    1) Unlawful killing (grossly negligent driving of the paparazzi);
    2) Unlawful killing (grossly negligent driving of the Mercedes);
    3) Unlawful killing (grossly negligent driving of the paparazzi and grossly negligent driving of the Mercedes);
    4) Accidental death;
    5) Open verdict.

These are my reasons. I have received written and oral submissions from Interested Persons and from Counsel to the Inquests. My reasons are necessarily in relatively summary form because of the limited time available and the need to prepare the summing-up. I shall not, therefore, deal with all the points made in over 450 pages of written submissions.

2) The inquests into the deaths of Diana, Princess of Wales, and Dodi Al Fayed heard evidence over a period of 5 ½ months. They have covered a wide range of topics. At the heart of the evidence has been detailed consideration of the circumstances of the crash in the Alma Tunnel in Paris just after midnight on 31 August 1997. We have heard from dozens of witnesses who saw some part of the journey of the Mercedes from the rear of the Ritz Hotel to the scene of the crash. Some have given oral evidence, others have had their evidence read under rule 37 of the Coroners Rules as uncontroversial. Yet more has been introduced as hearsay evidence when it has not been possible to secure the attendance of a witness. The circumstances of the crash have also been considered in detail by a range of experts, whose opinions have been explained to the jury. There was considerable agreement between those experts. Similarly, we have heard an enormous quantity of evidence that goes, in one way or another, to conspiracy theories that have abounded since the crash. [...]

4) There is some common ground on the verdicts which should be left. All are agreed that the verdicts accidental death and open verdict should be left to the jury. All are agreed that, whatever "short-form" verdict is returned by the jury, it can and should be supplemented by a short, non-judgmental narrative conclusion. The debate has focussed on the following questions:

i) Should unlawful killing be left to the jury on the basis that the crash was deliberately staged, with the intention of killing, harming or scaring? Deliberately causing the crash with the intention of killing the occupants of the car or causing them serious injury would support a verdict of unlawful killing by murder. Deliberately causing the crash with a view to scaring the occupants of the car would support a verdict of unlawful killing on the basis of unlawful act manslaughter. Mr Al Fayed submits that such a verdict should be left to the jury, whereas the Metropolitan Police submit that it should not.

ii) Should unlawful killing be left to the jury on the basis of gross negligence manslaughter by the driving of following paparazzi? The Ritz Hotel submits that it should, while the Metropolitan Police disagree. There is a subsidiary issue. The Ritz contends that this verdict should be left both on the basis of gross negligence manslaughter and on the basis of unlawful act manslaughter; the latter founded on a hypothetical offence under the Protection from Harassment Act 1997.

iii) Should unlawful killing be left to the jury on the basis of gross negligence manslaughter by the driver of the Mercedes (Henri Paul)? The Metropolitan Police say that this verdict should be left, while the family of Henri Paul argue that it should not.

[...]

Unlawful Killing: Staged Accident

12) For some years, Mr Al Fayed has expressed the firm belief that his son and the Princess of Wales were murdered in furtherance of a conspiracy to kill them or do them serious harm. This "broad and overarching allegation" was elaborated in written submissions before the inquest began. Mr Al Fayed believes that the conspiracy was orchestrated by the Duke of Edinburgh and executed by the Secret Intelligence Service on his orders. In the light of the evidence, Mr Mansfield QC has, quite

properly, accepted that there is no direct evidence that the Duke played any part in the deaths and has accepted that there is no direct evidence of any involvement of the SIS. Mr Mansfield now submits that the jury should consider an alternative scenario, which he terms the "troublesome priest thesis": a plan by unknown individuals (perhaps rogue SIS operatives) to stage the crash in order to serve the perceived interests or wishes of the Royal Family or "the Establishment", as he and Mr Al Fayed term it. He also now submits that the aim of the plot may have been to scare the Princess. That submission may rest in part on a realistic acceptance that there could have been no certainty that the Princess and Mr Al Fayed would die or be seriously harmed. The lethal forces that resulted in the deaths of Diana, Dodi and Henri Paul resulted from the high speed of the Mercedes (about 65 mph at the moment of the collision) and the fact that it impacted with the corner of a pillar. Had the Mercedes hit the side of the pillar or gone out of control and hit the wall on the other side of its carriageway, it would probably have been deflected and the outcome may well have been different. Additionally, the occupants were not wearing seat belts. The expert evidence was that wearing a seat belt would either have prevented or at the very least diminished the prospect of a fatal injury.

13) As I said in my Reasons regarding the decision not to call the Duke of Edinburgh to give evidence, the question of whether this was a staged crash is different from the question of whether the Duke could have been involved. But because it is impossible for anyone to argue that particular individuals or agencies were involved, beyond what amounts to speculation, it is necessary to focus on the issue whether the circumstances of the crash point to a staged accident. In other words, would the evidence of the events on the evening of 30/31 August 1997 enable the jury to be sure that the crash was staged by somebody

of whose identity there is no evidence? In my judgment it would not.

14) It is common ground between the reconstruction experts, and has not been disputed by anybody, that, either at the entrance to the Alma underpass or shortly into it, the Mercedes had a glancing collision with a white, slower moving Fiat Uno. The collision was between the right front corner of the Mercedes and the left rear corner of the Uno. There was a 17 cm overlap between the vehicles at the time of collision, and the point of impact was around the dividing line between the two lanes of the carriageway. Debris from the rear left light cluster of the Fiat was found at the scene, as was debris from the front right light cluster of the Mercedes. Additionally, the Fiat left a smear of paint on the Mercedes. There is some doubt about where precisely the collision took place, but of the fact that an impact took place between the Mercedes and the Fiat there is no doubt. The Mercedes clipped the slower moving Fiat as it went past. It would, in my view, be irrational for the jury to come to any conclusion other than that the presence of the Fiat was a potent contributory factor in the loss of control of the Mercedes and thus the crash and the deaths.

15) Mr Mansfield made clear in his oral submissions that the driver of the Fiat Uno, who has never been traced, was not involved in any plot. That is obviously right. The evidence to which he pointed as supporting a staged accident was different. He argued that there was evidence of a dark-coloured vehicle in front of the Mercedes in the left hand lane and evidence of a motorcycle behind it in that lane. As a result, he says that the Mercedes was "boxed in" and, on the evidence, collided with the dark vehicle. He also argues that there is evidence to support a conclusion that a bright light of some kind was deliberately flashed in the eyes of Henri Paul to disorientate him, and that this light may have been flashed by the

motorcycle rider or from elsewhere. These are the physical features which he identifies as pointing to a plot.

16) As regards the "blocking vehicle" and the motorcycle, the difficulties with the argument are as follows.

a) Given the speed of the Mercedes, any vehicle ahead in its lane and observing the speed limit, or even driving close to the limit, would have impeded its progress and would have appeared to be blocking it. The witness who used the term "blocking" (Olivier Partouche) said in his first statement to French police that he thought the car in front was being used to slow the Mercedes down to allow paparazzi to take photographs from behind. When asked specific questions in the French investigation, he said that he could not say whether or not the car in front was deliberately being driven slowly. In any event, he maintained that it did not perform any dangerous manoeuvre. See 24/10/07 at p. 10–11, 23–24 and 33–34. The evidence of his colleague, M. Gooroovadoo, was to similar effect (12/3/08, p. 93).

b) The other witnesses who saw a vehicle in front of the Mercedes in its lane were the driver and passenger of a car in the opposite carriageway: Benoit Boura and Gaelle L'Hostis. They did not conclude that the car was being driven deliberately slowly or manoeuvring dangerously. They described the car as being in front of the Mercedes as it was going out of control, and then driving off. See 24/10/07 at p. 47–48, 63–64, 72–74, 83–84, 85–86. In that regard, their evidence should be seen in the context of the evidence of Mohamed Medjahdi and Souad Mouffakir [sic], who were in a car ahead of the Mercedes. See 6/11/07 at p.57ff; 12/3/08 at p. 108ff. They gave evidence that they were in the tunnel when they saw the Mercedes behind them out of control, and that there was no vehicle between their car and the Mercedes. They drove on. Their evidence would seem to suggest that their car was the closest in front of the Mercedes when it lost control in the tunnel. M. Boura and Mlle L'Hostis describe the car in front of the Mercedes as rather different from M. Medjahdi's car, but their descriptions of the car are also inconsistent from each other. They say that there was a shorter distance between the Mercedes and the car in front than M. Medjahdi and Mlle Mouffakir [sic] say separated their car from the Mercedes, but judgment of distances in these circumstances can be very problematic.

c) The experts on road traffic reconstruction all agree that the Mercedes collided with the Uno (because of the debris at the scene) and all agree that the Mercedes lost control at around the time that collision occurred. There is some dispute about the extent to which that collision influenced the course of the Mercedes. However, Mr Mansfield suggests that a collision which M. Boura heard between the Mercedes and a car ahead of it, and described as sounding like "bumper-to-bumper" and not involving metal, was an impact between the Mercedes and the hypothetical "blocking vehicle". Yet there is no debris from that collision and none of the experts has put forward a thesis which involves such a collision.

d) The presence of a motorcycle relatively close behind the Mercedes does not point to a plot. M. Partouche and M. Gooroovadoo, who saw the motorcycle behind, gave evidence about seeing camera flashes from a pillion passenger on the motorcycle (24/10/07 at p. 14 and 26; 12/3/08 at p. 77 and 83). This would be consistent with the motorcycle of Rat and Darmon, who were among the paparazzi closest to the Mercedes. Although Boura and L'Hostis recall only one person on the motorcycle, and that is not consistent with any known paparazzo believed to have been near the Mercedes, they could well be wrong. And even if they were right, it does not go to prove that the motorcycle was deliberately doing anything dangerous.

17) While various witnesses recall "bright lights", the evidence is simply not sufficient for a jury to conclude that a light was flashed deliberately to disorientate Henri Paul. Mr Mansfield relies upon the evidence of: Boura; Partouche; Levistre; and Moufakkir. He does not rely upon the evidence of Brian Anderson, and for good reason. The following points need to be made.

a) On his approach to the tunnel in the opposite direction from the Mercedes, M. Boura saw flashes which he initially thought were like speed camera or radar flashes. On reflection, he thought that they were camera flashes (24/10/07, p. 44).

b) As mentioned above, M. Partouche also thought the flashes were from paparazzi cameras (24/10/07, p. 36–37).

c) Mr Mansfield relies upon one witness who gave evidence that, in general, paparazzi do not take pictures on the move. However, various eyewitnesses (including some paparazzi) have given evidence that they saw camera flashes on the journey in this particular case, not only close to the scene of the crash but also earlier when the Mercedes was in the Place de la Concorde.

d) Mlle Moufakkir gave evidence of seeing bright lights behind her (6/11/07, p. 74). However, she immediately acknowledged that those lights could have been the lights of the Mercedes as it swung around after Henri Paul had begun to lose control. Also, she only looked around to see the Mercedes after it was out of control, so her evidence is of limited value as to the cause of the loss of control. Her account about bright lights was not mentioned to the French police or in a television interview.

e) M. Levistre gave evidence about seeing a blinding flash as a motorcycle overtook the Mercedes. However, his evidence plainly falls into the category of "inherently weak evidence" (in Galbraith terms). He spoke about seeing the riders of the motorcycle dismounting and making mysterious signals to each other; a description which is not supported by any other witness. He gave inconsistent accounts about what he saw, and gave an account of his own speed and angle of vision which was difficult to accept. After giving evidence, he contacted the Inquests secretariat with a bizarre story involving bullet casings at the scene of the crash. In short, his evidence could not be a proper foundation for the jury to form any view.

f) A large number of witnesses did not see any flashing light, despite being specifically questioned on the point. The Metropolitan Police have listed 17 such witnesses. Mr Mansfield points out that some (though not all) of these witnesses would not, or might not, have had a view of the Mercedes after it had actually entered the tunnel. However, some of the witnesses on whose evidence Mr Mansfield relies concerning bright lights (such as Partouche) did not have a view into the tunnel either.

g) The jury have been shown a video of vehicles entering and leaving the Alma tunnel. The headlamps of vehicles can appear as bright lights as they ascend the slope.

18) In any event, as Mr Mansfield concedes, one cannot look at the circumstances of the collision in isolation from the immediate preparations for the journey of the Mercedes. This is because the jury could only be sure that there was a plot if they were sure that the supposed plotters knew in advance where to stage the crash. In other words, they would have had to know in advance that the Princess and Dodi Al Fayed would be driven in a single car along the embankment road, and not in a convoy of two vehicles (as was usual) or on some different route. The most direct route to the apartment was not along the embankment road, although there was evidence that professional

drivers would use it to avoid heavy traffic in the Champs Elysées. Only one source has been or can be suggested for the plotters' knowledge of the decoy plan and route: Henri Paul.

19) Henri Paul's movements cannot be accounted for between when he went off duty and left the Ritz at 7.00 p.m. and when he returned at 10.00 p.m. However, this period of time is of little relevance. M. Paul could not have imparted the information to the supposed plotters during that period. The incontrovertible evidence is that when he went off duty he was not expecting to return. Neither was it expected that Dodi and Diana would return to the Ritz. Their plan was to have dinner at a restaurant called Chez Benoit and then return to the apartment. It was as a result of the attentions of the paparazzi when they set off for the restaurant that Dodi diverted the convoy to the Ritz at the last moment. Henri Paul was then called back. He was first told of the plan to use a third car from the rear of the hotel at 10.30 p.m. The plan was conceived by Dodi Al Fayed, and communicated at that time by Thierry Rocher to Henri Paul. That is the evidence of M. Rocher, it is supported by CCTV evidence and it has been accepted by all Interested Persons.

20) Between that conversation with Rocher and the departure of the Mercedes from the rear of the Ritz, Henri Paul is visible on CCTV footage for all the time except 8½ minutes. Shortly after 10.30 p.m., he is seen to make one of his several walks out into Place Vendome and he cannot be located on the screen for those few minutes. However, Henri Paul could have been in the Place Vendome and outside the range of the cameras. Equally, he could have been within the range of the cameras and indistinct because his movements could not be followed in the darkness. It is theoretically possible that he could have made the three-minute walk to a call box,

telephoned "the plotters" and walked back, but this is pure speculation, unsupported by any kind of evidence. That is the difficulty with this hypothesis. There is nothing from which the jury could properly infer that Henri Paul had passed on information about the plan to leave from the rear of the Ritz in a third car. The distinction between a legitimate inference and speculation or guesswork is important.

21) For this hypothesis of Henri Paul aiding the assassins to be accepted, the jury would also have to conclude that Henri Paul assured them that the Mercedes would be driven along the embankment road. In other words, Henri Paul must have told the assassins that he would drive the car and he must then have ensured that he would do so. Mr Mansfield does not say that this was a suicide mission, but that Henri Paul had been paid and duped into believing that he was giving information to allow others to arrange protection for the Princess. It is true that Henri Paul had money on him that has not been accounted for and also that in the months before the crash (it is to be noted before Diana and Dodi were even together) Henri Paul was in receipt of income from somewhere other than his Ritz wages. But it is again a matter of speculation, not proper inference, that the source of the money on the evening (about £1,250 in French Francs) was someone interested in the movements of Dodi and Diana and interested in a sinister sense.

22) One also has to consider the inherent difficulties with the plot thesis. On any view, a staged crash would have had to be arranged at less than two hours' notice. As conceived, it would have been an extremely risky operation for the assassins, especially if it was not calculated to kill. The two vehicles supposedly involved in the plot could so easily have been involved in the collision. Additionally, everything that occurred was likely to be seen, especially in view of the considerable paparazzi interest. There were

many potential witnesses who gave evidence of the various vehicles they saw in addition to the Mercedes (albeit, as it turned out, confused and conflicting). Had the deceased occupants of the car survived, or Trevor Rees not lost his memory as a result of a serious head injury, the prospects of clear evidence of anything untoward being available through the occupants of the car were strong.

23) I take full account of the fact that the assessment of witnesses is the province of the jury. But I also bear in mind that the decision on what verdicts to leave must be taken in the light of all the evidence and that it must not be fudged. I confess that I was strongly tempted to leave this verdict so that the jury could pronounce upon the matter; but I have decided that for me to do so would be unlawful. It became apparent that this was not a viable option when I asked myself what evidence I could identify to the jury on which they could safely conclude this was a staged accident. I have concluded that, on the evidence taken at its highest, a jury properly directed could not properly be sure that this was a staged crash. In those circumstances, it is my clear legal duty to withdraw the verdict.

24) That is not to say that I shall not sum up to the jury the evidence elicited in relation to the conspiracy allegations. I propose to direct them to consider all the verdicts I leave, in the proper order. Then, if they are unable to reach one of those verdicts, they should return an open verdict. If, on the evidence, the jury were to conclude that there may be something in the staged accident thesis that conclusion might, for example, impact on whether they considered that the crash was, on balance of probability, an accident.

Unlawful Killing: Driving of the Paparazzi

25) Should the verdict of unlawful killing be left to the jury on the basis of the driving of the following vehicles? I

shall refer to these as the paparazzi, because the only identified following vehicles are paparazzi and, with the exception of the motorcycle considered above, there has been no submission that the driver of any chasing vehicle was trying to do anything other than get photographs. In relation to these vehicles, I need to consider two possible legal footings for the verdict: gross negligence manslaughter and unlawful act manslaughter. It does not matter that there are now statutory road traffic offences in this country to deal with conduct of this kind; the ordinary law of manslaughter must still be applied for the purposes of these inquests.

Gross Negligence Manslaughter
[...]

27) In this regard, I should remind myself that gross negligence manslaughter requires something more than even a very bad error. It requires very serious misconduct amounting to disregard of a serious risk to life. See: *R* v. *Misra and Srivastava* [2005] 1 Cr App R 21. Before leaving this verdict to the jury on this basis, I would have to conclude that the jury could properly form the view that one or more specific paparazzi drove in a criminally negligent fashion which contributed to the crash, or that the actions of a group of paparazzi combined to cause the crash and that they were part of a joint enterprise.

28) The features of the evidence which could support such a conclusion are as follows. First, there is evidence that individual paparazzi drove or rode very close to the Mercedes, thereby limiting its freedom of movement and restricting Henri Paul's options at the critical time. M. Hackett recalled at least 2–3 motorcycles riding close to the Mercedes in the Alexandre III tunnel (11/10/07, p. 6). He was scared when he saw them. M. Partouche recalled a "compact group" of vehicles, including motorcycles "just behind" the Mercedes (24/10/07, p. 8).

M. Gooroovadoo remembered one motorcycle following "very closely" (12/3/08, p. 83, p. 101).

29) Secondly, there is evidence that the paparazzi continually accelerated to follow the Mercedes, while it must have been plain that Henri Paul intended to outrun them. Also, M. Lucard gave evidence that Henri Paul, at the rear of the Ritz, told the paparazzi there not to try to follow him, because they would not keep up. There is evidence that a number of paparazzi vehicles followed the Mercedes to the Place de la Concorde and that a number were still behind it in the Alexandre III tunnel and on the approach to the Alma tunnel. Speed was plainly an important factor in the causes of the crash and also in the deaths.

30) Thirdly, it is necessary to take account of the scene. This was a challenging urban road environment at night. As the driver approaches the Alma underpass, there is a turn to the left which causes many drivers to go off their line. There is a slip road from the right, described by one witness as the most dangerous junction in Paris. There is a significant incline down. The wall and pillars in the tunnel present particular hazards, as the road traffic experts accepted. Because of the darkness, visibility would have been limited.

31) In view of all those features, I consider that the driving of certain paparazzi could be regarded by the jury as criminally negligent. This is a borderline case in Galbraith terms, but the verdict should be left to the jury. On one view of the evidence, the conduct could be fairly characterised as participating in a race through the centre of Paris at twice the speed limit. Some statements of the paparazzi themselves could lead to this conclusion. In addition, the cross-examination of M. Darmon provided some support for a conclusion that, after the crash, the paparazzi continued to seek the best picture without regard to helping the injured. This could be relied upon by the jury as indicative of their state of mind before the crash.

Unlawful Act Manslaughter
[...]

34) The argument of Mr Croxford QC is that the conduct of
the paparazzi, from the arrival at Le Bourget airport, can
properly be characterised as harassment. He submits that
that conduct can then be regarded as the basis for an
offence of manslaughter by an unlawful and dangerous
act, as set out in *DPP* v. *Newbury* [1977] AC 500 at
506–7. The principal reason he urges me to leave a
verdict on this basis is that a verdict of unlawful killing
could be returned in relation to the paparazzi without the
jury having to find a criminal degree of negligence in the
way in which one or more of the paparazzi drove at or
about the time of the crash.

35) There is certainly evidence that a number of the paparazzi
followed Diana and Dodi for some hours that day. There
is evidence that some pursued them by road. There is
evidence that some of the paparazzi were involved in a
stand-off with security staff outside Dodi's apartment.
Mr Horwell QC argued that this conduct could not be
"harassment" for the purposes of the Act. He made reference to *Tuppen* v. *Microsoft Corporation* [2000] QBD,
where Douglas Brown J. concluded that the Act was
directed at conduct such as stalking, persistent anti-social
conduct by neighbours and racial harassment. In the
event, it is not necessary for me to determine whether the
conduct of specific paparazzi could amount to harassment, because I have decided that the verdict should not
be left on this basis for other reasons.

[...]

36) Mr Burnett QC submits that the conduct of the paparazzi
(following people using vehicles and taking photographs)
was not inherently unlawful. If it was criminal, that was
by virtue of the manner of its execution (persistent and

liable to distress). He says that this course of conduct is a fortiori Lord Atkin's driving analogy. I accept his submissions. Where a series of acts, some not dangerous and all individually legal in themselves, are rendered criminal because they form a course of conduct and are performed in a particular way, that cannot form the basis of unlawful act manslaughter. If two paparazzi drove in exactly the same way on the final journey, why should one be guilty of manslaughter and the other not guilty, simply because the first took photographs with greater zeal earlier in the day?

[...]

Unlawful Killing: Driving of the Mercedes

41) This verdict should only be left to the jury if they could properly find that Henri Paul's driving was grossly negligent (in the sense considered above) and caused the crash. In the course of argument the question arose whether, if unlawful killing by gross negligence were left on the part of the paparazzi, it logically should also be left in respect of Henri Paul. To put it simply, as I have already indicated, the jury could conclude that Henri Paul and a number of paparazzi were engaged in a race through central Paris. Each could have broken off the chase at any time. It seems to me that, although there may be differences when the jury comes to consider questions of culpability, when one considers whether the verdict should be left at all there is, in truth, no great difference. I understood Mr Croxford to accept that on behalf of the Ritz. The essential features of the driving of Henri Paul that go to the question of his culpability are as follows.

42) First, M. Paul undoubtedly drove at around twice the speed limit on a busy urban road. There is evidence that he did so as a result of a deliberate decision to outrun the paparazzi. He could have slowed down at any time,

without risking anything worse than some photographs being taken. By driving at this speed, he knowingly impaired his ability to react to situations in the road, such as the presence of the Fiat Uno ahead. The presence of the paparazzi behind could be regarded as an aggravating factor. It may be thought more dangerous to drive fast when one knows that other vehicles will be driven close behind. The jury could conclude that he was racing. I am quite unable to accept the submission of Mr Keen QC that speed was not a causative factor in the crash.

43) Secondly, there is evidence on which the jury could conclude that Henri Paul had consumed alcohol up to twice the UK drink driving limit. There were real flaws in the chain of custody of samples and the recording of results by the French pathologists and toxicologists. Furthermore, the results of tests for carboxyhaemoglobin were difficult for anyone to explain. On the other hand, only one of the four experts called to give evidence thought the test results for alcohol were probably unreliable (as to the other three, see: (i) 22/1/08, p.54 (Forrest "comfortably satisfied" as to reliability); (ii) 30/1/08, p.158 (Vanezis had "nagging doubts" but preferred not to answer questions about probability); (iii) 31/1/08, p.41 (Oliver thought that the combination of toxicology findings was "strongly indicative" that the samples came from Henri Paul)). After they gave their evidence, further evidence was called which could be regarded as establishing that the sample tested for carboxyhaemoglobin was matched with Henri Paul by DNA profiling (see 6/3/08, p.124–9). It will be for the jury to consider all that evidence in the round, and in the context of witness evidence about Henri Paul's demeanour at the Ritz and about his medical history. In any event, the toxicological evidence has to be considered in the context of the whole of the evidence concerning his consumption of alcohol.

44) If the jury formed the view that Henri Paul had drunk something like that amount of alcohol, they could certainly decide that he had behaved negligently in choosing to drive a car. Given the speed of events on the approach to the Alma underpass, it is open to the jury to find that Henri Paul's reactions were impaired and that this contributed to his loss of control of the car.

45) Thirdly, as with the paparazzi, the jury is entitled to take account of the features of the road environment which presented additional hazards (see above).

46) Overall, while one has to distinguish the supposed negligence of the paparazzi and the supposed negligence of Henri Paul, there would be something unrealistic about my determining that one could be viewed as criminal while the other could not be so viewed. All these drivers were facing the same road conditions. All were free agents and had the choice to slow down, without any real adverse consequence.

47) For all these reasons, I have decided that this verdict should also be left to the jury.

[...]

The Jury's Verdict:
7 April 2008 – Verdict of the jury
(4.25 p.m.)
(Jury present)
VERDICTS
  [#]

LORD JUSTICE SCOTT BAKER: I would ask that nobody leaves the court until the reading of both inquisitions is complete, please.
SECRETARY TO THE INQUEST: Would the jury foreman please rise? Madam Foreman, in the matter of the death of

Mr Emad El-Din Mohamed Abdel Moneim Al Fayed, have you reached a verdict on which a majority of the nine of you have agreed?

THE JURY FOREMAN: We have.

SECRETARY TO THE INQUEST: Could you give us the verdict and indicate the number of jurors assenting to the verdict?

THE JURY FOREMAN: The verdict is unlawful killing, grossly negligent driving of the following vehicles and of the Mercedes.

SECRETARY TO THE INQUEST: Thank you. Could you now read the rest of the narrative on the inquisition, indicating as appropriate the—

LORD JUSTICE SCOTT BAKER: How many agreed and how many dissented?

THE JURY FOREMAN: Nine, sir. The deceased is Emad El-Din Mohamed Abdel Moneim Al Fayed. The injury causing death: multiple injuries, including severe impact injury to the chest and the transaction of the aorta. Dodi Al Fayed died in the Alma Underpass in Paris at around 12.22 a.m. on 31st August 1997 as a result of a motor crash. The crash was caused or contributed to by the speed and manner of driving of the Mercedes, the speed and manner of driving of the following vehicles, the impairment of the judgment of the driver of the Mercedes through alcohol. There are nine of those who agree on those conclusions. In addition, the death of the deceased was caused or contributed to by the fact that the deceased was not wearing a seat belt, the fact that the Mercedes struck the pillar in the Alma Tunnel rather than colliding with something else, and we are unanimous on those, sir.

SECRETARY TO THE INQUEST: Is that the conclusion of your narrative verdict?

THE JURY FOREMAN: It is.

SECRETARY TO THE INQUEST: In the matter of Diana, Princess of Wales, have you reached a verdict on which at least nine of you have agreed?

THE JURY FOREMAN: We have.

SECRETARY TO THE INQUEST: Could you give us the verdict, indicating the number of jurors that have dissented to that?

THE JURY FOREMAN: The verdict is unlawful killing, grossly negligent driving of the following vehicles and of the Mercedes, and that is nine of us, sir.

SECRETARY TO THE INQUEST: Could you please read the rest of the narrative of your inquisition, indicating, where appropriate, the number of jurors who have assented to the verdict?

THE JURY FOREMAN: The deceased is Diana, Princess of Wales. The cause of death is chest injury, laceration within the left pulmonary vein and the immediate adjacent portion of the left atrium of the heart. Diana, Princess of Wales, died La Pitié-Salpêtrière Hospital in Paris at around 4.00 a.m. on 31st August 1997 as a result of a motor crash which occurred in the Alma Underpass in Paris on 31st August 1997 at around 12.22 a.m. The crash was caused or contributed to by the speed and manner of driving of the Mercedes, the speed and manner of driving of the following vehicles, the impairment of the judgment of the driver of the Mercedes through alcohol. Nine of us are agreed on those points, sir. In addition, the death of the deceased was caused or contributed to by the fact that the deceased was not wearing a seat belt, the fact that the Mercedes struck the pillar in the Alma Tunnel, rather than colliding with something else, and we are unanimously agreed on that.

SECRETARY TO THE INQUEST: Have the assenting jurors signed both inquisition forms?

THE JURY FOREMAN: They have.

SECRETARY TO THE INQUEST: Could you pass the forms to the usher? You may be seated.

LORD JUSTICE SCOTT BAKER: Thank you very much.

PROJECT COAST

"Project Coast" was the code name for a top secret chemical and biological weapons (CBW) programme developed in 1981 by the South African apartheid regime for use against its enemies. While some of apartheid's CB weapons were relatively innocuous – tear gas, for example – others were designed for the extermination of individuals, even whole groups. Coast numbered among its satanic armoury an infertility toxin to sterilize the black population of uppity townships and – shades of the CIA's wackiest plans to whack Castro – poisons that could be concealed within chocolates. And cigarettes. Needless to say, Coast explicitly violated every international agreement you could shake a pipette at, chiefly the 1925 Geneva Convention and the 1972 Biological and Toxin Weapons Convention.

Ordered up in 1981 by Prime Minister P. W. Botha, Coast was headed by Wouter Basson, of whom it might be said that he honoured the Hippocratic Oath only in the breaching: he was also a medical doctor, Botha's personal heart specialist, and a member of the 7th South African Medical Service's Battalion. To maintain secrecy and make it difficult to link CBWs with the South African Defence Force, Coast operated through four front organizations: Delta G, Roodeplast Research Laboratories, Protechnik, Infladel. Coast's annual budget was $10 million, which was strictly off the treasury's books.

Under Basson's tutelage – allegedly – Coast was involved in lethal covert operations "Barnacle" and "Duel" in the 1980s in which hundreds of regime opponents, notably captured ANC guerrillas, were murdered by use of toxins, their bodies then dumped at sea. Coast has also been linked to biochemical experiments on captured ANC members and the mass killing of Marxist rebels in Rhodesia (now Zimbabwe) by providing the government there with cholera and anthrax. In 1979, the world's largest outbreak of anthrax took place in Rhodesia. Eighty-two people died.

When F. W. de Klerk became South Africa's president in 1989 he quickly scuppered Project Coast's offensive programme, since it hardly sat well with his desire to end apartheid. Numerous Coast officials were fired, incriminating documents and CBWs destroyed. Thereafter, Coast was devoted to manufacturing crowd control substances, some of which were drugs more usually associated with recreational use. Between 1992 and 1993, more than 900 hundred kilos of a crystalline form of Ecstasy was produced under Project Coast.

Old, murderous habits, it seems, died hard. In January 1992, Mozambican government forces were purportedly attacked with CBWs by the South African apartheid regime; several hundred soldiers claimed to have been exposed to a substance released from a plane flying above them. Four of them later died. It was widely suspected that the Coast front company Protechnik was the likely source of the lethal agent; the UK and US afterwards heavily pressured South Africa to terminate Project Coast, partly for humanitarian reasons, partly because it was feared that Coast's know-how would fall into terrorist hands.

Basson was given a one-year contract to dissolve Project Coast, after which he became an independent CBW consultant, but his subsequent globe-trotting occasioned the US and Britain to make démarches expressing their concern that the good doctor was selling his knowledge of CBWs to pariah states such as Libya. To keep Basson under control, the South African Government hired him as the head of an uncontroversial official department in 1995. As a method of keeping the dog on the chain, this was not entirely successful; two years later, after a tip-off from the CIA that Basson was about to flee the country, Basson was caught with a thousand Ecstasy pills and four trunks full of secret documents related to Project Coast. The Es were almost certainly from stock manufactured by Coast for non-lethal crowd control. After some heavy persuasion, Basson testified before the Truth and Reconciliation Commission (TRC) in 1998; he was the TRC's last witness and gave limited, evasive testimony, with his lawyers making frequent interjections. Enough was heard, however, for Dr Wouter Basson to be tried on sixty-seven charges, ranging from fraud to murder whilst working on Coast. Basson denied all charges, and the judge, one Mr Hartzenberg, dismissed many of them, ruling that because they had occurred in Namibia and other foreign terrains, Basson could not be tried on them. Then, after thirty months of trial, Hartzenberg grandly rejected the testimony of all of the prosecution's 153 witnesses (which included Coast scientists and operatives) and granted "Dr Death", as the media had nicknamed Basson, amnesty

To date, there remain concerns over whether or not Basson actually destroyed the CBW agents or merely relocated them. Hundreds of kilos of chemicals and agents were unaccounted for when inventory was later taken by the Government.

South Africa continues to have a CBW programme but says it is strictly defensive. The country is now a member of the Biological and Toxin Weapons Convention and the Chemical Weapons Convention.

Apartheid regime used chemical/germ warfare against opponents: ALERT LEVEL 10

Further Reading
Stephen Burges and Helen Purkitt, *The Rollback of South Africa's Chemical and Biological Warfare Program*, 2001
Chandré Gould, Peter I. Folb et al, *Project Coast: Apartheid's Chemical and Biological Warfare Programme*, 2003

PROJECT MONTAUK

Or, fast forward to the future without a Delorean car.

Conspiracy wonks believe that a series of top-secret experiments conducted in a vast cavernous underground laboratory built beneath the Montauk Air Force Station on the eastern tip of Long Island enabled teleportation and time travel.

Whispers about strange happenings at Montauk began circulating in the early 1980s when one Preston Nichols claimed to have recovered suppressed memories of his involvement with the lab. Around the same time, a man called Al Bielek began lecturing on his own recovered memories which linked Montauk to the Philadelphia experiment, the US Navy's supposed invisibility experiment in the forties. Bielek maintained that the USS *Eldridge*, on which he had served as matelot, had been teleported forty years hence to Montauk, where the lab's supremo was none other that Nikola Tesla, inventor of **Free Electricity**. (A busy boy was Al; he was confusingly also Ed Cameron, who worked on the Manhattan atomic bomb project, or so he says.) The lab's time tunnel allowed travel forwards and backwards and to alien planets. The website of Al Bielek – www.bielek.com – contains a timeline of his travels: he got to to 2,749.

The secrets of Montauk contain some other conspiracy favourites. Genetic engineering? Tick. PSI ops experiments? Tick. The giant Surface Air Ground Environment (SAGE) radar on the site was reportedly used for mind-control tests on abducted teenagers.

Alas, there is no documented evidence that Montauk is, or ever has been, a lab for a real-life version of TV's *Time Tunnel* show. Bielek's website is a classic case of the self-referential "proofs" offered by the weird wing of conspiracy. Al says Preston Nichols worked at Montauk; Preston says Al worked at Montauk; Stewart Swerdlow says Al and Preston toiled at the Montauk base; Al and Preston say Stewart worked there ... Bielek's website states that he "paid a big price for the privilege" of travelling in time and meeting little green creatures.

You'll also pay a high price if you want to know more about his adventures. His PC-DVD costs $39.99. Visa and Mastercard both accepted.

The Montauk base closed down several years back. The site is now home to Camp Hero State Park.

Montauk base developed time travel machine: ALERT LEVEL 1

Further Reading
www.bielek.com

PROJECT PAPERCLIP

As US forces advanced through the Wagnerian ruins of the Third Reich in May 1945, they stumbled upon research facility after facility that indicated that the Germans had technologies far beyond their own.

This was especially the case in aeronautics and rocket science – which in itself led to the conspiracy theory that the Nazis of the **Thule Society** had hitched up with aliens – and so the US deemed it advantageous to "relocate" leading German scientists and technicians across the Atlantic, where their expertise could be put to work on behalf of Uncle Sam. Or, as Major-General Hugh Knerr, deputy commander of the US Air Force in Europe put it:

> Occupation of German scientific and industrial establishments has revealed the fact that we have been alarmingly backward in many fields of research. If we do not take the opportunity to seize the apparatus and the brains that developed it and put the combination back to work promptly, we will remain several years behind while we attempt to cover a field already exploited.

Importing the German boffins Stateside also denied their use to the perfidious Russians, who were quickly going from being friends to foes. (Actually, America also wanted to deny the technology to the British, who remained so-called "friends".) There was a little local difficulty, however, in that some of the German scientists were full-blown members of the SS, even war criminals – and Truman had expressly ordered that anyone found "to have been a member of the Nazi Party and more than a nominal participant in its activities, or an active supporter of Nazi militarism" would be excluded from a welcome in the Land of the Free. To circumvent this tiresome legal and moral objection, in 1946 the US War Department began Project Paperclip, named after the technique of identifying useful German personnel by putting a paperclip on their file; sought-after German scientists had their records cleansed of mentions of war crimes/SS and Nazi membership or were given wholly false records to enable their entry into the US. During Paperclip more than 1,600 German technicians and scientists were hired in, many of them beginning their new lives at the military research facility of Fort Bliss, Texas.

Werner von Braun, the V-2 rocket man, was one of the most prominent SS members whitewashed and recycled by the Truman government. He ended up playing a leading role in NASA, masterminding many of the moonshots. A number of those processed through Paperclip had partaken in medical "experiments" in Dachau and other Nazi concentration/death camps; Hubertus Strughold, later called "the father of space medicine" and designer of Nasa's on-board life-support system, had headed a team at Dachau and Auschwitz which had frozen inmates and put them in low-pressure chambers to study the effects. Paperclip hireling Arthur Rudolph was hardly higher on the moral scale; another die-hard Nazi, he was chief operations director at Nordhausen, where 20,000 slave labourers died producing V-2 missiles.

So dense was the Paperclip paper trail cover-up that many of the SS/Nazi hirelings were never properly identified thereafter.

Project Paperclip. Or how the US establishment learned to stop worrying about morals and love the bomb.

> The US Government gave useful Nazis false papers to enable them to enter America: ALERT LEVEL 10

Further Reading
Clarence G. Lasby, *Project Paperclip: German Scientists and the Cold War*, 1975

PROPAGANDA DUE (P2)

During a raid on the Arezzo villa of Italian businessman Licio Gelli in March 1981 for evidence of his possible link to the Vatican Bank's laundering of Mafia money police turned up something far more sinister about Signor Gelli than dealings with dodgy money. He was the leader of the banned Masonic Lodge Propaganda Due (Propagation Two). And Propaganda Due (P2) was scheming to take over Italy.

A list of 962 P2 conspirators found in Gelli's safe included three cabinet ministers, forty MPs, the heads of the Army and Navy, police chiefs, intelligence officers, fourteen judges, numerous industrialists (among them one Silvio Berlusconi) and Victor Emmanuel, Prince of Naples. Shortly afterwards, police found under the false bottom in Gelli's daughter's briefcase a copy of a document entitled *Piana di Rinascita Democratica* ("A Plan for the Rebirth of Democracy"). The title was a misnomer: the document set out a plan for a fascist coup in which unions would be banned and the media put under state control. The fallout from the discovery of the P2 list and *Piana di Rinascita Democratica* was enough to bring down the Italian Government. Later a court indictment charged that P2's infiltration of the Italian state had "the incredible capacity to control a state's institutions to the point of virtually becoming a state-within-a-state".

The origins of P2 date back to 1877 when a Masonic Lodge was chartered by the Grand Orient of Italy as Propaganda Due; a century later the Lodge had become so infiltrated by the *Mafiosi* that the Master of Grand Orient shut it down and expelled its Worshipful Master, Licio Gelli. The response of

Gelli? To pick up the Lodge's membership list and set up his own, essentially private Lodge, P2.

Born in 1919, Gelli was a Mussolini-era fascist who had fought with the SS on the Eastern Front before fleeing to South America, where he was a financial backer of Argentinian dictator Juan Peron. Returning to Italy, he became a Mason in 1963 before taking over P2 in 1966. Under his tutelage P2 expanded nearly a hundredfold to 1,000 members, including branches – all funded by Mafia lira – in Argentina, Uruguay and Brazil. Raul Lastiri, Argentina's president during part of the "Dirty War" in the seventies was a P2 member, So was Jose Lopez Rega, the Social Welfare minister under Peron.

The Mafia wasn't P2's only financial provider. According to P2 supergrass Mino Pecorelli, the Lodge was funded by the CIA, and Gelli himself was a CIA officer. (Pecorelli was later found shot dead.) A 1990 article in the London *Observer* cited declassified US secret papers which linked Gelli to the CIA's Rome station and the continuance of the notorious Operation Gladio, the CIA-funded and (armed) anti-Communist network set up in Italy in the wake of the Second World War. There have been frequent accusations of P2 complicity in the 1978 assassination of Italian Prime Minister Aldo Moro and the 1980 Bologna railway bombing, events which were part of the "*strategia della tensione*" intended to create the conditions for a P2 coup.

Two of Gelli's principal sidekicks were Michele "The Shark" Sindora, a banker in the clutches of the Mafia, and Roberto Calvi, chairman of Banco Ambrosiano, Italy's largest private bank. Sindora and Calvi were duly hired by another P2 member Archbishop Marcinkus, head of the Vatican bank, to manage the Vatican's money; when police raided Gelli's safe in Arezzo they found evidence that Calvi had created hundreds of fictitious bank accounts to launder Mafia drug money. An ensuing audit of Banco Ambriosiano, Italy's largest bank, revealed that 1.3 billion dollars was missing from the bank's account. Calvi fled to London. On 18 June 1982, Calvi was found hanging at the end of a rope under Blackfriar's Bridge, his pockets stuffed with bricks. It is widely assumed that "God's Banker" was "suicided" by either P2 or the Mafia because he intended to name P2 members involved in corruption. The London coroner's conclusion was "cause of death" unknown; an Italian court, meanwhile, formally indicted Gelli for conspiring to murder Roberto Calvi.

Calvi is just one of the few associated with the P2 scandal to have died a mysterious death or disappeared off the face of the Earth. Sindona died in a Milan prison cell complaining he had been poisoned. Gelli vanished from a Swiss prison where he was being held for extradition, and has never been seen since.

Some investigators charge P2 with the mysterious death of John Paul I. After announcing on 28 September 1978 that he intended to remove Archbishop Marcinkus from the Vatican bank, John Paul I was found dead next morning.

P2 was formally banned by the Italian authorities in 1981. Its "work" might be said to linger on. Just before he disappeared into thin air, Gelli told *La Repubblica* newspaper: "I look at the country [Italy under Silvio Berlusconi], read the newspaper, and think: 'All [the *Piana di Rinascita Democratica*] is becoming a reality little by little, piece by piece.' "

P2 Masonic Lodge plotted coup d'état: ALERT LEVEL 9

Further Reading

Luigi DiFonzo, *St Peter's Banker*, 1983

Philip Willan, *The Last Supper: The Mafia, the Masons and the Killing of Roberto Calvi*, 2007

David Yallop, *In God's Name*, 1984

REPTILIAN HUMANOIDS

Long, long ago, David Icke (rhymes with bike) was a soccer player for Coventry City in England. Thereafter, it was all down-hill in a handcart. He played for Hereford United, became a BBC sports commentator, became a Green Party activist, before dressing entirely in turquoise and informing the world that he, Dave Icke, was the Son of God. Could one go lower?

David Icke answered that himself with his book *The Biggest Secret* (1999), in which he claimed that a race of 12-foot lizards known as the Babylonian Brotherhood from planet Draco have colonized Earth. If you think that 12-foot lizards might be easy to spot, more fool you; the critters can shape-shift by day to look like humans.

Got a feeling of déjà vu? Yes, that's right: the TV SF series *V* had much the same premise.

Icke's twist is to put a little Marx into the mix. The reptilians are the ruling class to the human proles, and the scaly-skinned ones make up all the past and present royal families, the presidents of the USA and entire crew of leading financiers. Just so that the poor proles don't catch on to what is going on, the reptilian humanoids rule through various front organizations, such as the Bilderberg Group, the Trilateral Commission, the Council on Foreign Relations, the **Bavarian Illuminati** and the Knights Templar. Naturally, the conspiratorial goal of the repto-humans is the **New World Order** (although their weakness for drinking human juice means that sometimes they have to have a blood-break from the great work).

In one mad moment Icke syntheses science fiction, New Age spiritualism and all popular conspiracy theories.

To be fair to Icke, he dislikes some lizards more than others. He has a particular downer on the British Royal Family, but then they did murder **Princess Diana** (who blurted out her in-laws' lizard nature to Icke) and they do control the gateway to the great underground reptilian city, which is situated on one of their Scottish estates. *Scotland*. A bit cold, surely, for lizards?

David Icke's books sell by the barn load and his meetings are well attended. Which only goes to prove that you can fool a lot of people a lot of the time.

Repto-humanoids rule the world: ALERT LEVEL 1

Further Reading
David Icke, *The Biggest Secret*, 1999
David Icke, *Children of the Matrix*, 2001

SARS

February 2003. A Chinese-American businessman flying from China to Singapore became severely ill with what appeared to be pneumonia, obliging his flight to land in Vietnam for his hospitalization. Despite the best efforts of the staff at the French Hospital of Hanoi, the 48-year-old businessman died. Realizing that they were dealing with a mysterious and highly infectious virus, the hospital contacted the World Health Organization (WHO), which issued an alert warning the world of the arrival of Severe Acute Respiratory Syndrome (SARS).

Panic – and face masks – spread across the world. The outbreak lasted until the summer of 2003 by which time over 8,000 cases had been confirmed, and 800 deaths reported.

Midway through the epidemic, Nikolai Filatov, head of Moscow's epidemiological services, stepped forward to inform reporters he thought SARS was not a natural occurrence, but man-made because "there is no vaccine for the virus, its makeup is unclear, it has not been very widespread, and the population is not immune to it".

His views were echoed by Sergei Kolesnikov, a member of Russia's Academy of Medicine, who asserted that the virus was a cocktail of mumps and measles. "We can only get that in a laboratory," he added.

Tests by Dutch and US scientists confirmed that the disease could be man-made.

If SARS was man-made, who could be behind such a dastardly plot? In China, at least, the baddies were identified as the USA in liaison with Taiwan, with the virus having been manufactured in Fort Detrick or **Plum Island** as a biological weapon to kibosh its Sino rival. According to financial giant J. P. Morgan, SARS did more damage to the Pacific Rim economies than the **Indian Ocean tsunami** because of the disruption it caused. Theorists maintain that the virus was specifically tailored to the Chinese race, pointing out that of the SARS cases just twenty-seven occurred in the US (with no fatalities), while China had the most reported cases by far. In *The Last Defense Line: Concerns About the Loss of Chinese Genes*, a Chinese businessman by the name of Tong Zheng claimed to have witnesses to American researchers collecting mainland Chinese people's blood and DNA in the 1990s from twenty-two provinces – the same twenty-two provinces mainly affected by SARS.

Then again, some point the finger of blame at China itself. A Chinese army doctor Jian Yanyong whistle-blew to the press that his unit had known about the disease since November 2002, and the authorities had suppressed the information. Although the scandal caused the heads of government ministers to roll, Yanyong himself was whisked away for "political re-education". Inevitably, the proven desperation of the Chinese to hide knowledge about SARS fed the belief that they themselves had concocted the virus. WHO's investigation was interesting in this respect: WHO concluded that the first cases of SARS were soldiers in Guangdong Province – the location of China's main biowarfare establishment.

Officially, WHO considers SARS to be a coronavirus which has jumped species. As with **Ebola**, the animal host may well be the bat. Civets – which are commonly eaten in Guangdong – are also in the frame. The explanation for the non-incidence of SARS deaths in the USA is the superiority of Stateside medical services.

SARS is a biowarfare weapon gone awry: ALERT LEVEL 6

Further Reading
Angela McLean (ed.), *SARS*, 2005

WILLIAM SHAKESPEARE

It was not Shakespeare as many liked it.

In 2011, Hollywood director Roland Emmerich released *Anonymous*, a movie about the Bard, the author of England's classic theatre pieces, *Macbeth, Hamlet, King Lear, Othello, The Tempest*, etc. Controversy was *Anonymous*'s trailer, because Emmerich rehashed the theory that "William Shakespeare" of Stratford-upon-Avon was not author of said works but rather Edward de Vere, Earl of Oxford, was the man with the talented quill pen. Since writing plays was beneath an aristocratic personage, and politically dangerous in turbulent times (those associated with *Richard II* were all interrogated, because Elizabeth perceived it as a personal attack), de Vere allowed Shakespeare, a humble theatre producer to stage his masterpieces and take the credit.

Emmerich is not the first, neither will he be the last, to suggest that de Vere was Shakespeare. And de Vere is only one of seventy-seven contenders put forward for the title of "real" Shakespeare. Sir Francis Bacon, Christopher Marlowe, the Earl of Rutland and the Earl of Derby all have strong supporters

The evidence for Shakespeare of Stratford not being the author of the plays is, essentially, the lack of evidence that he *was* the author of the plays. Aside from a birth certificate, some legal documents, and a fleeting mention in contemporary chronicles next to nothing is known about Wm. Shakespeare, Esq. His death in 1616 was a non-event outside Stratford, to which he had returned after his career as a comic actor, friend of criminal lowlifes (the Elizabeth/Stuart state was excellent at recording wrongdoings) and manager of the Globe Theatre in London. His life – and this is the killer argument, for the Shakespeare conspiracists – is almost impossible to square with the literary brilliance and erudition of the Shakespeare plays, which are rich in allusions to classical literature, much of it actually only available in the Classical languages of Greek and Latin. The books are full of Cambridge University slang, show a deep knowledge of the law, display a knowledge of foreign countries (north Italy especially) and a ready familiarity with the mores and tropes of the aristocracy, down to the technical terminology of falconry. None of this makes sense if the plays were penned by William Shakespere, son of a glover from a backwater Midlands town, the staple trade of which was sheep-selling. This line of reasoning was first developed by J. Thomas Looney in *"Shakespeare" Identified* as far back as 1920 (see Document, p.479).

Edward de Vere, on the other hand, studied law at Cambridge, travelled much, was a first-rate poet and supported a theatre company. The sonnets attributed to Shakespeare are heavy ammunition on de Vere's behalf, because they reference his life, and contain anagrams (the Elizabethans loved riddles) that identify him. The lines "That every word doth almost tell my name" from Sonnet 76 being the prime case; "every word" is almost exactly an anagram of "Edward Vere".

One difficulty in establishing the identity of Shakespeare is that even orthodox scholars agree that not all the plays in the canon are his own work; *Titus Andronicus* is a reheat of another play. Hence Ben Johnson slyly referring to Shakespeare as "Poet-Ape, that would be thought our chief".

Quite plausibly, William Shakespeare the Bard was not William Shakespeare of Stratford. The vocabulary in the plays is twice that of any writer in English, comprising as many as 29,000 words. The man who died in Stratford in 1616 did not, according to his extremely detailed will, leave a single book. Would the fertile, enquiring mind that conjured the Prince of Denmark, Henry V at Agincourt, the mischievous Puck not have possessed a single cowskin-covered tome at home?

Much ado about something: the works of Shakespeare
were written by another hand: ALERT LEVEL 6

Further reading:
H. N. Gibson, *The Shakespeare Claimants*, 2005
John Michell, *Who wrote Shakespeare?*, 1996

DOCUMENT: J. THOMAS LOONEY, *"SHAKESPEAR"' IDENTIFIED IN EDWARD DE VERE, THE SEVENTEENTH EARL OF OXFORD*, 1920 [EXTRACT]

It is hardly necessary to insist at the present day that
Shakespeare has preserved for all time, in living human characters, much of what was best worth remembering and retaining in the social relationship of the Feudal order of the Middle
Ages. Whatever conclusion we may have to come to about his
religion, it is undeniable that, from the social and political
point of view, Shakespeare is essentially a medievalist. The
following sentence from Carlyle may be taken as representative of much that might be quoted from several writers bearing
in the same direction: "As Dante the Italian man was sent
into our world to embody musically the Religion of the
Middle Ages, the Religion of our Modern Europe, its Inner
Life; so Shakespeare we may say embodies for us the Outer
Life of our Europe as developed then, its chivalries, cour-
tesies, humours, ambitions, what practical way of thinking,
acting, looking at the world, men then had."

When, therefore, we find that the great Shakespearean
plays were written at a time when men were revelling in what
they considered to be a newly-found liberation from
Medievalism, it is evident that Shakespeare was one whose
sympathies, and probably his antecedents, linked him on
more closely to the old order than to the new: not the kind of
man we should expect to rise from the lower middle-class

population of the towns. Whether as a lord or a dependent we should expect to find him one who saw life habitually from the standpoint of Feudal relationships in which he had been born and bred: and in view of what has been said of his education it would, of course, be as lord rather than as a dependent that we should expect to meet him.

It might be, however, that he was only linked to Shakespearean Feudalism by cherished family traditions; a surviving Aristocrat, representative, maybe, of some decayed family. A close inspection of his work, however, reveals a more intimate personal connection with aristocracy than would be furnished by mere family tradition. Kings and queens, earls and countesses, knights and ladies move on and off his stage "as to the manner born". They are no mere tinselled models representing mechanically the class to which they belong, but living men and women. It is rather his ordinary "citizens" that are the automata walking woodenly on to the stage to speak for their class. His "lower-orders" never display that virile dignity and largeness of character which poets like Burns, who know the class from within, portray in their writings. Even Scott comes much nearer to truth in this matter than does Shakespeare. It is, therefore, not merely his power of representing royalty and the nobility in vital, passionate characters, but his failure to do the same in respect to other classes that marks Shakespeare as a member of the higher aristocracy. The defects of the playwriter become in this instance more illuminating and instructive than do his qualities. Genius may undoubtedly enable a man to represent with some fidelity classes to which he does not belong; it will hardly at the same time weaken his power of representing truly his own class. In a great dramatic artist we demand universality of power within his province; but he shows that catholicity, not by representing human society in all its forms and phases, but by depicting our common human nature in the entire range of its multiple and complex forces; and he does this best when he shows us that human nature at work in the classes with which he is most intimate. The suggestion of an aristocratic author for the plays is, therefore, the simple common sense of the situation, and is no more in opposition to modern democratic tendencies, as one writer loosely hints, than the belief that William Shakespeare was indebted to aristocratic patrons and participated in the enclosure of common lands.

An aristocratic outlook upon life marks the plays of other dramatists of the time besides Shakespeare. These were known, however, in most cases to have been university men, with a pronounced contempt for the particular class to which William Shakspere of Stratford belonged. It is a curious fact, however, that a writer like Creizenach, who seems never to doubt the Stratfordian view, nevertheless recognizes that "Shakespeare" was more purely and truly aristocratic in his outlook than were the others. In a word, the plays which are recognized as having the most distinct marks of aristocracy about them, are supposed to have been produced by the playwright furthest removed from aristocracy in his origin and antecedents.

We feel entitled, therefore, to claim for Shakespeare high social rank, and even a close proximity to royalty itself.

Assuming him to have been an Englishman of the Lancastrian higher aristocracy, we turn now to these parts of his writings that may be said to deal with his own phase of life, namely, his English historical plays, to seek for distinctive traces of position and personality. Putting aside the greater part of the plays *Henry VI, Parts I* and *II*, as not being from Shakespeare's pen, and also the first acts of *Henry VI, Part III*, for the same reason, we may say that he deals mainly with the troubled period between the upheaval in the reign of Richard II and the ending of the Wars of the Roses by the downfall of Richard III at the Battle of Bosworth. The outstanding feature of this work is his pronounced sympathy with the Lancastrian cause.

Even the play of *Richard II*, which shows a measure of sympathy with the king whom the Lancastrians ousted, is full of Lancastrian partialities. "Shakespeare" had no sympathy with revolutionary movements and the overturning of established governments. Usurpation of sovereignty would, therefore, be repugnant to him, and his aversion is forcibly expressed in the play; but Henry of Lancaster is represented as merely concerned with claiming his rights, desiring to uphold the authority of the crown, but driven by the injustice and perversity of Richard into an antagonism he strove to avoid. Finally, it is the erratic wilfulness of the king, coupled with Henry's belief that the king had voluntarily abdicated, that induces Bolingbroke to accept the throne. In a word, the play of *Richard II* is a kind of dramatic apologia for the Lancastrians. Then comes the glorification of Prince Hal, "Shakespeare's" historic hero. Henry VI is the victim of misfortunes and machinations, and is handled with great tenderness and respect. The play of *Richard III* lays bare the internal discord of the Yorkist faction, the downfall and destruction of the Yorkist arch-villain, and the triumph of Henry of Richmond, the representative of the House of Lancaster, who had received the nomination and benediction of Henry VI. We might naturally expect, therefore, to find Shakespeare a member of some family with distinct Lancastrian leanings.

Having turned our attention to the different classes we are again faced with the question of his Italianism. Not only are we impressed by the large number of plays with an Italian setting or derived from Italian sources, but we feel that these plays carry us to Italy in a way that *Hamlet* never succeeds in carrying us to Denmark, nor his French plays in carrying us to France. Even in *Hamlet* he seems almost to go out of his way to drag in a reference to Italy. Those who know Italy and are familiar with *The Merchant of Venice* tell us that there are clear indications that Shakespeare knew Venice and Milan personally. However that may be, it is impossible for those who have had, at any time, an interest in nothing more than the language and literature of Italy, to resist the feeling that there is thrown about these plays an Italian atmosphere suggestive of one who knew and felt attracted towards the country. Everything bespeaks an Italian enthusiast.

Going still more closely into detail, it has often been observed that Shakespeare's interest in animals is seldom that of the naturalist, almost invariably that of the sportsman; and some of the supporters of the Stratfordian tradition have sought to establish a connection between this fact and the poaching of William Shakspere. When, however, we look closely into the references we are struck with his easy familiarity with all the terms relating to the chase. Take Shakespeare's entire sportsman's vocabulary, find out the precise significance of each unusual term, and the reader will probably get a more distinct vision of the sporting pastimes of the aristocracy of that day than he would get in any other way. Add to this all the varied vocabulary relating to hawks and falconry, observe the insistence with which similes, metaphors and illustrations drawn from the chase and hawking appear throughout his work, and it becomes impossible to resist the belief that he was a man who had at one time found his recreation and delight in these aristocratic pastimes.

His keen susceptibility to the influence of music is another characteristic that frequently meets us; and most people will agree that the whole range of English literature may be searched in vain for passages that more accurately or more fittingly describe the charm and power of music than do certain lines in the pages of Shakespeare. The entire passage on music in the final act of *The Merchant of Venice*, beginning "Look how the floor of heaven," right on to the closing words "Let no such man be trusted," is itself music, and is probably as grand a paeon in honour of music as can be found in any language.

Nothing could well be clearer in itself, nor more at Money variance with what is known of the man than the dramatist's attitude towards money. It is the man who lends money gratis, and so "pulls down the rate of usuance" in Venice, that is the hero of the play just mentioned. His friend is the incorrigible spendthrift and borrower Bassanio, who has "disabled his estate by showing a more swelling port than his faint means would grant continuance," and who at last repairs his broken fortunes by marriage. Almost every reference to money and purses is of the loosest description, and, by implication, teach an improvidence that would soon involve any man's financial affairs in complete chaos. It is the arch-villain, Iago, who urges "put money in thy purse," and the contemptible politician, Polonius, who gives the careful advice "neither a borrower nor a lender be"; whilst the money-grabbing Shylock, hoist with his own petard, is the villain whose circumvention seems to fill the writer with an absolute joy.

It ought not to surprise us if the author himself turned out to be one who had felt the grip of the money-lender, rather than a man like the Stratford Shakspere, who, after he had himself become prosperous, prosecuted others for the recovery of petty sums.

Of the Stratford man, Pope asserts that "Gain not glory winged his roving flight."And Sir Sidney Lee amplifies this by saying that "his literary attainments and successes were chiefly valued as serving the prosaic end of providing permanently for himself and his daughters". Yet in one of his early plays (*Henry IV, Part II*) "Shakespeare" expresses himself thus:

> How quickly nature falls into revolt
> When gold becomes her object.
> For this the foolish over-careful fathers
> Have broke their sleep with thoughts, their brains with
>   care,
> Their bones with industry;
> For this they have engrossed and piled up
> The cankcr'd hcaps of strange achieved gold.

From its setting the passage is evidently the expression of the writer's own thought rather than an element of the dramatization.

Finally we have, again in an early play, his great hero of tragic love, Romeo, exclaiming:

> There is thy gold, worse poison to men's souls,
> Doing more murders in this loathsome world
> Than these poor compounds.

In a word, the Stratfordian view requires us to write our great dramatist down as a hypocrite. The attitude of William Shakspere to money matters may have had about it all the "sobriety of personal aims and sanity of mental attitude" claimed for it. In which case, the more clearly he had represented his own attitude in his works the greater would have been their fidelity to objective fact. Money is a social institution, created by the genius of the human race to facilitate the conduct of life; and, under normal conditions, it is entitled to proper attention and respect. Under given conditions, however, it may so imperil the highest human interests, as to justify an intense reaction against it, and even to call for repudiation and contempt from those moral guides, amongst whom we include the great poets, who are concerned with the higher creations of man's intellectual and moral nature. Such, we judge, was the dramatist's attitude to money.

The points treated so far have been somewhat on the surface; and most, if not all, might be found adequately supported by other writers. There are, however, two other matters on which it would be well to have Shakespeare's attitude defined, if such were possible, before proceeding to the next stage of the enquiry. These are his mental attitude towards Woman, and his relation to Catholicism.

Ruskin's treatment of the former point in *Sesame and Lilies* is well known, but not altogether convincing. He, and others who adopt the same line of thought, seem not sufficiently to discriminate between what comes as a kind of aura from the medieval chivalries and what is distinctly personal. Moreover, the business of a dramatist being to represent every variety of human character, it must be doubtful whether any characterization represents his views as a whole, or whether, indeed, it may not only represent a kind of Utopian idealism. Some deference, too, must be paid by a playwriter to the mind and requirements of his contemporary public; and the literature of the days of Queen Elizabeth does certainly attest a respectful treatment of Woman at that period. In quotations from Shakespeare on this theme, however, one is more frequently met with suggestions of Woman's frailty and changeableness. In his greatest play, *Hamlet*, there are but two women; one weak in character, the other weak in intellect, and Hamlet trusts neither.

Shakespeare, however, is a writer of other things besides dramas. He has left us a large number of sonnets, and the sonnet, possibly more than any other form of composition, has been the vehicle for the expression of the most intimate thoughts and feelings of poets. Almost infallibly, one might say, do a man's sonnets directly reveal his soul. The sonnets of "Shakespeare", especially, have a ring of reality about them quite inconsistent with the fanciful non-biographical interpretation which Stratfordianism would attach to them. Examining, then, these sonnets we find that there are, in fact, two sets of them. By far the larger and more important set embracing no less than one hundred and twenty-six out of a total of one hundred and fifty-four, is addressed to a young man, and express a tenderness, which is probably without parallel in the recorded expressions of emotional attachment of one man to another. At the same time there occurs in this very set the following reference to woman:

A woman's face with Nature's own hand painted,
  Mistrust
Hast thou, the master mistress of my passion; and
A woman's gentle heart, but not acquainted affection.
With shifting change, as is false woman's fashion;
An eye more bright than theirs, less false unrolling.

The second set of sonnets, comprising only twenty-eight, as against one hundred and twenty-six in the first set, is probably the most painful for Shakespeare admirers to read, of all that "Shakespeare" has written. It is the expression of an intensely passionate love for some woman; but love of a kind which cannot be accurately described otherwise than as morbid emotion; a combination of affection and bitterness; tenderness, without a touch of faith or of true admiration.

Two loves I have of comfort and despair,
Which, like two spirits, do suggest me still.
The better angel is a man right fair.
The worser spirit, a woman, coloured ill.

In loving thee (the woman) thou knowest I am
  forsworn,
And all my honest faith in thee is lost.

I have sworn thee fair and thought thee bright,
Who art as black as bell and dark as night.

Whether this mistrust was constitutional or the outcome of unfortunate experiences is irrelevant to our present purpose. The fact of its existence is what matters. Whilst, then, we have comparatively so little bearing on the subject, and that little of such a nature, we shall not be guilty of over-statement if we say that though he was capable of great affection, and had a high sense of the ideal in womanhood, his faith in the women with whom he was directly associated was weak, and his relationship towards them far from perfect.

To deduce the dramatist's religious point of view from his plays is perhaps the most difficult task of all. Taking the general religious conditions of his time into consideration there are only two broad currents to be reckoned with. Puritanism had no doubt already assumed appreciable proportions as a further development of the Protestant idea; but, for our present purpose, the broader currents of Catholicism and Protestantism are all that need be considered. In view of the fact that Protestantism was at that time in the ascendant, whilst Catholicism was under a cloud, a writer of plays intended for immediate representation whose leanings were Protestant would be quite at liberty to expose his personal leanings, whilst a pronounced Roman Catholic would need to exercise greater personal restraint. Now it is impossible to detect in "Shakespeare" any Protestant bias or any support of those principles of individualism in which Protestantism has its roots. On the other hand, he seems as catholic as the circumstances of his times and the conditions under which he worked would allow him to be. Macaulay has the following interesting passage on the point:

The partiality of Shakespeare for Friars is well known. In "Hamlet" the ghost complains that he died without extreme unction, and, in defiance of the article which condemns the doctrine of purgatory, declares that he is "Confined to fast in fires,/ Till the foul crimes, done in his days of nature, Are burnt and purged away." These lines, we suspect, would have raised a tremendous storm in the theatre at any time during the reign of Charles the Second. They were clearly not written by a zealous Protestant for zealous Protestants.

We may leave his attitude towards Catholicism at that; except to add that, if he was really a Catholic, the higher calls of his religion to devotion and to discipline probably met with only an indifferent response. It is necessary, moreover, to point out that Auguste Comte in his "Positive Polity" refers to "Shakespeare" as a sceptic.

To the nine points enumerated at the end of the last chapter we may therefore add the following:

1) A man with Feudal connections.
2) A member of the higher aristocracy.
3) Connected with Lancastrian supporters.
4) An enthusiast for Italy.
5) A follower of sport (including falconry).
6) A lover of music.
7) Loose and improvident in money matters.
8) Doubtful and somewhat conflicting in his attitude to woman.
9) Of probable Catholic leanings, but touched with scepticism.

THE SHRINERS

Less well known as the Ancient Arabic Order of Nobles of the Mystic Shrine, the Shriners are a group of Freemasons fond of a drink. Seriously: the order was founded in New York City in 1871 by Doctor Walter Fleming as a club for Freemasons who liked to wine and dine at the Knickerbocker Cottage, a popular eaterie.

Numbers remained small until Fleming decided to give the Shriners an exotic makeover, and invented a long and completely specious pedigree which stretched all the way back to Arabia in the Middle Ages. He also devised a salutation (*Es Selamu Aleikum!*) and decided that members needed to wear a red fez. Offering "water from the well of ZumZum" (alcohol), fun, fraternity and dressing-up, the Shriner order expanded dramatically. A sobering up of a sort came in the late 1880s when the order, perhaps in recompense for its previous wild partying, turned to charitable works on a heroic scale. Currently, more than twenty Shriner hospitals and clinics provide free treatment for children in the USA.

Money was no object for Shriners, who tended to be well-off businessmen, willing to pay for the local Shriner Temple's country club-like facilities, in addition to giving handsome donations to the order's charitable projects. Unfortunately for the Shriners they, like other Masonic Orders composed primarily of WASPs, found themselves out of step with society by about 1972, and membership began to decline. To make joining easier, in 2000 the order dropped the long-standing requirement that Shriners must hold either the York Rite or high Scottish Rite degrees of Freemasonry. Still the membership dwindles.

The oddity is that the more the Shriners have lessened in real numbers, the more their role in conspiracy theory has grown. Aside from the small matter of being the *real* gang behind the **New World Order**/the **Bavarian Illuminati,** the Shriners also happen to house a working model of the Ark of the Covenant – yes, the Ark of the Covenant made by Moses to God's specifications – in their HQ. Unsurprisingly, ownership of the Ark facsimile gives the order special powers, though Yahweh may be surprised that the Shriners use it to communicate with aliens.

Outsiders may consider this less embarrassing than the clowning around in small cars that Shriners do on parades across America, usually likened in horror to watching dads dance at weddings.

> Frat-pack Masons wearing fezzes are disguised Illuminati: ALERT LEVEL 1

Further Reading
www.shrinershq.org

SOCIETY OF JESUS

The "Societas Jesu" was founded in Paris in 1534 by Basque priest Ignatius Lopez de Loyola, later canonized as Saint Ignatius of Loyola. Their original charter ordered them to "Enter upon hospital and missionary work in Jerusalem" – so far so good – but also "to go without questioning wherever the pope might direct". The "extreme oath" of absolute fealty sworn by the Jesuits to an infallible pope, started up the earliest conspiracy theories about the order, namely that they were the white robed one's personal political instruments. The accusation was not baseless; in Stuart Britain, the Jesuits were absolutely implicated in the most unChristian-like Gunpowder Plot to blow up James I in 1603.

Yet, even in Catholic countries the Jesuits ran foul of the authorities, who distrusted their missionary zeal, while the so-called Monita Secreta, a set of instructions from the Jesuits' "Superior General" detailing how the ascetic Society could gain illicit wealth and power, condemned them as hypocrites and megalomaniacs. The Monita Secreta was almost certainly a forgery, but the damage was done; by 1773, half the national governments of Europe had successfully lobbied for the order to be suppressed. When the Jesuits were allowed to reform in 1814, allegations that the Jesuits under their "Black Pope" ran the Catholic Church – and not vice versa – went wild. The Black Pope nickname for the Superior General originally came from his dark vestments; in anti-Jesuit circles the "Black" referred to his dabbling in the devil's arts. Murder, assassination, civil war, revolution, coups were all assumed to be the stock-in-trades of the Black Pope. And so, the Jesuits had their moment on the stage as the bogeymen of the Western world: in Eugene Sue's 1844 novel *The Wandering Jew*, the Society was depicted as being "bent on world domination by all available means". According to Sue, the Society was even more dangerous than ... the Freemasons and the Jews.

Even the Society's enemies like Sue grudgingly acknowledged its remarkable internal cohesion. Loyola had been a soldier, and ran the Jesuits in military fashion; in their own eyes, the early Jesuits were "Soldiers of Christ" in the Counter-Reformation against the Protestantism sweeping sixteenth-century Europe.

In the twenty-first century, allegations about Catholic conspiracy have tended to shift onto Opus Dei, although voices of alarm are periodically raised over the "Jesuit Oath" taken by Society members. It is damning stuff:

> I do ... promise and declare that I will, when opportunity presents, make and wage relentless war, secretly and openly, against all heretics, Protestants and Masons ... that I will spare neither age, sex nor condition, and that I will hang, burn, waste, boil, flay, strangle, and bury alive these infamous heretics; rip up the stomachs and wombs of their women, and crush their infants' heads against the walls in order to annihilate their execrable race. That when the same cannot be done openly I will secretly use the poisonous cup, the strangulation cord, the steel of the poniard, or the leaden bullet.

Luckily for all heretics, Protestants and Masons – and their wives and children – the oath was a forgery by one Robert Ware, aimed at stymieing the accession of the Catholic James II in England in the seventeenth century. Today, the Society of Jesuits has 20,000 members, and announces on its website: "We are still men on the move, ready to change place, occupation, method – whatever will advance our mission in the Church of teaching Jesus Christ and preaching his Good News ..." The website is a little less forthcoming about one conspiracy the Jesuits have unquestionably run: a conspiracy of silence about the paedophilia practised by the Society's priests. The old Jesuit boast "Give us the child for seven years, and we will give you the man" took on a grim twist when child abuse by Jesuit priests was uncovered in America, Germany and Latin America. In the Pacific Northwest of the USA, the Jesuit branch was required in 2011 to pay $166.1 million in compensation to 450 victims who had been sexually abused by Jesuit priests over a fifty-year period.

> The Jesuit "Black Pope" runs the world: ALERT LEVEL 2

Further Reading
Malachi Martin, *The Jesuits*, 1988
Edmond Paris, *The Secret History of the Jesuits*, 1986

SOCIETY OF THE ELECT

The Illuminati, the Bilderberg Group, the Trilateral Commission, *le Cercle* – all are favourites for the title of "The Secret Society That Really Runs the World". Most of the covert cabals are either fictions in paranoid nightmares or impotent talking shops, but there is one shadowy organization that really did want to take over the globe. This is the Society of the Elect, founded by Cecil Rhodes.

Born in 1853, Rhodes was the son of an English vicar who journeyed to Africa as a young man and made a mountain of money from diamond mining. He became a major force in African politics – Rhodesia (now Zimbabwe) was named for him.

Now, Rhodes might have found fame and fortune on the Dark Continent but his heart belonged to Blighty – and to the expansion of Victoria's empire so the whole map of the world would be coloured pink. In 1877, Rhodes wrote in his *Confessions of Faith*: "Why should we not form a secret society with but one object: the furtherance of the British Empire and the bringing of the whole uncivilized world under British rule for the recovery of the United States for making the Anglo-Saxon race but one Empire" (See Document, p.497).

Rhodes seems to have put his money where his belief was. One of his wills contains a provision for

> ... the establishment, promotion and development of a Secret Society, the true aim and object whereof shall be for the extension of British rule throughout the world, the perfecting

of a system of emigration from the United Kingdom, and of colonisation by British subjects of all lands where the means of livelihood are attainable by energy, labour and enterprise, and especially the occupation by British settlers of the entire Continent of Africa, the Holy Land, the Valley of the Euphrates, the Islands of Cyprus and Candia, the whole of South America, the Islands of the Pacific not heretofore possessed by Great Britain, the whole of the Malay Archipelago, the seaboard of China and Japan, the ultimate recovery of the United States of America as an integral part of the British Empire, the inauguration of a system of Colonial representation in the Imperial Parliament which may tend to weld together the disjointed members of the Empire and, finally, the foundation of so great a Power as to render wars impossible and promote the best interests of humanity.

The resultant Society of the Elect was formed in 1891, and according to the respected American historian Carroll Quigley, the Society had an inner and outer membership structure. Rhodes himself was the "General" of the Society, and sitting on its executive committee was the British High Commissioner in South Africa, the journalist William T. Stead and the banker Nathan Rothschild. Serving alongside the committee in the heart of the Society were the "initiates". The outer circle of backers was called the Association of Helpers.

Although Rhodes died in 1902 (one of his wills, incidentally, established the Rhodes scholarships at Oxford University, the recipients of which have included Bill Clinton), his vision was carried forward by Alfred Milner who founded the Round Table groups, also known as the Rhodes–Milner Round Table groups, a.k.a. the Moot. The Round Table groups – which were the Association of Helpers under another guise – spread across the English-speaking world, and gained great influence in the period after the First World War. According to historian of secret societies, Michael Streeter "They were closely associated with the establishment of the Union of South Africa, the British Commonwealth and the League of Nations."

The Round Tables were also likely behind the 1917 "Balfour Declaration", written by British Foreign Secretary Arthur

Balfour to Lord Rothschild (the son of Nathan Rothschild), stating Britain's support for a Jewish homeland in Palestine.

Aside from Milner, the dominant figure in the Society of the Elect/Round Tables in the decades after Rhodes's demise was Lionel Curtis, who founded the Royal Institute of International Affairs in 1920, known today as "Chatham House" after its premises in London. Although Chatham House advertises itself as nothing more sinister than a think tank on international affairs, to a large number of conspiracists Chatham House is a front for the Society of the Elect. They take their cue from Professor Carroll Quigley's *Tragedy and Hope*, in which he names Chatham House as Rhodes's secret society, no bones about it.

The vast bulk of historians believe the Society folded long ago, and may never got off paper. Quigley himself rowed back from the allegation in private. What is beyond supposition is the close tie between Chatham House and the American Council on Foreign Relations, which is another organization owing its existence to Rhodes. In 1919, Edward Mandel House, wingman to US President Woodrow Wilson at the Versailles peace conference, met with members of the Round Tables, whose ideals he shared. However, House believed that Americans would not accept the leadership of a British-dominated organization, so constituted instead the Council on Foreign Relations.

As Professor Kees van der Pijl observed in *Transnational Classes and International Relations*, "As a structure of socialisation through which a momentary ruling class consensus is shaped, transmitted and transformed into policy, the Rhodes–Milner Group became the model for all subsequent groups."

In other words, Rhodes failed dismally to create a secret society capable of taking over the world, but he did indirectly spawn the clubbable think tanks which seek to shape national and international policy. Unquestionably the NY-based CFR and Chatham House are major policy-making institutions, but to stretch their role to being the power behind the **New World Order** is breaking credibility.

If the Society of the Elect/CFR/Chatham House rule the world why, you might ask the edge-of-reason conspiracists, do they need a secret plot to take over what they already have?

Cecil Rhodes's Society of the Elect are the Masters of the Universe: ALERT LEVEL 3

Further Reading
Cecil J. Rhodes, *The Last Will and Testament of Cecil John Rhodes*,
  ed. W.T. Stead, 1902
Carroll Quigley, *Tragedy and Hope*, 1966
www.moot.org.uk

DOCUMENT: CECIL RHODES, *CONFESSION OF FAITH*, 1877

The spelling and grammar errors are as the the original.

It often strikes a man to inquire what is the chief good in life; to one the thought comes that it is a happy marriage, to another great wealth, and as each seizes on his idea, for that he more or less works for the rest of his existence. To myself thinking over the same question the wish came to render myself useful to my country. I then asked myself how could I and after reviewing the various methods I have felt that at the present day we are actually limiting our children and perhaps bringing into the world half the human beings we might owing to the lack of country for them to inhabit that if we had retained America there would at this moment be millions more of English living. I contend that we are the finest race in the world and that the more of the world we inhabit the better it is for the human race. Just fancy those parts that are at present inhabited by the most despicable specimens of human beings what an alteration there would be if they were brought under Anglo-Saxon influence, look again at the extra employment a new country added to our dominions gives. I contend that every acre added to our territory means in the future birth to some more of the English race who otherwise would not be brought into existence. Added to this the absorption of the greater portion of the world under our rule simply means the end of all wars, at this moment had we not lost America I believe we could have stopped the Russian-Turkish war by merely refusing money and supplies. Having these ideas what scheme could we think of to forward this object. I look into history and I read the story of the Jesuits I see what they were able to do in a bad cause and I might say under bad leaders.

At the present day I become a member of the Masonic order I see the wealth and power they possess the influence they hold and I think over their ceremonies and I wonder that a large body of men can devote themselves to what at times appear the most ridiculous and absurd rites without an object and without an end.

The idea gleaming and dancing before ones eyes like a will-of-the-wisp at last frames itself into a plan. Why should we not form a secret society with but one object the furtherance of the British Empire and the bringing of the whole uncivilised world under British rule for the recovery of the United States for the making the Anglo-Saxon race but one Empire. What a dream, but yet it is probable, it is possible. I once heard it argued by a fellow in my own college, I am sorry to own it by an Englishman, that it was good thing for us that we have lost the United States. There are some subjects on which there can be no arguments, and to an Englishman this is one of them, but even from an American's point of view just picture what they have lost, look at their government, are not the frauds that yearly come before the public view a disgrace to any country and especially their's which is the finest in the world. Would they have occurred had they remained under English rule great as they have become how infinitely greater they would have been with the softening and elevating influences of English rule, think of those countless 000's of Englishmen that during the last 100 years would have crossed the Atlantic and settled and populated the United States. Would they have not made without any prejudice a finer country of it than the low class Irish and German emigrants? All this we have lost and that country loses owing to whom? Owing to two or three ignorant pig-headed statesmen of the last century, at their door lies the blame. Do you ever feel mad? do you ever feel murderous. I think I do with those men. I bring facts to prove my assertion. Does an English father when his sons wish to emigrate ever think of suggesting emigration to a country under another flag, never – it would seem a disgrace to suggest such a thing I think that we all think that poverty is better under our own flag than wealth under a foreign one.

Put your mind into another train of thought. Fancy Australia discovered and colonised under the French flag, what would it mean merely several millions of English unborn that at present exist we learn from the past and to form our future. We learn from having lost to cling to what we possess. We know the size of the world we know the total extent. Africa is still lying ready for us it is our duty to take it. It is our duty to seize every opportunity of acquiring more territory and we should keep this one idea steadily before our eyes that more territory simply means more of the Anglo-Saxon race more of the best the most human, most honourable race the world possesses.

To forward such a scheme what a splendid help a secret society would be a society not openly acknowledged but who would work in secret for such an object.

I contend that there are at the present moment numbers of the ablest men in the world who would devote their whole lives to it. I often think what a loss to the English nation in some respects the abolition of the Rotten Borough System has been. What thought strikes a man entering the house of commons, the assembly that rule the whole world? I think it is the mediocrity of the men but what is the cause. It is simply – an assembly of wealth of men whose lives have been spent in the accumulation of money and whose time has been too much engaged to be able to spare any for the study of past history. And yet in hands of such men rest our destinies. Do men like the great Pitt, and Burke and Sheridan not now to exist. I contend they do. There are men now living with I know no other term the [Greek term] of Aristotle but there are not ways for enabling them to serve their Country. They live and die unused unemployed. What has the main cause of the success of the Romish Church? The fact that every enthusiast, call it if you like every madman finds employment in it. Let us form the same kind of society a Church for the extension of the British Empire. A society which should have members in every part of the British Empire working with one object and one idea we should have its members placed at our universities and our schools and should watch the English youth passing through their hands just one perhaps in every thousand would have the mind and feelings for such an object, he should be tried in every way, he should be tested whether he is endurant, possessed of eloquence, disregardful of the petty details of life, and if found to be such, then elected and bound by oath to serve for the rest of his life in his County. He should then be supported if without means by the Society and sent to that part of the Empire where it was felt he was needed.

Take another case, let us fancy a man who finds himself his own master with ample means of attaining his majority whether he puts the question directly to himself or not, still like the old story of virtue and vice in the Memorabilia a fight goes on in him as to what he should do. Take if he plunges into dissipation there is nothing too reckless he does not attempt but after a time his life palls on him, he mentally says this is not good enough, he changes his life, he reforms, he travels, he thinks now I have found the chief good in life, the novelty wears off, and he tires, to change again, he goes into the far interior after the wild game he thinks at last I've found that in life of which I cannot tire, again he is disappointed. He returns he thinks is there nothing I can do in life? Here I am with means, with a good house, with everything that is to be envied and yet I am not happy I am tired of life he possesses within him a portion of the [Greek term] of Aristotle but he knows it not, to such a man the Society should go, should test, and should finally show him the greatness of the scheme and list him as a member.

Take one more case of the younger son with high thoughts, high aspirations, endowed by nature with all the faculties to make a great man, and with the sole wish in life to serve his Country but he lacks two things the means and the opportunity, ever troubled by a sort of inward deity urging him on to high and noble deeds, he is compelled to pass his time in some occupation which furnishes him with mere existence, he lives unhappily and dies miserably. Such men as these the Society should search out and use for the furtherance of their object.

(In every Colonial legislature the Society should attempt to have its members prepared at all times to vote or speak and advocate the closer union of England and the colonies, to crush all disloyalty and every movement for the severance of our Empire. The Society should inspire and even own portions of the press for the press rules the mind of the people. The Society should always be searching for members who might by their position in the world by their energies or character forward the object but the ballot and test for admittance should be severe.)

Once make it common and it fails. Take a man of great wealth who is bereft of his children perhaps having his mind soured by some bitter disappointment who shuts himself up separate from his neighbours and makes up his mind to a miserable existence. To such men as these the society should go gradually disclose the greatness of their scheme and entreat him to throw in his life and property with them for this object. I think that there are thousands now existing who would eagerly grasp at the opportunity. Such are the heads of my scheme.

For fear that death might cut me off before the time for attempting its development I leave all my worldly goods in trust to S. G. Shippard and the Secretary for the Colonies at the time of my death to try to form such a Society with such an object.

SPACE MONOLITH

If *Star Trek* taught us anything it was that the *Enterprise* would take much more, Captain, and that pretty much anything was possible on the final frontier.

But space monoliths?

When Soviet cosmonaut Yuri Gagarin entered space in 1961 he is said to have observed an alien communication beacon, dubbed the Monolith, which continued in orbit until 1972 when it was retrieved by a US military shuttle and taken for study at a clandestine base, probably **Area 51**. In between these dates, the Monolith almost caused the demise of the 1969 Apollo 10 mission, which took a top secret detour from its schedule as the "dress rehearsal" for the moon landings to photograph the celestial map carved on the Monolith's surface. As Apollo 10 approached the Monolith, the crew of Stafford, Young and Cernan suffered communications and technical malfunctions resulting in a re-entry to Earth at a dangerously high speed which the crew were lucky to survive.

Remember Stanley Kubrick's classic 1968 film *2001: A Space Odyssey*, itself based on Arthur C. Clarke's short story *The Sentinel*? The one with the alien monoliths that mark (if not kick-start) the various stages of human evolution? The monolith conspiracists surely do.

The evidence for the monolith theory is scant. Neither Gagarin nor the Apollo 10 crew ever mentioned seeing a monolith. Apollo 10 splashed down within thirty-five seconds of its scheduled landing time, meaning that the technical problems suffered were indeed very minor – and that there cannot have been time for a detour to investigate an alien artefact. One of the fuller expositions of the monolith conspiracy, by Richard Boylan in the pages of abovetopsecret.com, is based on information "disclosed to me by a reliable confidential informant, who previously worked on contract for the National Security Agency, and maintains connections within the Intelligence community. This informant, whom I shall call 'Jesse', has over 40 years of notes from a very close relative, who served as CIA liaison officer to the National Council on UFO/ET matters." In other words, the "information" is third-hand from unnamed, unidentified sources.

For years the Monolith theory went into abeyance, and just when it seemed dead in space a camera from the University of Arizona's HiRise (High Resolution Imaging Science Experiment) project took a photograph of a "monolith" on Mars in 2011. Veteran astronaut Buzz Aldrin then stoked the space conspiracy theory by announcing that a similar monolith had been detected on Mars's moon Phobos. The University of Arizona, however, roundly rejected any notion that the monolith was an alien-made structure. Alfred McEwen, professor of planetary science at the university and HiRise's principal investigator, said: "Layering from rock deposition combined with tectonic fractures creates right-angle planes of weakness such that rectangular blocks tend to weather out and separate from the bedrock … It is not that unusual. There are lots of rectangular structures on Mars. It is striking when you see one that is isolated, but they are common."

Buzz Aldrin suggested that the only way to prove the matter of the Mars monolith one way or another was to pump money into space exploration and go there.

Monoliths in space are alien-made beacons: ALERT LEVEL 2

SPACE SHUTTLE COLUMBIA

At around 2.00 p.m. GMT on 1 February 2003, the Space Shuttle Columbia disintegrated while re-entering the Earth's atmosphere after sixteen days in space. Tragically all seven crew members taking part in mission STS-107 were killed. Barely had Columbia's debris finished showering down on the East Texas town of Palestine (pop. 18, 458) than the conspiracy theories lifted off.

As to whodunnit, there is an embarrassment of choices:

- There was some irony – or maybe a clue – in the falling of the wreckage on "Palestine", because *the* major league Columbia conspiracy points the finger at Israel. One of the Columbia seven was Ilan Ramon, an Israeli Air Force officer who had taken part in the bombing of the Iraqi nuclear facility at Osirsk in 1981. After Ramon's death at Mach 18 it was rumoured that he had been included in the Columbia crew so he could covertly photograph Iraq on behalf of Israel's Institute of Biological Research military in preparation for a biowarfare attack on Saddam Hussein. In this view, Ramon was "martyred" by the Israelis and US to ramp up global support for an Israeli invasion of Palestine (the one in the Middle East), Lebanon, and Iraq itself.

   The son of Holocaust survivors Colonel Ramon was the first Israeli to enter space, taking with him a scroll of the Torah. This read: "Has any nation ever heard the voice of God speaking out of the mist of the fire, as you have, and yet lived?" On due consideration of this, Palestinian organizations and the Islamic press decided that Allah had waved his hand to destroy Columbia and stop the Jews entering the celestial sphere. In the words of Abu Hamza Al-Masri, Islamic fundamentalist preacher (and terrorist, and benefit fraudster) in an interview with *Al-Sharq Al-Awsat* in 2003:

The target of this event was the trinity of evil, as the shuttle carried Americans, an Israeli, and a Hindu, the trinity of evil against Islam. This is a message to the American people that Bush's term is nothing but a string of curses cast upon them, and that it will lead to the exhaustion of their resources and the elimination of the false American dream ... This is a divine message to the Israelis, saying that they are not welcome in space.

- The Russian news service PRAVDA suggested that China or North Korea had hacked into Columbia's onboard computer and uploaded a virus or worm that caused Columbia to malfunction.
- An amateur astronomer by the name of Peter Goldie took photographs of Columbia seconds before its break-up which purportedly show a purple bolt heading towards the craft. Numerous conspiracists thus maintain that Columbia was shot down by a particle beam destroyer or some form of HAARP-like ray device employed by the US military. Thus a classic "false-flag" operation, the downing of Columbia was designed to create grief and anger amongst the American "sheeple" so they would support the upcoming Iraq War. There was, as every good conspiracist knew, a precedent for such a dubious mission, **Operation Northwoods**, which had been drawn up by the Joint Chiefs of Staff and intended to blame Cuba if anything went amiss with John Glenn's orbit of Earth in 1962.
- Aliens shoot down Columbia.

The official investigating body, the Columbia Accident Investigation Board (which comprised independent experts from academia, the space industry, the military) mundanely concluded:

The physical cause of the loss of Columbia and its crew was a breach in the Thermal Protection System on the leading edge of the left wing, caused by a piece of insulating foam which separated from the left bipod ramp section of the External Tank at 81.7 seconds after launch, and struck the wing in the vicinity of the lower half of Reinforced Carbon-Carbon panel number 8. During re-entry this breach in the Thermal Protection System allowed superheated air to penetrate through the leading edge insulation and progressively melt the aluminium structure of the left wing, resulting in a weakening of the structure until increasing aerodynamic forces caused loss of control, failure of the wing, and break-up of the Orbiter. This breakup occurred in a flight regime in which, given the current design of the Orbiter, there was no possibility for the crew to survive.

Similar incidents concerning debris breaking off had occurred before, but never with major consequences. If, the CAIB determined, a proper analysis of the damage to Columbia had occurred while the craft was still in orbit, a rescue of the shuttle's crew might have been effected, either by boarding Atlantis or undertaking an emergency spacewalk to attempt repairs to the left wing thermal protection.

As to the snaps of a purple ray hitting Columbia, the CAIB concluded that these were the result of camera wobble during a long exposure.

Space shuttle Columbia was intentionally destroyed by human and/or aliens: ALERT LEVEL 1

STOLEN ELECTIONS

It was the election that gave us the "hanging chad".

The seventh of November 2000 was presidential election night in the US and just after 8.00 p.m. TV networks "called" the election for Democrat Al Gore when exit polls showed he had taken the key state of Florida.

A few hours later TV anchormen had to red-facedly retract the estimate. They weren't the only ones to make retractions. At first Gore conceded the election to rival George H. W. Bush, then when Bush's lead in Florida near disappeared, Gore withdrew his concession. Meanwhile, the votes in Florida were recounted by machine, by hand, and Republicans and Democrats alike threw court cases around like confetti. At one stage there were no less than thirty separate court cases underway concerning the Florida count.

Eventually, the US Supreme Court forced Florida to stop counting ballots and gave the state's votes to Bush. As trial lawyer Vincent Bugliosi acidly observed, it was a "judicial coup d'etat" that allowed Bush to become the first Republican president for eight years.

Back in Florida, the air was also heavy with the smell of a political fix. Journalists and lawyers turned up dubious electoral practice after dubious electoral practice, beginning with the voting system in Palm Beach County where the punch card "butterfly ballot" was so flawed that 5,000 votes went to the unholy (and improbable) alliance of Gore and Reform Party candidate Pat Buchanan. Then there were the endless disputes over whether punch-card votes counted if bits of paper were left on the card – the infamous "hanging chads". Over in Gadsen County, which had a high proportion of black and predominantly Democrat voters, there was an unfeasibly high excess of spoiled votes. There, ballot papers were read by an "Accuvote" machine which rejected any with extra marks on them. Unfortunately, the machine recording the votes made marks, meaning that around 15 per cent of Gadsen votes were discounted. In predominantly white Tallahassee, however, voters were warned about machine marks and asked to try again. The percentage of spoiled votes was 1 per cent.

Black voters were also on the dubious end of so-called "scrubbing", as the USS Commission on Civil Rights discovered (see Document, p.510). In the run-up to the election Florida's governor – who happened to be Jeb Bush, bro of George – and others commissioned a company called DBT to remove ("scrub") from the electoral register convicted felons. This turned out to be a wholly flawed exercise because DBT's computer did not include people's middle initials, meaning there were numerous counts of mistaken identity. According to journalist Greg Palast at least 15 per cent of DBT's scrub list was erroneous and, guess what, a disproportionate number of those were black or Hispanic. DBT's computer might not have been sufficiently clever to record middle initials, but it could do race.

Talking of electronic errors, the voting machines in Volusia did very strange things on November 7/8. At first the Volusia machines gave Bush a 51,000 lead – the announcement of which started the "Bush victory" juggernaut – then apparently suffered a "memory error" which reduced his lead by 16,022. There were stories too of voting records hidden in the trash cans at Volusia County offices.

It was of course coincidence that the Volusia County machines were made by Diebold Inc., which just happens to be owned by Republican businessman Walden O'Dell. Diebold Direct Record Electronic machines are environmentally friendly, and leave no paper receipt. Meaning votes cannot be properly checked.

The cry of "stolen election" was heard again in 2004. Exit polls trumpeted a huge victory for Bush's opponent, the lantern-jawed Senator Kerry. But somehow by midnight, Bush had taken the lead. This time Ohio was the state under scrutiny. From 12.20 in the morning until around 2.00 a.m., the flow of information in Ohio stopped and in that time Bush went from underdog to top dog, emerging with a 118,000-vote-plus official margin. "There is no evidence of vote theft or errors on a large scale," the oily *New York Times* announced.

Robert Kennedy Jr, among many others disagreed: "Officials there [Ohio] purged tens of thousands of eligible voters from the rolls, neglected to process registration cards generated by Democratic voter drives, short-changed Democratic precincts when they allocated voting machines, and illegally derailed a recount that could have given Kerry the presidency."

Once again, electronic voting machines were in the main frame. Of the three private companies supplying electronic voting machines, three had close ties to the Grand Old Party (Republicans), one of them being Diebold. O'Dell had promised in an email to deliver Ohio to Bush. Ohio went to Bush. Coincidence? Or collusion.

The man in charge of vote counting in the state was J. Kenneth Blackwell. Blackwell just happened to be the co-chair of the Bush-Cheney re-election committee in the state. On the night of the election, Blackwell okayed a 124 per cent (!) turnout in two Republican precincts. But he was even busier in the run-up, challenging the credentials of 35,000 newly registered voters until a federal judge stopped him. On looking into the Ohio vote, Congressman John Conyers concluded that there had been "massive and unprecedented voter irregularities and anomalies in Ohio ... caused by intentional misconduct and illegal behavior, much of it involving Secretary of State J. Kenneth Blackwell".

The plot thickened. When a case alleging vote tampering in Ohio during the 2004 US election proceeded, one of the main witnesses, Republican IT guru Michael Connell, died in a plane crash. Connell had been involved in the setting up of a duplicate voting electronic counter for Blackwell so the latter could monitor the Ohio count in real time. The contract for the duplicate counter contained the stipulation that it must fit "a hardware VPN device [that] will allow access to a private network connecting the servers for database replication services as well as remote admin[istration]".

Remote administration meant that the votes could be *altered* as well as watched. Some claim that Connell was about to blow the whistle on Ohio wrongdoings and that his Piper plane crash was more than coincidence, and that like **Paul Wellstone**, his craft was downed by an electromagnetic pulse that caused essential systems to fail.

Whether Connell was assassinated or not, the Florida and Ohio counts in 2000 and 2004 were better suited to a banana republic than a great democracy.

> The 2000 and 2004 US presidential elections were "stolen" from the Democrats: ALERT LEVEL 7

Further Reading
Vincent Bugliosi, *The Betrayal of America*, 2001
Greg Palast, *The Best Democracy Money Can Buy*, 2002

DOCUMENT: REPORT FROM THE US COMMISSION ON CIVIL RIGHTS: THE 2000 VOTE AND ELECTORAL REFORM [EXTRACTS]

Voting Irregularities in Florida During the 2000 Presidential Election

Chapter 1
Voting System Controls and Failures

No right is more precious in a free country than that of having a voice in the election of those who make the laws under which, as good citizens, we must live.
To ensure that every eligible citizen in Florida has an opportunity to exercise his or her right to vote, the state established a system of checks and balances that extends from the governor

to the local poll worker. This system of control is codified in many of the provisions of the election laws of the state of Florida and, in part, is intended to help guarantee the rights granted to voters by the Voting Rights Act of 1965 will be protected. During the November 2000 election, a wide range of errors, including the insufficient provision of adequate resources, caused a significant breakdown in the state's plan, which resulted in a variety of problems that permeated the election process in Florida. Large numbers of Florida voters experienced frustration and anger on Election Day as they endured excessive delays, misinformation, and confusion, which resulted in the denial of their right to vote or to have their vote counted. While some maintain that what occurred in Florida was nothing out of the ordinary, but rather was simply amplified by the closeness of the election, the overwhelming evidence provided to the Commission proves otherwise.

It is impossible to determine the total number of voters turned away from the polls or deprived of their right to vote. It is clear that the 2000 presidential election generated a large number of complaints about voting irregularities in Florida. The Florida attorney general's office alone received more than 3,600 allegations – 2,600 complaints and 1,000 letters. In addition, both the Democratic and Republican parties received many complaints from Floridians who either could not vote or experienced difficulty when attempting to vote. These widespread complaints prompted Florida's governor to sign an executive order creating the Select Task Force on Election Procedures, Standards and Technology. The task force was formed to examine the concerns that had been raised about Florida's election process and to recommend reforms where necessary.

Several advocacy group representatives testified about the disproportionate number of complaints they received from their constituents in Florida. Jackson Chin, associate counsel at the Puerto Rican Legal Defense and Education Fund in New York City, explained that his group's preliminary investigation revealed that certain election practices in central Florida might have led to the widespread voter disenfranchisement of up to several thousand Latino voters. D. P. Misra, former president of the Association of Indians in America, and Venghan Winnie Tang, president of the South Florida chapter of the Organization of Chinese Americans, both testified that immigration and language assistance problems prevented many East Indians and Asians from being able to vote in Florida.

Other advocacy groups formed coalitions to investigate or to take action against the election problems that surfaced in Florida. For example, the NAACP filed a federal class-action lawsuit on behalf of voters in Florida who allege their right to vote in the election was unlawfully denied or abridged. The Florida Justice Institute joined with the ACLU of Florida and Florida Legal Services to develop statewide electoral reform that focuses on the concerns of Florida's racial and language minorities and those who live in poverty, "considerations that are probably long overdue in this state." According to JoNel Newman of the Florida Justice Institute, "[w]hen new or vulnerable voters from traditionally disenfranchised groups are wrongly prevented from going to the polls and from voting, they feel often a humiliation and a stigma or a disaffection that has the effect in many cases of causing them never to return to the voting booth."

The complaints from those denied the right to vote during the 2000 Florida presidential election were anything but isolated or episodic. Credible evidence shows many Floridians were denied the right to vote. Analysis of the testimony and evidence gathered by the Commission show that these denials fell most squarely on persons of color.

[...]

The Commission heard from several experts regarding potential violations of the VRA during the Florida presidential election, including Professors Allan Lichtman and Darryl Paulson.

Professor Lichtman, applying the results test, said, "The key is whether a system, regardless of why it was adopted or why it was held in place, has the effect of diminishing minority voting opportunities." Professor Lichtman explained:

> We do not have to demonstrate an intent to discriminate. We do not have to demonstrate that there was some kind of conspiracy against minorities or that anyone involved in the administration of elections today or yesterday had any intent whatever to discriminate against minorities, because indeed under the Voting Rights Act, practices can be illegal so long as they have the effect of diminishing minority opportunities to participate fully in the political process and elect candidates of their choice.

Professor Lichtman testified that a violation occurs if the following two criteria are satisfied:

- if there are "differences in voting procedures and voting technologies between white areas and minority areas"; and
- if voting procedures and voting technologies used in minority areas "give minorities less of an opportunity to have their votes counted."

Referring to a *New York Times* study showing that voting systems in Florida's poorer, predominantly minority areas are less likely to allow a voter to cast a properly tallied ballot, Professor Lichtman testified:

> In other words, minorities perhaps can go to the polls unimpeded, but their votes are less likely to count because of the disparate technology than are the votes of whites ... That is the very thing the Voting Rights Act was trying to avoid – that for whatever reason and whatever the intent, the Voting Rights Act is trying to avoid different treatment of whites and minorities when it comes to having one's vote counted ... If your vote isn't being tallied, that in effect is like having your franchise denied fundamentally.

Professor Lichtman testified that one remedy in such a case would be to equalize the technology across all voting places in the state of Florida – "to have technologies equalized such that there are no systematic correlations between technologies and whites and minorities, and a minority vote is as likely to be tallied as a white vote." The professor acknowledged this would require spending additional funds in certain parts of the state.

Darryl Paulson testified he did not believe *intentional* discrimination occurred in Florida against people of color during the 2000 vote – meaning "some sort of collusion among public officials, some sort of agreement in principle, some sort of mechanism to impose" discrimination. However, Professor Paulson agreed with Professor Lichtman on the voter spoilage issue, testifying that the "real scandal" in Florida was "the inequities that existed from county to county. Disparities between wealthy and poor counties were reflected in the types of voting machinery used. Poor counties, whether in Florida or elsewhere, have always had a disproportionate number of votes not counted."

Spoiled Ballots

An analysis of the incidence of spoiled ballots (votes cast but not counted) shows a correlation between the number of registered African American voters and the rate at which ballots were spoiled. The higher the percentage of African American residents and of African American voters, the higher the chance of the vote being spoiled.

[...]

In a very small part, the county-level relationship between race and rates of ballot rejection can be attributed to the fact that a greater percentage of African American registered voters live in counties with technologies that produce the greatest rates of rejected ballots. About 70 percent of African American registrants resided in counties using technology with the highest ballot rejection rates – punch cards and optical scan systems recorded centrally – compared with 64 percent of non-African American registrants. Counties using punch card or optical scan methods recorded centrally rejected about 4 percent of all ballots cast, compared with about 0.8 percent for counties using optical scan methods recorded by precinct. The vast majority of rejected votes were recorded in counties using punch cards or optical scan methods recorded centrally. Such counties included about 162,000 out of 180,000 unrecorded votes in Florida's 2000 presidential election. These counties that used punch cards or optical scan technology recorded centrally included 65 percent of all ballots cast in Florida's 2000 presidential election, but 90 percent of rejected ballots.

Table 1-2 Ecological Regression Estimates of Statewide Ballot Rejection Rates by Race

	Invalid votes*		Overvotes		Undervotes	
	Black voters	Nonblack voters	Black voters	Nonblack voters	Black voters	Nonblack voters
Punch card & central-record counties	19.4%	2.2%	17.1%	0.8%	2.4%	1.3%
Precinct-record counties	5.2%	0.4%	2.5%	0.2%	2.1%	0.1%
All counties combined	14.4%	1.6%	12.0%	0.6%	2.3%	1.2%

[...]

Impact of the Purge List

A similar effect upon African Americans is presented based on an analysis of the state-mandated purge list. In 1998, the Florida legislature enacted a statute that required the Division of Elections to contract with a private entity to purge its voter file of any deceased persons, duplicate registrants, individuals declared mentally incompetent, and convicted felons without civil rights restoration, i.e., remove ineligible voter registrants from voter registration rolls. What occurred in Miami-Dade County provides a vivid example of the use of these purge lists. According to the supervisor of elections for Miami-Dade County, David Leahy, the state provides his office with a list of convicted felons who have not had their rights restored. It is the responsibility of Mr. Leahy's office to verify such information and remove those individuals from the voter rolls "[i]f the supervisor *does not* determine that the information provided by the division is *incorrect* ..." In practice, this places the burden on voters to prove that they are incorrectly placed on the purge list. Mr. Leahy's office sends a notice to the individuals requiring them to inform the office if they were improperly placed on the list.

Many people appear on the list incorrectly. For example, in the 2000 election, the supervisor of elections office for Miami-Dade received two lists – one in June 1999 and another in January 2000 – from which his office identified persons to be removed from the voter rolls. Of the 5,762 persons on the June 1999 list, 327 successfully appealed and, therefore, remained on the voter rolls (see table 1-4, p.517). Another 485 names were later identified as persons who either had their rights restored or who should not have been on the list. Thus at least 14.1 percent of the persons whose names appeared on the Miami-Dade County list appeared on the list in error. Similarly, 13.3 percent of the names on the January 2000 list were eligible to vote. In other words, almost one out of every seven people on this list were there in error and risked being disenfranchised.

In addition to the possibility of persons being placed on the list in error, the use of such lists has a disparate impact on African Americans. African Americans in Florida were more likely to find their names on the list than persons of other races. African Americans represented the majority of persons – over 65 percent – on both the June 1999 and the January 2000 lists (see table 1-4). This percentage far exceeds the African American population of Miami-Dade County, which is only 20.4 percent. Comparatively, 77.6 percent of the persons residing in Miami-Dade County are white; yet whites accounted for only 17.6 percent of the persons on the June 1999 convicted felons list. Hispanics account for only 16.6 percent of the persons on that list, yet comprise 57.4 percent of the population. The proportions of African Americans, whites, and Hispanics on the January 2000 list were similar to the June 1999 list.

This discrepancy between the population and the percentage of persons of color affected by the list indicates that the use of such lists – and the fact that the individuals bear the burden of having their names removed from the list – has a disproportionate impact on African Americans.

TABLE 1-4 Convicted Felons List, Miami-Dade County, 1999 and 2000

	June 1999		January 2000		Combined totals	
	Number	Percent	Number	Percent	Number	Percent
Names on list	5,762	100%	1,388	100%	7,150	100%
Appealed & removed	327	5.7%	142	10.2%	469	6.6%
Names on list in error	485	8.4%	N/A	N/A	485	6.8%
Total names removed	812	14.1%	N/A	N/A	954	13.3%
White	1,013	17.6%	251	18.1%	1,264	17.7%
Black	3,794	65.8%	884	63.7%	4,678	65.4%
Hispanic	955	16.6%	253	18.2%	1,208	16.9%
Total	5,762	100%	1,388	100%	7,150	100%
Successful appeals						
White	98	30.0%	27	19.0%	125	26.7%
Black	155	47.4%	84	59.2%	239	51.0%
Hispanic	74	22.6%	31	21.8%	105	22.4%
Total	327	100%	142	100%	469	100%

Indeed, the persons who successfully appealed to have their names removed from the list provided to Miami-Dade County by the Florida Division of Elections are also disproportionately African American. One hundred fifty-five African Americans (47.4 percent of the total) successfully appealed in response to the June 1999 list, and 84 African Americans (59.2 percent of the total) successfully appealed in response to the January 2000 list. Hispanics accounted for approximately 22 percent of those who appealed in response to both lists. White Americans accounted for 30 percent of those who appealed in 1999 and 26.7 percent of those who appealed in 2000 (see table 1-4). Based on the experience in Miami-Dade County, the most populous county in the state, it appears as if African Americans were more likely than whites and Hispanics to be incorrectly placed on the convicted felons list.

CONCLUSION

The Voting Rights Act prohibits both intentional discrimination and "results" discrimination. It is within the jurisdictional province of the Justice Department to pursue and a court of competent jurisdiction to decide whether the facts prove or disprove illegal discrimination under either standard. The U.S. Commission on Civil Rights does not adjudicate violations of the law. It does not hold trials or determine civil or criminal liability. It is clearly within the mandate of the Commission, however, to find facts that may be used subsequently as a basis for legislative or executive action designed to protect the voting rights of all eligible persons.

Accordingly, the Commission is duty bound to report, without equivocation, that the analysis presented here supports a disturbing impression that Florida's reliance on a flawed voter exclusion list, combined with the state law placing the burden of removal from the list on the voter, had the result of denying African Americans the right to vote. This analysis also shows that the chance of being placed on this list in error is greater for African Americans. Similarly, the analysis shows a direct correlation between race and having one's vote discounted as a spoiled ballot. In other words, an African American's chance of having his or her vote rejected as a spoiled ballot was significantly greater than a white voter's. Based on the evidence presented to the Commission, there is a strong basis for concluding that section 2 of the VRA was violated.

Chapter 2
First-Hand Accounts of Voter Disenfranchisement

Who are to be the electors of the Federal Representatives? Not the rich more than the poor; not the learned more than the ignorant; not the haughty heirs of distinguished names, more than the humble sons of obscure and unpropitious fortune. The electors are to be the great body of the people of the United States.

Although statistics on spoiled ballots and voter purge lists point to problems in Florida's election, perhaps the most compelling evidence of election irregularities the Commission heard was the first-hand accounts by citizens who encountered obstacles to voting. The following chapter presents individual accounts of voting system failures.

VOTERS NOT ON THE ROLLS AND UNABLE TO APPEAL

On November 7, 2000, millions of Florida voters arrived at their designated polling places to cast their votes. Unfortunately, countless voters were denied the opportunity to vote because their names did not appear on the lists of registered voters. When poll workers attempted to call the supervisors of elections offices to verify voter registration status, they were often met with continuous busy signals or no answer. In accordance with their training, most poll workers refused to permit persons to vote whose names did not appear on the rolls at their precinct. Thus, numerous Floridians were turned away from the polls on Election Day without being allowed to vote and with no opportunity to appeal the poll workers' refusal. The following are a few examples of experiences that Floridians had who were turned away from their polling places.

Citizens Who Were Not Permitted to Vote

Cathy Jackson, an African American woman, has been a registered voter in Broward County since 1996. Upon registering in Broward County, Ms. Jackson was told that if she ever experienced a problem with her voter registration card, she would be allowed to vote if she could produce a valid driver's license. Ms. Jackson voted in Broward without any incident using her driver's license since 1996. However, when she went to her polling place, Precinct 52Z, on November 7, 2000, she was told that her name was not on the list. The poll workers suggested that she travel back to her old precinct in Miami-Dade County to vote. Ms. Jackson did as she was advised even though she had voted in Broward County since she moved from Miami-Dade County in 1996. After waiting 45 minutes at her old precinct, the poll workers in Miami-Dade told Ms. Jackson that her name was not on the rolls and referred her back to Broward to vote.

When Ms. Jackson returned to the Broward precinct, the poll workers advised her to wait while they checked her registration status. While she waited, Ms. Jackson observed a poll worker from another precinct within the same polling place allow an elderly white voter, whose name did not appear on the rolls, to fill out an affidavit and vote. When Ms. Jackson asked if she could do the same, the poll workers explained that she could fill out an affidavit, but that she could not vote until they had verified her registration. The phone lines to the supervisor of elections office, however, remained busy for several hours. Ms. Jackson became upset and eventually left to go to work. Undeterred by these delays, Ms. Jackson returned to her precinct after work to try to vote again, but the poll workers were never able to verify her registration status and refused to allow her to vote.

Donnise DeSouza, an African American, has been registered to vote since 1982 in Miami-Dade County. When she entered the Richmond Fire Station in Miami-Dade County at 6.50 p.m. and showed her identification to the poll worker, Ms. DeSouza was told that her name was not on the rolls. The poll worker directed her to the "problem line," so that her registration status could be verified with the supervisor of elections office. Ms. DeSouza recalled that the line of about 15 people did not move, but at 7.00 p.m. when the poll began to close, a poll worker announced to the group "if our name was not on the roll that she could not let us vote and that there was nothing she could do." The poll workers stopped their attempts to verify the registration status of the voters who had been standing in line. When Ms. DeSouza asked if there was an absentee ballot that would allow her to cast her vote, the poll worker explained that there was nothing he could do.

Ms. DeSouza testified to the Commission that she was "very agitated" and the next day began to register complaints with various sources about her experience. Upon further investigation with the office of the supervisor of elections, she discovered that the poll workers should have continued their efforts to resolve the problems of those voters who were in the precinct prior to the 7.00 p.m. closing time. Furthermore, Ms. DeSouza learned that her name was actually on the rolls of registered voters, because subsequently a worker at the elections office showed her the sheet that contained her name where she should have been allowed to sign. But Ms. DeSouza explained, "at that point [the election was over so] there was nothing they could do and I was deprived of my right to vote."

Angenora Ramsey, an African American former poll worker with 18 years' experience, had changed her address prior to November 7. Based on her familiarity with election procedures, when Ms. Ramsey went to vote at Precinct 62 in Palm Beach County, she completed a change of address affidavit. But when the poll worker tried to call the office of the supervisor of elections to verify Ms. Ramsey's registration status, she was unable to get through. According to Ms. Ramsey, the phone lines remained busy for three and a half hours – a delay she had never experienced during her time as a poll worker. Ultimately, the poll workers refused to allow her to vote because they could not verify her voter status.

Margarita Green, a 75-year-old Cuban American woman, went to vote at the same precinct in Miami-Dade County where she had always voted since becoming a citizen in 1966. When Mrs. Green showed her registration card to the poll worker, she was told that her name was not on the rolls and that she must speak with another poll worker who would look into the problem. Mrs. Green recalled that it took a long time for the poll worker to reach the supervisor of elections because the phone line was busy. When she finally got through, the worker explained that according to their records Mrs. Green had called in 1998 and "erased" herself from the voter list. Although Mrs. Green insisted that she had not called and showed the poll worker her registration card, the poll worker refused to allow her to vote.

R. Jai Howard, vice president of the Florida Agricultural and Mechanical University Student Government Association, testified on behalf of more than 12,000 predominantly African American students. She described the massive voter registration efforts that took place at the school in the months preceding the November 2000 election. The association's efforts continued until October 10, 2000 (the last day to register before the election) and included a rally in which Reverend Jesse Jackson and Ion Sancho, the Leon County supervisor of elections, participated. Despite its efforts, the Student Government Association learned in the days following the election that large numbers of students had problems voting, "including one student who had two voter registration cards with two different precincts, some students who received no voter registration cards, switching of precincts without prior notification, misinformation at precincts, and students who had attempted to register numerous times and never received registration [cards] and were never entered into the system." As a result of these combined problems, many students who believed they had been properly registered were not allowed to vote.

[...]

POLLING PLACES CLOSED OR EARLY OR MOVED WITHOUT NOTICE

Many Floridians experienced extreme frustration on November 7 when they reported to the precincts where they had been voting regularly, in some cases for many years, and discovered that their precincts were no longer being used or had moved to another location without notice from the county supervisor of elections. In other instances, some voters who had been standing in line to vote at their precincts prior to 7.00 p.m. were told that they could not vote because the poll was closed. Under these circumstances, the patience of many Floridians was exhausted.

Polling Places Closed Early

When **Lavonna Lewis**, an African American first-time voter, went to her polling place to vote, she was told by a white poll worker standing outside that the poll was closed. As she turned to leave, the poll worker allowed a white gentleman to walk in and get in line to vote.

Donnise DeSouza arrived at her assigned precinct at 6.30 p.m., but she could not enter until 6.50 p.m., due to the long line of cars parked on the street waiting to gain access to the polling place. Once Ms. DeSouza was finally able to enter the polling place, she waited for another 10 minutes while poll workers verified her registration status. At 7.00 p.m., however, the poll workers announced to Ms. DeSouza and about 15 other voters who were waiting to be helped that they could not vote because the poll was closed.

Susan and **Joel Newman** arrived at the Water Works Department in Palm Beach to vote at approximately 6.15 p.m. Upon their arrival, they noticed:

[T]he iron gates at the entrance were closed, preventing entrance ... Several cars pulled into the entrance lane and tried to attract attention by honking horns and ringing an intercom. We waited 5–10 minutes but no one showed up and the gates remained locked. We drove off thinking we were wrong about the closing time – that the polls must have closed at 6.00. A few blocks away we spotted a police car and pulled up to check. He verified that the polls were open until 7.00. We complained about the situation we had just experienced and he told us to go to the Board of Elections (some 20 minutes away). We drove there and met a policeman as we entered the building. He listened to our complaint and politely told us there was nothing he could do. We would

have to register our complaint with the [supervisor] of elections, Theresa LePore. Unfortunately, he told us her office
had closed at 5.00 p.m. and her staff went home [and] we
would have to complain the following day. We left, realizing
that we would have no opportunity to vote this year.

Millard Suid, a poll worker at the Water Works Department
on John Road in Boynton Beach, confirmed the above poll
closing. He explained that the gates to the property are on an
automatic timer that shuts them every day at 6.15 p.m. When
the automatic timer shut the gates at 6.15 p.m. on Election
Day, however, Mr. Suid stated, "It was a disaster. The people
at the Water Works Department should have known about it
or the people, Theresa LePore, who runs that particular district, should have known about that." When asked if he called
the supervisor of elections to report that the gates had closed,
Mr. Suid testified, "That wouldn't do any good, couldn't get
in. I had called 911 and told the police. Now there was a
young lady at the Water Works Department who worked
there all day and she left at like 5.30 and she said, 'I'll be back
at 7.30 to lock up.' Now she should have known this gate's
going to lock automatically ... That wasn't the first time they
used that. So somebody screwed up."

Robert Weisman, the county administrator for Palm
Beach County, stated in a response to an interrogatory issued
by the Commission after the February 16, 2001, hearing, that
he did not know about the gate-closing incident until the
Commission hearing. He further acknowledged that a subsequent investigation by representatives of the supervisor of
elections office determined that the gate indeed had closed.
Mr. Weisman did not dispute that the automatic locking of
the gate blocked access to the Palm Beach County polling
place before the official closing.
[...]

POLICE PRESENCE AT OR NEAR POLLING SITES
Several Florida voters reported seeing Florida Highway Patrol
(FHP) troopers in and around polling places. Troopers

conducted an unauthorized vehicle checkpoint within a few miles of a polling place in a predominantly African American neighborhood. In another area, trooper vehicles were reportedly parked within sight of at least two polling places, which one resident characterized as "unusual." The FHP reported that troopers only visited polling places to vote on Election Day. In light of the high voter turnout that was expected during the 2000 presidential election, particularly among communities of color that may have a strained relationship with law enforcement, some Floridians questioned the timing of and the motivation for the FHP's actions.

The Florida Election Code provides:

> No person, whether acting under color of law or otherwise, shall intimidate, threaten, or coerce, or attempt to intimidate, threaten or coerce, any other person for the purpose of interfering with the right of such other person to vote or not to vote as that person may choose.

The state of Florida also restricts the presence of law enforcement officers at polling places. Specifically, unless he or she enters the polling place to cast a ballot, no law enforcement officer may enter a polling place without the permission of the clerk or a majority of the inspectors. The clerk or inspectors are required to make an affidavit for the arrest of any law enforcement officer who does not comply with the law. Sheriffs also have a duty under Florida election law to "exercise strict vigilance in the detection of any violations of the election laws and in apprehending the violators."

Charles Hall, director of the Florida Highway Patrol, testified at the Commission's Tallahassee hearing. He explained that the history of increased checkpoints by the FHP began in the early 1980s, when the vehicle inspection laws were repealed. The FHP determined that the most effective way to inspect a large number of vehicles was through driver's license/faulty vehicle equipment checkpoints. He also noted that he had no conversations with the office of the governor, the office of the attorney general, or the office of the secretary of state in preparation for the 2000 presidential election.

Colonel Hall admitted that on November 7, 2000, the FHP established a checkpoint on Oak Ridge Road in Southern Leon County between the hours of 10.00 a.m. and 11.30 a.m. The demographic makeup of the precincts surrounding the Oak Ridge Road checkpoint are as follows: (1) Precinct 107 is 82 percent Caucasian and 13 percent African American; (2) Precinct 109 is 37 percent Caucasian and 57 percent African American; and (3) Precinct 110 is 70 percent Caucasian and 24 percent African American. Approximately 150 vehicles were stopped as a result of the Oak Ridge Road checkpoint that day. According to FHP records, of the 16 citizens who received notices of faulty equipment, six (37 percent) were people of color.

On the afternoon of Election Day, the FHP received notice of a complaint to the attorney general's office that FHP troopers had hindered people of color from arriving at polling places due to the Oak Ridge Road checkpoint. Colonel Hall indicated that "the FHP was the first statewide law enforcement agency in the county to voluntarily begin collecting data concerning traffic stops in response to the racial profiling issue." The racial breakdown of the 150 drivers stopped at that checkpoint on Election Day, however, is not available.

As a result of its investigation, the FHP found that some policy violations had occurred, but concluded that no citizen was unreasonably delayed or prohibited from voting as a result of the Oak Ridge Road checkpoint. The policy violations cited by FHP's investigators included the fact that the checkpoint site was not on the monthly preapproved list and the media notification policy was not followed. The investigators recommended "counseling" for the sergeant in charge of the checkpoint and the district commander in charge of the media notification.

Colonel Hall stated the FHP was "very concerned about the perception people may have about what the patrol did that day." The Commission heard testimony from voters in Tallahassee regarding their reaction to the FHP's actions on

Election Day. Roberta Tucker, an African American woman and a longtime resident of Tallahassee, was driving along Oak Ridge Road on her way to vote. Before Ms. Tucker could reach her polling place, she was stopped at an FHP vehicle checkpoint conducted by approximately five white troopers. According to Ms. Tucker, the checkpoint was located at the only main road leading to her assigned polling place. One of the troopers approached Ms. Tucker's car, asked for her driver's license, and after looking at it, returned it to her and allowed her to proceed. Ms. Tucker considered the trooper's actions to be "suspicious" because "nothing was checked, my lights, signals, or anything that [the state patrol] usually check." She also recalled being "curious" about the checkpoint because she had never seen a checkpoint at this location. Ms. Tucker added that she felt "intimidated" because "it was an Election Day and it was a big election and there were only white officers there and like I said, they didn't ask me for anything else, so I was suspicious at that."

In response to the allegations of voter intimidation surrounding this checkpoint, Colonel Hall stated that "the checkpoint was properly conducted, and it was not anywhere near a polling facility, and I don't see how that could affect anybody's ability to vote." He added that he was "not really" surprised to learn that a trooper may have asked for a driver's license and not registration. He explained that such an action could occur if vehicles had begun to back up. Moreover, Colonel Hall stated he was "disappointed" that the FHP could not speak with Ms. Tucker because she refused to cooperate with their investigation. Ms. Tucker testified, however, that she reported the incident to her local NAACP and never returned the FHP's calls because "I felt it was a civil rights issue ... I felt like it was sort of discriminatory."
[...]

CONCLUSION

A wide variety of concerns have been raised regarding the use and effectiveness of Florida's voting system controls during the 2000 presidential election. Many Floridians were denied their opportunity to vote, in what proved to be a historic general election because of the narrow vote margin separating the candidates. Some voters were turned away from their designated polling places because their names did not appear on the lists of registered voters. Other voters discovered that their precincts were no longer being used or had moved to another location, without notice from the supervisor of elections office. In other instances, voters who had been standing in line to vote at their precincts prior to closing, were told that they could not vote because the poll was closed. In addition, thousands of voters who had registered at motor vehicle licensing offices were not on the rolls when they came to vote. The Commission also heard from several voters who saw Florida Highway Patrol troopers in and around polling places, while other troopers conducted an unauthorized vehicle checkpoint within a few miles of a polling place in a predominantly African American neighborhood.

The Commission's investigation demonstrated an urgent need for attention to this issue by Florida's state and local officials, particularly as it relates to the implementation of statewide election reforms. Without some effective redress, the pervasive problems that surfaced in the 2000 election will be repeated.

DOMINIQUE STRAUSS-KAHN

Alors. It was the middle of the night in Paris on 14 May 2011 when the news broke that Dominique Strauss-Kahn, the Chief of the International Monetary Fund had been pulled off Air France flight 23 in New York and arrested for sexual assault on a hotel maid at the city's Sofitel Hotel. Strauss-Kahn – or "DSK" as he is widely known in his homeland of *la Belle* France – protested his innocence, stated that the incident was consensual, and lo! conspiracy theories asserting that he was the victim of a "honey trap" immediately viralled over the blogosphere. And not just the blogosphere; one opinion poll found that nearly 60 per cent of French society believed that a sting operation had placed the West African immigrant maid in a $3,000 a night Sofitel suite to discredit DSK. No less than Vladimir Putin, the Russian prime minister, hinted that DSK had likely fallen victim of a shadowy plot: "It is hard for me to evaluate the real political underlying reasons and I do not even want to get into that subject, but I cannot believe that everything is as it seems and how it was initially presented … It does not sit right in my head."

The most believable conspiracy theory as to *why* DSK was framed concerns the French presidential election: the silver-haired politician had been set to announce his candidacy for the 2012 French presidential elections – and was likely to be the Parti Socialiste's strongest runner against President Sarkozy. By this version of the DSK conspiracy, Sarkozy wanted to eliminate DSK from the race, so set him up for a sex-baited trap.

The evidence? The most interesting "proof" from proponents of the Sarko-dunnit theory is the curious timing of a Tweet.

Before the media broke the story of Strauss-Kahn's arrest, Jonathan Pinet, a youth activist in Sarkozy's UMP party tweeted "a friend in the US just told me that #DSK was arrested by the police in a NYC hotel one hour ago". The tweet was posted at 4.59 p.m. New York time, just ten minutes after Mr Strauss-Kahn was seized, raising questions on how Pinet had obtained the information so fast. And why he tweeted "hotel" when DSK was arrested on an Air France jet. Pinet's tweet was almost immediately retweeted by Arnaud Dassier, a journalist known to be a DSK-loather, and who had published an infamous anti-DSK article featuring the IMF chief in a Porsche with his wife – not great publicity for a socialist man of the people. The first website to mention the news was 24heuresactu.com, a conservative operation. Meanwhile *Le Monde* quoted an unnamed "right-wing heavyweight" as saying, "It happened as planned," and a user of Post.fr accused Pinet of participating in "a carefully orchestrated operation" by the UMP.

Interestingly, Strauss-Kahn had previously given an off-the-record interview with France's *Libération* newspaper saying he suspected that his enemies would plot to destroy his career. He imagined "a woman (who I supposedly) raped in a car park and who had been promised 500,000 or a million euros to invent such a story." A woman like the Sofitel maid Nafissatou Diallo, perhaps, who was not quite the innocent mother portrayed by the prosecutor's office, having apparently lied in her asylum application and married a drug-dealer.

By the weird coincidence every good conspiracy needs, DSK's room number at the Sofitel was 2806, which corresponds to the date of the opening of the Socialist Party primaries in France, 28 June.

According to another, minority, strand of the "*l'affaire* DSK", the sixty-three-year-old Frenchman was an innocent victim in a much bigger scheme. Michelle Sabban, a supporter of Strauss-Kahn and Vice-President of the Regional Council of Ile-de-France, told *Le Monde*: "I am convinced it is an international conspiracy. It's not like him. Everyone knows that his weakness is seduction, women. That's how they got him ... It's the IMF that they wanted to decapitate, not just the candidate in the Socialist primary."

A number of prominent economists stepped forward to explain that under Socialist DSK the IMF had taken a pro-left, pro-Third World tilt. They quoted his words in an address at George Washington University: "Globalisation has delivered a lot ... but it also has a dark side, a large and growing chasm between the rich and the poor. Clearly we need a new form of globalisation to prevent the 'invisible hand' of loosely regulated markets from becoming 'an invisible fist'."

Paul Craig Roberts, Assistant Secretary of the US Treasury in Reagan's time, added his dime's worth in a syndicated column: "Strauss-Kahn is being framed up because the IMF recently announced that 'the age of America is over', that China will be the number one economy within five years. This was a massive blow to Washington, and they are taking their revenge."

Meanwhile, news reports from Russia suggested that DSK was arrested because he had discovered that the USA was stalling in its pledged delivery of 191.3 tons of gold to fund the Special Drawing Rights. Another report out of Russia, picked up by the *EU Times*, stated that: "a new report prepared for Prime Minister Putin by the Federal Security Service (FSB) says that former International Monetary Fund (IMF) Chief Dominique Strauss-Kahn was charged and jailed in the US for sex crimes on May 14th after his discovery that all of the gold held in the United States Bullion Depository located at Fort Knox was 'missing and/or unaccounted' for."

The verdict on *l'affaire* DSK: there is little reason to suspect that Pinet's tweet was anything other that what he said it was – message from a friend working at the Sofitel in Manhattan. Dessaier, as a known opponent of DSK, could hardly be expected to have done anything other than retweet with glee. Although bluffing cannot be ruled out, it is significant that the French interior minister, Claude Guéant – a close associate of President Nicolas Sarkozy – dismissed as "scandalous" suggestions made by DSK's Socialist pals that his arrest in New York was organized in Paris. Guéant advised Socialist politicians to "make a formal legal complaint ... or shut up." Similarly, the French Accor hotel group, which owns the Sofitel Hotel in Manhattan where the sexual attack allegedly took place, threatened legal action against anyone who suggested that the company had been involved in a plot against Mr Strauss-Kahn. And the idea that DSK was a tribune of the people at the IMF is risible. Ask the people of Greece.

The most likely explanation of the DSK affair is the most obvious one. DSK had a reputation as a predatory womanizer. "The only real problem with Strauss-Kahn," Jean Quatremer of *Libération* had noted in 2007, "is his attitude to women. He is too insistent ..." Despite being married to French TV reporter (and multi-millionairess) Anne Sinclair, he had an affair with a junior Hungarian colleague at the IMF. After DSK's arrest at JFK airport, the French journalist Tristane Banon came forward to announce that DSK had made a sexual attack on her a number of years before. Strauss-Kahn was not helped by the news that Nicolas Sarkozy, the man who put him up as IMF president, advised him to keep his trousers zipped in America and not to get into elevators with interns.

The criminal charges against DSK were eventually dismissed at the request of the prosecution due to serious doubts about Diallo's credibility (see Document, p.533). At this point, supporters of Ms Diallo suggested that *she* was the victim of conspiracy involving the best lawyers and muckrakers money can buy.

Oh, and DSK's nickname? Le Perv.

Dominique Strauss-Kahn, IMF big *fromage*, was victim of a "honey pot" sting operation designed to bring down his presidential candidacy/headship of IMF: ALERT LEVEL 4

DOCUMENT: RECOMMENDATION FOR DISMISSAL: THE PEOPLE OF THE STATE OF NEW YORK AGAINST DOMINIQUE STRAUSS-KAHN

The People of the State of New York move to dismiss the above-captioned indictment, which charges the defendant with sexually assaulting the complainant at a hotel in midtown Manhattan on May 14, 2011. The crimes charged in the indictment require the People to prove beyond a reasonable doubt that the defendant engaged in a sexual act with the complainant using forcible compulsion and without her consent. After an extensive investigation, it is clear that proof of two critical elements – force and lack of consent – would rest solely on the testimony of the complaining witness at trial. The physical, scientific, and other evidence establishes that the defendant engaged in a hurried sexual encounter with the complainant, but it does not independently establish her claim of a forcible, nonconsensual encounter. Aside from the complainant and the defendant, there are no other eye-witnesses to the incident. Undeniably, then, for a trial jury to find the defendant guilty, it must be persuaded beyond a reasonable doubt that the complainant is credible. Indeed, the case rises and falls on her testimony. At the time of the indictment, all available evidence satisfied us that the complainant was reliable. But evidence gathered in our post-indictment investigation severely undermined her reliability as a witness in this case. That an individual has lied in the past or committed criminal acts does not necessarily render them unbelievable to us as prosecutors, or keep us from putting them on the witness stand at trial. But the nature and number of the complainant's falsehoods leave us unable to credit her version of events beyond a reasonable doubt, whatever the truth may be about the encounter between the complainant and the defendant. If we do not believe her beyond a reasonable doubt, we cannot ask a jury to do so.

We have summarized below the circumstances that have led us to this conclusion. This is is not a case where undue scrutiny or a heightened standard is being imposed on a complainant. Instead, we are confronted with a situation in which it has become increasingly clear that the complainant's credibility cannot withstand the most basic evaluation. In short, the complainant has provided shifting and inconsistent versions of the events surrounding the alleged assault, and as a result, we cannot be sufficiently certain of what actually happened on May 14, 2011, or what account of these events the complainant would give at trial. In virtually every substantive interview with prosecutors, despite entreaties to simply be truthful, she has not been truthful, on matters great and small, many pertaining to her background and some relating to the circumstances of the incident itself. Over the course of two interviews, for example, the complainant gave a vivid, highly detailed, and convincing account of having been raped in her native country, which she now admits is entirely false. She also gave prosecutors and the grand jury accounts of her actions immediately after the encounter with the defendant that she now admits are false. This longstanding pattern of untruthfulness predates the complainant's contact with this Office. Our investigation revealed that the complainant has made numerous prior false statements, including ones contained in government filings, some of which were made under oath or penalty of perjury. All of these falsehoods would, of course, need to be disclosed to a jury at trial, and their cumulative effect would be devastating. Finally, we have conducted a thorough investigation in an effort to uncover any evidence that might speak to the nature of the sexual encounter between the complainant and the defendant. All of the evidence that might be relevant to the contested issues of force and lack of consent is simply inconclusive. We do not make this recommendation lightly. Our grave concerns about the complainant's reliability make it impossible to resolve the question of what exactly happened in the defendant's hotel suite on May 14, 2011, and therefore preclude further prosecution of this case. Accordingly, we respectfully recommend that the indictment be dismissed.

SUBLIMINAL ADVERTISING

RATS.

Just one of the dirty tricks George W. Bush was accused of in the **Stolen Elections** of 2000 and 2004 was using subliminal messages – something near imperceptible to the eye, but which the brain records anyway. In a Republican advert dissing Al Gore the word "RATS" appeared for a second before morphing into "THE GORE PRESCRIPTION PLAN: BUREAUCRATS DECIDE". You can pick out R-A-T-S from "BUREAUCRATS" yourself. The advert was shown 4,400 times.

Subliminal messages first hit the headlines, however, with another horror story, *The Exorcist*, back in 1973. When it was shown in cinemas, people flocked out vomiting and screaming. Eventually, the filmmakers confessed to having added single frames, lasting for a mere 1/48 of a second, with demon faces into the movie. Conversely, the images of a topless woman in Disney's *The Rescuers* presumably had dads glued to their seats.

The power of subliminal messaging inevitably appealed to advertisers who, as Vance Packard's classic *The Hidden Persuaders* recorded, manipulated customers by the million. A follow up tome by Dr Wilson Bryan Key, *Subliminal Seduction*, contained even more lurid tales of advertising companies sticking in secret messages, mostly of sexual gratification if they want you to buy it. (Sex sells: Coca-Cola's Australian ad which headlined "Feel the Curves" and had a drawing of a girl practising fellatio hidden in the ice cubes is now a collector's item.) The ensuing public panic led the Federal Communications Commission to sit and stroke their chins before deciding on 29 January 1974:

Subliminal Programming. The FCC sometimes receives complaints regarding the alleged use of subliminal techniques in radio and television programming. Subliminal programming is designed to be perceived on a subconscious level only. The Commission has held that the use of subliminal perception is inconsistent with the obligations of a licensee and contrary to the public interest because, whether effective or not, such broadcasts are intended to be deceptive.

Under this regulation, FCC-licensed TV and radio stations are banned from knowingly broadcasting programming containing subliminal messages. The FCC issued its regulation in response to a 1974 TV commercial for the toy Husker Du which repeatedly flashed the phrase "Get It".

End of story? Not quite. Because as the Gore case highlighted, hidden symbols can be dismissed by the accused as a mistake or as coincidence. And so everyone pretty much carried on as before.

But all this selling commodities or denigrating political opponents is penny ante stuff, because the truly important hidden messages are the symbols of the **Bavarian Illuminati** and its satanic project. Take a look at CBS's logo with its ocular image, which conspiracists insist is the All-Seeing Eye, the emblem of Freemasonry, the middle-aged white men's front for the Illuminati. Then turn McDonald's golden arches clockwise by ninety degrees and you get the number three – a sacred number in Freemasonry, because it symbolizes the Deity. Adidas? Run and have a look at the sports manufacturer's logo, it is a triangle – another form of three. Texaco's logo is a pentagram (well, almost), the sign the Illuminati use to mark their territory in much the way a dog pees on a lamppost.

Freakiest of all subliminal messages is on US $20 bill. When folded in half there can be seen the image of the World Trade Center in flames. And so the evil Illuminati announced their intention to the world ...

Mmm.

Illuminati hide symbols of their satanic power and plots in corporate logos: ALERT LEVEL 1

Further Reading
Vance Packard, *The Hidden Persuaders*, 1957

SYNARCHY

Alexandre Saint-Yves d'Alveydre was a nineteenth-century French conservative *philosophe* who, looking at the world around him, believed that there was too much competition between the spheres of Economics, Politics, and Religion. Dire Anarchy was about to ensue. To avoid this dread fate, d'Alveydre prescribed a system of rule whereby the top men from all three spheres would work together in a secret circle for peace and prosperity. He lashed together the Greek "syn" (together) and "archy" (rule) to describe this system of harmonious governance by an elite. Come to think of it, he lashed bits of Plato together to make up the philosophy in the first place.

Anyway, so far so explicable; thereafter synarchism became a term that meant almost anything to any *homme*.

- Some theorists suggest that d'Alveydre was an occultist who telepathically communicated with "ascended masters" of the universe, whose HQ is a cave called Agarttha. For alternative historians Lynn Picknett and Clive Prince d'Alveydre's occult synarchy is the big conspiratorial beast behind the Priory of Sion, the European Union ... Umberto Eco treads similar ground in his novel *Foucault's Pendulum*.
- In 1922, or thereabouts, a Mouvement Synarchtique d'Empire was reportedly formed to replace French democracy with a right-wing dictatorship. The proto-fascists of the "Movement for a Synarchist Empire" were joined in the thirties by a military clique around Admiral Darlan and businessmen who wanted collaboration with Hitler. Vichy

France has been defined as synarchy in action. The fullest account of the MSE is contained in a document entitled "Pacte Synarchique". Which may well be a hoax. A number of academic studies, including Olivier Dard's *La synarchie, le mythe du complot permanent* (1998), suggest that French synarchism was non-existent hooey, although the French fascist **Cagoule** group did draw for "inspiration" on d'Alveydre's ideas.

- The *Executive Intelligence Review* of Lyndon LaRouche Jr has published copiously on synarchism, where it is defined as:

> a name adopted during the Twentieth Century for an occult freemasonic sect, known as the Martinists, based on worship of the tradition of the Emperor Napoleon Bonaparte. During the interval from the early 1920s through 1945, it was officially classed by U.S.A. and other nations' intelligence services under the file name of "Synarchism: Nazi/Communist," so defined because of its deploying simultaneously both ostensibly opposing pro-communist and extreme right-wing forces for encirclement of a targeted government. Twentieth-Century and later fascist movements, like most terrorist movements, are all Synarchist creation ... It is typified by the followers of the late Leo Strauss and Alexandre Kojève today ... is found among both nominally left-wing and also extreme right-wing factions such as the editorial board of the *Wall Street Journal* ... The underlying authority behind these cults is a contemporary network of private banks of that medieval Venetian model known as *fondi*.

The neo-Conservative thinker Leo Strauss has certainly wielded influence in the twentieth century, especially in America where economist Paul Wolfowitz and historian Francis Fukuyama might both be termed "Straussians". Disappointingly, there is little verifiable evidence of an actual synarchist cabal, which is what you would expect from a super-shadowy super-elite. Or a fantasy.

Quasi-fascists in plot to take over the globe: ALERT
LEVEL 3

Further Reading
Umberto Eco, *Foucault's Pendulum*, 1988
Alexandre Saint-Yves d'Alveydre, *La France vraie ou la Mission
   des Français*, 1887

THE THIRD SECRET OF FÁTIMA

On 13 July 1917, at around noon, a vision of the Virgin Mary appeared (allegedly) before three young shepherd girls at Fátima in Portugal. It was not the first or last time the Madonna revealed herself to the children, Lucia Santos and her cousins Francisco and Jacinta Marto, but on this occasion She entrusted them with three secrets. Although the Roman Catholic Church generally pooh-poohs visions, the children were so convincing that their account received Vatican approval and the site where "Our Lady of Fátima" had descended became a holy shrine. Of course, authentication was helped by the fact that 50,000 people also saw the Marian visions, and the sun was said to dance in the sky.

The Marto children both died in the great flu pandemic of 1919, but Lucia went on to become a nun, and in 1941 was prevailed upon by the Bishop of Leira, Jose da Silva, to reveal the first two prophecies to assist with the canonization of Francisco and Marta. The first secret was a vision of Hell, complete with demons and blackened human souls; the second prophecy predicted the end of World War I and the start-up of World War II (which of course was already well under way by 1941); the third secret revealed ... Well, Lucia on considered reflection decided that this was a secret not to be told.

Two years later, however, as Lucia teetered on the edge of death, da Silva persuaded her to write down the third secret so it could be known in case of her death. She did so, and the written prophecy was dispatched forthwith to the Vatican with the proviso that 1960 was the earliest year in which it could be opened for general gaze. Before then, the secret was for the pope's eyes only.

The year 1960 came – and the Vatican failed to release the text of the third vision. Then, 1961 passed with no release of the secret text, 1962, 1963 ... Not until 2000 was the Third Secret of Fátima revealed, by which time suspicions about what it foretold had gone into overdrive. The publication of the text (see Document, p.543) did little to quell the queries. According to the official Vatican line, the text foretold the attempted assassination of **Pope John Paul II**, centring as it did on "a man clothed in white who falls to the ground apparently dead". (John Paul II had a special affinity with Our Lady of Fátima; Mehmet Ağca tried to whack him on the 13 July, the anniversary of the Madonna granting the secrets to the girls, and the pontiff believed that Mary's hand guided the bullets away from his vital organs.) Admittedly an attempted assassination of a pope is a Bad Thing, but Cardinal Ratzinger, later Pope Benedict XVI, had once stated on the record that the third secret dealt with nothing less than "the End Times". And why had Sister Lucia – who was still alive in 2000, having recovered from her illness in the 1940s – been sworn to secrecy about a secret that was now no longer secret? And was a prophecy about a papal whacking really worth hiding for forty years?

Very helpfully, the Vatican issued an image of the four pages of Lucia's handwritten account of the Third Secret. This was petrol to the flames of controversy: Lucia herself, along with a bevy of Vatican prelates who had sighted the text, all commented that it was written down as a one-page letter. These witnesses included Father Joaquin Alonso, the official Fátima archivist for sixteen years.

Many "Fátamists", as those in the Catholic Church who are cynical of the Vatican's line on the Third Secret are dubbed, believe that there are two Third Secret texts, with the first a single page containing the words of the Blessed Virgin and the other a description of the vision. All this, of course, begs the question – what is in the suppressed portion? According to arch-Fátamist Father Nicholas Gruener, the secret portion is a prophecy that the Vatican itself will be taken over by Satan and the Roman Catholic Church will suffer a crisis of faith.

Little wonder, then, that the top men of the Vatican City have kept the important bit of the third prophecy locked tightly away in the archives.

Vatican is covering up prophecy predicting Fall of the
Vatican to Apostasy: ALERT LEVEL 9

Further Reading
Christopher Ferrara, *The Secret Still Hidden*, 2008
Antonio Socci, *Il Quatrro Segretto di Fátima*, 2006

DOCUMENT: SISTER LUCIA, THE THIRD PART OF THE SECRET REVEALED AT THE COVA DA IRIA-FÁTIMA ON 13 JULY 1917

I write in obedience to you, my God, who command me to do
so through his Excellency the Bishop of Leiria and through
your Most Holy Mother and mine.

After the two parts which I have already explained, at the
left of Our Lady and a little above, we saw an Angel with a
flaming sword in his left hand; flashing, it gave out flames that
looked as though they would set the world on fire; but they
died out in contact with the splendour that Our Lady radiated towards him from her right hand: pointing to the earth
with his right hand, the Angel cried out in a loud voice:
"Penance, Penance, Penance!" And we saw in an immense
light that is God: "something similar to how people appear in
a mirror when they pass in front of it" a Bishop dressed in
White "we had the impression that it was the Holy Father".

Other Bishops, Priests, men and women Religious going
up a steep mountain, at the top of which there was a big Cross
of rough-hewn trunks as of a cork-tree with the bark; before
reaching there the Holy Father passed through a big city half
in ruins and half trembling with halting step, afflicted with
pain and sorrow, he prayed for the souls of the corpses he met
on his way; having reached the top of the mountain, on his
knees at the foot of the big Cross he was killed by a group of
soldiers who fired bullets and arrows at him, and in the same
way there died one after another the other Bishops, Priests,

men and women Religious, and various lay people of different ranks and positions. Beneath the two arms of the Cross there were two Angels each with a crystal aspersorium in his hand, in which they gathered up the blood of the Martyrs and with it sprinkled the souls that were making their way to God.

THE THULE SOCIETY

Occult-loving Nazis piloting flying saucers? You couldn't make it up.

Could you?

In 1912 veteran German occultist Rudolf von Sebottendorf set up the Thule Society, the name taken from the legendary continent in the Far North where, by repute, had lived the original Aryan civilization – who had divined the secrets of the Universe. By means of mystical rituals, Sebottendorf sought to imbibe said ancient wisdoms of Thule, which would accordingly endow Sebottendorf and his fellow initiates with superior powers.

Sebottendorf was also a virulent anti-Semite, so rather more of the Thule Society's energy went into denouncing Jews than communing with the spirits of the original master race. Despite damning Freemasonry as a Jewish plot, the Thule Society ironically modelled its structures and symbolisms on Freemasonry. It also adopted the swastika as its emblem.

The connection between the Thule Society and the Nazi Party extended to rather more than a liking for the swastika. Two Thule Society members, Anton Drexler and Karl Harrer, set up the fledgling German Workers Party, soon to become the National Socialist German Workers Party – the Nazi Party. Ernst Rohm and Rudolf Hess, both key players in the early Nazi Party, were also Thule Society members.

Under the tutelage of the Nazis, Germany made significant advances in military and aviation technology – far more so than the Allied powers who fought her between 1939 and 1945. By the end of the Second World War, the Germans had fielded the first jet fighter, the "cruise missile" V-1, the ballistic V-2, not to mention the Me163 rocket plane.

Advancing into the ruins of Nazi Germany, the Americans were quick to notice the superiority of Nazi avionics, and promptly recruited hundreds of scientists and technicians in **Project Paperclip**.

But was German military technology so far advanced because Nazi mystics were in contact with the inhabitants of the Isle of Thule? And did the Nazis even get as far as building flying saucers? Someone who believes all the above is UFO researcher Vladimir Terziski, President of the American Academy of Dissident Sciences. According to Terziski, the occult Thule Society (and the **Vril Society**, too) established clear lines of communication with the "Thulians" in the inter-war period, who then generously passed on their superior technical knowledge to SS Military Technical Branch E-IV. In turn SS Military Branch E-IV was not only able to build jets and rockets, but flying saucers which reached the Moon in 1942. And Mars a little later.

A more mundane use for the saucers came in 1945, when they whisked Adolf Hitler from his Berlin bunker to a secret underground base in Antarctica. Terziski has the film footage of the base, known as "New Schwabia".

If all this was not extraordinary enough, it turns out that the beings from Thule were not actually humans – but aliens.

What proto-Nazis like Rudolf von Sebottendorf would have made of the knowledge that they were descended from little green men and not white supermen can only be guessed at. What can be said with certainty is that the Luftwaffe did not need alien technology for its futuristic designs. The Treaty of Versailles at the end of World War I forbade Germany to build military aircraft. So, frustrated aircraft designers turned their attention to designing extreme shapes for the new sport of gliding. The case in point were the Horten brothers, who were building delta-winged gliders in the 1930s. When Germany under Hitler re-armed, the Horton boys built "flying wing" jet planes for the Luftwaffe. Then there was Professor Heinrich Focke who patented a flying-disc design in 1939, Alexander

Lippisch who helped build the delta-winged Me163 rocket plane, Arthur Sack who constructed an aircraft with a circular wing ... The Germans did not need alien technology. They could do it all by themselves. Vorsprung durch Technik, as they say.

Occult German society communed with inhabitants of lost land to learn flying saucer technology: ALERT 1

THE TONKIN GULF INCIDENT

By early 1964 South Vietnam seemed to be losing the war against its Communist insurgency, sponsored by Ho Chi Minh's regime in North Vietnam. This was a major concern to the US, which feared a "domino effect" should the South fall, in which country after country in Asia would turn Red. To aid the South Vietnamese effort, President Lyndon B. Johnson provided a number of fast patrol boats; ostensibly these were for defensive purposes, but secret OPLAN-34A sanctioned them for covert attacks on North Vietnamese military targets. US warships, operating in international waters just off the North's coast, were to direct the operations.

On the night of 4 August, two US Navy destroyers, the *C. Turner Joy* and the *Maddox*, were patrolling the Gulf of Tonkin off the North Vietnamese coast when they came under apparent torpedo-attack from North Vietnamese PT boats. President Johnson, after assessing North Vietnamese radio intercepts and on the advice of Admiral Ulysses S. Grant Sharp, went on national TV to denounce North Vietnam's "open aggression on the open seas". Within three days Congress had passed the Gulf of Tonkin Resolution (there were just two dissensions in the Senate, see Document, p.550), which authorized the president "To take all necessary measures to repel any armed attack against the forces of the United States and to prevent further aggression ... [and] to take all necessary steps, including the use of armed force, to assist any member or protocol state of the Southeast Asia Collective Defense Treaty requesting assistance in defense of its freedom."

Up to 7 August 1964, the US had only been "advising" in the Vietnam War. From that day forth, it was fighting it. A campaign of heavy bombing was ordered immediately, and by early 1965 thousands of US troops were arriving in theatre almost daily.

According to the *Los Angeles Times*, "the Communists, by their attack on American vessels in international waters, have themselves escalated hostilities". The North Vietnamese started it!

Or, perhaps, not. Even on 4 August there were doubts that the *Maddox* and *C. Turner Joy* had actually come under attack. The *Maddox*'s captain blamed "freak weather conditions" for affecting the radio, while Admiral Grant Sharp of the Pacific Fleet cited edgy personnel, adding in a communiqué to the White House, "A lot of these torpedo attacks were from the sonar operators!"

The personnel on the US ships were definitely hyped up, because the *Maddox* had come under attack two days previously. Why did the US Government not denounce North Vietnamese aggression on that occasion? Because the *Maddox* had been operating illegally and provocatively *inside* North Vietnamese waters. The radio decrypts used to justify the official account of the Gulf of Tonkin almost definitely relate to 2 August, not 4 August.

Nearly fifty years later, the weight of evidence is that the "incident" in the Gulf of Tonkin was a fabricated pretext for the US to step up its involvement in Vietnam. In the words of the US Navy Historical Center, "North Vietnamese naval forces did not attack *Maddox* and *Turner Joy* that night.' The defense secretary at the time, Robert McNamara, admitted in a 2001 TV documentary *The Fog of War: Eleven Lessons from the Life of Robert S. McNamara*, that the US "initiated the action". The same documentary revealed that five weeks before Tonkin, Johnson had told McNamara over the phone, "I want to be able to trap these people [the North Vietnamese]."

Lyndon B. Johnson was gunning for war. By the tramlines of his morality, Johnson acted justifiably in escalating the conflict with a "white lie" because he hoped to keep the people of South Vietnam free of Communist totalitarianism. Less generously,

Professor Peter Dale Scott has suggested that Johnson was encouraged by the oil corporations to intervene, since they wanted control of the "considerable offshore oil deposits in the South China Sea". In this oily scenario President **John F. Kennedy** had been assassinated for his peacenik signing of National Security Action Memorandum 263, which reduced the number of military advisors in South Vietnam. The oil boys wanted more army boots on the ground, not less.

Why exactly the Tonkin Gulf incident was faked up may never be known, but faked it was.

President Lyndon B. Johnson fabricated the Gulf of Tonkin Incident in order to justify escalation of the Vietnam War: ALERT LEVEL 10

Further Reading
Peter Dale Scott, *The War Conspiracy*, 1972

DOCUMENT: TONKIN GULF RESOLUTION AND US SENTATE DEBATE

Eighty-eighth Congress of the United States of America
AT THE SECOND SESSION
Begun and held at the City of Washington on Tuesday, the seventh day of January, one thousand nine hundred and sixty-four

Joint Resolution
To promote the maintenance of international peace and security in southeast Asia.

Whereas naval units of the Communist regime in Vietnam, in violation of the principles of the Charter of the United Nations and of international law, have deliberately and repeatedly attacked United States naval vessels lawfully present in international waters, and have thereby created a serious threat to international peace; and Whereas these attackers are part of deliberate and systematic campaign of aggression that the Communist regime in North Vietnam has been waging against its neighbors and the nations joined with them in the collective defense of their freedom; and Whereas the United States is assisting the peoples of southeast Asia to protect their freedom and has no territorial, military or political ambitions in that area, but desires only that these people should be left in peace to work out their destinies in their own way: Now, therefore be it *Resolved by the Senate and House of Representatives of the United States of America in Congress assembled,* That the Congress approves and supports the determination of the President, as Commander in Chief, to take all necessary measures to repel any armed attack against the forces of the United States and to prevent further aggression.

Section 2. The United States regards as vital to its national interest and to world peace the maintenance of international peace and security in southeast Asia. Consonant with the Constitution of the United States and the Charter of the United Nations and in accordance with its obligations under the Southeast Asia Collective Defense Treaty, the United States is, therefore, prepared, as the President determines, to take all necessary steps, including the use of armed force, to assist any member or protocol state of the Southeast Asia Collective Defense Treaty requesting assistance in defense of its freedom.

Section 3. This resolution shall expire when the President shall determine that the peace and security of the area is reasonably assured by international conditions created by action of the United Nations or otherwise, except that it may be terminated earlier by concurrent resolution of the Congress

Senate Debate: [Extracts]
MR. NELSON:
[Gaylord Nelson, Dem.–Wis.] ... Am I to understand that it is the sense of Congress that we are saying to the executive branch: "If it becomes necessary to prevent further

aggression, we agree now, in advance, that you may land as many divisions as deemed necessary, and engage in a direct military assault on North Vietnam if it becomes the judgment of the Executive, the Commander in Chief, that this is the only way to prevent further aggression"?

MR. FULBRIGHT:

[William Fulbright, Dem.–Ark] As I stated, section 1 is intended to deal primarily with aggression against our forces ... I do not know what the limits are. I do not think this resolution can be determinative of that fact. I think it would indicate that he [the President] would take reasonable means first to prevent any further aggression, or repel further aggression against our own forces ... I do not know how to answer the Senator's question and give him an absolute assurance that large numbers of troops would not be put ashore. I would deplore it ...

MR. NELSON: ... My concern is that we in Congress could give the impression to the public that we are prepared at this time to change our mission and substantially expand our commitment. If that is what the sense of Congress is, I am opposed to the resolution. I therefore ask the distinguished Senator from Arkansas if he would consent to accept an amendment [that explicitly says Congress wants no extension of the present military conflict and no U.S. direct military involvement].

MR. FULBRIGHT: ... The Senator has put into his amendment a statement of policy that is unobjectionable. However, I cannot accept the amendment under the circumstances. I do not believe it is contrary to the joint resolution, but it is an enlargement. I am informed that the House is now voting on this resolution. The House joint resolution is about to be presented to us. I cannot accept the amendment and go to conference with it, and thus take responsibility for delaying matters .

MR. GRUENING: [Ernest Gruening, Dem.–Alaska] ... Regrettably, I find myself in disagreement with the President's Southeast Asian policy ... The serious events of the past few days, the attack by North Vietnamese vessels on American warships and our reprisal, strikes me as the inevitable and foreseeable concomitant and consequence of U.S. unilateral military aggressive policy in Southeast Asia ... We now are about to authorize the President if he sees fit to move our Armed Forces ... not only into South Vietnam, but also into North Vietnam, Laos, Cambodia, Thailand, and of course the authorization includes all the rest of the SEATO nations. That means sending our American boys into combat in a war in which we have no business. which is not our war, into which we have been misguidedly drawn, which is steadily being escalated. This resolution is a further authorization for escalation unlimited. I am opposed to sacrificing a single American boy in this venture. We have lost far too many already ...

MR. MORSE: [Wayne Morse, Dem.–Ore.] ... I believe that history will record that we have made a great mistake in subverting and circumventing the Constitution of the United States ... I believe this resolution to be a historic mistake. I believe that within the next century, future generations will look with dismay and great disappointment upon a Congress which is now about to make such a historic mistake.

SOURCE: Congressional Record. August 6–7, 1964. Pp. 18132–33, 18406–7, 18458–59, and 18470–71.

TURIN SHROUD

The Turin Shroud is a 14-feet long strip of linen that carries the faint image of a long-haired man with a beard. A man with wounds consistent with crucifixion. A man with the mark of a lance wound in his side. A man with cuts along his forehead as though he had worn a crown of thorns.

Jesus Christ! (As it were.) The Shroud of Turin is the shroud in which the Saviour was buried, his image being transferred onto the cloth!

Well, maybe.

Ever since the shroud appeared in northern France around 1350, there have been doubts about its authenticity. One of its first caretakers, local Bishop Pierre d'Arcis, was convinced it was a fraud, just one of the forty or so doing the round of medieval cathedrals to entice the pilgrim trade. A papal edict even banned its owners from calling it the real shroud of Jesus.

Not until the 1960s did anyone much care about the shroud, when the Catholic Church set up a commission to determine the relic's authenticity. The commission's report, issued in 1976, found that pollen in the shroud suggested that the relic might have come from Palestine but the red on the cloth was paint not blood. In 1988, radiocarbon dating of small samples of the relic by three different teams of researchers (viz. Oxford University, Arizona University, Swiss Institute of Technology) all concluded that the cloth was woven between AD 1260 and 1390. Case for it's-a-fake closed? Not quite. Other scientists assert that the carbon14-dating was thrown off course by 1,300 years because of the use of a bioplastic coating. And the red paint is from pilgrims holding pictures against the cloth in the hope of miraculous powers being transferred. Historian Ian Wilson, author of *The Blood and the Shroud: New Evidence that the World's Most Sacred Relic is Real*, accounts for the gaping lack of mentions of the shroud before 1389 by claiming it was the Edessan icon relocated. Meanwhile, Richard Levi-Setti of the Enrico Fermi Institute and Joseph Kohlbeck from the Hercules Aerospace Company in Utah found tiny particles of travertine aragonite limestone on the relic; the chemical signatures of the Shroud samples and the limestone from ancient tombs around Jerusalem were identical.

Muddying the matter are alternative historians who mate the Turin Shroud mystery with their own pet conspiracy. Here Kersten and Gruber take the prize with *The Jesus Conspiracy: The Turin Shroud and the Truth About the Resurrection*. According to Kersten and Gruber science proves that the Shroud is real and that Jesus was wrapped in it whilst ... alive. After three days of rest and recuperation Jesus then went off with **Mary Magdalene**. Second prize for conspiracy crossbreeding goes to Knights Templar occultists who claim that the shroud is that of Grand Master Jacques de Molya, burned at the stake in 1314 by the Inquisition.

The Turin Shroud is a riddle wrapped in a mystery. Even if it was forged in the fourteenth century, the maker's method befuddles contemporary scientists because the image looks like a photographic negative.

On this one, the jury is still out.

> Shroud of Turin is burial cloth of Christ: ALERT LEVEL 5

Further Reading

Holger Kersten and Elmar R. Gruber, *The Jesus Conspiracy: The Turin Shroud and the Truth About the Resurrection*, 1992

Joe Nickell, *Inquest on the Shroud of Turin: Latest Scientific Findings*, 1998

Brendan Whiting, *The Shroud Story*, 2006

Ian Wilson, *The Shroud: The 2000-Year-Old Mystery Solved*, 2010

TUSKEGEE SYPHILIS STUDY

There are conspiracies that make you nervous, there are conspiracies that make you mad. The Tuskegee Syphilis Study is the conspiracy that will make you weep with grief.

Syphilis is a sexually transmitted disease which, if untreated, can lead to blindness, crippling loss of muscle control, devastating internal damage, followed by an excruciatingly painful death.

In 1932, a clinical study by the Public Health Department began in Tuskegee, Alabama, on 399 syphilitic black men. Mostly poor, illiterate sharecroppers, the men were informed that they were being treated for "bad blood", and were enticed into participation by free meals, a "Thank You" certificate from the surgeon general's office, and a $50 insurance payment to cover their funeral fees. The research programme, properly the "Tuskagee Study of Untreated Syphilis in the Negro Male", was modelled on a study of white men in Norway, and started off with at least some legitimate intentions: at the time there was no viable cure for syphilis and proper questions were asked about treatments, some of which were likely doing more harm than good. Arsenic, for instance, was a popular "cure". A sponsor of the study was the prestigious black college the Tuskagee Institute, founded by Booker T. Washington.

Fast forward to 1947. By then, the wonder drug penicillin was widely available, and was extremely effective in treating syphilis. Obviously, the Tuskagee researchers offered penicillin – in effect, life – to the black subjects of the study. Didn't they?

No, they did not. Instead the "doctors" allowed the disease to run its course in the affected men, so they could record what would happen. There is also evidence that the doctors contacted the personal physicians of the men to ensure that they did not administer antibiotics.

Eventually, in 1966, Peter Buxtun, a PHS venereal-disease investigator from San Francisco discovered what was going down in Tuskegee and sent a letter to the director of the Division of Venereal Diseases to express his concerns about the morality of the study. The Center for Disease Control (CDC), which by then controlled the study, reaffirmed the necessity of continuing the study until all the subjects were dead. When he failed to alter the CDC's mind, Buxtun blew the whistle, and in July 1972 the story broke in the *Washington Star*. It became front page news in the *New York Times*, which called the Tuskegee Syphilis Study "the longest nontherapeutic experiment on human beings in medical history".

A public outcry ensured that the "research" ceased, and in time laws were passed governing medical experiments. Of the original 399 Tuskagee men, there were seventy-four survivors; twenty-eight had died of syphilis and a hundred of syphilis-related illnesses; over forty of their wives were infected, and nineteen children were born with congenital syphilis. A compensation package of $9 million was awarded to the Tuskagee men and their families. It was agreed to provide free medical treatment to surviving participants and to surviving family members infected as a consequence of the study. On 16 May 1997, President Bill Clinton formally apologized and held a ceremony for the survivors in the White House.

US Public Health Service allowed Afro-American males with syphilis to go untreated as part of a medical experiment: ALERT LEVEL 10

DOCUMENT: THE WHITE HOUSE PRESS RELEASE, MAY 16, 1997 [EXTRACTS]

REMARKS BY THE PRESIDENT IN APOLOGY FOR STUDY DONE IN TUSKEGEE

The East Room 2.26 P.M. EDT

THE PRESIDENT: Ladies and gentlemen, on Sunday, Mr. Shaw will celebrate his 95th birthday. (Applause.) I would like to recognize the other survivors who are here today and their families: Mr. Charlie Pollard is here. (Applause.) Mr. Carter Howard. (Applause.) Mr. Fred Simmons. (Applause.) Mr. Simmons just took his first airplane ride, and he reckons he's about 110 years old, so I think it's time for him to take a chance or two. (Laughter.) I'm glad he did. And Mr. Frederick Moss, thank you, sir. (Applause.)

I would also like to ask three family representatives who are here – Sam Doner is represented by his daughter, Gwendolyn Cox. Thank you, Gwendolyn. (Applause.) Ernest Hendon, who is watching in Tuskegee, is represented by his brother, North Hendon. Thank you, sir, for being here. (Applause.) And George Key is represented by his grandson, Christopher Monroe. Thank you, Chris. (Applause.)

I also acknowledge the families, community leaders, teachers and students watching today by satellite from Tuskegee. The White House is the people's house; we are glad to have all of you here today. I thank Dr. David Satcher for his role in this. I thank Congresswoman Waters and Congressman Hilliard, Congressman Stokes, the entire Congressional Black Caucus. Dr. Satcher, members of the Cabinet who are here, Secretary Herman, Secretary Slater, members of the Cabinet who are here, Secretary Herman, Secretary Slater. A great friend of freedom, Fred Gray, thank you for fighting this long battle all these long years.

The eight men who are survivors of the syphilis study at Tuskegee are a living link to a time not so very long ago that many Americans would prefer not to remember, but we dare not forget. It was a time when our nation failed to live up to its ideals, when our nation broke the trust with our people that is the very foundation of our democracy. It is not only in remembering that shameful past that we can make amends and repair our nation, but it is in remembering that past that we can build a better present and a better future. And without remembering it, we cannot make amends and we cannot go forward.

So today America does remember the hundreds of men used in research without their knowledge and consent. We remember them and their family members. Men who were poor and African American, without resources and with few alternatives, they believed they had found hope when they were offered free medical care by the United States Public Health Service. They were betrayed.

Medical people are supposed to help when we need care, but even once a cure was discovered, they were denied help, and they were lied to by their government. Our government is supposed to protect the rights of its citizens; their rights were trampled upon. Forty years, hundreds of men betrayed, along with their wives and children, along with the community in Macon County, Alabama, the City of Tuskegee, the fine university there, and the larger African American community.

The United States government did something that was wrong – deeply, profoundly, morally wrong. It was an outrage to our commitment to integrity and equality for all our citizens. To the survivors, to the wives and family members, the children and the grandchildren, I say what you know: No power on Earth can give you back the lives lost, the pain suffered, the years of internal torment and anguish. What was done cannot be undone. But we can end the silence. We can stop turning our heads away. We can look at you in the eye and finally say on behalf of the American people, what the United States government did was shameful, and I am sorry. (Applause.)

The American people are sorry – for the loss, for the years of hurt. You did nothing wrong, but you were grievously wronged. I apologize and I am sorry that this apology has been so long in coming. (Applause.)

To Macon County, to Tuskegee, to the doctors who have been wrongly associated with the events there, you have our apology, as well. To our African American citizens, I am sorry that your federal government orchestrated a study so clearly racist. That can never be allowed to happen again. It is against everything our country stands for and what we must stand against is what it was.

So let us resolve to hold forever in our hearts and minds the memory of a time not long ago in Macon County, Alabama, so that we can always see how adrift we can become when the rights of any citizens are neglected, ignored and betrayed. And let us resolve here and now to move forward together.

The legacy of the study at Tuskegee has reached far and deep, in ways that hurt our progress and divide our nation. We cannot be one America when a whole segment of our nation has no trust in America. An apology is the first step, and we take it with a commitment to rebuild that broken trust. We can begin by making sure there is never again another episode like this one. We need to do more to ensure that medical research practices are sound and ethical, and that researchers work more closely with communities...

The people who ran the study at Tuskegee diminished the stature of man by abandoning the most basic ethical precepts. They forgot their pledge to heal and repair. They had the power to heal the survivors and all the others and they did not. Today, all we can do is apologize. But you have the power, for only you – Mr. Shaw, the others who are here, the family members who are with us in Tuskegee – only you have the power to forgive. Your presence here shows us that you have chosen a better path than your government did so long ago. You have not withheld the power to forgive. I hope today and tomorrow every American will remember your lesson.

Thank you, and God bless you. (Applause.)

UNIT 731

Officially known under the gloriously misleading name of the "Anti-Epidemic Prevention and Water Purification Department of the Kwantung Army", Unit 731 was a covert Japanese biological and chemical warfare group set up in 1936. The unit's main base was a six kilometre square compound at Pingfang in Manchuria, complete with a railway line, barracks, dungeons, laboratories, operating rooms, crematoria, bar, airport, cinema and Shinto temple. At this Auschwitz of the East, Unit 731 conducted medical and biological warfare (BW) experiments on criminals, political opponents, Allied POWs and Chinese civilians. Known to staff as "logs", the victims were subjected to a Dante-like range of horrors – live vivisection, food deprivation, injection with horse urine, hanging upside down until death, frostbite, electrocution, incarceration in high pressure chambers (until the victim's eyes popped out) but mostly injection with the germ cultures of cholera, botulism, anthrax, smallpox, plague and VD. Unit 731 planes dropped plague-infected flea "bombs" on the Chinese populations of Yunnan, Ningbo and Changde in which over 400,000 people died. A clear case, you might think, for Unit 731 scientists to be tried for war crimes? Especially the Unit's leader, Lieutenant-General Shiro Ishii?

The Soviets thought so, and hauled captured Unit 731 personnel before the Khabarovsk War Crimes Trial in 1949, with those found guilty being sent to a gulag. And the Americans? The US Army sent several investigators from its BW base, Fort Detrick, to Japan after the war to interrogate Japanese scientists from 731; the US interrogators concluded that, although Unit 731 members were guilty of contravening the rules of land warfare, their BW knowledge was so essential – and so far in advance of the USA's – that some deal should be done with them. And reported to this effect to General MacArthur, Supreme Commander of Allied Forces. He, in turn, wrote to Washington DC in 1947, suggesting that "additional data, possibly some statements from Ishii, probably can be obtained by informing Japanese involved that information will be retained in intelligence channels and will not be employed as 'War Crimes' evidence".

Replying to MacArthur, the State-War-Navy Coordinating Committee agreed that Ishii and his scientists would receive immunity from prosecution for war crimes if they gave up all their deadly data. Unsurprisingly, they said "*Hai.*" So: in return for acquiring the expertise of Unit 731's scientists, the US covered up the evidence of its crimes, which may well have included torture and experimentation on captured GIs (see Congressional Research Report document, p.563). No charges were ever brought by the prosecutor at the Tokyo War Crimes trial, and many of the Unit's personnel went on to play a prominent role in Japanese society; Ishii's successor as head of 731, Dr Masaji Kitano, became head of the Green Cross pharmaceutical giant. Ishii himself was transported to the USA to carry on his bioweapons research, this time for Uncle Sam, in much the same way useful Nazi war criminals were under **Project Paperclip**.

To this day, Japan refuses Chinese demands for an apology and compensation for what happened at Pingfang on the grounds that there is no legal basis for them.

The site at Pingfang is now a museum.

> US covered up Japanese germ warfare crimes: ALERT LEVEL 10

Further Reading
Sheldon Harris, *Factories of Death*, 1994
Peter Williams and David Wallace, *Unit 731: Japan's Secret Biological Warfare in World War II*, 1989

DOCUMENT: CONGRESSIONAL RESEARCH SERVICE REPORT FOR CONGRESS: US PRISONERS OF WAR AND CIVILIAN AMERICAN CITIZENS CAPTURED AND INTERNED BY JAPAN IN WORLD WAR II: THE ISSUE OF COMPENSATION BY JAPAN

Starting with the 1980 publication of "Japan's Germ Warfare: The U.S. Cover-up of a War Crime", in *The Bulletin of Concerned Asian Scholars*, information on alleged Japanese Army biological warfare experiments on POWs has slowly been revealed, contributing to the continuing intensity of the WWII POW issue.

According to Sheldon Harris, there were apparently at least two different chemical and biological warfare units centered in Manchuria, each commanded by a different officer. One organization was Unit 100, with a central headquarters at Changchun, 150 miles south of Harbin: it was commanded by Major, later Major General, Wakamatsu Yujiro. Although, Harris reported, it experimented on humans, it has gotten little attention so far. The experiments about which the most is known are the biological warfare (BW) as well as some chemical warfare (CW) experiments, reportedly directed by a military doctor named Shiro Ishii. From the mid-1930s through 1945, Dr. Ishii, who eventually rose to the rank of Lieutenant General, reportedly directed BW experiment organizations under various names at a number of locations in and around the northern Manchurian city of Harbin, capital of Heilongjiang province. His main organization, Unit 731, was based in Manchuria, 15 miles south of Harbin at Ping Fan [sic]. The base at Ping Fan [sic] had a perimeter of almost four miles, an airfield, and a rail spur from Harbin, 150 buildings, and 3,000 employees. Ping Fan [sic] was declared a Special Military Region and was very securely fortified and guarded.

Three books have been written about the activities of Unit 731, and it has been the subject of frequent mentions in U.S. newspaper articles in the late 1990s. A one-hour television documentary on Unit 731, entitled *History Undercover: Unit 731, Nightmare in Manchuria*, was broadcast on the History Channel on March 7, 1999, and was rebroadcast an additional three times. Books have been written about Unit 731 in Japan, former members have come forward to tell of their activities, and a traveling exhibit about it has been seen by some 200,000 Japanese.

Ongoing private investigations by scholars have described Unit 731 as spreading disease and causing epidemics in field experiments that may have killed tens or even hundreds of thousands of Chinese. Although exact numbers are unknown, various researchers have alleged that Unit 731 performed laboratory experiments on somewhere between 850 to 10,000 or more subjects, and that none of them survived. According to author Sheldon Harris, victims consisted mostly of Han Chinese inhabitants of the area around Harbin but also included stateless White Russians, Harbin Jews, criminals, communist guerrillas or spies, Mongolians, Koreans, the mentally handicapped, and also Soviet soldiers captured in border skirmishes. Newspaper articles also state that Allied soldiers, possibly including some Americans, might have been experimented on.

Experiments on humans reportedly not only included infection with anthrax, typhoid, and other infectious diseases but also live dissections of prisoners without anesthesia, exposing prisoners to low air pressure, freezing of prisoners, removal of limbs, blood, and organs (often without anesthesia) to see the results, exposing humans to fragmentation rounds containing infectious agents, and other experiments.

Reports of Experimentation on POWs

News accounts have indicated possibly as many as 1,500 U.S. POWs, many of them survivors of the Bataan Death March, were among Allied POWs sent to a POW camp at Mukden (also known as Shenyang) in Manchuria, more than 300 miles southwest of Harbin. The first testimony by a U.S. POW about his experiences at Mukden apparently occurred in the brief testimony of Warren W. Whelchel in a 1982 field hearing on Veterans Administration health care in Montana. At the hearing, Whelchel testified that different men were given different injections and, thereafter, the Japanese took careful note of each man's condition.

At a half-day hearing of the Compensation Subcommittee of the House Veterans Affairs Committee, held in 1986 on treatment of U.S. POWs in Mukden, much of the discussion focused on compensation issues. There were four witnesses at the 1986 hearing, only one of whom was a former POW. The first witness, John H. Hatcher, Chief of Army Records Management and Army Archivist, testified that no primary records had been found by the Army dealing with what might have happened at Mukden and that Japanese Army records which could have contained such information had been returned unread to Japan. He stated that the Army had no records which could confirm or deny claims that had been made. Former POW James Frank, the second witness, testified that he had been sent to Mukden and that he believed he had been experimented on. He described what he saw when he was assigned to help Unit 731 personnel with autopsies of those who died and he stated that Unit 731 functionaries were interested in only certain of the dead POWs. He also testified that after he had been liberated, he and others had been required by the Army to sign papers promising not to reveal what had gone on at the camp under penalty of court martial. He also spoke of the difficulty in getting the VA to accept claims for illnesses he believed were caused by his time at Mukden when the VA said no medical records of such time existed.

The third witness at the 1986 hearing, Greg Rodriguez, Jr., was the son of a deceased POW and had previously testified at the 1982 hearing in Montana. He stated he believed his father's many ailments stemmed from being experimented on at Mukden, talked of his father's struggle to get veterans' benefits and about the records the son had found about Mukden. The last witness, William Triplett, who had written a book focusing on involvement of Unit 731 personnel in the Tokyo Imperial Bank murders in 1948, said that in his research he

had found declassified DOD documents which he believed
attested to the existence of Unit 731, to the fact that it performed biological warfare experiments on human beings, and
that Army occupation officials knew about these facts when
dealing with former members of Unit 731. He quoted from a
State Department memorandum that was part of a U.S. War
Department Judge Advocate General document, which said,
"It should be kept in mind that there is a remote possibility
that the independent investigation conducted by the Soviets
in the Mukden area may have already disclosed evidence that
American prisoners of war were used to experimental purposes of a BW nature and that they lost their lives as a result
of these experiments." Mr. Triplett stated that he believed
that the government was in possession of records about what
happened to POWs at Mukden that could help the VA in
diagnosing POWs' ailments. Since 1994, there have been
newspaper accounts discussing the experiences of several
American POWs who were interned at Mukden.

In his 1994 book, *Factories of Death*, Sheldon Harris analyzed the fragmentary and sparse available data and concluded that "... the evidence, while inconclusive, suggests
strongly that they [U.S. POWs] were not [among those] subjected to human BW experiments at Mukden".

In *Unjust Enrichment*, Linda Goetz Holmes lays out in
much more detail than Harris the reported incidents that led
to POWs' claims that they were experimented on at Mukden
and elsewhere.

U.S. Agreement Not to Prosecute Unit 731 Members

One of the most persistent allegations surrounding Unit 731 is
one made in the initial 1980 article, "Japan's Germ Warfare:
The U.S. Cover-up of a War Crime" (in *The Bulletin of
Concerned Asian Scholars*), in Harris's *Factories of Death*, and
elsewhere – that General Ishii and his staff were given immunity against prosecution as war criminals by the United States
in exchange for the scientific information gathered during Unit
731's experiments. In a letter to Rabbi Abraham Cooper of the
Simon Wiesenthal Center in Los Angeles, dated December 8,

1998, Eli M. Rosenbaum, Director of the Department of Justice's Office of Special Investigations, indicated that such a deal was struck. Mr. Rosenbaum wrote that "Two of these [formerly classified] reports [about biological warfare data collected by the Japanese and the arrangement made between the United States and Lieutenant General Shiro Ishii, the commander of Unit 731], dated November 17, 1981, and May 5, 1982, confirm that Ishii and his colleagues received immunity from prosecution and that, in exchange, they provided a great deal of information to U.S. authorities."

According to news accounts, Gen. Ishii returned to Japan after the war where he was permitted to continue medical research, was paid a Japanese government pension, and died of cancer in 1959. Moreover, many of Ishii's chief lieutenants occupied prominent positions in post-war Japanese society. According to one news account, the several hundred remaining members of Unit 731 were still holding their annual reunion in Japan as of 1999.

Missing Records

In the 20-year controversy over whether Americans were experimented on, the chief problem has been the lack of documentary evidence to support anecdotal accounts. According to U.S. Army testimony in the 1986 hearing on treatment of U.S. POWs in Mukden, the United States captured the records of the Imperial Army when it occupied Japan. These very hard-to-translate records were brought to this country, remained here for some 13 years largely untranslated and unread, and were then returned to Japan. However, according to a 1999 *New York Times* article, in 1948 the Central Intelligence Agency screened the records before they were turned over to the National Archives. Later 5% of the records were hurriedly microfilmed by a group including scholars from Harvard and Georgetown University, between the time they were ordered returned to Japan in 1957 and when they were actually put on a boat in February 1958. Japan has denied access to these records to those trying to document the actions of Unit 731. Author Sheldon Harris is quoted in the *New York Times* article as saying that he learned from Freedom of Information Act requests for military debriefing records dealing with this issue that relevant records were lost in the fire at the St. Louis Military Personnel Records Center in 1973. In 1995 an article in the *Washington Times* quoted Ken McKinnon, spokesman for the Department of Veterans Affairs, as saying, "The Veterans Administration has never seen evidence that research was done on the U.S. POWs. We would be more than willing to see new information on how POWs were treated and review the causes of injury and death." Mr. McKinnon said that the VA depends on DOD for analysis and documentation in this area. The article then went on to say that a Pentagon spokesman said he had never heard about U.S. POWs and the germ-warfare experiments at Mukden.

Efforts to Obtain an Apology

Several times since the end of WWII, Japanese government officials made statements that they regarded as an apology for their conduct in WWII, but that other nations did not accept as a full, direct, and unambiguous apology. These statements have evolved. In 1989, Prime Minister Noboru Takeshita stated that, "We cannot say in affirmative terms whether the Japanese state was an aggressor nation. That is a matter for future historians to judge." But, in 1991, on the 50th anniversary of the Japanese attack on Pearl Harbor, Japanese Prime Minister Kiichi Miyazawa apologized to the United States by expressing his "deep remorse ... that we inflicted an unbearable blow on the people of America and the Asian countries." In 1992, Prime Minister Kiichi Miyazawa apologized to the people of the Asia-Pacific Region, saying, "During a period in the past, the people of the Asia-Pacific region experienced unbearable suffering and pain due to our country's behavior. I would like to express again deep remorse and regret." According to the article citing his apology, this apology to the people of the Asia-Pacific region was the first apology by a Japanese prime minister in a policy speech. A senior government official said that this apology to the people of the Asia-Pacific region was also meant to apply to the United States.

However, a month before this apology, the Japanese parliament rejected a bill which called specifically for a Japanese apology on the anniversary of the attack on Pearl Harbor. In August 1993, Japanese Prime Minister Morihiro Hosokawa stated that the Japanese "... state clearly before all the world our remorse at our past history and our renewed determination to do better."

In 1994 the Japanese Foreign Ministry apologized for the "deeply regrettable" conduct of failing to break off diplomatic relations before their attack on Pearl Harbor. However, a Japanese Foreign Ministry spokesman said that this apology was to the Japanese people and not to the people of the United States.

On August 15, 1995, Japanese Prime Minister Tomiichi Murayama made the following statement, "During a certain period in the not too distant past, Japan, following a mistaken national policy, advanced along the road to war, only to ensnare the Japanese people in a fateful crisis, and through its colonial rule and aggression caused tremendous damage and suffering to the people of many countries, particularly to those of Asian nations." He went on to say, "In the hope that no such mistake be made in the future, I regard, in a spirit of humility, these irrefutable facts of history, and express here once again my feelings of deep remorse and state my heartfelt apology." However, some observers pointed out that he made his apology in the first person, on his behalf, and not that of Japan. This statement was not seen as adequate by various victims' groups because, they said, it was not endorsed by the Japanese parliament. According to newspaper accounts Prime Minister Murayama's apology obtained a tepid reaction in Asia. Speaking to veterans in Honolulu on the 50th anniversary of V-J Day, a few days after Murayama's remarks, President Clinton said, "... let me say especially how much the American people appreciate the recent powerful words of the Japanese Prime Minister, Mr. Murayama, when he expressed his nation's regret for its past aggression and its gratitude for the hand of reconciliation that this, the World War II generation, extended 50 years ago."

In her September 8, 2001, speech given on the 50th anniversary of the signing of the Multilateral Treaty of Peace with Japan in San Francisco, Japanese Foreign Minister Makiko Tanaka echoed the statement of Murayama by saying, "Facing the facts of history in a spirit of humility, I reaffirm today our feeling of deep remorse and heartfelt apology expressed in Prime Minister Muryama's statement of 1995." She also said in her speech, without elaboration, that the war has left an incurable scar on many people, including former prisoners of war – apparently the first such mentions of POWs. According to newspaper accounts, many protestors, Chinese-American groups, former U.S. prisoners of war, and others staged a conference demanding apologies and reparations from Japan. Speaking of reparations, Tanaka told reporters that based on the Peace Treaty, "the entire issue was settled." Secretary of State Colin Powell, who joined in the celebration, said, "The treaty dealt with the matter 50 years ago," but added, "at the same time we have the utmost compassion for the veterans who suffered." Powell is also quoted as saying, "It is the United States position that those claims were extinguished in the San Francisco Treaty."

USS *COLE*

On the sweltering morning of 12 October 2000, an inflatable boat packed to the gunnel with explosives slammed into the side of USS *Cole* as she was anchored in the port of Aden, Yemen. Seventeen US sailors died, as well as the two bombers.

The Yemeni police soon arrested six men, who confessed to having been trained in Osma bin-Laden's Jihad Camp No. 1 in Afghanistan and being under telephone orders from an al-Qaeda commander in Dubai. Satellite records confirmed that the arrested men had made dozens of calls to other al-Qaeda members in Africa.

Despite the weight of evidence pointing to bin Laden's outfit, not everyone was convinced of its guilt. The hole in the side of *Cole* was 40 × 60 feet, too big and too shaped (some believed) to be made by a rubber dingy full of fertilizer, and seemed to suggest a party with more bomb-making know-how and kit than al-Qaeda boasted. Who had the wherewithal to make the supposedly necessary military, shaped charge?

Shalom, Mossad. Rumours – especially in the Muslim world – became rampant that the Israeli secret service sank *Cole* with a cruise missile fired from a Dolphin-class submarine. That Israel should be willing to shed the blood of its American ally was not implausible: in 1967, Israeli jets and motor torpedo boats attacked the US intelligence ship USS *Liberty* for seventy-five minutes. The Israelis pleaded that the incident was a case of mistaken identity; since the *Liberty* was flying the American flag in international waters no one, up to US Secretary of State Dean Rusk, believed them. The best guess was that the Israeli Defence

Force was trying to stop the Americans knowing what it was up to in the Six Day War.

According to conspiracists, the Aden attack was a "black flag" operation in which Mossad sought to frame the Yemen. Worried about improving Washington–Aden relations, Mossad staged the bombing in order to persuade the Americans that Yemen was unreliable, and a breeding ground for terrorism.

Then again, in "The Truth About the USS *Cole* Bombing", Lloyd T. Vance and Steven Johnson have the US itself waving the black flag, suggesting at worst that Washington used al-Qaeda as patsy bombers, or at best a refuelling accident was opportunistically turned into a chance to blame al-Qaeda.

You may ask *why* the US sank its own ship? Vance and Johnson posit the reason as the desirability of getting the "Bush/ Cheney junta" into the White House. The *Cole* calamity made Clinton/Gore look useless (just as poor Jimmy Carter had seemed in the Tehran hostage debacle) so good ol' kick-ass boys Bush and Cheney became shoo-ins.

Mmm. Reagan might – just – have managed to persuade the Iranians not to release the Tehran hostages for his electoral benefit in **October Surprise**, but Bush 'n' Cheney hiring in al-Qaeda (even if Osama was a family friend of George's) stretches credulity.

> Mossad blew up USS *Cole* in false-flag op: ALERT LEVEL 4

Further Reading
www.scribd.com/doc/53626841/
  The-Truth-About-the-USS-Cole-Bombing

VRIL SOCIETY

In 1947 an article by rocket engineer Willy Ley in *Astounding Science Fiction* remarked on an occult Berlin group in the 1930s which "called itself Wahrheitsgesellschaft – Society for Truth – and which was more or less localized in Berlin, devoted its spare time looking for Vril."

After issuing two pamphlets, *Vril: The Primal Cosmic Power* and *World Dynamism* (about Atlantean free energy technology), and one issue of a magazine, the group seems to have gone kaput.

From these slender sources, post-War conspiracists have woven a thesis that the "Vril Society" was in contact with alien forces from Aldebaran, who instructed on flying saucer technology (shades of the **Thule Society**), with the power for craft supplied by said Vril. According to French authors Jacques Bergier and Louis Pauwels in *The Morning of the Magicians*, the Berlin Vril group was the inner circle of the Thule Society and connected to the English Hermetic Order of the Golden Dawn. Bergier and Pauwels are amongst the most unreliable guides to the esoteric you could fear or find, but Vril does have an English connection, because the originator of "Vril" was Edward Bulwer-Lytton, who wrote *Vril: The Power of the Coming Race* in 1871.

This is an account of a super race, the Vril-ya, that live in caves inside the Earth and use a near magical form of magnetism/electricity, the Vril Force, described by Bulwer-Lytton thus:

> ... there is no word in any language I know which is an exact synonym for Vril (*prana*, *chi*, or *qi*). I should call it electricity,

except that it comprehends in its manifold branches other forces of nature, to which, in our scientific nomenclature, differing names are assigned, such as magnetism, galvanism, &c. These people consider that in Vril they have arrived at the unity in natural energic agencies, which has been conjectured by many philosophers above ground.

Vril is derived from the Black Sun, a ball of Prima Materia, that supposedly exists in the centre of the Earth. Served by robots and able to fly on Vril-powered wings, the vegetarian Vril-ya can use Vril rods to wipe out barbarians a thousand times their number. (There was some irony in the vegetarianism of the Vril; a smart ad man in the Victorian era combined bovine with "vril" to make "Bovril", the branded meat extract.)

Bulwer-Lytton's book is a fiction. This notwithstanding, the Berlin group believed it to be an occult bible, as do handfuls of contemporary conspiracists. Naturally, no German secret society is worth its salt unless Adolf Hitler was a member – and, guess what, historian Michael Fitzgerald has discovered that Herr Schicklgruber ("*Heil*, Schicklgruber!" doesn't have quite the right ring about it, does it?) was a member of the Vril Society. A busy boy Adolf, organizing putschs, running the NSDAP, running the Third Reich, attending Vril meetings.

In *The Unknown Hitler*, Wulf Schwarzwaller, goes even further, declaring that Alfred, Rosenberg, Himmler, Goring and Hitler's personal physician Dr Morell were in the same Vril Lodge as their führer. And in *UFO Secrets of the Third Reich*, Vladimir Terziski traces how the Third Reich made contact with the Vril through a hole in Antarctica, which allowed the Nazis to develop a series of antigravity machines culminating in the Andromeda space station.

Vril-powered moon rockets? Now there's an idea that really is out of this world.

Proto-Nazi occult group discovers reverse-engineering alien technology: ALERT LEVEL 0

Further Reading
Edward Bulwer-Lytton, *Vril: The Power of the Coming Race*, 1871
Michael FitzGerald, *Storm Troopers of Satan*, 1990
Michael FitzGerald, *Adolf Hitler: A Portrait*, 2006
Nicholas Goodrick-Clarke, *Black Sun*, 2002
John Michael Greer, *The Element Encyclopedia of Secret Societies*, 2006

DOCUMENT: EDWARD BULWER-LYTTON, *VRIL: THE POWER OF THE COMING RACE*, 1871 [EXTRACT]

I have spoken so much of the Vril Staff that my readers may expect me to describe it. This I cannot do accurately, for I was never allowed to handle it for fear of some terrible accident occasioned by my ignorance of its use; and I have no doubt that it requires much skill and practice in the exercise of its various powers. It is hollow, and has in the handle several stops, keys, or springs by which its force can be altered, modified, or directed – so that by one process it destroys, by another it heals – by one it can rend the rock, by another disperse the vapour – by one it affects bodies, by another it can exercise a certain influence over minds. It is usually carried in the convenient size of a walking-staff, but it has slides by which it can be lengthened or shortened at will. When used for special purposes, the upper part rests in the hollow of the palm with the fore and middle fingers protruded. I was assured, however, that its power was not equal in all, but proportioned to the amount of certain Vril properties in the wearer in affinity, or "rapport" with the purposes to be effected. Some were more potent to destroy, others to heal, &c.; much also depended on the calm and steadiness of volition in the manipulator. They assert that the full exercise of Vril power can only be acquired by the constitutional temperament – i.e., by hereditarily transmitted organisation – and that a female infant of four years old belonging to the Vril-ya races can accomplish feats which a life spent in its practice would not enable the strongest and most skilled mechanician, born out of the pale of the Vril-ya to achieve. All these wands are not equally complicated; those intrusted to children are much simpler than those borne by sages of either sex, and constructed with a view to the special object on which the children are employed; which as I have before said, is among the youngest children the most destructive. In the wands of wives and mothers the correlative destroying force is usually abstracted, the healing power fully charged. I wish I could say more in detail of this singular conductor of the Vril fluid, but its machinery is as exquisite as its effects are marvellous.

I should say, however, that this people have invented certain tubes by which the Vril fluid can be conducted towards the object it is meant to destroy, throughout a distance almost indefinite; at least I put it modestly when I say from 500 to 1,000 miles. And their mathematical science as applied to such purpose is so nicely accurate, that on the report of some observer in an air-boat, any member of the Vril department can estimate unerringly the nature of intervening obstacles, the height to which the projectile instrument should be raised, and the extent to which it should be charged, so as to reduce to ashes within a space of time too short for me to venture to specify it, a capital twice as vast as London.

Certainly these Ana are wonderful mathematicians – wonderful for the adaptation of the inventive faculty to practical uses.

I went with my host and his daughter Zee over the great public museum, which occupies a wing in the College of Sages, and in which are hoarded, as curious specimens of the ignorant and blundering experiments of ancient times, many contrivances on which we pride ourselves as recent achievements. In one department, carelessly thrown aside as obsolete lumber, are tubes for destroying life by metallic balls and an inflammable powder, on the principle of our cannons and catapults, and even still more murderous than our latest improvements.

My host spoke of these with a smile of contempt, such as an artillery officer might bestow on the bows and arrows of the Chinese. In another department there were models of vehicles and vessels worked by steam, and of an air-balloon which might have been constructed by Montgolfier.

"Such," said Zee, with an air of meditative wisdom – "such were the feeble triflings with nature of our savage forefathers, ere they had even a glimmering perception of the properties of Vril!"

WATER CONTROL

Water, water everywhere and not a drop to drink.

Multinational companies taking control of the world's water supply? Sounds like a Blofeld plotline in an 007 movie of Sean Connery vintage – but it is real. The globe's water is being privatized at a staggering rate. Blue water is the new black. The Bushes and Pickens of Texas are far from being the only oil baronage buying up aquifers, and some of the water industry players are way bigger than Bush Inc. They include Swiss combine Nestlé, French conglomerate Veolia, and US agribusiness giant Monsanto.

Why buy into water? Easy. H_2O is a commodity that is scarcer by the day. On the Blue Planet just 3 per cent of the water is freshwater and this, on the one hand, is being contaminated by agri-chemicals and industrial pollution, and on the other hand is being "abstracted" by farmers, factories (the average auto uses 350,000 litres of water in its manufacture) and an ever-increasing number of thirsty people. There is less water, and it is often bad water beyond human use. About 2.5 billion people in the world lack access to safe drinking water. Control of this vital resource will, especially in the industrialized and emerging industrialized world (India, China, Brazil), be a source of guaranteed profits. Already the water business is worth over a cool $100 billion per annum.

Where's the conspiracy? Well, most people consider water a natural resource, free, and even God given. Few, if any of the speculators or companies buying water admit to buying water. They just happen to buy the land above – and when they own the land above they own the water below. The effect on the communal environment can be catastrophic. Take Nestlé's pumps for "Ice mountain" bottling plant at Stanwood, Michigan. These suck up the groundwater that should feed Lake Michigan. Truthout.org reports the following, which may be a tad connected to Nestlé's pumping, pumping, pumping:

> That the water levels in the upper lakes are falling is certain. Data from the Army Corps of Engineers website indicates that Lake Superior has almost reached its record low, set in 1926. Roger Gauthier, a project manager at the Great Lakes Commission, an intergovernmental body representing eight states and two Canadian provinces, said water levels in Lakes Michigan and Huron had dropped three feet since 1999 and were about seven inches above the record low set in 1964. The persistence of low water in *Lakes* Huron and Michigan has been out of keeping with the larger cycles of high and low water in the basin.

For the right to withdraw water from near Lake Michigan Nestlé plays a paltry $100 a year.

Of course, he who controls the water controls what goes into the water. About 60 per cent of Americans, and 10 per cent of Brits have fluoride added to their drinking H_2O. Now, some elements in the dental industry consider fluoridation a good thing because it (allegedly) prevents tooth decay, particularly in children. On the other hand, General Jack D. Ripper in *Dr Strangelove*, memorably asked, "Do you realize that fluoridation is the most monstrously conceived and dangerous Communist plot we have ever had to face?"

Contra Jack D. Ripper, some conspiracists consider that fluoridation is a plot by the candy industry to allow kids to eat all the confectionery they want. Or is even a CIA-inspired campaign to make a mindless America, with a little help from some old Nazi friends. Sodium fluoride was used in Nazi mind-control experiments in the Third Reich; in 1945, US scientist Charles Perkins visited the IG Farben chemical works in Deutschland and concluded about the work done there: "Repeated doses of infinitesimal amounts of fluoride will in time reduce an individual's power to resist domination, by slowly poisoning and narcotizing a certain area of the brain, thus making him submissive to the will of those who wish to govern him."

IG Farben chemists were then reputedly exported to the USA under **Project Paperclip** to show the CIA MKULTRA teams how to make a **Manchurian Candidate**.

The list of alleged fluoridation conspirators goes way beyond the Commies, the Nazis, the CIA. Fluoride is a by-product of aluminium/uranium/steel production, and is estimated by many scientists to be a toxin. Putting fluoride in the people's drinking water is simply a way of the metal industry dumping its toxic waste under the cover of improving health.

In their view.

Big business is taking over the world's water supply: ALERT LEVEL 9

Further Reading
Maude Barlow and Tony Clarke, *Blue Gold: The Battle Against Corporate Theft of the World's Water*, 2003

PAUL WELLSTONE

I'm for the little fellers, not the Rockefellers.

Senator Paul Wellstone, Democratic Party

On 25 October 2002, Senator Paul Wellstone of Minnesota was killed as his private jet came within two miles of Eveleth–Virginia Municipal Airport. In normal circumstances few would have given the cause of the crash a second thought. But October 2002 was not a normal time, and Wellstone was no normal senator. Paul Wellstone was the first (and maybe the last) sixties radical elected to the US Senate. Wellstone was the only member of the Senate to have voted against George W. Bush's plans to go to war in Iraq. In October 2002, Wellstone was nearing the end of his re-election campaign to the Senate, and looking like the winner. In a Senate likely to be evenly split, Wellstone was perhaps a one-man obstacle to President Bush's stated desire to secure passage of the Homeland Security measure.

Wellstone's death seemed too convenient to be an accident, especially as Dick Cheney, Bush's enforcer, had reputedly told the Senator: "If you vote against the war in Iraq, the Bush administration will do whatever is necessary to get you. There will be severe ramifications for you and the state of Minnesota."

Did "severe ramifications" include murder? No one without a large wallet, the heart of a lion and a good lawyer was going to accuse Cheney of orchestrating an offing, but speculation – including by nervous Democrats on Capitol Hill – that right-wingers and/or the CIA had hit Wellstone was rampant. Two researchers into the case, Four Arrows and Jim Fetzer, dug up some odd happenings around the time of the Wellstone downing. Firstly, the FBI arrived at the crash scene at 11.00 a.m., only an hour or so after the ambulances – and in order to do that, the FBI would have needed to leave their St Paul office at 9.30, the same time that Wellstone's flight was taking off.

Secondly, around the time of the crash cell phones and electronic instruments in the vicinity wildly malfunctioned.

The NTSB (National Transportation Safety Board), despite queries raised by individual officials, initially determined that icy conditions were responsible for the tragedy. However, other craft were taking off and landing at Eveleth–Virginia just fine that morning. Besides, the Beechcraft King Air A-10 boasted an elaborate de-icing system, which records showed was fully operational.

Obliged to disqualify ice, the NTSB suggested that the main pilot, Richard Conry, was to blame because his approach speed was too slow. But Conry was a massively experienced pilot, who had passed a routine assessment two days before, and the King Air had an alarm to alert pilots about low airspeed. As to why the King Air was heading south instead of west the NTSB magnificently failed to address.

Four Arrows and Fetzer believe the King Air stopped communicating and went off course because an electromagnetic pulse was aimed at the plane, which prevented the electronics from operating. The same pulse also screwed up cell phone calls locally; the interference was described by one man driving within a couple of blocks of the airport as being "between a roar and loud humming voice ... oscillating ... screeching and humming noise".

This is maybe the place to make the point that Four Arrows and Fetzer are not your usual conspiracy nuts. They are university professors. In maintaining that Wellstone was assassinated they are in plentiful company; in one poll of Minnesotans 69 per cent of respondents said they had a hunch that a "GOP Conspiracy" (Grand Old Party, a.k.a. the Republicans) had arranged Senator Wellstone's death.

Wellstone had been the target of an assassination before. In 2000, during a visit to Colombia, a bomb was found along his route from the airport. He was also sprayed with the herbicide glyphosate by a helicopter while sojourning in that Latin American country.

Wellstone is far from being the only American politician from the awkward squad to die in a "mysterious" plane crash: Democratic Governor of Missouri, Mel Carnahan was killed during a close Senate race when his small plane crashed in 2000; John F. Kennedy Jr. died in a 1999 plane crash; Commerce Secretary Ron Brown perished in a 1996 "accident" (there is a widely reproduced photograph of Brown with a bullet wound in his head at the post-mortem); and John Tower, Republican, was writing a revealing book about the Iran-Contra affair when he conveniently died in a plane accident in 1991.

According to the website From the Wilderness of twenty-two air crashes involving federal and state officials, 64 per cent were Democrats and 36 per cent Republicans.

So, if you're scared of flying, make sure you don't have a dissident Democrat aboard your plane.

Senator Paul Wellstone was assassinated: ALERT LEVEL 8

Further Reading
Four Arrows and Jim Fetzer, *American Assassination: The Strange Death of Senator Paul Wellstone,* 2004
http://www.fromthewilderness.com/free/ww3/110102_wellstone.html

THE WHITE HOUSE PUTSCH

What was behind the plot was shrouded in a silence which has not been broken to this day. Even a generation later, those who are still alive and know all the facts have kept their silence so well that the conspiracy is not even a footnote in American histories.

So wrote the journalist John L. Spivak in his book *A Man in His Time*. The conspiracy Spivak was referring to was the attempted 1934 overthrow of the Great Depression presidency of Franklin Delano Roosevelt by a clique of bankers and industrialists. Not just any Wall Street financiers and manufacturers either, but big-corporate names, among them DuPont and Morgan Bank. And what did these money-men wish to replace FDR's Democratic government with? Nothing less than a full-blown fascist dictatorship on the model of Mussolini in Italy.

Time has done little to diminish Spivak's observation that the putsch against the White House is hardly known to the public. It remains un-footnoted in standard histories of the US of A.

In all probability, the 1934 plot was the *second* attempted coup d'etat against Roosevelt. In the previous year, there had been an assassination attempt against him from which he had escaped unscathed but Chicago Mayor Anton Cermak had died. The assassin, Giuseppe Zangara, was captured and pronounced to be a lone killer. (Shades of Lee Harvey Oswald.) Scuttlebutt on the street, though, was that he was in the pay of the Mafia or a Wall Street cabal.

Certainly in summer 1933, General Smedley Darlington Butler, war hero and former Marine, was approached by bondsman and fascist-sympathizer Gerald C. MacGuire and offered the opportunity of leading a coup against Roosevelt. The veterans' association, the American Legion, MacGuire boasted to Butler, was to be transformed into a 500,000-strong army. MacGuire also promised a $3 million war, courtesy of DuPont, General Motors and Morgan Bank. Arms and ammunition were to be supplied by DuPont's subsidiary, Remington.

Fortunately for American democracy, MacGuire and his fellow conspirators chose the wrong man. And how. Butler, the "fighting Quaker", was an instinctive anti-authoritarian, a man of integrity and a railer against capitalist greed. As a loyal soldier, he complained that he had:

> helped make Mexico, especially Tampico, safe for American oil interests in 1914. I helped make Haiti and Cuba a decent place for the National City Bank boys to collect revenues in. I helped in the raping of half a dozen Central American republics for the benefits of Wall Street. The record of racketeering is long. I helped purify Nicaragua for the international banking house of Brown Brothers in 1909-1912. I brought light to the Dominican Republic for American sugar interests in 1916. In China I helped to see to it that Standard Oil went its way unmolested.

Butler played along with MacGuire with the aim of drawing his "friends" out of the woodwork and into the light.

The friends turned out to be a list of American great and bad, and included:

- John W. Davis, senior attorney for J. P. Morgan
- Robert Sterling Clark, Wall Street stockbroker
- Grayson Murphy, director of Morgan Bank, Bethlehem Steel and Goodyear. He also ran the brokerage firm where MacGuire worked
- Al Smith, former governor of New York, and the co-director of the newly founded American Liberty League.

According to MacGuire the American Liberty League was the crucible of the coup. Grayson Murphy was its treasurer, DuPont executive John J. Raskob was its other co-director, and its founder was the industrialist Irénée DuPont.

DuPont was an out-and-out fascist. What is extraordinary is the number of big beasts from FDR's own Democratic Party who were in on the plot, such was their hatred for him and his radical "New Deal" policies. Davis was a former Democratic presidential candidate, and Raskob a former chairman of the party.

As soon as Butler had the names of the plotters, he reported to the White House. Roosevelt's initial instinct was to arrest the conspirators, but the American economy was in the doldrums. He had to assume that a mass imprisoning of Wall Street financiers might trigger another stock market crash. So, Roosevelt defused the plot by leaking the story to the press, taking the gamble that a public outing would make the cabal back off. He also tipped off the House of Representatives' McCormack–Dickstein Committee (the forerunner of the House Un-American Activities Committee) to launch an investigation. The plotters were asked to appear and, to no great surprise, denied any knowledge of an intended coup to replace the president. The McCormack–Dickstein Committee took four years to release its report on the coup d'etat, and marked it for "restricted circulation". Publicly, the committee claimed "no evidence" other than "hearsay" linked MacGuire, Clark, Davis, DuPont et all to the putsch. This was a direct contradiction of its internal summation to the House, which concluded: "these attempts [at a fascist coup] were discussed, were planned, and might have been placed in execution when and if the financial backers deemed it expedient ..."(See Document, p.587.)

The committee also suppressed parts of General Butler's (and others') testimony in its published report (see Document.)

Why did the committee say one thing in public and another in private? Why were none of the conspirators hauled before a court? Almost certainly, because Roosevelt, having headed off the coup at the pass, wanted to save the Democratic Party from embarrassment.

The putschists, meanwhile, went back to captaining finance and industry, their only admonishment the embarrassment of having their Nazi sentiments exposed.

Smedley D. Butler was twice awarded the Medal of Honor and once the so-called "Brevet medal". But the bravest thing he ever did was putting down the White House putsch.

Wall Street/US fascists plotted coup to overthrow Roosevelt: ALERT LEVEL 10

Further Reading
Jules Archer, *The Plot to Seize the White House*, 1973
John L. Spivak, *A Man in His Time*, 1967

DOCUMENT: REPORT OF THE MCCORMACK–DICKSTEIN COMMITTEE INVESTIGATION OF NAZI AND OTHER PROPAGANDA, FEBRUARY 15, 1935 [EXTRACTS] AND THE TESTIMONY OF GENERAL SMEDLEY D. BUTLER BEFORE THE COMMITTEE.

There have been isolated cases of activity by organizations which seemed to be guided by fascist principle, which the committee investigated and found that they had made no progress ...

In the last few weeks of the committee's official life it received evidence showing that certain persons had made an attempt to establish a fascist organization in this country. No evidence was presented and this committee had none to show a connection between this effort and any fascist activity of any European country.

There is no question that these attempts were discussed, were planned, and might have been placed in execution when and if the financial backers deemed it expedient.

This committee received evidence from Maj. Gen. Smedley D. Butler (retired), twice decorated by the Congress of the United States. He testified before the committee as to conversations with one Gerald C. MacGuire in which the latter is alleged to have suggested the formation of a fascist army under the leadership of General Butler (p. 8–114 D.C. 6 II).

MacGuire denied these allegations under oath, but your committee was able to verify all the pertinent statements made by General Butler, with the exception of the direct statement suggesting the creation of the organization. This, however, was corroborated in the correspondence of MacGuire with his principal, Robert Sterling Clark, of New York City, while MacGuire was abroad studying the various forms of veterans' organizations of Fascist character (p. III D.C. 6 II).

The following is an excerpt from one of MacGuire's letters:

I had a very interesting talk last evening with a man who is quite well up on affairs here and he seems to be of the opinion that the Croix de Feu will be very patriotic during this crisis and will take the cuts or be the moving spirit in the veterans to accept the cuts. Therefore they will, in all probability, be in opposition to the Socialists and functionaries. The general spirit among the functionaries seems to be that the correct way to regain recovery is to spend more money and increase wages, rather than to put more people out of work and cut salaries.

The Croix de Feu is getting a great number of new recruits, and I recently attended a meeting of this organization and was quite impressed with the type of men belonging. These fellows are interested only in the salvation of France, and I feel sure that the country could not be in better hands because they are not politicians, they are a cross-section of the best people of the country from all walks of life, people who gave their "all" between 1914 and 1918 that France might be saved, and I feel sure that if a crucial test ever comes to the Republic that these men will be the bulwark upon which France will be served.

There may be more uprisings, there may be more difficulties, but as is evidenced right now when the emergency arises and part difficulties are forgotten as far as France is concerned, and all become united in the one desire and purpose to keep this country as it is, the most democratic, and the country of the greatest freedom on the European Continent (p. III D.C. 6 II).

This committee asserts that any efforts based on lines as suggested in the foregoing and leading off to the extreme right, are just as bad as efforts which would lead to the extreme left. Armed forces for the purpose of establishing a dictatorship by means of Fascism or a dictatorship through the instrumentality of the proletariat, or a dictatorship predicated in part on racial and religious hatreds, have no place in this country.

Testimony of Maj. Gen. S. D. Butler (Retired)

Redacted sections are reinserted in italics.

(The witness was duly sworn by the chairman.)

The CHAIRMAN. General, you are a retired Commandant of the Marine Corps?

General BUTLER. No, I was never Commandant.

The CHAIRMAN. You were in the Army how long?

General BUTLER. I was in the Marine Corps 33 years and 4 months on the active list.

The CHAIRMAN. As I remember, you are a Congressional Medal of Honor man; received the Congressional Medal of Honor on two occasions?

General BUTLER. Yes.

The CHAIRMAN. General, you know what the purpose of your visit here is today?

General BUTLER. Yes.

The CHAIRMAN. Without my asking you any further questions, will you just go ahead and tell in your own way all that you know about an attempted Fascist movement in this country?

General BUTLER. May I preface my remarks by saying, sir, that I have one interest in all of this, and that is to try to do my best to see that a democracy is maintained in this country.

The CHAIRMAN. Nobody who has either read about or known about General Butler would have anything but that understanding.

General BUTLER. It is nice of you to say that, sir.

But that is my only interest.

I think I had probably better go back and give you the background. This has been going on for a year and a half. Along – I think it must have been about the 1st of July 1933, two men came to see me. First there was a telephone message from Washington, from a man who I did not know well. His first name was Jack. He was an American Legionnaire, but I cannot remember his last name – cannot recall it now accurately. Anyhow, he asked me if I would receive 2 soldiers – 2 veterans—

If they called on me that afternoon. I said I would.

About 5 hours later a Packard limousine came up into my yard and 2 men got out. This limousine was driven by a chauffeur. They came into the house and introduced themselves. One said his name was Bill Doyle, who was then the department commander of the Legion in Massachusetts. The other said his name was Jerry MacGuire.

The CHAIRMAN. Where did MacGuire come from?

General BUTLER. MacGuire said he had been State commander the year before of the department of Connecticut and was then living in Connecticut. Doyle was living in Massachusetts.

The CHAIRMAN. Had you met either of these men before?

General BUTLER. Never had seen them before, as I recollect. I might have done so; but as far as my impression then was, they were absolute strangers. The substance of the conversation, which lasted about 2 hours, was this: That they were very desirous of unseating the royal family in control of the American Legion, at the convention to be held in Chicago, and very anxious to have me take part in it. They said that they were not in sympathy with the then administration – that is, the present administration's treatment of the soldiers.

They presented to me rather a confused picture, and I could not make up my mind exactly what they wanted me to do or what their objective was, but it had something to do with weakening the influence of the administration with the soldiers.

They asked me to go to the convention, and I said I did not want to go – that I had not been invited and did not care anything about going.

Then MacGuire said that he was the chairman of the distinguished-guest committee of the American Legion, on Louis Johnson's staff; that Louis Johnson had, at MacGuire's suggestion, put my name down to be invited as a distinguished guest of the Chicago convention. *that Johnson had then taken this list, presented by MacGuire, of distinguished guests, to the White House for approval; that Louis Howe, one of the secretaries to the President, had crossed my name off and said that I was not to be invited – that the President would not have it.* I thought I smelled a rat, right away – that they were trying to get me mad – to get my goat. I said nothing.

They said, "We represent the plain soldiers, and we want you to come to this convention." They said, "We want you to come there and stampede the convention in a speech and help us in our fight to dislodge the royal family."

The CHAIRMAN. When you say you smelled a rat, you mean you had an idea that they were not telling the truth?

General BUTLER. I could not reconcile and from the very beginning I was never able to reconcile their desire to serve the ordinary man in the ranks, with their other aims. They did not seem to be the same. It looked to me as if they were trying to embarrass the administration in some way. They had not gone far enough yet but I could not reconcile the two objectives; they seemed to be diametrically opposed. One was to embarrass the administration of the American Legion, when I did not want to go anyhow, and the other object will appear here in a little while. I do not know that at that moment I had formed any particular opinion. I was just fishing to see what they had in mind. So many queer people come to my house all the time and I like to feel them all out.

Finally they said, "Now, we have arranged a way for you to come to this convention."

I said, "How is that, without being invited?"

They said, "Well, you are to come as a delegate from Hawaii."

I said, "I do not live in Hawaii."

"Well, it does not make any difference. There is to be no delegate from one of the American Legion posts there in Honolulu, and we have arranged to have you appointed by cable, by radio, to represent them at the convention. You will be a delegate."

I said, "Yes; but I will not go in the back door."

They said, "That will not be the back door. You must come."

I said, "No; I will not do this."

"Well," they said, "are you in sympathy with unhorsing the royal family?"

I said, "Yes; because they have been selling out the common soldier in this Legion for years. These fellows have been getting political plums and jobs and cheating the enlisted man in the Army, and I am for putting them out. But I cannot do it by going in through the back door."

"Well," they said, "we are going to get them out. We will arrange this."

That was all that happened the first day, as I recollect it. There were several days of it, and I will tell you everything that happened, but I cannot check it with the specific days. So they went away. Two or three days later, they came back in the same car, both together, the second time. Doyle dropped out of the picture, he appeared only twice.

The CHAIRMAN. What was the second talk?

General BUTLER. The substance of the second talk was this, that they had given up this delegate idea, and I was to get two or three hundred legionnaires from around that part of the country and bring them on a special train to Chicago with me; that they would sit around in the audience, be planted here and there, and I was to be nothing but an ordinary legionnaire, going to my own convention as an onlooker; not as a participant at all. I was to appear in the gallery. These planted fellows were to begin to cheer and start a stampede and yell for a speech. Then I was to go to the platform and make a speech. I said, "Make a speech about what?"

"Oh," they said, "we have one here."

This conversation lasted a couple of hours, but this is the substance of it. They pulled out this speech. They said, "We will leave it here with you to read over, and you see if you can get these fellows to come."

I said, "Listen. These friends of mine that I know around here, even if they wanted to go, could not afford to go. It would cost them a hundred to a hundred and fifty dollars to go out there and stay for 5 days and come back."

They said, "Well, we will pay that."

I said, "How can you pay it? You are disabled soldiers. How do you get the money to do that?"

"Oh, we have friends. We will get the money."

Then I began to smell a rat for fair. I said, "I do not believe you have got this money."

It was either then or the next time, or one of the times, they hauled out a bank-deposit book and showed me, I think it was $42,000 in deposits on that occasion, and on another occasion it was $64,000.

The CHAIRMAN: They took out a bank book and showed you what?

General BUTLER. They took out a bank book and showed me deposits of $42,000 on one occasion and $64,000 on another.

The CHAIRMAN. Do you know on what bank that was?

General BUTLER. I do not. They just flipped the pages over. So, I have had some experience as a policeman in Philadelphia. I wanted to get to the bottom of this thing and not scare them off, because I felt then that they had something real. They had so much money and a limousine. Wounded soldiers do not have limousines or that kind of money. They said, "We will pay the bill. Look around and see if you cannot get two or three hundred men and we'll bring them out there and we will have accommodations for them."

This was getting along about the first of August, I should say. Well, I did not do anything about it. MacGuire made one other trip to see me, this time by himself, to see how things were getting along, I said that I had been busy and had not had time to get the soldiers together. Then on this occasion I asked him where he got this money. He was by himself when I asked him that. Doyle was not around.

"Where did you get all this money? It cannot be yours."

He said that it was given to him by nine men, that the biggest contributor had given $9,000 and that the donations ran all the way from $2,500 to $9,000.

I said, "What is the object?"

He said the object was to take care of the rank and file of the soldiers, to get them their bonus and get them properly cared for.

Well, I knew that people who had $9,000 to give away were not in favor of the bonus. That looked fishy right away.

He gave me the names of two men: Colonel Murphy, Grayson M.P. Murphy, for whom he worked, was one. He said, "I work for him. I am in his office."

I said to him, "How did you happen to be associated with that kind of people if you are for the ordinary soldier and his bonus and his proper care? You know damn well that these bankers are not going to swallow that. There is something in this, Jerry MacGuire, besides what you have told me. I can see that."

He said, "Well, I am a business man. I have got a wife and family to keep, and they took good care of them, and if you would take my advice, you would be a business man, too."

I said, "What has Murphy got to do with this?"

"Well," he said, "don't you know who he is?"

I said, "Just indirectly. He is a broker in New York. But I do not know any of his connections."

"Well," he said, "he is the man who underwrote the formation of the American Legion for $125,000. He underwrote it, paid for the field work of organizing it, and had not gotten all of it back yet."

"That is the reason he makes the kings, is it? Pie has still got a club over their heads."

"He is on our side, though. He wants to see the soldiers cared for."

"Is he responsible, too, for making the Legion a strike breaking outfit?"

"No, no. He does not control anything in the Legion now."

I said: "You know very well that it is nothing but a strike breaking outfit used by capital for that purpose and that is, the reason they have all those big club-houses and that is the reasons I pulled out from it. They have been using these dumb soldiers to break strikes.

He said: "Murphy hasn't anything to do with that. He is a very fine fellow."

I said, "I do not doubt that, but there is some reason for him putting $125,000 into this."

Well, that was the end of that conversation. I think it was then that he showed me the deposit of $64,000.

The CHAIRMAN. MacGuire had the money?

General BUTLER. MacGuire had the bank book. He did not have any money yet. No money had appeared yet. There was nothing but a bank book showing deposits. It was in his name.

The CHAIRMAN. In his name?

General BUTLER. Yes.

The CHAIRMAN. Not in Doyle's name?

General BUTLER. No. Doyle had faded out of the picture and his name was never mentioned again and has never been mentioned since I do not know but what Doyle just rode along with him.

The next time I saw him was about the 1st of September, in a hotel in Newark. I went over to the convention of the Twenty-ninth Division. Sunday morning he walked into my room and he asked me if I was getting ready now to take these men out to Chicago, that the convention was pretty close. I said, "No; I am not going to Chicago."

"Why not?"

I said, "You people are bluffing. You have not got any money." Whereupon he took out a big wallet; out of his hip pocket, and a great, big mass of thousand dollar bills and threw them out on the bed.

I said, "What's all this?"

He says, "This is for you, for expenses. You will need some money to pay them."

"How much money have you got there?"

He said, "$18,000."

"Where did you get those thousand dollar bills?"

"Oh," he said, "last night some contributions were made. I just have not had a chance to deposit them, so I brought them along with me."

I said, "Don't you try to give me any thousand dollar bills. Remember, I was a cop once. Every one of the numbers on these bills has been taken. I know you people and what you are trying to do. You are just trying to get me by the neck. If I try to cash one of those thousand dollar bills, you would have me by the neck."

"Oh," he said, "we can change them into smaller denominations."

I said, "You put that money away before somebody walks in here and sees that money around, because I do not want to be tied up with it at all. I told you distinctly I am not going to take these men to Chicago."

"Well, are you going yourself?"

I said, "Oh, I do not know. But I know one thing. Somebody is using you. You are a wounded man. You are a bluejacket. You have got a silver plate in your head. I looked you up. You were wounded. You are being used by somebody, and I want to know the fellows who are using you. I am not going to talk to you any more. You are only an agent. I want some of the principals."

He said, "Well, I will send one of them over to see you." I said, "Who?" He said, "I will send Mr. Clark."

"Who is Mr. Clark?"

"Well, he is one of our people. He put up some money."

"Who is he?"

"Well, his name is R. S. Clark. He is a banker. He used to be in the Army."

"How old a man is he?" He told me.

"Would it be possible that he was a second lieutenant in the Ninth Infantry in China during the Boxer campaign?"

He said, "That is the fellow."

He was known as the "millionaire lieutenant" and was sort of batty, sort of queer, did all sorts of extravagant things. He used to go exploring around China and wrote a book on it, on

THE WHITE HOUSE PUTSCH

explorations. He was never taken seriously by anybody. But he had a lot of money. An aunt and an uncle died and left him $10,000,000. That was the story at the time. So he said, "I will send him over to see you." I said, "All right, you send him over."

I thought no more about it until the end of the week, when Clark called up and asked if he might spend Sunday with me. I said, "Yes," and he said, "I will take the 9 o'clock train from New York." I said, "All right; I will meet you at the station."

Well, this was getting down to something real. I was there on time, and he stepped off the train, and I recognized him. I had not seen him for 34 years, but I could see that he was the same man, a long, gangling fellow. His hair had turned gray, but it was the same man. We got in the car and drove out home and had lunch. He did not approach the subject until after lunch. Then we went out on the porch and he began to talk about my going to the convention along with him; that he had reservations. He said something about a private car attached to the Pennsylvania Limited; that we could get on at Paoli and go right out with him, and that he had a suite of rooms for me at the Palmer House and he would see that I had a chance to speak.

He said, "You have got the speech?" I said, "Yes. These fellows, Doyle and MacGuire, gave me the speech." I said, "They wrote a hell of a good speech, too." He said, "Did those fellows say that they wrote that speech?" I said, "Yes; they did. They told me that that was their business, writing speeches." He laughed and said, "That speech cost a lot of money." Clark told me that it had cost him a lot of money. *Now either from what he said then or from what MacGuire had said, I got the impression that the speech had been written by John W. Davis – one or the other of them told me that – but he* thought that it was a big joke that these fellows were claiming the authorship of that speech.

I said, "The speech has nothing to do with what I am going to Chicago for. The speech urges the convention to adopt the resolution that the United States shall return to the gold standard." MacGuire had said, "We want to see the soldiers' bonus paid in gold. We do not want the soldier to have rubber money or paper money. We want the gold. That is the reason for this speech."

"Yes," I said, "but it looks as if it were a big-business speech. There is something funny about that speech, Mr. Clark."

The conversations were almost the same with both of them.

That was the end of that and we talked pleasantly on personal matters after that. I took him to the train about 6 o'clock and he went home.

The convention came off and the gold standard was endorsed by the convention. I read about it with a great deal of interest. There was some talk about a flood of telegrams that came in and influenced them and I was so much amused, because it happened right in my room.

Then MacGuire stopped to see me on his way back from the convention. This time he came in a hired limousine. It was not a private one this time. He came out to the house and told me that they had been successful in putting over their move.

I said, "Yes, but you did not endorse the soldiers' bonus."

He said, "Well, we have got to get sound currency before it is worthwhile to endorse a bonus."

He then went away and the campaign here in New York started. They were electing municipal officers, a political campaign. A marine was running for public office over here in Brooklyn and I came over to make a speech for him.

I was met at the train by MacGuire. He seemed to know just where I was going and he said he wanted to go with me, and he did.

I think there was one other visit to the house because he (MacGuire) proposed that I go to Boston to a soldiers' dinner to be given *by Governor Ely* for the soldiers, and that I was to go with Al Smith. He said, "We will have a private car for you on the end of the train *and have your picture taken with Governor Smith.* You will make a speech at this dinner and it will be worth a thousand dollars to you."

I said, "I never got a thousand dollars for making a speech."

He said, "You will get it this time."

"Who is going to pay for this dinner and this ride up in the private car?"

"Oh, we will pay for it out of our funds. *You will have your picture taken with Governor Smith.*"

I said, "*I do not want to have my picture taken with Governor Smith. I do not like him.*"

"*Well, then, he can meet you up there.*"

I said, "*No, there is something wrong in this. There is no connection that I have with Al Smith, that we should be riding along together to a soldiers' dinner. He is not for the soldiers' either.* I am not going to Boston *to any dinner given by Governor Ely for the soldiers.* If the soldiers of Massachusetts want to give a dinner and want me to come, I will come. But there is no thousand dollars in it."

So he said, "Well, then, we will think of something else."

I said, "What is the idea of Al Smith in this?"

"*Well,*" he said, "*Al Smith is getting ready to assault the Administration in his magazine. It will appear in a month or so. He is going to take a shot at the money question. He has definitely broken with the President.*"

I was interested to note that about a month later he did, and the New Outlook *took the shot that he told me a month before they were going to take. Let me say that this fellow has been able to tell me a month or weeks ahead of time everything that happened. That made him interesting. I wanted to see if he was going to come out right.*

So I said at this time, "So I am going to be dragged in as a sort of publicity agent for Al Smith to get him to sell magazines by having our picture taken on the rear platform of a private car, is that the idea?"

"*Well, you are to sit next to each other at dinner and you are both going to make speeches. You will speak for the soldiers without assaulting the Administration, because this Administration has cut their throats. Al Smith will make a speech, and they will both be very much alike.*"

I said, "I am not going. You just cross that out."

[...]

"... cannot keep this racket up much longer. He has got to do something about it. He has either got to get more money out of us or he has got to change the method of financing the Government, and we are going to see to it that he does not change that method. He will not change it."

I said, "The idea of this great group of soldiers, then, is to sort of frighten him, is it?"

"No, no, no; not to frighten him. This is to sustain him when others assault him."

I said, "Well, I do not know about that. How would the President explain it?"

He said: "He will not necessarily have to explain it, because we are going to help him out. Now, did it ever occur to you that the President is overworked? We might have an Assistant President somebody to take the blame; and it things do not work out, he can drop him."

He went on to say that it did not take any constitutional change to authorize another Cabinet official, somebody to take over the details of the office – take them off the President's shoulders. He mentioned that the position would be a secretary of general affairs – a sort of a super secretary.

The CHAIRMAN. A secretary of general affairs?

General BUTLER. That is the term used by him – or a secretary of general welfare – I cannot recall which. I came out of the interview with that name in my head. I got that idea from talking to both of them, you see. They had both talked about the same kind of relief that ought to be given the President, and he said: "You know the American people will swallow that. We have got the newspaper. We will start a campaign that the President's health is failing. Everybody can tell that by looking at him, and the dumb American people will fall for it in a second."

And I could see it. They had that sympathy racket, that they were going to have somebody take the patronage off of his shoulders and take all the worries and details off of his shoulders, and then he will be like the President of France. I said, "So that is where you got this idea?"

He said, "I have been traveling around – looking around. Now about this superorganization – would you be interested in heading it?"

I said, "I am interested in it, but I do not know about heading it. I am very greatly interested in it, because you know, Jerry, my interest is, my one hobby is, maintaining a democracy. If you get these 500,000 soldiers advocating anything smelling of Fascism, I am going to get 500,000 more and lick the hell out of you, and we will have a real war right at home. You know that."

"Oh, no. We do not want that. We want to ease up on the President."

He is going to ease up on him.

"Yes; and then you will put somebody in there you can run; is that the idea? The President will go around and christen babies and dedicate bridges, and kiss children. Mr. Roosevelt will never agree to that himself."

"Oh, yes; he will. He will agree to that."

I said, "I do not believe he will." I said, "Don't you know that this will cost money, what you are talking about?"

He says, "Yes; we have got $3,000,000 to start with, on the line, and we can get $300,000,000, if we need it."

"Who is going to put all this money up?"

"Well," he said, "you heard Clark tell you he was willing to put up $15,000,000 to save the other $15,000,000."

"How are you going to care for all these men?"

He said, "Well, the Government will not give them pensions, or anything of that kind, but we will give it to them. We will give privates $10 a month and destitute captains $35. We will get them all right."

"It will cost you a lot of money to do that."

He said, "We will only have to do that for a year, and then everything will be all right again."

Now, I cannot recall which one of these fellows told me about the rule of succession, about the Secretary of State becoming President when the Vice President is eliminated. There was something said in one of the conversations that I had *either with MacGuire or with Flagg, whom I met in*

Indianapolis, that the President's health was bad, and he might resign, and that Garner did not want it anyhow, and then this super secretary would take the place of the Secretary of State and in the order of succession would become President. *He made some remark about the President being very thin-skinned and did not like criticism, and it would be very much easier to pin it on somebody else. He could say that he was a foot stuck in routine matters and let the other fellow take care of it and then get rid of him if necessary.* That was the idea. He said that they had this money to spend on it, and he wanted to know again if I would head it, and I said, "No; I was interested in it, but I would not head it."

He said "When I was in Paris, my headquarters were Morgan & Hodges. We had a meeting over there. I might as well tell you that our group is for you, for the head of this organization. Morgan & Hodges are against you. The Morgan interests say that you cannot be trusted, that you will be too radical, and so forth, that you are too much on the side of the little fellow; you cannot be trusted. *They are for Douglas MacArthur as the head of it. Douglas MacArthur's term expires in November, and if he is not reappointed it is to be presumed that he will be disappointed and sore and they are for getting him to head it.*"

I said, "I do not think that you will get the soldiers to follow him, Jerry. He is in bad odor, because he put on a uniform with medals to march down the street in Washington. I know the soldiers."

"Well, then, we will get Hanford MacNider. They want either MacArthur or MacNider. They do not want you. But our group tells them that you are the only fellow in America who can get the soldiers together. They say, 'Yes, but he will get them together and go in the wrong way.' That is what they say if you take charge of them."

He said, "MacNider won't do either. He will not get the soldiers to follow him, because he has been opposed to the bonus."

"Yes, but we will have him in change (charge?)"

And it is interesting to note that three weeks later after this conversation MacNider changed and turned around for the bonus. It is interesting to note that.

He said, "There is going to be a big quarrel over the reappoint-
ment of MacArthur," and he said, "You watch the President
reappoint him. He is going to go right and if he does not reappoint
him he is going to go left."

I have been watching with a great deal of interest this quarrel
over his reappointment to see how it comes out. He said, "You
know as well as I do that MacArthur is Stotesbury's son-in-law in
Philadelphia – Morgan's representative in Philadelphia. You just
see how it goes and if I am not telling you the truth."

I noticed that MacNider turned around for the bonus, and that
there is a row over the reappointment of MacArthur.

So he left me, saying, "I am going down to Miami and I
will get in touch with you after the convention is over, and we
are going to make a fight down there for the gold standard,
and we are going to organize."

So since then, in talking to Paul French here – I had not
said anything about this other thing, it did not make any
difference about fiddling with the gold standard resolution,
but this looked to me as though it might be getting near, that
they were going to stir some of these soldiers up to hurt our
Government. I did not know anything about this committee,
so I told Paul to let his newspaper see what they could find
out about the background of these fellows. I felt that it
was just a racket, that these fellows were working one another
and getting money out of the rich, selling them cold bricks. I
have been in 752 different towns in the United States in
3 years and 1 month, and I made 1,022 speeches. I have
seen absolutely no sign of anything showing a trend for a
change of our form of Government. So it has never appealed
to me at all. But as long as there was a lot of money stirring
around – and I had noticed some of them with money to
whom I have talked were dissatisfied and talking about having
dictators – I thought that perhaps they might be tempted to
put up money.

Now there is one point that I have forgotten which I think
is the most important of all. I said, "What are you going to
call this organization?"

He said, "Well, I do not know."

I said, "Is there anything stirring about it yet." "Yes," he says; "you watch, in 2 or 3 weeks you will see it come out in the paper. There will be big fellows in it. This is to be the background of it. These are to be the villagers in the opera. The papers will come out with it." He did not give me the name of it, but he said that it would all be made public; a society to maintain the Constitution, and so forth ... *and in about two weeks the American Liberty League appeared, which was just about what he described it to be. We might have an assistant President, somebody to take the blame; and if things do not work out, he can drop him. He said, "That is what he was building up Hugh Johnson for. Hugh Johnson talked too damn much and got him into a hole, and he is going to fire him in the next three or four weeks." I said, "How do you know all this?" "Oh," he said, "we are in with him all the time. We know what is going to happen."* They had a lot of talk this time about maintaining the constitution. I said, "I do not see that the Constitution is in any danger," and I asked him again, "Why are you in this thing?" He said, "I am a businessman. I have got a wife and children."

In other words, he had had a nice trip to Europe with his family, for 9 months, and he said that that cost plenty, too.

The CHAIRMAN. Did you have any further talks with him?

General BUTLER. NO. The only other time I saw or heard from him was when I wanted Paul to uncover him. He talked to me and he telephoned Paul, saying he wanted to see him. He called me up and asked if Paul was a reputable person, and I said he was. That is the last thing I heard from him.

The CHAIRMAN. The last talk you had with MacGuire was in the Bellevue in August of this year?

General BUTLER. August 22; yes. The date can be identified,

The CHAIRMAN. We thank you, General Butler, for coming here this morning.

HAROLD WILSON

The Soviet KGB surreptitiously assassinate a British political leader so their man can replace him and eventually end up in 10 Downing Street.

It's a scenario that thriller writer John le Carré might hesitate to use for his Smiley novels, yet it is exactly what some in MI5 believed happened in Britain in 1963, when Hugh Gaitskell suddenly resigned as leader of the Labour Party and died shortly afterwards from a baffling illness. Taking over from Gaitskell was Harold Wilson, about whom MI5 had long held the deepest suspicions.

A brilliant economist, Wilson had been at Oxford University in the thirties which was almost enough evidence of his being a red-under-the-bed in itself, since this had been the time and place that the KGB had recruited a host of spies. But what really alarmed MI5 was Wilson's post-Second World War role as a junior trade minister, when he became the cheerleader for more commerce with the USSR. A 1947 visit to Moscow by Comrade Harold was rumoured to have entrapped him in a "honey pot", after which he was most definitely the KGB's man. Then there was Gaitskell's curious demise; his doctor is said to have approached MI5 with concerns about the responsible disease, lupus disseminata, which was hardly known in the UK. Gaitskell had just come back from the USSR. Information filtered through to MI5 from Russian defector Anatoli Golitsin that the KGB's Assassination Department 13 had killed a European leader and installed their man in his place. According to Peter Wright, former deputy director of MI5, in his autobiography *Spycatcher*, the strange death of Gaitskell added to Golitsin's rumour equalled a certainty that Wilson was a Moscow mole. The context and the timing was right too; the ruling Conservative Party was imploding in the aftermath of the Profumo affair, and Labour was a shoo-in for winning the General Election.

Was Wilsonski a double-agent, even the Fifth Man in the spy ring that included Philby, Burgess, Maclean and Blunt? Certainly sections of MI5 believed so and put him under surveillance. More, as detailed in Wright's *Spycatcher* tome, they then set about conspiring to remove Wilson from Downing Street, steadily dripping snippets of "black propaganda" to the press, in particular the satirical/investigative magazine *Private Eye*, about Wilson's "Communism" and his supposed dalliance with his secretary Marcia Williams. According to Colin Wallace, an intelligence officer with the British Army's Information Policy Unit in Northern Ireland, he was asked to cooperate in this smearing campaign against Wilson, known to MI5 insiders as "Clockwork Orange". (When Wallace refused to cooperate with the "unconstitutional" Clockwork Orange plot, he was framed for manslaughter, a case highlighted by journalist Paul Foot in *Who Framed Colin Wallace?*) MI5 was additionally alleged to have worked with the Conservative Party to bring about Wilson's downfall. Wilson himself became border-edge paranoid about the "dark forces" gathering against him; later, on his retirement, he would accuse Lord Mountbatten, Admiral of the Fleet and Prince Philip's uncle, of having plotted a coup d'état in 1968.

Wilson's delusional character – it was said of him that he made Walter Mitty look unimaginative – make some of his claims of "subversion from the right" difficult to take seriously, while Wright's *Spycatcher* is more colourful than reliable (by the author's own admission). An official government report *MI5: The Security Service* found that "no such plot [against Wilson] had ever existed". But they would say that, wouldn't they?

There is small doubt that some in MI5, with a little judicious outsourcing to Army and Conservative Party allies, sought by illegal means to bring down the elected prime minister of Britain. What is harder to determine is whether Wilson himself was actually a Soviet stooge. Golitsin's accusation holds no water; the defector had been briefing the CIA/MI5 for a decade before discovering, ooops!, he had forgotten to mention the biggest secret of all, Britain's PM is Moscow's man. More likely, given he was paid for information, he felt the need to invent some good material. The claim of Oleg Lyalin, a KGB defector, is marginally damning: Joseph Kagan, Wilson's friend and financier, regularly met agents from the Czech secret service. Most troubling of all is Wilson's resignation. Forty years after the event, no one has ever put forward a convincing reason why Wilson suddenly quit as PM just after starting his fourth term in office. And at the relatively sprightly age of 60.

"Tiredness" was the official stated reason. Meanwhile, the rumour mill energetically cranked out the word that Wilsonski had been obliged to step down because of incriminating evidence against him.

Harold Wilson is that rare thing in conspiracy theory, an alleged conspirator, an alleged conspiratee. Predator and victim.

British PM Harold Wilson was a KGB stooge: ALERT LEVEL 4

Labour prime minister was subject of MI5 "dirty tricks" campaign to remove him from office: ALERT LEVEL 9

Further Reading
Paul Foot, *Who Framed Colin Wallace?*, 1990
Ben Pimlott, *Harold Wilson*, 1992
Peter Wright, *Spycatcher: The Candid Autobiography of a Senior Intelligence Officer*, 1987